AIRPORT PLANNING

A Practical Guide for Planners and Airport Managers

by Lynn S. Bezilla

Copyright © 2009 Lynn S. Bezilla

All rights reserved

Lynn S. Bezilla
6273 Centre Stone Ring
Columbia, MD 21044

printed in the USA
by CreateSpace.com

*This book is dedicated to my mentors:
the late G. Frederick Young, who tried to teach me how to write;
Isaac W. Shafran, who tried to teach me how to think;
and to the memory of my mother-in-law,
R. Geraldine (Frazier) Benes,
who did so much.*

Acknowledgments

I must extend my sincere appreciation to Charles Flood, who encouraged me (repeatedly) to write this book, and to Kelly Lyles, whose enthusiasm and support helped me get it done.

I am also indebted to the following people, who provided valuable assistance in the preparation of this book: Shawn Ames, Joanne Brooks, Eric Buncher, Cliff Burnette, Tim Campbell, Gary Davies, Tom Davis, Tim Deike, Danielle DelBalso, Bill Flanagan, Doug Ganey, Wayne Heibeck, Mike Henry, Paula Hochstetler, John Kirby, Michelle Krummel, Mark Lang, Mindy Lee, Steve Lucchesi, Carol Lurie, Susan McDonald, Barbara Michael, Carolyn Motz, Chirantan Mukhopadhyayay, Ron Price, Carlos Rece, Bill Richardson, Juan Rivera, Elaine Roberts, Brian Rodgers, Ellen Sample, Wayne Schuster, Isaac Shafran, Paul Shank, John Silva, Ashish Solanki, Mike Steer, John Stewart, Eileen Straughan, Beverly Swaim-Staley, Fred Testa, Joe Varrone, Jim Walsh, and Len Wood.

Some gave of their valuable time to sit down with me and talk about airports and airport planning; others read over portions of draft materials. Their insights and real-world experiences contributed significantly to the usefulness of this book.

I also extend my sincere appreciation to Vince Scarano, who performed a detailed technical review and uncovered numerous errors, both of fact and judgment.

And finally, I want to thank my editor, Julia Johnson of Wordsworth Communications, whose enthusiasm, knowledge, and clear thinking improved the quality and readability of this book and made the process stress-free.

Contents

INTRODUCTION 1
   Overview 1
   Additional Sources of Detailed Guidance 2

CHAPTER 1: OVERVIEW OF AIRPORT PLANNING 5
   You Just Have to Think…of Everything 5
   Understand Uses and Users 7
   Be Proactive Amid Uncertainties 7
   An Open and Honest Process 9
   A Guide to Future Development 9
   Types of Plans 10
   Different Customers with Different Priorities 11
   Organized Thinking about the Future 12

CHAPTER 2: AIRPORTS 13
   Airports from Different Perspectives 13
      Transportation Connection 13
      Economic Engine 13
      Unwelcome Neighbor? 14
      Airports are for People—So Keep Them Happy 14
   Airport Components 15
      Airside 15
      Terminals 33
      Landside 49
      Land Use 56

**CHAPTER 3: AIRPORT MANAGEMENT, OPERATIONS,
AND FINANCE** 63
   Background 63
      Types of Airports 63
      Airport Ownership 66
      Airport Oversight 66
   Airport Management and Operation 67
      Management Staff 67
      Operations Staff 69
      Maintenance Staff 70
      Finance Staff 71

    Engineering Staff *72*
    Planning Staff *73*
    Environmental Staff *73*
    Marketing and Communications Staff *75*
    Human Resources Staff *76*
Airport Finance 77
    Federal Funding *77*
    Grant Assurances *83*
    State and Local Funding *87*

CHAPTER 4: STRATEGIC PLANNING 97
What is a Strategic Plan? 97
    The Overall Vision—for Various Possible Futures *97*
    Goals, Objectives, Actions *98*
    Comprehensive, Yet Focused *99*
    The Planning Horizon *100*
    The Local Context *100*
    Identifying Funding, Supporters, and Opposition *101*
    Team-Building Opportunity *101*
    What a Strategic Plan is Not *102*
    Avoid Fatal Flaws *103*
The Strategic Planning Process 104
    Facilitator *105*
    Stakeholders *106*
    SWOT Analysis *109*
    Goals and Objectives *110*
    Monitoring and Updating *114*
    The Final Plan *114*

CHAPTER 5: MASTER PLANNING 117
Background 117
    A Plan, Not a Blueprint *118*
    Is It Worth It? *120*
The Master Planning Process 121
    Step 1: Pre-Planning *123*
    Step 2: Public Involvement *138*
    Step 3: Environmental Considerations *140*
    Step 4: Existing Conditions *143*
    Step 5: Aviation Forecasts *147*
    Step 6: Facility Requirements *151*
    Step 7: Alternatives Development and Evaluation *154*

Contents

    Step 8: Airport Layout Plans *166*
    Step 9: Facilities Implementation Plan *167*
    Step 10: Financial Feasibility Analysis *170*

CHAPTER 6: SYSTEM PLANNING 175

  Background 175
    NPIAS *176*
    State Airport System Plans *177*
    Regional Airport System Plans *180*
    Continuous Planning and Special Studies *181*
  The System Planning Process 182
    Step A: Pre-Planning *184*
    Step B: Issues Identification *184*
    Step C: Study Design *185*
    Step D: System Inventory *187*
    Step E: System Goals and Performance Measures *190*
    Step F: System Demand Forecasts *191*
    Step G: Definition of Airport Roles *194*
    Step H: System Needs Identification *195*
    Step I: Alternative Systems Development *197*
    Step J: System Priorities *199*
    Step K: Recommended System Plan *201*
    Step L: Implementation Plan *203*
    Step M: Executive Summary *205*
    Additional Factors *205*

CHAPTER 7: FORECASTING 217

  Why Do We Forecast? 217
  What Should We Look For in a Forecast? 221
  What Do We Forecast? 224
    Passengers *226*
    Air Cargo *229*
    Aircraft Operations *230*
    Based Aircraft *231*
    Fleet Mix *232*
    Socioeconomic Data *232*
  Forecast Methodologies 233
    Qualitative Methods *234*
    Quantitative Methods *235*
  How Can We Tell if the Forecast is Good? 243

CHAPTER 8: ENVIRONMENTAL CONSIDERATIONS 247
   Background 248
   The NEPA Process 253
      Categorical Exclusions *253*
      Environmental Assessments *254*
      Environmental Impact Statements *255*
      Environmental Streamlining *257*
   Environmental Practice 258
      Overview *258*
      Noise *260*
      Air Quality *265*
      Water Quality *269*
      Wetlands *272*
      Cumulative Impacts *274*
   Sustainability 275
      Noise *278*
      Air Quality *278*
      Water Consumption and Quality *279*
      Waste and Recycling *279*
      Energy Consumption *280*
      Ground Transportation *281*
      Buildings *281*
      Community Relations *282*

CHAPTER 9: COORDINATION AND COMMUNICATION 287
   Coordination 288
      The Planner's Role *288*
      Listen First, Plan Later *289*
      Building Support for the Plan *290*
      Launching the Discussion *290*
      Knowing Where the Land Mines Are *291*
      Coordinating Discretely *292*
   Public Involvement 293
      Building Trust *293*
      Consider the Many Publics *294*
      When is it Mandatory? *295*
      Public Involvement versus Public Hearings *295*
      Encouraging Productive Discussion *296*
      Speak Their Language *297*
      How Much Information? *297*

Contents

    Public Outreach 298
    Dealing with Plan Opposition 299
        Resistance to Change. *299*
        Resistance to Competition. *299*
        Political Opposition *300*
        Emphasize the Benefits. *300*
        Work With Elected Officials *302*
        Work With the Public *304*
        Give a Little. *305*
        Don't Give Up *305*
    Presentation 306
        Presentation Format *306*
        Tailor Your Message to Your Audience *306*
        Written Presentations. *307*
        Oral Presentations. *309*
        Listen! *309*
        Short and to the Point *310*
        Be Prepared *310*
        Visual Aids *311*
        Designing the Graphics *312*
        Simplest is Best *313*
        Graphs, Charts, and Drawings. *313*

**CHAPTER 10: MENTORING, MANAGING,
AND TEAM BUILDING** **317**
    Mentoring 317
        Finding the Ideal Apprentice *319*
        The Time Commitment. *320*
        The First Steps *321*
        The Real World of Airports. *322*
        Effective Hands-On Learning. *323*
        Shaping Organizational and Interpersonal Skills *324*
        A Mentoring Plan. *325*
        Mentoring by Objectives *326*
        Learning by Doing. *326*
        Thinking and Imagining *327*
        Avoiding Boredom. *328*
        Empowerment *329*
        The Apprentice's Responsibilities *330*

Managing 331
   Managing People *331*
   Managing Projects *332*
   Schedule Challenges *333*
   Managing Reviews *334*
   Avoiding Delay Pitfalls *335*
   Budget Challenges *335*
   Project Reporting *336*
Team Building 338
   Teamwork versus Personal Friendships *338*
   Understanding the Bigger Picture *338*
   The Benefits of Diverse Skills *339*
   Leading through Inspiration *340*

CHAPTER 11: CONCLUSION 341

Think! 341
Flexibility 341
Overlapping Phases 341
Completeness 342
Judgment 342
Your Most Important Tools 342

BIBLIOGRAPHY 343

INTRODUCTION

This book defines and examines airport planning and offers insight and direction aimed at improving the planning process. In it I try to give some idea of what both planning and airports are all about—what we do and why we do it. Throughout I have tried to be as objective as possible. The information and ideas in this book are based on my background, education, and 37 years of experience working and learning in this ever-changing field. Many are based on mistakes I have made, or have seen others make, in the hope that this will help you avoid the same pitfalls. Because I was the Director of Planning and Environmental Services at Baltimore/Washington International Airport (BWI) for 20 years, the information in this book is generally presented from an airport's perspective. My experiences and observations are supplemented by conversations and formal interviews with airport directors, managers, staff members, consultants, and individuals in the Federal Aviation Administration (FAA).

Overview

Chapter 1 of this book provides an overview of planning in general and airport planning in particular. Chapter 2 discusses the various components of airports: airside, terminal, landside, and use of surrounding lands. Chapter 3 describes how airports are owned, operated, managed, and financed, and emphasizes those areas and issues that are of interest to an airport planner. Understanding how airports are operated and financed helps in the development of a more realistic and implementable plan.

Chapter 4 is devoted to strategic planning—establishing a vision for the future and identifying the steps that must be accomplished to achieve this vision. A strategic plan provides a basis for follow-on master plans and helps set the direction for future development. Airport master plans and other, smaller-scale or focused plans for specific airport facilities such as terminals or runway safety areas are discussed in Chapter 5. The discussion covers each of the steps in the master planning process, from initial concept development and consultant selection through the facilities implementation plan and financial feasibility analysis. Chapter 6 deals with airport system planning, i.e., planning for airports covering a broad geographical area such as a state or region.

Chapter 7 is devoted to forecasts, which are a critical element in the planning process. The discussion attempts to take some of the mystery out of the aviation demand forecasting process. Chapter 8 covers the environmental aspects of airport planning and some of the basic environmental concerns and issues encountered in the day-to-day operation of an airport. It also discusses the need for, and how to plan for, sustainability in the airport environment.

Chapters 9 and 10 address aspects of airport planning that are important but often do not receive adequate attention. Chapter 9 deals with coordination and communication, i.e., how to present and gain acceptance for the plan. The chapter emphasizes that coordination and communication should begin at the outset of the planning process, not after the plan is completed. This includes gaining public acceptance of the plan from various interests in the airport community as well as the general public. Chapter 10 deals with mentoring, managing, and team building. It provides guidance on training new planners, since there seem to be no schools that offer degrees in airport planning. Chapter 10 also deals with techniques for managing both staff and projects and shows how mentoring and managing are part of team building.

Additional Sources of Detailed Guidance

As noted throughout the text, the FAA has a number of Advisory Circulars (ACs) and Orders that provide guidance on various aspects of airport planning. For the most part this book does not duplicate the material contained in ACs, because they are free and available online. They are also updated from time to time, so always be sure you are referring to the latest edition.

It is important to note that the ACs lay out the processes that should be followed for such activities as master planning and system planning, but they do not tell planners *how to think*, although they do contain a lot of things to *think about* during the planning process. Much of what is presented in this book is thus based on my experience with, and interpretation of, published FAA planning guidance.

Most of what we do as airport planners is based upon FAA requirements and guidelines. The FAA plays a key role in virtually every aspect of the development and operation of airports. Specifically, federal statutes charge the FAA with developing U.S. standards for the design and construction of airports. The FAA began developing such standards in the mid-1900s and revises them continuously based on testing and research as well as field experience. The efficacy of FAA standards is attested to by the fact that they are considered the worldwide benchmark.

The U.S. government provides grants for airport planning, design, and construction, subject to the availability of funds, certain specified requirements, and other priority considerations. These grants are administered by the FAA under the Airport Improvement Program (AIP); the money comes from the Aviation Trust Fund which is supported by various aviation taxes. One of the prerequisites for receiving AIP funding is that the recipient airport must comply with FAA standards. Also, the federal regulation of air carriers stipulates that a properly certificated air carrier may provide airline service only to those airports which have been certificated by the FAA. One of the airport certification requirements is that it is in compliance with FAA design standards.

CHAPTER 1

OVERVIEW OF AIRPORT PLANNING

Planning is a world of ideas. Planning is about thinking and imagining. It is about having a vision for the future, and following through in a systematic and organized way to achieve that vision. The ACs provide guidance on how to organize your ideas in a systematic, coherent, and coordinated manner, but without having an idea—a vision—a planner can follow established planning processes yet produce a plan that does not adequately address an airport's issues or meet its needs. This book attempts to describe and explain the kinds of things that planners should be thinking about while they are going through the AC processes and how the guidance contained in the ACs applies to day-to-day airport situations.

Planning is simply looking ahead, envisioning the future, and deciding how you will act or what you will be in the future. Typically more than one future will be envisioned; thus, you will have to decide how you will act in each of the possible futures. A simple example of looking ahead: someone wonders what the weather will be tomorrow. For possible futures, it will either be cold or warm. How will they act in the alternative futures? They will either dress for cold weather, with a coat, hat, and gloves, or they will dress for warm weather, with light, comfortable clothing. Therefore everyone is a planner in one way or another, but *how* they plan, or *how well* they plan, i.e., how accurately they envision the future, determines whether they and their plans will be successful. It may not be possible to teach someone how to be a good planner in the sense that planning requires imagination and certain other innate qualities. However, in my opinion it is possible to encourage imaginative thinking, and that is really one of the main purposes of this book.

You Just Have to Think…of Everything
It seems that when architects are asked for their ideas on airport development, they talk about how the airport should look, how future facilities

should blend with the existing architecture and the immediate airport surroundings, and how the airport's structures should reflect the community it serves. Eventually they get around to talking about how the facility should be attractive to and amenable to use by air passengers and other airport visitors. When engineers are asked for their views about airport development they start looking for places to build things, usually attempting to keep construction complexity and costs to a minimum. They seem to regard airports and airport users in terms of quantitative units, e.g., linear feet of curb, cubic feet of fill, and so many peak hour aircraft operations, passengers, and so on. Planners, on the other hand, tend to think more of possibilities, imagining all kinds of futures in which all kinds of airport improvements are possible. Unfortunately, many planners don't seem to spend much effort on whether the improvements are actually needed, and whether or not there is somebody out there who is willing to pay for them. To develop an airport properly, all three skills are needed: architecture, engineering, and planning. And of course a good construction manager is always needed to straighten out everybody else's mistakes and omissions. Ultimately, architects, engineers, and planners need to work together throughout the planning process in order to develop a plan that will be functional, implementable, and customer-friendly.

Because this book is about airport planning, and because a good airport development program usually begins with a good plan, the focus is primarily on airport planners in the context of airport planning. Planning of any kind, airport planning included, is really all about thinking. In essence, planning is easy; all a planner has to do is think. The only complicating factor is that a planner has to think of *everything*. As discussed throughout this book, planners are often criticized because their plans are not practical, or cannot be easily implemented in a real airport operating environment. Planners should know what kinds of things happen at airports, what issues are of major concern to airport operators,* and how planning should reflect those issues and concerns to help ensure a useful end product. Good planners should also be able to develop accurate cost estimates, along with an indication of where the money will come from to pay for the planned improvements.

Planners should always keep in mind that airport facilities go through several stages: planning, design, construction, operation, and maintenance. In a sense, planning, design, and construction can be thought of as the conception, gestation, and birthing process; once the facility goes into operation its real life begins—it is born. An airport facility is built to be used and the more it is used the more successful it is. On the other hand, the more it is used the more it has to be maintained. Just as the genetic makeup of a human being, a plant, or a puppy is locked in at conception, the makeup of an airport facility is rooted in the conception of the plan.

---

* Strictly speaking, the airport operator is the authority responsible for operating the airport and the airport sponsor is the authority responsible with respect to FAA programs. In the case of most airports they are the same, and the terms are used interchangeably in this book.

Understand Uses and Users

To develop a good plan, planners must understand the environment into which they are bringing this new facility. Planners need to talk to the people who will be leasing, operating, and maintaining the new facility after it is constructed to find out what their concerns are, what is important to them, and how they operate. The initial discussions should take place at the outset of the planning process. For example, as soon as it appears that the passenger terminal might need to be expanded, discussions should begin with the people who handle the leasing to see what they will need, or would like to have, in terms of space—both size and location. Discuss their needs in terms of how they operate now and how they might operate in the future. Talk to airport operations to see how they would use the gates and parking ramps and learn what they need for airline ground support equipment parking and airside roadways. Operations and the Transportation Security Administration (TSA) can also help determine the location and amount of space needed to support appropriate security procedures and equipment. The maintenance staff can state what their needs are for airside, terminal, and landside space, equipment, and storage of supplies. Planners should also keep in mind how the facility will be used once it becomes operational; therefore, it is imperative to know the characteristics of the types of facility *uses* as well as the actual *users*.

Be Proactive Amid Uncertainties

Planning should be active, not passive. A good planner should anticipate future events, not simply react to current ones. This can be a daunting task given such challenges as the dynamics of the aviation industry, airlines that are not willing to share their plans, and a political structure that can change with every election. What will be happening 10 years from now will very likely not be the same as what is happening today. A traveler passing through Chicago O'Hare in 1971 would have seen many B-747s but very few B-737s. A good many knowledgeable people stated that the B-737 was an airplane with no future. A few years later most of the airlines that had B-747s were either selling them or installing piano bars on the upper decks because they couldn't fill the airplanes. This was during the OPEC oil embargo, when ticket prices were up and air travel demand was down.

Some years later, People Express was thought to be the wave of the future— and using 737s at that. Then a few years later the airline was gone. At one point Piedmont made history with its revolutionary concept of hubbing, i.e., an airline's use of an intermediate airport as a transfer point to get passengers to their final destination. Of course all the other major airlines followed suit, each insisting that it was in fact the carrier that had originated the concept of hubbing. Piedmont flew B-737s too, and most of the other airlines started ordering them as well. The B-737 and its various offspring are now the world's leading airliners.

There was a time when the aviation industry was excited about something called *wayports*—airports that were designed and built primarily to handle airline hubbing. Then somebody asked, "Why should I fly from Baltimore to Pittsburgh, when I really want to go to Orlando?" And then the concept of point-to-point service was born. Reborn, actually; that is how most airlines originally operated. Hubbing gradually faded from the scene. More recently most industry experts have stated that any airlines that don't reduce their costs by cutting crew salaries and reducing in-flight amenities won't survive. They emphasize that people want to get from Point A to Point B, safely and on time, and that is the essence of air travel in the future.

All of these examples show that nothing stays the same, and the future is usually not what we expect it will be. Thus plans should be flexible.

Having said that, planners still must always look to the future; that's what planning is all about. When a planner goes to an airport he should see the airport not as it is today, but as it will be 5 or 10 years from now, and even beyond. As noted above, this is difficult because the future is unknown and filled with uncertainties, and most future events cannot be predicted with a high degree of confidence. But planners can make themselves aware of some of these uncertainties by trying to identify emerging trends and applying them to facility planning. This can be done by developing scenarios or possible different futures. As a simple example, Future A may be an optimistic scenario, assuming that the market the airport serves will grow and prosper, perhaps at a rate even faster than that seen historically. Future B may be somewhat more pessimistic, assuming that the market area will show little or no growth for the next 5 to 10 years. Future C may be a scenario that assumes that the market area will actually decline, with business closures and relatively high unemployment. Obviously these are highly simplified scenarios, and there are a number of others that can fit between A and B, and between B and C. Looking at the bright side can give a planner a sense of what it would be like if the airport had to grow to meet increased aviation demand associated with economic growth, such as new businesses, higher employment, etc. It is a good idea to lay out a concept for airport growth under a relatively optimistic scenario such as this. It gives an idea of how much land may need to be acquired and how much existing airport land should be reserved for various airport uses. Looking next at a relatively pessimistic scenario, a planner can get an idea of how much overbuilding would result if a plan were developed under an optimistic scenario and then circumstances dramatically changed, such as if a major employer were to close a nearby manufacturing plant. This kind of thinking and examples of how to conduct airport planning with an eye to alternative scenarios are discussed in Chapter 4: Strategic Planning, Chapter 5: Master Planning, and Chapter 6: System Planning.

An Open and Honest Process

The planning process should also be transparent, i.e., the key assumptions, methodologies, and conclusions should be stated clearly in a manner that can be understood by the audience for which they are intended. It should identify the issues to be addressed and describe why they are issues, or why they are important to the airport and the community it serves.

Planning should also be honest. As noted in the following chapters, there are ways to cheat—ways to set up a methodology or evaluation process in such a manner that it produces the answer someone wants, but not necessarily the true answer. For example, the businesses and elected officials in a community may want to establish scheduled airline service or attract a major company, and they may want the airport to be improved to accommodate such service. Overly optimistic forecasts may be used in an attempt to justify the desired improvements. But if the market truly isn't there, and if the community cannot generate enough air traffic to support airline service, then a lot of time and money will be spent for nothing.

The bottom line is that if the underlying data and analysis do not support the need for additional, improved, or expanded facilities, none should be proposed. Sometimes telling the truth is difficult, but if planning is to remain credible and if planners expect to be trusted, honesty should be the only policy.

A Guide to Future Development

The dictionary defines a plan as "a detailed scheme, program, or method worked out beforehand for the accomplishment of an objective, …a proposed or tentative project or purpose."[1] Some, including many in the FAA, engineering, or even in finance, regard a plan as a blueprint for the phased development of an airport. That would actually be an Airport Layout Plan, as defined by the FAA. Others, such as Richard de Neufville (Founding Chairman of the Technology and Policy Program at the Massachusetts Institute of Technology), consider a plan to be "a collection of possible local suggestions of what airports might like to do, all of which are debatable or negotiable."[2] To my mind, both of these general definitions are correct. For now, let's define a plan as a guide to future development. Thus it follows that an airport plan is a guide to the future development of an airport.

In the airport planning context the "future" usually refers to a 20-year planning horizon. Many planning critics say this horizon is too distant and that nobody can predict what things will be like 20 years from now. Therefore, they argue, it is impossible to determine what facilities will be needed in two decades. They believe airport planning should focus on the near term, such as a five-year future. Unfortunately this will not always work because it often takes more than five years to get a major project started, let alone completed. Still other critics claim that a 20-year look into the future does not go far enough; planning should consider what the airport might need, and what it might look like, 30 or 40 or more years into the future. Good airport planning should balance these two extremes. Planners should develop a 20-year program for airport development, with an emphasis on the 5- to 10-year near term. But planners should also consider what might happen to the airport beyond 20 years. This will certainly be a very broad, nondetailed assessment, but it will help keep options open with the aim of preventing near-term development from precluding potential longer-range options.

Types of Plans

Airport planning involves a number of different types of plans, including strategic plans, master plans, system plans, airport layout plans, terminal area plans, environmental plans, financial plans, air service development plans, and on and on. This book deals primarily with the first three listed above, but also touches on airport layout plans and terminal area plans because they are parts of (or products of) airport master plans.

A *strategic plan* can be defined as "…a disciplined effort to produce fundamental decisions and actions that shape and guide what an organization (or other entity) is, what it does, and why it does it."[3] A strategic plan establishes a long-term vision for the airport, and results in a set of recommended actions, one of which is usually a recommendation to prepare a master plan or facility development plan within the context of the airport future established in the strategic plan. In effect, the strategic plan sets the stage for future facility development. It is essential that a strategic plan, or at least some concentrated strategic thinking, be done prior to embarking on any facility planning study. Strategic plans are discussed in detail in Chapter 4.

In AC 150/5070-6B, *Airport Master Plans*, the FAA defines an *airport master plan* as "…a comprehensive study of an airport [that] usually describes short-, medium-, and long-term development plans to meet future aviation demand."[4] Airport master plans vary in detail and complexity, depending upon the nature of the facilities being studied. If the airport issues are limited in scope, such as the proposed development of a general aviation aircraft parking and hangar area, or runway/taxiway system improvements, the study may be referred to as a "master plan update." Master plan updates generally follow the same process as master plans; both are discussed in Chapter 5. One of the major products of a master plan study is the Airport Layout Plan (ALP). The ALP is a graphic representation of current and proposed airport facilities. The ALP is one of the most important documents that results from the planning process because a current, approved ALP is required in order to obtain federal Airport Improvement Program (AIP) funds. One of the AIP grant assurance requirements is that the airport must keep the ALP current and follow that plan.

An *airport system plan* is a summary of facility requirements for individual airports considered and evaluated in the context of a larger geographic area such as a state or a region. System plans also provide the context and documentation for establishing airport roles and lay the groundwork for strategic and policy planning. Chapter 6 follows the general outline for airport system planning as presented in AC 150/5070-7, *The Airport System Planning Process*.[5] In many cases the state or regional airport system plan is a compilation of individual airport master plans; in some cases, however, fresh planning work may be needed. The end product of a system plan is a summary and prioritization of state or regional airport system needs.

Airports also generate a variety of other plans—there are probably as many plans as there are issues to be addressed. The ALP includes a *terminal development plan*, an *airport land use plan*, and an *airport access plan*, among others. Airports with scheduled air service or airports wishing to obtain scheduled air service usually prepare an *air service development plan*, which lays out some air service objectives and some strategies to achieve those objectives. A number of Web sites for larger airports include what they identify as a strategic plan but is really an air service development plan. Most airports, especially the larger and busier ones, prepare an *airport financial plan*. The financial plan shows how the airport operates financially and how it expects to fund future facility improvements.

Different Customers with Different Priorities

Airports are developed and operated primarily to serve their customers. Airports basically have two sets of customers: the airlines and the traveling public. Both types of customers have their own sets of needs and wants. The airport operator has its own set of needs and wants that may differ from those of the customers. Trying to meet the needs and wants of both sets of customers, as well as the airport operator, can be challenging, but it can also be very exciting. Passengers want everything to be perfect for them; they want a seamless connection from their car (or other access mode) to the airplane, and from the airplane to ground transportation at the end of their trip. They want a pleasant, hassle-free experience. Airlines want facilities that will enable them to maximize their traffic and revenues at minimal cost to them. Many airport operators would say that the airlines seem to want everything but don't want to pay for anything. And finally, airport operators want facilities that have sufficient capacity to serve aviation needs and maximize revenues while reducing costs.

As the preceding discussion shows, airport planning encompasses at least three potential areas of conflict: passenger wants, airline wants (or aircraft operator wants at general aviation airports), and airport wants. On top of all this is the fact that virtually every operation and type of activity at an airport is subject to some form of federal regulation and various state and local regulations. Further, special interest groups and the general public seem to have more influence in airport plans and development programs than in years past.

Organized Thinking about the Future

At its core, planning is organized thinking about the future. Airport planning is thus organized thinking about the future of an airport—and how it should be developed to fit efficiently into that future. The "planning process" is often referred to, written about, and discussed at conferences. But planning is more than a process; it is having a vision for an airport, not as it exists today, but how it will exist—and how it will function—tomorrow.

Endnotes

1. *Webster's II New Riverside University Dictionary.* Boston: Houghton-Mifflin, 1998.

2. de Neufville, Richard, and Amedeo Odoni, *Airport Systems Planning, Design, and Management.* New York: McGraw-Hill, 2003, p. 60.

3. Bryson, John M., *Strategic Planning for Public and Nonprofit Organizations,* 3rd Edition. San Francisco: Jossey-Bass, an imprint of John Wiley & Sons, 2004.

4. *Airport Master Plans,* AC 150/5070-6B. Washington, D.C.: Federal Aviation Administration, 2005. Accessed April 2008, from http://www.faa.gov/airports_airtraffic/airports/resources/advisory_circulars/

5. *The Airport System Planning Process,* AC 150/5070-7. Washington, D.C.: Federal Aviation Administration, November 11, 2004. Accessed August 2007, from http://www.faa.gov/airports_airtraffic/airports/resources/advisory_circulars/

CHAPTER 2

AIRPORTS

Airports are fairly complex places, and the larger and busier the airport, the larger and more complex the facilities and services provided. This chapter discusses the three major components of airports: airside, terminal, and landside. It also discusses land use compatibility in the vicinity of airports, which is another critical aspect of airport planning. It provides an introduction to the functions, planning parameters, and measures of effectiveness of each component. It also includes references to the appropriate advisory circulars and other publications that provide specialized guidance for each component.

Airports from Different Perspectives

The definition of an airport reflects various points of view and it is important for the airport planner to consider these perspectives in the planning process. Airport planning in this environment can be both extremely challenging and extremely rewarding.

Transportation Connection

Stated simply, airports should be thought of as a place to go *through*, not to go *to*. Most airport planners would probably define an airport as a place that provides "a safe and efficient connection between air and ground transportation." The FAA defines an airport as "...an area of land or water that is used or intended to be used for the landing and take-off of aircraft, and includes its buildings and facilities, if any."[1]

Economic Engine

The business and economic development communities tend to regard an airport as an economic engine. The local airport gives local citizens and businesses quick and convenient access to global markets. The airport is also a local employment center, providing a wide range of diverse jobs. It also provides a source of revenue, because people pay to park at the airport and pay for food, magazines, and other consumer goods; and airlines rent ticket counter space and baggage handling areas, pay landing fees, and purchase fuel for aircraft and ground support equipment. And of course, wherever you find revenue, you also find taxes. Airport-related businesses and employees are significant contributors to federal, state, and local tax revenues. Because airports contribute to the vitality and viability of the local community, many local businesses can be counted on to support airport improvements.

Unwelcome Neighbor?

Although they provide economic benefits, airports can be noisy, especially during peak arrival and departure periods. For that reason, and because they generate a considerable amount of traffic on local roadways, airports are often regarded by their neighbors as a nuisance. Some might resent them as only a place where rich people keep their expensive toys. As one airport planner once stated, "Airports are a major intrusion into a larger community." The people living around an airport can typically be counted upon to oppose any airport expansion plans, regardless of the potential benefits. This situation is just another part of airport life.

Airports are for People—So Keep Them Happy

Regardless of how airports are defined in various situations by different entities or user groups, the main point to remember is that *airports are for people*. Airports enable people to travel safely, efficiently, and quickly to conduct business, visit friends and family, or just take a vacation. Airport planners should always keep this in mind; we are here to help ensure people's travel needs will be met in the future.

Customer satisfaction is thus a very important consideration during the planning process. According to a press release by J.D. Power and Associates announcing the results of their 2008 North America Airport Satisfaction Study^{SM}, customer satisfaction with airports was down significantly in 2008.[2] The study rates airports on a number of factors, including accessibility, the check-in/baggage check process, terminal facilities, security check, food and retail services, and baggage claim. The press release states that customer satisfaction with airports increased steadily between 2002 and 2006, but by 2008, overall satisfaction was down 14 points from 2007, earning 675 on a 1,000-point scale. More than one in five passengers reported experiencing a delay.[3] Moreover, among those reporting a delayed flight, the average length of delay was 68 minutes. The press release also stated:

> When air passengers are forced to wait out delays in airports for departing flights, they are essentially a captive audience, and their frustration and stress levels affect their satisfaction with airport operations and amenities.... Those airports that are best equipped to handle delayed passengers with comfortable seating, a variety of food and beverage options, and restrooms located near departure gates are the ones that will perform better in customer satisfaction in these trying times. When delayed passengers arrive at their destination airports, they are seeking efficient service at baggage claim and an expedient exit. Any ad-

ditional inconveniences will only compound their dissatisfaction with the airport experience.[4]

Also, according to a survey conducted for the Travel Industry Association of America (TIA), "…deep frustration with the air travel process, including inefficient security screening and flight delays and cancellations, caused travelers to avoid 41 million trips over the past year" [2007].[5]

Clearly, air passengers are not satisfied with the nation's air transportation services for a variety of reasons. Planners cannot solve all of these problems, but planners can play a major role in the overall travel experience as discussed throughout this book. As noted above, *airports are for people*. They exist primarily because people want to get from one place to another safely, quickly, and conveniently. The planner's job is to make sure these movements continue to take place in the future—safely, conveniently, and efficiently.

Airport Components

Airports are usually thought of in three components: airside, terminal, and landside. From an airport planning standpoint, a fourth can be added: surrounding land use. The airside component is the sexy part, with great silver birds roaring down the runways and lots of noise and excitement. The terminal is where passengers get "processed," eat, shop, tinkle, wait, and sometimes find out that their luggage did not happen to make the same flight. The landside component consists of public parking lots, maintenance buildings, cargo facilities, access and circulation roadways, and everything else around an airport. Sometimes roadways are grouped into a fourth airport component called "ground access." Note that landside and land use are not the same, although the terms are sometimes incorrectly used interchangeably. Land use in the context of airport planning specifically refers to what type of development surrounds the airport that may affect, or be affected by, the airport and its operation.

Airside

The airside of an airport consists primarily of runways, taxiways, taxilanes, and their surrounding surfaces, including such zones and surfaces as safety areas, object free areas, and the like. This part of the airport accommodates aircraft take-offs and landings, as well as ground circulation to and from the terminal gates and aircraft parking ramps. The airside of an airport with an air traffic control tower (ATCT) can be divided into two major components: a *movement area* and a *non-movement area*. The movement area is controlled by the tower and requires a controller's permission to enter; all airplane, vehicle, and pedestrian activities inside the movement area must be approved by the tower. In the non-movement area, airplanes, authorized vehicles, and pedestrians are free to move about without tower permission. This is something that should be kept in mind during the planning process, particularly when laying out taxiways and aircraft parking ramps. The control tower should have an unobstructed view of all parts of the movement area.

Generally speaking, taxiways are part of the movement area; taxilanes usually are not. A taxiway provides a connection between a runway and various parts of the airport such as the terminal area or an aircraft parking ramp. A taxilane provides access between taxiways and aircraft parking positions.

Airside Geometry Considerations

The geometry or layout of the runway and taxiway system is critical because it controls how the terminal and landside components can be laid out, developed, and operated. The runways and taxiways need to be designed with safety, efficiency, and future growth in mind. The FAA has numerous advisory circulars dealing with airside geometry, lighting, marking, obstruction removal, and just about anything else you can think of, and probably even some things you can't. The primary FAA source is AC 150/5300-13, *Airport Design*.[6] Most airport design standards can be found there. They are not duplicated in this book because standards change from time-to-time; the current advisory circular should always be used for planning any airport improvements.

Airspace

Airport plans and plans for land uses surrounding the airport must ensure that no development, activities, or natural objects will interfere with the airspace needed by aircraft landing and taking off from the airport. Obviously if a skyscraper were located too close to the end of a runway, it would be an obstruction to airspace. To determine exactly how much airspace needs to be "preserved" (with no skyscrapers, construction cranes, terminal buildings, or tall trees poking into it), the FAA has developed a detailed set of requirements, which are set forth in Subpart C of Federal Aviation Regulations (FAR) Part 77, of Title 14 of the Code of Federal Regulations (CFR).[7] The airspace to be preserved surrounding an airport is described by a set of imaginary surfaces, which are planes (as in geometry, not aircraft) of specific sizes and slopes, or angles. Logically, the closer to the runway, the lower to the ground these imaginary surfaces are—tall buildings can't be built close to runways. Moving away from the runway in various directions, the planes generally angle upward—a one-story maintenance building could be safely constructed closer to a runway than could a skyscraper or communications tower, which would poke through the imaginary surface. The imaginary surfaces don't simply angle up and out like stadium seating—they are a fairly complex set of planes based on potential movements of aircraft. Their size and slope also depend on the type of runway, because runways used for large, heavy aircraft need more preserved airspace than short runways used by prop planes.

Part 77 identifies four different runway types:

- Utility: runways designed for use by propeller-driven aircraft with a maximum gross weight of 12,500 pounds or less.
- Visual: runways intended only for the operation of aircraft using visual approach procedures.

Chapter 2 – Airports 17

- Nonprecision Instrument: runways having a published instrument approach procedure using air navigation facilities with only lateral (horizontal or localizer) guidance.
- Precision Instrument: runways with an instrument landing system that provides both lateral and vertical (vertical or glide slope) guidance.

The imaginary surfaces defined in Part 77 are summarized below and schematic examples are shown in Figures 2-1 and 2-2. These drawings are only intended to illustrate the concept of imaginary surfaces—Part 77 should be consulted to identify the specific details associated with each of the surfaces for any of the specific existing or planned runway types.

Figure 2-1: FAR Imaginary Surfaces

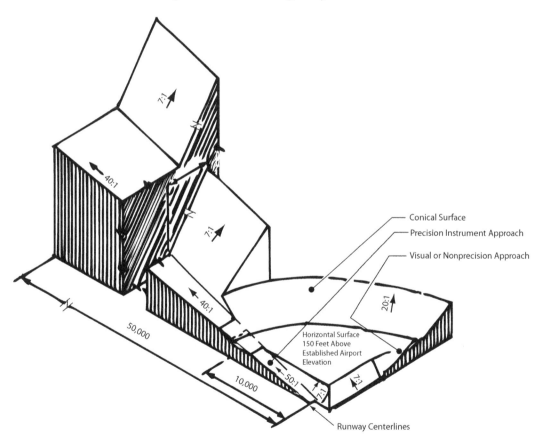

Source: Federal Aviation Administration

Figure 2-2: FAR Imaginary Surfaces

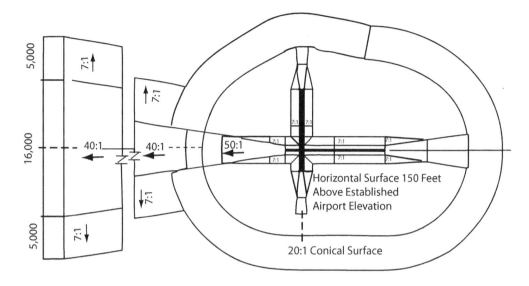

Source: Federal Aviation Administration

Imaginary surfaces:

- Horizontal surface: a horizontal plane 150 feet above the established airport elevation. The perimeter of the plane is constructed by swinging arcs of specified radii from the center of each end of the primary surface of each runway, and then connecting the adjacent arcs by lines tangent to those arcs. The radius of each arc is 5,000 feet for utility and visual runways, and 10,000 feet for all other runways.
- Conical surface: a surface extending outward and upward from the periphery of the horizontal surface at a slope of 20:1 for a horizontal distance of 4,000 feet.
- Primary surface: a surface longitudinally centered on a runway. For a runway with specially-prepared hard surface, the primary surface extends 200 feet beyond each end of the runway. For other runways the primary surface ends at the end of each runway. The width of the primary surface is:
    - 250 feet for utility runways having only visual approaches.
    - 500 feet for utility runways having nonprecision instrument approaches.
    - For other than utility runways the width is:
        - 500 feet for visual runways having only visual approaches and for nonprecision instrument runways having minimums greater than ¾ of a statute mile.

- 1,000 feet for precision instrument runways and for nonprecision instrument runways with visibility minimums as low as ¾ of a statute mile.
- Approach surface: The approach surface is defined for each end of each runway based upon the type of approach for that runway. The surface is longitudinally centered on the extended runway centerline and extends outward and upward from each end of the primary surface. The inner edge of the approach surface is the same width as the primary surface and expands uniformly to a width of:
    - 1,250 feet for a utility runway with visual approaches only.
    - 1,500 feet for other runways with visual approaches only.
    - 2,000 feet for a utility runway with a nonprecision instrument approach.
    - 3,500 feet for a nonprecision instrument runway, other than utility, having visibility minimums greater than ¾ of a statute mile.
    - 4,000 feet for a nonprecision instrument runway, other than utility, having visibility minimums as low as ¾ of a statute mile.
    - 16,000 feet for precision instrument runways.

  The approach surface extends for a horizontal distance of:
    - 5,000 feet at a slope of 20:1 for utility and visual runways.
    - 10,000 feet at a slope of 34:1 for all nonprecision instrument runways other than utility.
    - 10,000 feet at a slope of 50:1, with an additional 40,000 feet at a slope of 40:1 for all precision instrument runways.
- Transitional surface: Surfaces extending outward and upward at right angles to the runway centerline, and the runway centerline extended at a slope of 7:1 from the sides of the primary surface and the approach surfaces. Transitional surfaces for those portions of the precision approach surface which project through and beyond the limits of the conical surface extend a distance of 5,000 feet horizontally from the edge of the approach surface and at right angles to the runway centerline.

The bottom line is that all airside facility plans should first ensure that the surrounding airspace is and remains clear of obstructions to air navigation (an object higher than any of the heights or surfaces outlined above and identified in Part 77). The FAA generally presumes that obstructions to air navigation are *hazards to air navigation* until an FAA aeronautical study has determined otherwise. A hazard to air navigation is an object which, as a result of an aeronautical study, is determined by the FAA to have a substantial adverse effect upon the safe and efficient use of navigable airspace by aircraft, operation of air navigation facilities, or existing or potential airport capacity. Unfortunately obstructions such as tall buildings, communications towers, and power lines are all too common around airports, and their presence can limit runway extensions or the location of new runways, because they would penetrate the imaginary surfaces associated with the proposed runway.

Large air carrier airports usually have more success in restricting the construction of such facilities than the smaller general aviation airports. As discussed in the next chapter, large air carrier airports are typically owned by an airport authority or by an agency of a city or county government. Most government officials and agencies are aware of the airport and the valuable services it provides. The airport usually (but not always) has influence or leverage with the local planning and zoning agencies to help ensure that construction permits are not granted for facilities that could be an obstruction or hazard to air navigation. The situation is rather different at many, perhaps most, small general aviation airports. Elected officials and government agencies are not always aware of the services such an airport provides, nor are they always aware of the critical need to maintain clear approaches to all runways. These small airports, especially privately-owned airports, typically do not have the leverage of larger airports, and struggle to keep their approaches clear.

The Design Aircraft
Airside geometry and the design standards for virtually all airside components are determined by something called an *Airport Reference Code* (ARC). This code relates airport design criteria to the operational and physical characteristics of the largest or most demanding aircraft expected to use the airport on a regular basis—regular being defined as 500 itinerant operations per year.[8] Note that this is equivalent to 250 departures per year, or one per business day. This is usually referred to as the *design aircraft* or *critical aircraft*. Aircraft operations are broken into two types: local and itinerant. Local operations are take-offs and landings by aircraft that have remained in the general vicinity of a particular airport without an intermediate stop at another airport. Flight training and local sightseeing or recreational flights are examples of local operations. Itinerant operations are operations that originate at, or are destined to, another airport. Also, operations by aircraft operating beyond 20 miles from the originating airport are usually classed as itinerant. Occasionally the term *touch-and-go operations* is used. Touch-and-go operations are those where the aircraft touches down and then takes off again without coming to a full stop. Such operations are usually associated with flight training activities. Touch-and-go operations are a subset of local operations. For most planning purposes the volume of itinerant operations is the key factor in determining facility requirements.

The ARC has two components: the *aircraft approach category* is determined by the speed of the aircraft on the landing approach (operational characteristic); the *airplane design group* is determined by the aircraft wingspan (physical characteristic). Both the approach speed and wingspan are based on the aircraft expected to be using the facility on a regular basis. Generally, runway standards are related to aircraft approach speed, aircraft wingspan, instrument approach types, and landing visibility minimums. Taxiway and taxilane standards are related to the airplane design group. Table 2-1 shows the parameters for the aircraft approach category and the airplane design group. The largest aircraft using the relatively small general aviation airports are usually the smaller business jets and these airports are usually designed to B-II standards. The B-737 and A-320 series aircraft operating at most air carrier airports are C-III aircraft, although an airport that is regularly served by a 737 could also expect to see service by a 757, which is a C-IV aircraft. Thus many of our air carrier airports are designed to C-III or C-IV standards. Aircraft such as the B-747, B-767, B-777, and A-340 fall into the D-V category, but as newer aircraft such as the Airbus A-380 begin to replace the current long-haul airline fleet, the largest airports—particularly those with transoceanic international service—should be designed to D-VI standards.

Note that these standards change occasionally, and modifications are sometimes granted. When the B-747 came into use it was designated a Design Group VI aircraft, due to its wingspan of 195.7 feet (213 feet for the 747-400). However, very few airports could be expanded to accommodate Group VI aircraft so the FAA raised the Group V limit to 214 feet to include the 747 series. More recently, the FAA and the European Aviation Safety Agency (EASA) approved the Airbus A-380, a Group VI aircraft with a wingspan of just over 261 feet, for operations on runways of 150 feet wide or greater, even though the current Group VI standard calls for a runway width of 200 feet.

Table 2-1: Aircraft Approach Categories and Design Groups

Aircraft Approach Category	
Category A	Speed less than 91 knots
Category B	Speed 91 knots or more but less than 121 knots
Category C	Speed 121 knots or more but less than 141 knots
Category D	Speed 141 knots or more but less than 166 knots
Category E	Speed 166 knots or more
Airplane Design Group	
Group I	Up to but not including 49 feet (15 m)
Group II	49 feet up to but not including 79 feet (24 m)
Group III	79 feet up to but not including 118 feet (36 m)
Group IV	118 feet up to but not including 171 feet (52 m)
Group V	171 feet up to but not including 214 feet (65 m)
Group VI	214 feet up to but not including 262 feet (80 m)

Runways and Taxiways

A general rule among airport planners is that, when designing a new airport, you start from the outside and work in. This means establishing the number of runways, their orientation, and the supporting system of taxiways first, and then locating the terminal, cargo, landside, and support components accordingly. This works fine when you are dealing with a greenfield (undeveloped) site, but the vast majority of the time planners have to work with airport property that is already intensely developed. This makes our work challenging and interesting. And it gives most of us gray hair after a few years.

The initial step in planning a new runway is to determine the orientation. Typically the runway should be oriented according to the prevailing winds so that aircraft do not have to operate with a strong crosswind component. The critical aircraft, as defined above, is usually used for the crosswind analysis. The manufacturer's performance manual should be consulted for specific information on crosswind operations, as well as for all other aircraft performance characteristics. AC 150/5300-13 states that 95 percent wind coverage is desired. That is, aircraft should be able to operate 95 percent of the time with a crosswind component within the allowable coverage, according to the operating standard for the particular aircraft. As the aircraft size increases, so does the allowable crosswind component, i.e., the aircraft can operate with a stronger crosswind. Thus wind coverage is not as critical for large airports or runways handling large air transport category aircraft as for those accommodating lighter aircraft.

Other factors can be just as important in determining runway orientation as wind coverage. For example, runways should be sited so that they will have clear approaches, i.e., approaches that are not blocked or potentially obstructed by tall buildings, mountain ranges, or intensely-developed residential areas. If one of the alternative locations for a new runway is oriented so that traffic arriving or departing on that runway will pass over an intensely-developed residential area, it would be ideal to shift the runway orientation to avoid the area, although this is not very often feasible. In some cases the wind coverage may drop to below 95 percent. If it only drops to 90 percent or so that may not be a problem, but if wind coverage goes down to the 75 percent range, the airport sponsor will be faced with the question of whether or not to invest in a runway that can only be used 75 percent of the time. If the runway cannot be shifted or reoriented to avoid a noise-sensitive area, the cost of buying or soundproofing the affected properties should be included as part of the cost of constructing the runway. This is discussed in more detail in the cost discussions in Chapter 5: Master Planning.

Most of the time planners have few choices for locating a new runway; thus, it is important to look at the big picture at the outset. Don't just look at the engineering solution, or how the runway can be made to fit at a reasonable cost. Think of how the runway will be used and how the rest of the airport will operate when that runway is in use. Remember when siting a new runway that a day may come when somebody wants to build a parallel runway,

Chapter 2 – Airports

a parallel taxiway, or some other facility next to it, so try to leave as much room as feasible. Even though it may seem at the time that an additional facility is not likely to be needed in the foreseeable future, remember that situations and requirements change over time, often in unexpected ways. For example, a number of large air carrier airports were built to accommodate Group IV aircraft, and runway and taxiway separations were planned, designed, and constructed accordingly. Then all of a sudden Group V aircraft began coming into service, and airport operators were faced with inadequate runway and taxiway separations, sprawling terminal complexes, and airports that no longer met FAA standards. And next, airport operators are faced with the potential of accommodating Group VI aircraft at airports that can barely handle Group V.

The length of a runway is determined by the type of aircraft that will be using it on a regular basis, i.e., the critical aircraft, which is typically the design aircraft for the airport. For determining runway length for planning purposes, AC 150/5325-4B, *Runway Length Requirements for Airport Design* should be used. The AC uses a five-step procedure to determine recommended runway lengths for a selected list of critical design airplanes. The AC notes that "…the information derived from this five-step procedure is for airport design and is not to be used for flight operations. Flight operations must be conducted per the applicable flight manual."[9] In calculating runway length the AC also assumes that the runway has no obstructions, calm winds, dry runway surfaces, and zero runway gradient, i.e., the difference between the elevations of both runway ends. If a more accurate runway length determination is required, the manufacturer's performance manuals should be consulted for the particular type of aircraft that will be designated as the critical aircraft. These manuals consider the stage length, i.e., the nonstop distance the aircraft will be flying to reach a particular destination, along with take-off weights, temperature, wind, runway gradient, runway surface condition, airport elevation, and other relevant factors.

When working on an analysis of runway length requirements as part of a long-range planning study, the big picture should be kept in mind—the possible future beyond the study's planning horizon. For example, calculations may show that a 7,000-foot runway is sufficient to meet the airport's needs for the foreseeable future. But remember that the future always has a degree of uncertainty. Therefore it is always a good idea to play "what if" and think about what would happen if the runway might need to be extended to 8,000 or 9,000 feet at some point in the future. Even though it is not included in the current planning study and federal aid is not being requested for it, and the longer runway is not even being shown on an ALP, some flexibility should be provided to avoid constraining the potential long-term runway length. This principle applies whether laying out the runway, or planning any other major facility improvement.

Runway and taxiway widths, centerline separations, safety areas, object free areas, obstacle free zones, and other airfield dimensional standards are defined in AC 150/5300-13. The details are not included in this book as the AC contains all the up-to-date details, definitions, and tables needed—remember to always reference the latest edition of the AC. Simply summarized, these dimensional standards are based on the aircraft approach category, the airplane design group, and the type of approach, e.g., visual or instrument. If a published instrument approach is available, the landing minimums associated with the approach, i.e., whether it is a precision or nonprecision approach, must be considered. By way of background, visual flight rules generally apply when the cloud ceiling is at least 1,000 feet above ground level and the visibility is at least three statute miles.[10]

The landing minimums associated with the various precision instrument approach categories are shown in Table 2-2. The approach categories are a function of weather conditions and the type of instrument landing aids available at the airport. This information, along with a plethora of other information regarding instrument approaches and associated flight requirements, can be found in the FAA's *Instrument Procedures Handbook* (TERPS).[11] Note that special authorization and equipment, both aircraft and airfield, are required for Category II and III operations. The decision height (DH) is a specified altitude at which a missed approach must be executed if the necessary visual reference to continue the approach has not been confirmed. The runway visual range (RVR) is the visibility at the runway, as opposed to tower visibility, which is the visibility as observed from the control tower.

Table 2-2: Precision Instrument Approach Categories[12]

Precision Instrument Approach Categories	
Category I	DH 200 feet and RVR 2,400 feet (with touchdown zone and centerline lighting: RVR 1,800 feet)
Category II	DH 100 feet and RVR 1,200 feet
Category IIIa	No DH or DH below 100 feet and RVR not less than 700 feet
Category IIIb	No DH or DH below 50 feet and RVR less than 700 feet but not less than 150 feet
Category IIIc	No DH and no RVR limitation

One of the most important things to remember is that these dimensional standards, e.g., runway and taxiway centerline separation distances, should be closely adhered to for safety reasons. Although the FAA does occasionally grant *modifications to standard* (sometimes informally referred to as *waivers*), it is not a good idea to develop an airside layout that depends on obtaining an FAA waiver. A modification to standard is defined by the FAA as any change to FAA design standards, other than dimensional standards for runway safety areas. Any modification to an airport design standard related to new construction, reconstruction, expansion, or upgrade on an airport that received federal funds requires FAA approval. The request for modification should show that the modification would provide an acceptable level of safety, economy, and durability. The standards are typically established based on sound reasoning, with operational safety as the primary concern. The ACs also specify clearing and grading requirements within the runway protection zones, runway safety areas, object free areas, etc. These also should be closely followed. Sometimes modifications have to be made to the rule in order to operate efficiently; however, in the interest of safety and long-term efficiency, planning should *not* be based on such exceptions. Also, when requesting a modification to standard, remember that the burden of proof lies with the planner. Planners need to prepare documentation to show that a modification is necessary, explain why it is necessary, and demonstrate that safety will not be compromised.

The planning process includes determining how the taxiway system will operate in any given runway configuration or usage pattern, including providing safe and efficient access to the passenger and/or cargo terminal areas. Every attempt should be made to avoid complicated or circuitous routings, particularly those that could lead to runway or taxiway incursions as discussed below. Taxiways that curve should be avoided wherever possible, as should the short taxiway sections that are often found at large airports that have been developed, expanded, and redeveloped over the years. Curves and short taxiway lengths can be very difficult to see in low-visibility conditions. Short taxiway lengths and frequent intersections usually lead to congestion points that can result in delays and unsafe operating conditions. When considering new taxiway layouts some thought (and imagination) should be given to how the planned configuration would look to a pilot or a controller on a dark, rainy night. Typically, planners do not have a good feel for how the airside system of an airport operates, even in daylight, let alone in inclement weather or nighttime conditions. Therefore it is necessary to talk with airport operations staff and especially with local air traffic control tower personnel early on in the planning process. Go up in the tower or out on the airfield in various places and see how things look and operate. Listen in on tower and ground control frequencies, especially during periods of bad weather, to see and hear what actually goes on, and what can go wrong.

It is also important to remember that the facilities located on the airside of the airport include aircraft approach and landing aids, their emergency or backup power generators, aircraft hold pads, remote aircraft parking and maintenance areas, and other aircraft and airport support facilities. Often these are facilities whose location is *fixed by function*. According to the FAA an air navigation aid (NAVAID) that must be positioned in a particular location in order to provide an essential benefit for civil aviation is considered to be fixed by function. The term NAVAID includes electrical and visual air navigational aids, lights, signs, and associated supporting equipment. It is important to note that there are "exceptions," as the FAA calls them. Equipment shelters, junction boxes, transformers, and other appurtenances that support a fixed by function NAVAID are *not* fixed by function unless operational requirements specify that they be located in close proximity to the NAVAID. Also, some NAVAIDs, such as localizers, can provide acceptable performance even when they are not located at their optimal location. These NAVAIDs are not fixed by function.

Aircraft Parking
Another example of a remotely-located facility that is not fixed by function is a remote aircraft parking ramp. A remote parking ramp is often needed at airports with crowded terminal ramp and apron areas—particularly airports that accommodate large numbers of aircraft parked overnight. When an airport also has a large number of charter flights, both passenger and cargo, these aircraft need a place to park, sometimes for several days, while they are waiting for their next trip or undergoing maintenance. Flight crews; aircraft provisioning, cleaning, and maintenance crews; and others such as U.S. Department of Agriculture inspectors require access to these areas. Frequently the people operating the service or transport vehicles do not have a lot of experience operating on an active airfield. Sometimes finding a site for a remote parking ramp can be a problem because these ramps should have convenient access to the terminal area. However, most terminal areas are probably already crowded and there may not be enough room, so the ramp must be put in a remote location. But in that case the aircraft support crews may have to cross active runways and taxiways to access the aircraft, and that leads to an increased potential for runway incursions (discussed further below), which are to be avoided at all cost. Also, these parking areas should be located so that aircraft tails do not penetrate critical airspace or block the air traffic controllers' line of sight or view of the air operations area. Balancing all these requirements makes life as an airport planner quite interesting.

Operations and Maintenance Factors
Once the runway (or runways), taxiways, parking ramps, etc., are laid out, it may appear that airfield planning is complete and attention can be shifted to the terminal area. Not so fast. All of the airside access and circulation roadways must be sited and appropriate routes determined. The next time you are at a large airport, spend some time looking out the terminal window and watch the number and variety of vehicles other than airplanes that are flitting around out there. The airside, especially in the vicinity of the terminal, teems with service and maintenance vehicles, cargo and baggage tugs, fuel trucks, operations and security vehicles, construction vehicles, and so on. Properly located and well-maintained roadways are necessary to accommodate all these vehicles, which have to be able to reach *everything* located on the airside of the airport, and that means *everything*, from parked aircraft to NAVAIDS, weather equipment, runway and taxiway lights, as well as their supporting buildings, conduits, etc. As a general rule remember that anything located on an airport that can break down or get dirty must have some way for a maintenance or inspection crew to get to it. Also remember that it is not a good idea to have ground vehicles using the runways or taxiways to get from one part of the airport to another. All airside roadways must remain clear of all safety areas, object free areas, and NAVAID critical areas.

Emergency Vehicle Access

Airport rescue and firefighting (ARFF) facilities are also a necessary component of an airport. Airports with scheduled airline service are required to maintain an ARFF facility according to accident response time standards set forth in Part 139 of the Federal Aviation Regulations, as shown below.

- Within 3 minutes from the time of the alarm, at least one required aircraft rescue and firefighting vehicle must reach the midpoint of the farthest runway serving air carrier aircraft from its assigned post or reach any other specified point of comparable distance on the movement area that is available to air carriers, and begin application of extinguishing agent.

- Within 4 minutes from the time of the alarm, all other required vehicles must reach the point specified in paragraph (h)(2)(i) of this section from their assigned posts and begin application of an extinguishing agent.[13]

Design criteria for ARFF facilities are set forth in AC 150/5210-15, *Airport Rescue and Firefighting Station Building Design*. It should also be kept in mind that many ARFF facilities also respond to accidents on airport area roadways and to medical emergencies, fires, and other incidents at the airport terminal, cargo facilities, airport and airline maintenance facilities, and general aviation areas. Thus ARFF facilities should be sited so that fire and rescue equipment can respond quickly to non-aircraft incidents on other parts of the airport.

Snow Removal

In areas that experience significant amounts of snowfall during the winter months it is important to find a location (or a number of different locations) for a snow dump site. All the snow that is removed from the runways, taxiways, and ramp and apron areas has to be put someplace so the snow piles do not interfere with aircraft maneuvering or control tower visibility. Snow dumps should be located so they are conveniently accessible for the snow removal crews in order to maximize efficiency during snow removal operations. Both airport operations and control tower staff should be involved in locating the snow dump sites, as well as the storage buildings for snow removal equipment and materials storage. The dump sites and buildings should be located to provide direct access to the runway and taxiway systems, without circuitous routings. The buildings should also be located to minimize runway and taxiway crossings (and the potential for incursions) by employee vehicles and snow and ice removal equipment.

In most areas snow dump sites will also have to meet some sort of environmental requirement, so coordination with the appropriate environmental review agency will be necessary. Larger airports often have snow melting equipment. These large mobile units are taken to the ramp, apron, or other areas where snow is being removed. Snow is dumped in, melted, and the liquid is then disposed of elsewhere. In most areas environmental regulations will require that the meltwater be treated before being discharged. When snow removal is completed in one area, the equipment is towed to another location to repeat the same procedure. At airports where portable snow melters are used, ramp and apron areas and taxiways should be planned to allow space for the operation of the equipment. Some airports have permanent snow melting facilities and their location should be planned with adequate access in mind. Providing adequate space for snow removal operations will help ensure that the airport stays operational during inclement weather conditions.

Detailed guidance on snow removal site selection and building design is provided in AC 150/5220-18A, *Buildings for Storage and Maintenance of Airport Snow and Ice Control Equipment and Materials*. The AC also provides guidance on support areas for personnel required for the airport's winter storm management plan.

Service Road Layout
It is a good idea to have a service roadway running around the perimeter of the airport, along the inside of the airport security fence. This roadway, and other service roads located on the airside, can provide access from various landside facilities (discussed below) to all parts of the airfield, including sites where navigation and landing aids are located. Service roads can also be used by security personnel making their periodic rounds, as well as by fire and rescue personnel and equipment responding to airfield emergencies.

Although planning airport roadways is not exactly rocket science, it can be a challenge. Ideally all roadways should be two lanes, and wide enough and strong enough to handle the largest and heaviest vehicles that can be expected to require airside access, including fire and rescue equipment. Of course, that kind of road can be expensive, so some extra time and common sense should be used in determining not only where the road will go, but also what kinds of vehicles will be using it. For example, the road leading to the localizer antenna will probably not see much in the way of heavy equipment, so it can be constructed with a light duty pavement, or even crushed stone, or simply be graded, depending on the weather conditions that the airport typically experiences. Consult with the expected users—chiefly airport operations and maintenance departments, and the local FAA personnel who service all the NAVAIDS—to make sure the airside ground access and circulation plan is sound and efficient. They will appreciate being consulted and the resulting plan will be much the better for the effort. It is also important to make sure that service roads provide adequate separation between ground vehicles and aircraft, and are not located in the movement area if at all possible. Every effort should be made to locate service roads so they are outside the airport design surfaces and air navigation aid clearance surfaces.

Runway Incursions
In recent years the FAA has been working diligently to reduce the number of runway incursions. According to the FAA, a runway incursion is defined as "any occurrence at an airport involving an aircraft, vehicle, person, or object

Chapter 2 – Airports

on the ground that creates a collision hazard or results in a loss of separation with an aircraft taking off, intending to take off, landing, or intending to land."[14] In this regard the FAA has recently published a memorandum with the subject "Engineering Brief No. 75: *Incorporation of Runway Incursion Prevention into Taxiway and Apron Design.*"[15] Although the memorandum states that "…these design strategies are only recommendations. They are not a set of standards that must be followed whenever possible…," it also states that "key elements of this Engineering Brief will be incorporated into the [forthcoming] comprehensive revisions to Advisory Circular 150/5300-13." Some of the main points noted in this memorandum are listed below.

- The use of runways as taxiways is not recommended.
- Limiting the number of aircraft crossing a runway is a priority in the design of the airport to enhance runway safety.
- Designers should avoid designating taxiway names by function.
- Avoid taxiway nomenclature assigning the same name to a taxiway making several turns along its route.
- Right-angle taxiways are the recommended standard for all runway/taxiway intersections, except where there is a need for high-speed exit taxiways.
- Keep taxiway intersections simple by reducing the number of taxiways intersecting at a single location.
- Taxiways should never go across the intersection of two runways.
- Full parallel taxiways are recommended as a standard airport design element when justified through planning.
- Design taxiways in a manner that reduces the number of active runway crossings.
- Use dual parallel taxiways to increase efficiency. Consider dual taxiways parallel to the runway for queuing departing aircraft instead of providing a large holding area at the runway end that requires large expanses of pavement.
- When possible, connect entrance taxiways to the runway end at a right angle.
- Where possible, avoid wide pavement areas such as expansive intersections or departure holding areas at runway ends extending through the runway holding position location.
- Avoid the use of short, nonstandard taxiway segments connecting to the runway.
- Terminate high-speed exit taxiways at a parallel taxiway if possible.
- Avoid runway high-speed exit taxiways from both directions meeting at the same point.
- Avoid acute-angled taxiways to exit the runway requiring turns in excess of 90 degrees whenever possible.[16]

Even though the FAA says that these strategies are only recommendations and not standards, they amount to some very good guidance that should be taken seriously. As noted above, what looks good on a drawing may look quite different from the cockpit of an aircraft on a rainy night.

Airside Capacity Considerations

The capacity of a runway or runway system is the volume of aircraft operations (arrivals and departures, e.g., one arrival and one departure equal two operations), that can be accommodated within a given time period. For most long-range planning studies runway capacity is presented in terms of annual operations and is sometimes referred to as *annual service volume* (ASV). The ASV is the volume of operational activity that an airport can accommodate under typical operating conditions throughout the year. According to the FAA, "Annual Capacity or Annual Service Volume, as reported in the NPIAS, is the level of annual activity at which the average delay per operation is four minutes."[17] (NPIAS is the National Plan for Integrated Airport Systems, and is discussed in Chapter 3: Airport Management, Operations, and Finance.) ASV is often used as a reference point in airport planning, but is not a particularly precise measure for discussing airfield capacity. For more detailed studies, peak hour capacity is used and is generally considered to be a more accurate representation of what is actually occurring on the airfield under various conditions. Runway capacity is a function of a number of factors, the most important of which are the aircraft fleet mix; the number, location, and configuration of runway exits; and the configuration of the taxiway system. Thus it is more accurate to speak of "airfield capacity" rather than "runway capacity." Key non-airport factors that can affect an airport's operating capacity are primarily weather conditions, airspace limitations, and the desire of the airlines to schedule all their flights to land and depart at the same time.

Fleet Mix

The fleet mix is important because different aircraft fly at different speeds on approach. In a mixed arrival stream, aircraft speeds must be reduced to the speed of the slowest aircraft. Thus faster jet and turboprop aircraft must slow down to the approach speed of a small single-engine aircraft. Most of the large jet aircraft cannot operate this slowly, thus they are directed to make "S" turns and other maneuvers to maintain adequate separation from the leading aircraft.

Also, different types of aircraft generate different levels of wake turbulence. Thus aircraft on approach have to be sequenced so that a trailing aircraft will not be affected by the wake turbulence generated by the preceding aircraft. If the arrival stream consists of aircraft having similar approach speeds and generating similar levels of wake turbulence, the arrival sequencing and flow can be kept fairly uniform and aircraft can arrive at a steady pace. When extremely slow aircraft or very large aircraft enter an otherwise uniform arrival mix, approach speeds must be reduced and the separation between aircraft must be increased. This means fewer aircraft can arrive within a given amount of time, thus reducing capacity.

Chapter 2 – Airports

Runway Exits

The number and type of runway exits is important because a landing aircraft must be able to exit the runway as safely and as soon as possible. The airport's taxiway system is a function of the airport's pavement widths, separations, and curve radii, and is thus ultimately based on the type of aircraft using the airport. The exit taxiways serve as a transition zone between the air movement and the ground movement of aircraft; therefore, the exits should be located and constructed to facilitate the expeditious movement of aircraft. The FAA recommends that the taxiway system have the ability to accommodate average aircraft taxi speeds of 20 miles per hour.[18] Specific guidance on the design of exit taxiways can be found in Chapter 4: Strategic Planning, and in Appendix 9 of AC 150/5300-13. The AC also notes that airport capacity can be enhanced by constructing angled or "high-speed" exits, but for airports with a design peak hour traffic volume of fewer than 30 operations, a right-angled exit will maintain an efficient traffic flow. Bear in mind, however, that a right-angled exit usually means that the landing aircraft will have to come to a full stop (or very nearly so) before turning onto the exit. The longer an aircraft must be on the runway after it touches down, the longer the next aircraft must wait to land. This separation distance, when added over the course of a day's aircraft operations, makes a significant difference in the capacity of the airport.

Non-Airport Factors

Non-airport factors can contribute significantly to airfield capacity limitations. In metropolitan areas in particular, the local airspace must often be shared by two or more airports, giving air traffic controllers less flexibility in the routing and maneuvering of aircraft. The effects of weather on airport capacity are obvious; under instrument flight rules (IFR) conditions aircraft have to fly more precise routings associated with instrument approach paths than under visual flight rules (VFR) conditions. Also, the separation distance between aircraft is increased. Specific weather occurrences such as thunderstorms and strong wind shear conditions also contribute significantly to delays.

Analyzing Airfield Capacity

Analyzing and quantifying airfield capacity is fairly simple at small airports, but can be a complicated process at larger, busier facilities. FAA AC 150/5060-5, *Airport Capacity and Delay*, provides guidance and sample problems for determining airport capacity using manual calculations and a series of runway configuration diagrams. This circular can be used effectively for smaller airports, but at larger, busier airports, computer simulation modeling is usually used. Simulation models give more accurate and detailed results than manual calculations, but they also require much more detailed information in terms of input data and can be expensive to operate because they require considerable skilled person-hours to collect, input, and analyze the data. Most simulation models have the advantage of being able to model airspace factors and gate use as well as runway and taxiway configurations.

One of the chief benefits of simulation models is the fact that planners can sit down with air traffic controllers and examine the model's results with regard to aircraft operations. Controllers can then make their own assessment of whether the model represents the reality they work with every day. And that goes a long way toward selling the plan (as discussed in Chapter 9: Coordination and Communication). The primary models currently being used are The Airport Machine™, the Airport and Airspace Simulation Model (SIMMOD™), and the Total Airport and Airspace Modeler (TAAM™). Simulation models can be used to simulate the functioning and interaction of various components of the airfield, such as one particular runway and its associated taxiways, or the entire airport, including runways, taxiways, apron areas, gates, and parking ramps. Most simulation models can also include an airport's associated terminal airspace or a regional system of airports and their airspace. The Massachusetts Institute of Technology has a Web site that provides an excellent summary of a number of airport and airspace simulation models, including those mentioned above.[19]

For general planning purposes it is usually sufficient to discuss airfield capacity in terms of annual or peak hour aircraft operations, but for busy airports such as large and medium air carrier hubs, and busy general aviation relievers, airfield capacity is discussed in terms of peak hour VFR and IFR operations.

When discussions get more detailed, and particularly when the point is reached in the planning process when the cost aspect of airfield improvement is being discussed, capacity is more often presented in terms of "delay." Aircraft delay is the difference in time between when an operation was supposed to occur and when it actually does occur. For example, if a flight is scheduled to depart at 10:05 a.m. and doesn't actually depart until 10:20 a.m., a delay of fifteen minutes is incurred. The discussion of airport delay gets a little complicated, however, by the fact that most flight delays are caused by weather. The FAA records flight delay data for flights departing or arriving fifteen minutes or more from the scheduled time. This information is published by airline and by airport by the U.S. Department of Transportation's Bureau of Transportation Statistics, but it does not differentiate between delays attributable to weather, congested airspace, equipment malfunctions, or airport configurations.[20] If used as part of an airport capacity study this information should thus be used with caution, and should be supplemented with additional airport-specific data that must be collected on site.

I recall seeing the difference in causes of delay demonstrated quite vividly at BWI Airport many years ago when Piedmont Airlines was operating its BWI hub. During a peak arrival period we noticed that aircraft arrivals were fairly constant and unconstrained as long as the arriving aircraft consisted almost exclusively of jet transport aircraft such as the B-737 or DC-9. But when slower-moving commuter turboprop aircraft entered the arrival stream we noticed that everything slowed down to the approach speed of the slowest arriving aircraft. When we lengthened our short general aviation runway to accommodate the commuter aircraft, arrival streams could be separated and arrival delay virtually dropped to zero. However, we still noticed delays during peak departure periods. It often seemed like things on the airfield were moving in slow motion. Upon further investigation we found that flights departing BWI, Washington National, and Washington Dulles bound for northeastern points such as New York, Boston, Providence, etc., were all routed to the SWANN intersection, an airway fix located about 20 miles east of Baltimore. The FAA maintains a five-mile longitudinal separation between aircraft, thus flights departing BWI, National, and Dulles had to be sequenced so that they had the proper in-trail separation at that fix. As a result, departures at each of the three airports were often delayed by a few minutes. If there were thunderstorms in the area the situation was a little worse. Compounding this problem was the fact that BWI had only a single taxiway leading to the primary instrument departure runway, plus a very small holdblock. Therefore flights departing BWI for destinations to the south and west were also held up because a leading flight headed northeast was delayed for traffic sequencing. If the delay for that flight was going to be significant, that aircraft was sometimes directed to "back-taxi" down the departure runway and hold on the ramp or re-enter the departure queue at the end of the line. Because the departure runway was also used for some flight arrivals during this period, delays could become acute. Our near-term fix was to expand the holdblock so that delayed aircraft had a place to wait while other flights could pass by and depart according to their schedule. A long-term fix was to program the construction of an additional, parallel taxiway; the dual taxiways could then be used to help with flight departure sequencing.

The point is that air traffic delays can be more complicated than they first appear, and before proposing major improvements such as parallel runways, planners need to understand exactly what is going on at the airport under study, as well as at neighboring airports, under varying weather conditions, modes of operation, and times of day.

To summarize the airside component: remember that the airside covers a lot of ground; a lot goes on out there; things can happen pretty quickly; and the primary concern should be safety.

Terminals

General Planning Considerations

As noted earlier in this chapter, to most people the airside is the sexy part of the airport, but to me the most challenging and sometimes even the most exciting part is the terminal. It is the heart of the airport. That is where people make that critical connection between air and ground modes of transportation, and to me that is where the airport passes or fails. Always remember: *airports are for people*.

In the early days of commercial aviation the typical trip through the airport was very close to the ideal implied above, with convenient up-front parking and short walking distances. Passengers walked in to the terminal, bought a ticket, checked in their bags, walked a short distance to the airplane, boarded, and went on their way. The return trip was usually a mirror image. However, as passenger traffic grew and terminals increased in size and complexity, passengers began to be faced with remote parking lots, shuttle buses, long queues, long walking distances, and above all, security checks. Faced with increasing terminal congestion and long processing times, many people have begun to get their tickets and boarding passes on a home or office computer, thereby reducing the importance of the ticketing function in airport terminals. Baggage processing is now becoming a key function, along with the security screening of both passengers and baggage. But the main purpose of terminals is still the same: getting people in one side of the building and out the other as quickly and conveniently as possible. The primary task of the airport terminal planner is to achieve that ideal as closely as possible. Yes, during busy periods there will be long lines, but this should be the exception, not the rule. When calculating the square footages required for queuing areas, baggage claim space, concession space, etc., remember that the passengers are the main reason the airport is there in the first place. As you read through the following paragraphs, think of how terminals operate now, and how some of the factors noted below might change over the next decade or so.

Satisfying all the Customer Groups
The most important thing to remember when airports plan new terminals or expansions to an existing terminal is that they are trying to satisfy the customer. Airport terminal planning is challenging because they have two groups of customers: the airlines that provide the air service and the passengers who use the air service. Between the two, satisfying the customers is the most important requirement; satisfying the airlines is usually the most difficult. Other airport users must be considered, such as meeters and greeters (people who accompany departing passengers and see them off, and people who come to the airport to meet arriving passengers) and the tenants who rent space in the terminal, such as the food and beverage and retail merchandise concessionaires. Nevertheless, the airlines and their passengers are the most important customers to try to satisfy. In addition, airport operators and management staff have their own needs and desires that must be considered. The interaction among these three entities makes for interesting dynamics.

Sometimes it is very difficult to figure out exactly what the airlines want, aside from as much room as possible at the lowest price possible. In other words, they want more space than their competitors and they want to pay less for it than their competitors do. Further, the airlines seemingly have always been afraid that airport authorities are going to build grandiose architectural monuments to civic pride, and that they (the airlines) will be stuck with the bill in terms of higher landing fees and facility rental charges. They are also afraid that airports will overbuild, providing too much space under the philosophy of "build it and they will come." Too much space from a carrier's perspective often means any space that they do not need, but that might be available to a competitor. Airlines have a tendency to focus on "value engineering," where value engineering results in cement block walls and a tarpaper roof. What the airlines actually *need* is enough room to serve—efficiently and economically—the needs of their passengers and baggage, with respect to ticket counter space, queuing space, baggage makeup and claim space, gate and holdroom space, and operations space, plus a relatively small area to house their administrative functions.

The other major customer group, passengers, wants whatever gets people through the building as quickly and comfortably as possible. Unfortunately, with increased security requirements, airlines advise passengers to arrive two hours before their flight is scheduled to depart. Most passengers understand this and have come to accept it, but still, they don't really want to spend time in the terminal, they want to get to where they are going. Spending time in the airport is not on most people's list of fun things to do—especially in the U.S., where time is money. The typical passenger would probably like to park their car right in front of the terminal, walk across the street, check in their bags (but only if they really *have* to—most seem to prefer taking everything they own on the plane with them), walk a short distance to the boarding gate, get on the plane, and go. And do it all in as little time as it took to read this, with a return flight that is just as simple. Although this ideal is not often realized at many large airports, the point here is that the terminal should be planned with the comfort and convenience of the passenger in mind. This consists chiefly of providing a pleasant and clean physical environment, with conveniently-located food service and retail facilities, and adequate restrooms. In all fairness to the airlines, they would probably agree with this but they are very concerned, and justifiably so, with how much it will cost them. Therefore airport terminals should be planned to provide the passengers with what they want and the airlines with what they need, as economically as possible. Therein lies the challenge.

The terminal planning process can get very complicated, mainly because it involves a lot of different people, who are working for a lot of different companies or organizations, with a lot of different ideas and objectives, all operating in a constantly changing environment. Airport operations staff, for example, desires a terminal that is easy to secure and/or evacuate in the event of a security threat or fire or similar emergency situation. They will also want a layout that is simple to sign for wayfinding purposes. Also keep in mind that the airport operations office at large airports is staffed 24 hours a day, every day. In bad weather or in emergency situations they don't get to go home; therefore, sleeping areas, a small kitchen, and perhaps shower facilities would be appreciated.

Airport maintenance will want adequate and conveniently-located storage space for all the disposable items that help a terminal function, such as paper products, soap, spare light bulbs, etc., as well as all the tools and equipment, such as bulky ladders, that are needed virtually every day.

Airport management will also want space for airport staff, particularly operations, maintenance, and security. And you can bet that the airport manager will also want an office with a nice view of his or her domain, no matter what they may say at the beginning of the terminal planning process. At larger airports, airport management will probably also want a fairly large conference room—perhaps something that would accommodate two dozen people comfortably—complete with all the space required for the latest audio-visual equipment. And an executive bathroom and small kitchen area would be nice too.

The commercial management or leasing office will also want to maximize the amount of space available for concessions, since concession space rentals and fees account for a significant portion of airport revenues. They and the prospective tenants will want to ensure that concessions are located so that they are easy to find (perhaps even hard to avoid) for as many people as possible. This raises the thorny issue of whether airports are transportation facilities or shopping malls, and can involve some pretty heated discussions. A balance is always struck, even though some people may not be happy with the outcome, but the balance will vary from airport to airport. The process of sizing and locating concession space can take a lot of time and effort, and in my experience the best answers come through negotiation rather than formulas.

It is important to make an accurate determination of the space required, and the facilities should also be categorized into "must have" and "nice to have." Again, this varies among airports and among individuals, but if planners are patient and flexible, and can show that they know what they are talking about, all will come out well in the end. As mentioned throughout this book (and discussed in detail in Chapter 9: Coordination and Communication), airport planning is half sales. If nobody buys into the final plan and accepts the analyses, methodologies, and results, a lot of time and money will have been wasted.

Safety and Security
Another key aspect of terminal planning is the safety/security factor. Planners must be sure to include the Transportation Security Administration (TSA) in decision-making. Because security is so critical and because security technologies and procedures are still evolving fairly quickly, TSA representatives must be involved in the planning process to make sure that they can function with the proposed alternatives, both now and in the future. The airport operations office should be included in these discussions, because these two groups frequently have common interests and work together on security, passenger processing, and overall terminal operations issues. From the safety standpoint, coordination with the local fire marshal is also important. Often the fire marshal will request (and sometimes try to require) some pretty extreme arrangements. For example, in more than one instance the local fire marshal has insisted that terminal concourses and holdrooms be made large enough to safely accommodate *all* the passengers that could

be expected to occupy the concourse under the assumption that *all of the aircraft gates would be occupied simultaneously by the largest aircraft type that each of the gates could accommodate*. In instances like these, an airport planner needs competent negotiating skills, along with a good bit of luck.

It is a good idea to work with the appropriate agencies to find a place where people in the terminal can go if there is an emergency, such as a fire, explosion, toxic gas release, or similar scenario. Evacuation is usually the responsibility of airport operations, but it is a big help to them if planners identify spaces or areas where evacuees could be directed and held until the emergency situation has been resolved. After all, airport operators really don't want people wandering around on the ramp or standing in the street in front of the terminal blocking traffic. It is usually not feasible to set aside a site for use only in the event of an emergency, but the planners should help identify areas where crowds could gather and be controlled safely without interfering with other airport activities.

Collaboration and Buy-in
Another complicating factor is that the airlines and other tenants will eventually wind up paying for all the space, and airlines in particular can be pretty stingy, especially if they are asked to pay for something that doesn't benefit them directly and exclusively. Again, some "sales" skills will be needed here, typically in support of airport management who will usually take the lead on the financial negotiations. Part of the problem is coordination. It seems that no matter how hard planners try to coordinate, somebody will come in when the plan is completed and say that it is not going to work for them. The subject of coordination is discussed in more detail in Chapter 5: Master Planning and Chapter 9: Coordination and Communication. Every effort should be made to talk with representatives of all the terminal users. They should be briefed at the beginning of the terminal planning study and periodically as the study progresses. Planners should not develop their plans in a vacuum and then present the final results to the users as something they have to accept and live with. If the appropriate representatives are not attending the briefings it is the responsibility of the planner to find out why (are they held at awkward times, are they boring, etc.) and correct the problem. Of course one can only go so far, and if people don't speak up they will have to live with the results, but keep in mind that they can make the planner's life miserable if they take their complaints to the airport director or the airport commission.

Lack of Current Guidance
Terminal planning is especially challenging because terminal planning guidance is rather difficult to come by. The FAA's advisory circulars that deal with terminal planning and design are outdated (as of 2009), particularly with regard to large airline terminals. The latest edition of AC 150/5360-13, *Planning and Design Guidelines for Airport Terminal Facilities*, was published in 1988. AC 150/5360-9, *Planning and Design of Airport Terminal Building Facilities at Non-hub Locations*, was published in 1980. Also, airport terminals, and the

airlines that serve them, are so different in how they are configured—and thus in how they operate—that it is difficult to come up with a standard "how to" manual.

These circulars should be applied in a very broad context. For example, AC 150/5360-13 suggests using between 0.08 and 0.12 square feet per annual enplaned passenger as a "rule of thumb" to determine gross terminal square footage requirements. Applying that to an airport that enplanes five million passengers annually comes up with the need for between 400,000 and 600,000 square feet, a difference of 50 percent. Planners should be more accurate than this. Note also that most terminal facilities are used by originating passengers rather than enplaned passengers, as discussed in Chapter 7: Forecasting, thus using enplanements to develop a value for terminal size can be misleading. On a brighter note, it appears that some help may be forthcoming. The Transportation Research Board is sponsoring a research study termed "Passenger Space Allocation Guidelines for Planning and Design of Airport Terminals" as an Airport Cooperative Research Project. The goal of the study "…is to identify passenger perceptions as they pertain to physical space and innovative solutions that can [be] used in the diverse phases of airport operations." The focus of the study "…is to determine how to best appropriate [sic], plan, and design airports to most efficiently serve their passengers, both now and in the future."[21]

Terminal Configuration Considerations

Part of the problem in terminal planning is that airport terminals are so different from each other that it would be hard to develop an overall planning guide that takes into consideration all the variations seen between airports and even between different parts of the terminal at the same airport. In his book on airport planning and design, Bob Horonjeff, late Professor of Transportation Engineering at the University of California, Berkeley, divides the terminal into three components: the *access interface*, the *processing component*, and the *flight interface*.[22] Other authors have developed similar schemes, but Horonjeff's will work quite nicely for us. In this context the access interface is where the passenger transfers between the ground access mode of travel and the processing component. It includes vehicular circulation, parking, and curbside loading and unloading of passengers and their luggage. The processing component consists of ticketing, baggage check-in, baggage claim, seat assignment, federal inspection, and security. The flight interface is where the passenger transfers from the processing component to the aircraft, or vice versa, depending on whether the passenger is inbound or outbound.

Configurations

There are probably as many different terminal configurations and combinations as there are airports. These are described in detail in ACs 150/5360-13 and 150/5360-9, in a book on airport planning and management by Alexander Wells (Professor Emeritus of Aviation at Embry-Riddle Aeronautical University), and in even greater detail in Horonjeff's book, so I will not belabor the subject here.[23] A brief but excellent summary of airport terminal layouts and an especially concise summary of terminal functions can be found in a presentation prepared by Eileen Poh, Assistant Director of ICAO Affairs (International Civil Aviation Organization).[24] Wells briefly describes seven basic terminal design concepts and Poh describes five. This book will cover three: gate arrival terminals, pier finger terminals, and satellite terminals, as shown in Figures 2-3, 2-4, and 2-5. Other terminal layouts are essentially variations on these three basic configurations.

Figure 2-3: Gate Arrival Terminal

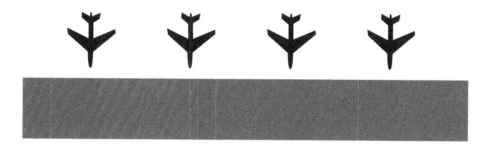

Figure 2-4: Pier Finger Terminal

Figure 2-5: Satellite Terminal

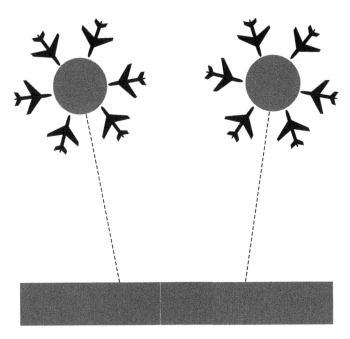

Gate Arrival Terminals are those where the aircraft pulls up to the terminal directly. This is the way most airports started and this is the way most smaller airports are configured today. If the terminal is small this is an ideal concept because the airplanes are literally on one side of the building and the cars on the other. As aircraft increase in size, the terminal must be widened to accommodate the same number of aircraft, and widened even more as the number of aircraft increases. In general the gate arrival design configuration works well at commercial airports with relatively low traffic volumes, but becomes inconvenient and inefficient as traffic increases.

Pier Finger Terminals are those where a pier or concourse extends out from the terminal and aircraft are parked on both sides, as well as at the end if sufficient room is available. This configuration can be modified to have a pier extension with a concourse at the end. Some airports even have a combination, with gates along both sides of the pier and around the end concourse. The pier finger configurations generally work well, but they have some limitations. Because the length of the concourse is often fixed, by the location of a taxiway for example, an increase in the size of the aircraft using the gates may result in the loss of one or more gate positions. Also, as the number of aircraft parked along the pier increases, so does the walking distance. Walking distance is not only the distance from the wall of the terminal building proper to a particular gate on the pier, but also the distance within the terminal from the ticket counter to the entrance to the pier. Walking distances become particularly important if the airport handles a lot of connecting passengers who must pass through the terminal to board another flight, particularly if the flights are on different concourses. There does not appear to be a hard and fast rule for maximum walking distances, but 1,000 feet seems to be widely used. The ICAO recommends 300 meters, which amounts to nearly the same thing. Considering that 1,000 feet is equivalent to more than three football fields, that is a pretty long hike, especially when lugging carry-on bags.

At some airports electric golf carts are used for people who might have difficulty walking the length of the pier. That helps, but the golf carts do take up space and passengers on foot have to be aware and accommodate the carts—and then there is the incessant beeping, which can get on people's nerves. At other airports moving walkways may be used. This is a nice idea and passengers seem to like them, but installing a moving walkway means the pier has to be widened to accommodate the walkway, and some ceiling height is lost on the lower level to accommodate the return loop and the mechanical and electrical devices required to make the moving walkway function. The lower levels of piers are commonly used for baggage sorting and airline operations space, so ceiling height may or may not be important, but it should be considered before any decision is made to construct a moving walkway. To complicate things further, grades can be a problem if the pier is very long. The grade slopes away from the terminal and the walkway must be installed accordingly.

Satellite Terminals are not physically connected to the main terminal building. There are two variations: the first is served by an underground connection, either a moving walkway or a people mover; the second is served by mobile lounges, i.e., bus-like vehicles that transport passengers between the main terminal and the satellite terminal, or sometimes between the terminal and the aircraft. Mobile lounges are usually used if there is a significant distance between the main terminal and the satellite. There are two important things to remember about mobile lounges: 1) make sure the plan includes an area where they can park when they are not in use, and 2) passengers seem to hate them. There isn't much that can be done about how passengers feel about mobile lounges, but something can be done about parking. The area should be located close to the terminal, or, if the aircraft being served by the mobile lounges will be parked on a remote ramp, close to that ramp. Also, the route between the terminal and the remotely-parked aircraft should be clear and provide safe and efficient access, and it should not cross runways or taxiways.

Start With the Operational Profile
Strictly speaking, terminal space planning is based on the operational profile of the airport, including the type of aircraft, gate utilization, load factors, volume of peak hour passengers, passenger mix (origin and destination [O&D] versus connecting, trip purpose), the relative volumes of charter and international service, and specific airline operational needs. Meeter/greeter ratios are also important in determining lobby space needs and should be

considered in the analysis of airport parking requirements. Although not a major determinant of terminal space requirements, the ratio of meeters and greeters to passengers can be significant at some airports. Ratios on the order of 1:1 and 2:1 are pretty commonly used, but ratios on the order of 10:1 or 20:1 can occur at major international airports. Thus it doesn't seem to be a very good idea to pick an average or typical ratio; if there is any indication that meeter/greeter volumes will be significant, planners should do some surveys at the individual airport under study to come up with a valid number. Terminal space requirements and measures to determine future space needs for each and every component of the terminal can be found in the Terminal Planning ACs, as well as in Horonjeff's book.

Basically, terminal space planning involves finding out how many passengers will be using a given area, such as ticket counter queuing or baggage claim, during a typical peak period and applying a square foot per passenger value to the passenger volume. Horonjeff goes into particular detail in determining passenger processing times and queue lengths, complete with charts and graphs.[25] Space must also be provided for concessions, airline operations, airport operations and management, police and other security, federal inspection services, building maintenance and storage, and a number of other uses that often vary from airport to airport.

Once all the relevant data have been collected and space needs quantified, this information is passed on to an architect to develop alternative layouts and configurations. That information is then passed on to an engineer who will change nearly everything to accommodate considerations such as the location of support columns, routes for utilities, space for mechanical and electrical vaults, and a dozen other things that planners seem to forget. And then the terminal plan is done. It is really a very simple process, except that no two airports are exactly alike, either physically or operationally. Good consultants take local factors into account, developing a customized terminal plan that meets the airport's unique needs.

Those Lines at the Loo
One point should be emphasized about restrooms. According to virtually all sources of terminal planning guidance public restroom facilities should be adequately sized and conveniently located. However, one mistake that we all see and about half of us experience nearly all the time in *any* public facility, not only airports, is that ladies' rooms tend to be overcrowded, i.e., there is always a line during busy periods. This seems to happen because restrooms are designed on a simple total square footage basis, without considering the fact that more "facilities" can be installed in a men's room than in an equally-sized women's restroom because some of the individual "facilities" don't require separate cubicles. Restrooms should be planned by calculating the number of "facilities" needed, and then doing a square footage space calculation based on an average "facility" size, rather than applying a simple quantity takeoff based on the number of people expected to use the restroom at any given time.

Changes in Passenger "Processing"
As for the interior of the terminal building itself, we can expect to see some major changes in the way terminals are laid out and used, and particularly, how passengers and baggage are processed through the building. Traditionally, passengers entered at the "front door" of the terminal, walked to the ticket counter to get their tickets and/or boarding passes, checked their bags, and proceeded on through to the rear (or airside) of the terminal, where the airplane would (hopefully) be waiting. To accommodate this process the standard airport terminal now contains an area between the front door and the ticket counters to provide for lateral circulation and queuing space at the ticket counters. Additional space is provided for ticketing and airline ticket office (ATO) functions, plus space for circulation to and from the gate and holdroom areas, with assorted niches for concessions of various types. But this layout developed when people went to the ticket counter to pick up their tickets, and sometimes even purchased them there. Airlines needed space behind the counter to store the cash associated with ticket purchases, as well as ticket stock and other assorted essentials and goodies. Now, however, many (perhaps most) passengers already have their ticket and their boarding pass before they even get to the airport, or else they walk up to a free-standing ticketing kiosk and make their purchase and get their pass at the kiosk. It appears that this will reduce the terminal space needed for passenger processing. In fact it has been said that one check-in kiosk can replace two or three ticket agent positions located at a traditional ticket counter. With the increased emphasis on security following 9/11, passengers tend to proceed immediately to security screening—not knowing how long they will wait in line—and thus spend more time in the concourse areas rather than in the main terminal ticketing area. Planners are therefore rethinking the location and amount of space designated for concessions. Passengers who have baggage to check still need to go to the ticket counter, but a good many people seem to prefer to hang on to their bags, no matter how large and cumbersome, and take them on the plane with them. In fact, according to the J.D. Power survey noted at the beginning of this chapter, the percentage of customers checking bags has declined considerably, from 77 percent in 2007 to 66 percent in 2008.[26] This is happening in spite of the more intensive security requirements after 9/11, and the longer times associated with screening carry-on bags. It may also be a result of the fact that, some airlines now charge a fee for a checked bag; some carriers charge for the first bag but others charge only for the second. With respect to security and baggage inspection, a good bit of terminal space is taken up these days by baggage screening equipment that is about the size of a minivan, but this is something that will probably change in the near future with the development of new screening technologies that result in much smaller equipment, including hand-held devices. Also, we are beginning to see remote baggage check-in, at downtown hotels and off-airport parking lots for example. Passengers who use this service and already have a boarding pass do not have to go to the ticket counter at all. These are just two examples of changes that will undoubtedly affect terminal planning and design. Planners should keep

their eyes and ears open—there are likely to be many more changes in the not-too-distant future.

Flexibility
Airport terminals have traditionally been designed with airline needs in mind. Passenger needs (and wants) are becoming at least as important, if not more so, than airline requirements. New technologies and operational procedures will enable the design and operation of airport terminals that are more closely based on passenger wants and needs. This will call for greater flexibility in terminal design. It is difficult to predict with any confidence what airport terminals will look like and how they will operate in the future. Terminal planners sometimes say that the terminal should be thought of as a box and the facilities as furniture that can be put anywhere as conditions change. This is an example of flexibility. There are, however, some basic factors that should be considered prior to and during the necessary square footage calculations, and should guide terminal planning and development now and in the future. These include accessibility and wayfinding, airport support systems, and expansion.

Wayfinding
Convenient access and wayfinding are very important because those are two of the factors that customers notice most. Wayfinding is just another term for signage, and that is more of a design issue than a planning issue. To the extent that planners get involved with terminal signage, they should make sure that all signs and markers are consistent throughout the terminal building. Keep in mind that people want to know where their flight will be, where their bags will be, where the restrooms are, and where the concessions are. Quite often an airport has a clear and consistent (or at least consistent) sign system in place and for some reason, when a section of the terminal is expanded or renovated, a new sign system is installed. It may be a good system and it may be a better system than the one it replaced, but it will not be consistent with the sign system in place throughout the rest of the terminal. Thus it may cause confusion and defeat the purpose of the overall signage program. Wayfinding and overall ease of access should always be kept in mind when laying out new terminals or expansions to existing terminals. Passage from the terminal entrance to ticketing/baggage check, security, and gates/holdrooms should be as direct as possible, keeping clear lines of sight, avoiding points where bottlenecks could occur, and avoiding the need for passengers to have to backtrack during the check-in/boarding process. For inbound or arriving passengers, the route from deplaning at the gate, through baggage claim, and on to ground transportation should also be clear and easy to follow.

Accommodating Future Systems
Planners should also keep in mind that new technologies show up on a regular basis, whether dealing with aircraft parking and gate monitoring systems, airline flight information and baggage claim, or security, to name

only a few technology-sensitive airport systems. Sufficient space should be provided for hardware, wiring, and maintenance. Consideration should also be given to the adequacy of existing power supply systems and the need for (and location of) backup power supplies. Many information systems at airports are becoming "common use," able to be used by any airline. Some years ago airlines said they would never agree to such an idea—they had to maintain a separate corporate identity. But now flight and baggage information shows all airlines in one display. Many sections of ticket counter are now being used by several carriers at various times throughout the day, particularly at airports where an airline only has a few flights.

Keeping Options Open
Most planners do not have the opportunity to plan brand new terminals; most terminal planning work seems to involve expansion to, or renovation of, existing terminal buildings. When the opportunity to plan a new terminal building does arise, however, it should be kept in mind that it will probably have to be expanded at some point. Thus the new building should be sited with expandability in mind. Terminals should also be sited with respect to the rest of the airfield. For example, a clear line of sight should be maintained from the control tower to all parts of the movement area, not only for the proposed structure but also for any potential expansions to that structure at some point in the future. In some cases cameras are used where a building or other object blocks a controller's view of the aircraft operations area. Note, however, that controllers do not like to rely on cameras unless absolutely necessary. Controllers really have enough to do without having another monitor to look at. Cameras have a tendency to get covered with snow or ice in northern climates, and ice can also cause the cameras to jam and not be able to be directed toward the particular area where the controller needs to see what is going on. Glare from ramp and terminal lighting can also interfere with camera visibility. In fact, the location of such lights should always be planned so that glare does not inhibit the controller's view, whether looking at a monitor or viewing an area directly from the tower. And finally, new terminal buildings should be sited so that taxiway access between the gates and the runways is as direct and convenient as possible.

When planning expansions to existing buildings, the above-mentioned factors also apply. But expanding an existing building presents some significant issues as well. The new addition to the structure should work well with the existing building in terms of wayfinding and ease of access, but it should also be remembered that an existing building is usually being expanded because the old building is too small. Therefore it is highly likely that the existing building must be kept in operation while the new construction is taking place. This is something that should be included when evaluating expansion alternatives. Also, planners should consider the fact that additional expansion may well be needed at some point in the future. So if a six-gate addition to an existing terminal building is needed, the expansion plan should account for the possibility that at some point in the future four more gates may be needed. Therefore it might be wise for the overall *concept* plan to show a

10-gate addition but to only include the first six gates in the *final* plan. This can be very helpful down the road if a new addition is needed in a hurry, which most terminal expansions are. Having developed a concept plan that shows that 10 gates are feasible, especially if an FAA airspace review is done for the full 10-gate addition, will save a lot of time and money. It will also give an early warning of any issues that may arise during the second phase of the expansion.

Terminal Capacity Considerations

An assessment of terminal capacity is an important part of the terminal planning process, just as a measure of runway capacity is important to airside planning. However, terminal capacity seems to be much more difficult to quantify accurately.

Level of Service: It's All Relative

Terminal capacity is usually presented in terms of a "level of service" (LOS), as opposed to a number of annual or peak hour passengers. At some point during the 1960s the Federal Highway Administration (FHWA) introduced a concept called level of service to show how well (or how poorly) a given section of highway was performing. In that context the LOS indicates the degree of congestion (resulting in delay) associated with categories ranging from A to F, with A being free-flow conditions (with no delay), and F being gridlock. In the 1980s the International Air Transport Association (IATA) developed a similar methodology to show how well (or how poorly) airport terminals were performing. Others have tinkered with the IATA system, but most versions are generally presented as shown below. The IATA LOS standards in terms of square footage per person for each terminal component are shown in Table 2-3.

LOS A: Excellent service, free flow, uncongested, no delay

LOS B: High-level service, stable flow, uncongested

LOS C: Good service, generally stable flow, some congestion and delay during peak periods

LOS D: Adequate service, periods of unstable flow, some congestion and delay occur at various times during the day

LOS E: Unacceptable service, unstable flow, congestion and delay are common throughout the day, usually presented as the terminal capacity limit

LOS F: System breakdown, unacceptable congestion and delay

Although this sounds like a reasonably accurate and objective measure of how well the terminal (or various parts of the terminal) is performing, a good bit of subjectivity actually goes into the calculations. For example, what do we mean by "congested" and "delay"? An LOS assessment can be made from direct observations or from videos, and it is pretty easy to distinguish free flow from gridlock. It becomes a bit more subjective (and less precise) to distinguish congestion during peak periods from occasional congestion throughout the day, and from common congestion throughout the day. Also keep in mind that airports serving tourist destinations can be near gridlock during peak travel seasons but experience free-flow conditions during the rest of the year. And to complicate things just a bit more, some parts of a large terminal may operate without congestion, while other parts experience serious congestion throughout the day.

Although LOS can be a valuable tool, it cannot provide all the answers all the time. Care should be used when analyzing and presenting airport terminal capacity information in terms of service levels because LOS does not provide all the answers—especially when someone asks you, "What is the capacity of the terminal? How many passengers a year can it handle?" It is possible to provide an answer, but it has to be qualified. For example, at LOS B the terminal could accommodate 10 million passengers per year, but if the airport operator is willing to put up with some congestion, delay, and dissatisfied customers, the terminal might be able to handle 12 or 15 million passengers a year. Remember: the fact that something can be presented numerically doesn't necessarily guarantee accuracy.

Table 2-3: IATA Airport Level of Service Standards[27]
(square footage per person)

LOS	A	B	C	D	E	F
Check-in Queue	19	17	15	13	11	--
Circulation	29	25	20	16	11	--
Holdroom	15	13	11	9	6	--
Baggage Claim	22	19	17	15	13	--
Federal Inspection	15	13	11	9	6	--

Note: Values converted from metric to English units and rounded to nearest whole number.

Terminal congestion can also be stated in terms of delay, but delay itself can be subjective. Surveys can time how long it takes an individual to get from one point to another, and how long an individual has to stand in line at security or baggage claim. But delay can be a relative term and does not include a "comfort" or "utility" component. Consider someone waiting in a security line carrying a heavy briefcase or laptop, or somebody waiting in baggage claim trying to keep a pair of unruly children under control. In these situations a 10-minute delay can seem like an hour. On the other hand, to someone sitting in a holdroom with a good book, or writing a report or checking stock prices on a laptop, even 20 minutes may be barely noticed.

The "Junkyard" Outside
Another issue that comes up when discussing terminal areas is the airside congestion that occurs immediately adjacent to the terminal building.

It seems that any tenant who has space in the terminal needs, or at least wants, some space adjacent to the terminal to park vehicles. This can include airport administration, the FAA, federal inspection services, concessionaires, and sometimes construction companies, particularly those who are doing construction management and inspection work. In addition, the airlines need space to park their tugs, baggage carts, ground power units (GPU), and other assorted vehicles and pieces of equipment. The airside of any airport should be limited to airplanes, and only those ground vehicles that are necessary to support airport or aircraft operations.

Obviously the airlines need space for their GPUs, baggage carts, and tugs, and airport management needs some space for the operations staff and the maintenance staff, but it can get out of hand unless airport management takes a firm stand. The problem is that everybody thinks all of their vehicles fall into the "essential equipment" category. So how can the space required for these purposes be determined? In reality it can't be planned for.

All terminal buildings have an airside wall, and tenants will be able to park vehicles adjacent to that wall. And they will take as much space as is available. In my experience there is always enough room to park aircraft service equipment, plus some left over for airport management and a few other essential users. It is also my experience that tenants will abuse this space by parking equipment that doesn't really need to be there, including equipment that they no longer use. In these cases airport management has to take a hard line and tell people that if they don't use the equipment they should move it to another location, sell it, or junk it. Some airport managers will do that and some will not. As a planner there is not really much you can do about this situation, but planners should not make extraordinary efforts to plan terminal parking areas that will wind up being used for junk storage. The airside should be for essential vehicles only; any extraneous equipment will only get in the way, and may compromise safety.

General Aviation Terminals

The preceding discussion of airport terminals applies primarily to large airports with air carrier service. Although many of the same principles and considerations apply to small general aviation airports, general aviation terminal planning has its own unique needs and requirements. A primary consideration at general aviation airports is that their terminals are generally not eligible for FAA funding; the costs must be borne by the local airport sponsor. At small general aviation airports where most flight activity is generated by locally-based aircraft and the number of transient (or visiting) aircraft is relatively low, a simple administration building will usually suffice. This building should be large enough to accommodate the airport manager and an assistant—if the manager is lucky enough to have one—along with a reception area where pilots can pay for gasoline and any other services. It should have a 24-hour public restroom and public telephone service (to enable pilots to contact the FAA to close flight plans or obtain weather briefings for upcom-

Chapter 2 – Airports

ing flights). Virtually every airport, regardless of size, will have a coffee pot, and many also have vending machines for snacks and beverages.

Busier general aviation airports, particularly those accommodating a significant number of transient aircraft, need a somewhat larger building that includes a lounge area where charter or corporate pilots can relax and wait for their passengers. At these airports the administration building is often large enough to be thought of as a terminal, with sufficient space and facilities to accommodate both visitors and airport users. Although most of these airports are too small to support rental car operators, the airport operator often has a "loaner" available for pilots who want to run into town for a quick bite to eat. Many of the busier general aviation airports also accommodate a fixed base operator (FBO). In some cases FBO services are provided by the airport operator, but where volume is sufficient, FBO services are contracted out to a private business. The FBOs typically provide aircraft support facilities and services such as parking, fueling, maintenance, and deicing; along with ground services such as catering, baggage handling, aircraft cleaning, hotel reservations, and car rentals. The busier general aviation airports often have two or more FBOs, sometimes with different specialties. For example, one FBO might provide all of the above services, while another specializes in flight training, and a third specializes in avionics repairs. At some airports the FBO is located in the main administration or terminal building but at others, particularly those with more than one FBO, the FBO operators have their own leased area and construct and maintain their own facilities. In any case the facilities, regardless of size, should be located such that public access is clear and convenient, with ample room for transient aircraft parking near the terminal (or FBO office location), and with convenient access from the aircraft parking ramp to the taxiway system.

Although planning general aviation airport terminals is not nearly as complex as planning large passenger terminals, it should be remembered that the terminal function is the same: to provide a safe, efficient, and convenient interface between air and ground transportation. Facilities should be located and sized to meet the needs of the people they serve.

In summary, terminal planning, especially at large air carrier airports, is complicated and requires some serious negotiating skills, but the most serious problem for terminal planners today is trying to figure out how the terminal will function tomorrow. In all cases planners must consider the needs of the terminal users; not only in terms of how they operate today, but also how they might operate tomorrow.

Landside

Everything Else

The landside component of an airport is regarded by some planners as the dull, dirty part. Landside facilities and functions include the airport maintenance facilities, equipment storage areas, public and employee parking lots, and auxiliary fire stations. Auxiliary fire stations are, for example, those whose primary function is responding to structure fires, such as at the terminal or in the cargo or maintenance areas, and providing emergency medical responses to accidents, heart attacks, and other day-to-day emergencies that occur where large numbers of people and/or moving vehicles are found. These stations can also provide support for airside accidents. The landside component of the airport handles the movement of ground vehicles for passengers, cargo, public parking, rental car activities, and myriad other airport and customer support services and facilities. Landside development also often includes all those things that are located at or around an airport that people don't know where else to put, such as storage areas for unused equipment. Airport maintenance facilities are usually classed as landside facilities, even though much of the equipment and materials kept there are used to support airside operations. The airport maintenance division needs an area where repairs and routine maintenance can be performed on maintenance and operations equipment such as snow plows and brooms; grass-cutting equipment; and assorted cars, vans, and trucks. Airlines and the tenants who support airline operations need areas where they can perform maintenance on their ground support equipment, including tractors and tugs, baggage carts, GPUs, sanitation trucks, food service vehicles, fuelers, etc. At larger airports, airport operators and tenants also need areas where they can locate a vehicle wash rack and sometimes a vehicle paint booth. Integrated air cargo carriers such as FedEx and UPS also need areas where they can perform maintenance on their aircraft support equipment, cargo tugs, and carts, as well as over-the-road delivery trucks. Often delivery trucks are serviced and maintained at off-airport locations, but occasionally the companies ask for some on-airport facilities.

Too often in the past planners located these types of airport and airline support facilities where they could find room, without regard for locational requirements of these facilities. Planners seemed to think that the operations and maintenance people will find some way to make do (or at least that is the way the ops and maintenance people often feel about it), and at a lot of airports that seemed to be the case. The reality is that the airside facilities are often the most site-critical and demanding, and the terminal comes next. Therefore, especially at airports located in developed metropolitan areas, there is simply not enough room to meet support facility needs in the way we would like. This means that locating these rather unglamorous facilities requires some serious thinking.

Avoid Creating Obstructions

All landside facilities should be located so that they are clear of all runway and taxiway safety areas, as well as critical areas for navigation aids such as glide slope and localizer antennas. They should not be located in areas where they might interfere with NAVAID and radar signal propagation. They should also be constructed so they do not penetrate Part 77 imaginary surfaces and so they do not obstruct the line of sight from the control tower. If an airport does not have a control tower, but may need one at some point in the future, maintenance and support facilities should be located with future line of sight requirements in mind. Constructing these kinds of facilities at random may preclude options for future control tower site locations.

Think Efficiency and Convenience

Airport operators and planners have both come to the realization that in order for these organizations and their facilities to function well, support facilities should be located in areas convenient for both landside and airside access, and for the needs of their particular users. For example, an airfield maintenance facility should be located so that it has convenient access from the public roadway system for the delivery of supplies, including salt and sand for terminal area roadways and walkways, runway and taxiway deicing materials, supplies for the terminal, spare parts for airport vehicles, topsoil and mulch for terminal area landscaping, and a seemingly infinite variety of other items required for the maintenance and operation of an airport. An airfield maintenance facility should also be located so that it has convenient access to the runway and taxiway system for easy access of runway deicing and snow removal equipment, as well as grass-cutting equipment. However, the airport maintenance area should also be located so that airport vehicles traveling to and from the maintenance complex do not have to cross active runways and taxiways. It can be challenging to meet all these requirements, so at some airports, the airport maintenance functions are divided among different sites, each of which is designed to function effectively. The airport maintenance staff may sometimes complain if they have to operate out of more than one location, but sometimes it can't be helped. Access to these kinds of facilities from the public roadway system should be well marked, and a clear demarcation should be made at points leading to areas that are not open to the public. This is particularly important at smaller airports where someone out for a drive may wind up motoring down the runway. This happens more often than you might think.

Similarly, areas designated for the storage and maintenance of airline aircraft service and support vehicles should be located with convenient access to the terminal, and again, without the need to cross runways and taxiways. Airport operators are often not very happy with the idea that they have to provide potentially valuable land to the airlines to store their equipment. They occasionally blame airlines for hanging on to equipment that they don't use (i.e., junk), just because they are too cheap to get rid of it. There is probably some truth in this, although it is probably not as widespread as airports sometimes think. Nonetheless, it is important to provide a location for airline equipment, if for no other reason than that if the airport doesn't provide a space, the airlines will just park it on the airside of the terminal, an area which has a tendency to be congested at any time.

Shelter Maintenance Equipment and Materials

Maintenance facilities should be planned with weather conditions in mind. In areas that are subject to rain, snow, ice, and freezing temperatures, some type of shelter should be provided for equipment and materials. Expensive maintenance equipment that has a life of 15 years or so may need to be overhauled in as little as five years if not sheltered. Parts such as belts, hoses, and hydraulic lines do not last nearly as long when they are exposed to frequent freezing and thawing. Sometimes a simple shelter is sufficient, and is certainly an improvement over open storage. But ideally the buildings that house equipment should be heated; a temperature of about 40 °F will suffice. Snowplow blades have a tendency to freeze up when covered with snow or ice, just when they are needed the most. Structures should also be provided for materials storage, similar to the domes used by many highway departments for storing salt, sand, and other materials. These are not really major planning issues, but planners should keep them in mind because they will be important when preparing cost estimates for new maintenance facilities. If a plan only calls for site preparation and an access road the construction estimate will be much too low to accommodate the maintenance director's need for a structure and utility services. Once the planner's cost estimate goes into the airport's capital improvement program it is very difficult to squeeze out any more money. It is often better to prepare a plan and cost estimate that calls for a good facility and let the airport director trim back if money is an issue.

Flexible Cargo Security Space

An emerging concern that can complicate landside planning is air cargo security. Generally speaking, cargo security is a function of procedures established by the TSA, and they are still evolving. Thus cargo facilities should be planned with security concerns in mind and should be closely coordinated with the TSA. Cargo ramps should be located so that it will be easy to establish clearly defined perimeters and control access. A complicating factor is that many airports that receive air cargo service do not have a leased cargo service area or leased cargo ramp space. Thus a ramp that is used for air cargo aircraft parking may also be used by other aircraft throughout the day.

Public Parking Realities

Public parking facilities are another aspect of landside planning, although parking demand is usually analyzed as part of the terminal planning process. Public parking lots owned by private operators are located off-airport and are usually considered a land use function, rather than a landside function. Parking lots and parking structures should be located with safe and convenient access from the public highway system, and should also have direct and convenient access for shuttle buses and vans operating between the parking facilities and the terminal building. Most airport planners seem to start off planning public parking facilities by trying to develop estimates of short-term and long-term demand. Short-term demand is usually meant to include those people who park for an hour or two while seeing off passengers or picking them up. But short-term demand (or at least parking areas intended to be used for short-term demand) also includes passengers who park for a day, leaving on a flight in the morning and returning in the evening. Long-term parking refers to people who are traveling for periods longer than a day, including longer business trips and vacations. Some estimate of true short-term demand is needed, i.e., parking for those who are only staying at the airport for an hour or two, to ensure that enough space is available. Someone who comes to the airport to pick up Aunt Nellie should not have to park in a remote long-term lot and take a shuttle to the terminal. It is easy to lose sight of the fact that people want to park as close to the terminal as they can, and most people do not seem to enjoy riding on a shuttle bus, whether from a remote parking lot or rental car lot or other location. Passengers going on long trips will park in the lot closest to the terminal, all other things being equal, especially if it means that they will not have to wait for a shuttle. The way most airports control short-term lot use is through their parking price structure. Short-term parkers get a reasonable hourly rate, but after a certain period, 12 hours or 24 hours for example, the rate goes up to something totally outrageous, thereby discouraging long-term use. There are always some high rollers who will pay just about anything for the convenience of a close-in parking space, but if the rate is set high enough, long-term parking in the short-term lot will be discouraged. The maximum rate will vary widely at airports around the country, but at current prices in a fairly affluent metropolitan area, something on the order of $20 to $25 dollars a day seems to be effective.

Most airport planners forecast parking demand by applying a rate of so many thousand spaces per so many million passengers. And unfortunately an *enplaned* passenger value is often used. Remember that *enplaned* passengers do not park cars; *originating* passengers park cars. Because the enplaned passenger total includes connecting passengers, any parking demand ratios that use enplanements, which include connections as well as originations, may be unreliable and should be applied carefully (enplanements, originations, and connections are discussed in more detail in Chapter 7: Forecasting). An enplaned passenger total should only be used to project public parking demand at airports with a very low level (10 percent or so) of connecting passenger traffic. In AC 150/5360-13 the FAA notes that the ratio of parking spaces to originating passengers varies between airports, especially at those enplaning more than 1.5 million passengers, and typically ranges from under 1,000 spaces per million originations to as high as 3,300 spaces per million.

The problem with using a ratio of spaces to passengers is that the data on the number of parking spaces actually available at airports is often of questionable accuracy. Attempts are often made to get an accurate base value from which to establish a ratio, but many airport operators don't really have a very accurate idea of how many parking spaces are actually available to airport customers. Many airports own their own parking lots and can provide an accurate count of the spaces they own. But most large airports are virtually surrounded by privately-owned parking lots. The number of spaces available at those lots is a little harder to estimate accurately. The easiest way to get a private parking space estimate is to ask the operator, and they may or may not be willing to provide an accurate answer—or they may not answer at all. An alternative is to count spaces using an aerial photograph, or to estimate spaces from a photo based on a certain number of cars per acre. A fairly accurate value seems to be about 125 cars per acre, including an allowance for access and circulation. But many of these lots could serve customers other than airport patrons. Many businesses, manufacturing establishments, etc., locate near airports, and a conveniently-located parking lot could be used by their customers as well as by airport patrons. In most cases it is possible to come up with a reasonably accurate ratio of parking spaces to passengers by assuming that the space count accurately accounts for a given portion of the spaces that might be available for airport parking. For example, one could say, "We believe we have a total of 1,800 parking spaces per million originations and, based on our analysis, we believe that accounts for 90 percent of total airport parking demand." Just keep in mind that this is an estimate.

Rather than using a ratio of spaces per million passengers, some planners have successfully used a method of estimating parking demand that involves multiplying the number of cars parked by the parking duration. For example, if 1,000 cars park for three days, 3,000 spaces are occupied. Bear in mind however, that this method works for the total volume of airport parking and is not always accurate for individual lots. I once had a lengthy discussion with someone who insisted that this method was not accurate, because if it was applied to a specific lot, and the data indicated that 1,000 cars parked in a given period for an average stay of three days, it would show that 3,000 cars were parked—but that was not possible because the lot only has 2,000 spaces. I told him it was not an estimate for an individual lot, but for the airport as a whole. I also pointed out that he probably did have a demand for 3,000 spaces but the demand was unserved because when his lot filled he closed it and additional cars were directed to other lots. His response was, "Oh. Yeah, that did happen like that. I guess it works after all."

Data on the number of cars parked is pretty easy to get since most airports that charge for parking have some method of recording transactions. At airports with fairly sophisticated revenue control systems, the parking duration is also recorded and it is a simple matter of getting a summary of that information for any given time period. In other cases it may be necessary to obtain the duration data from individual ticket stubs; in this case, unless an accurate count is really necessary, it may be more appropriate to say to heck with it and use a ratio.

To summarize the subject of parking demand forecasts, if all that is needed is a long-range forecast of parking demand, the ratio of spaces per million passengers will suffice, if the base data are sufficiently accurate. But if there is a need for a short-term estimate that requires more accuracy (e.g., the airport director asks you in May how many cars will be parking over the coming Thanksgiving and Christmas holidays), it would be necessary to use a more detailed and more accurate methodology.

Rental Car Requirements

Airport rental car operations are closely related to public parking and rental car demand is usually analyzed as part of a terminal planning study. Rental car operations used to be located near the terminal building at most airports, and at many airports they still are. Passengers could rent a car at a counter in the terminal, usually located near baggage claim. Returning rental cars were driven to the same location and passengers could just walk across the street to the terminal. Ready/return spaces were located across the street from or adjacent to the terminal building and gas/wash facilities were often located nearby—sometimes at the same site. As car rentals increased, both in volume and in the number of rental car companies, rental car operators found that they did not have enough room to accommodate all the cars needed for peak-hour rental demand, and needed more space yet for fueling, washing, and cleaning the returned cars. At many large airports rental car operations were moved to remote locations and passengers were transported between the rental car facilities and the terminal by shuttle bus. For the most part each rental car company operated its own shuttle and that contributed significantly to roadway congestion, particularly in the terminal area including curbside. More recently the trend has been for the rental car operators to locate at a common site, off-airport. These are sometimes referred to as consolidated rental car facilities, or "conracs." In this sense rental car facilities have become more of a land use function rather than landside. The conracs are typically served by common-use shuttle buses. The consolidated shuttle bus operations have reduced traffic congestion on terminal roadways. Rental car operators should be involved in any rental car facility planning efforts, because they have some unique needs and are highly competitive, to say the least.

Leased Landside Property

There are some fortunate airports that have land available for uses not directly related to the operation of the airport. Airport operators have come to realize that this land can be leased out to private concerns that are usually related in some way to airport activities and services and, perhaps more importantly, can generate revenue for the airport. The important point to keep in mind is that the development should not interfere with airport activities, and that the land should be *leased* rather than being sold outright. People sometimes say that leasing will not be attractive because a business will not want to put up a building on land it doesn't own, but this has happened at many airports. Remember that airport land is valuable and a business or industry that needs airport access will usually be willing to pay a higher rent to be on-airport rather than at a remote location. From the point of view of the business owner, they get a site and can put up a building, and if something changes and they wind up having to relocate to another part of the country (or another part of the world), they will not be left with a piece of land that they have to dispose of. From the airport operator's point of view, even if an immediate need for the land is not apparent, the future is highly uncertain and the last thing they want to have to do is to buy back land they sold. As long as the development and associated activity is compatible with airport operations, just about anything could be acceptable as long as it helps pay the rent. But just because something is compatible, it doesn't necessarily follow that it is the best use of the land, as discussed below.

Land Use

Airport *landside* planning should not be confused with airport *land use* planning. Landside planning covers those parts of the airport proper that are not used for the operation of aircraft, or for passenger terminals. Land use planning covers the uses of land surrounding the airport proper, and can either be land that is owned by the airport or land that is owned by others, including the private sector. The FAA guidelines on land use planning focus primarily on controlling uses so that they are compatible with airport operations. Specifically, CFR Part 150 of the Federal Aviation Regulations covers the noise aspects of land use compatibility.[28] Part 150 provides guidance on the types of land uses that are considered compatible with the noise levels generated by aircraft operations, as shown in Table 2-4. Other land use controls, specifically CFR Part 77, are directed toward restricting uses that would compromise the safety of aircraft operations, including tall structures, light emissions, wildlife attractants, and sources of bright light emissions and electronic interference. Very little guidance is available with respect to how the various land uses interact with the airport and with each other from a functional standpoint. Fortunately some serious thought is now being given to the different kinds of land use development that could benefit from or complement the activities and services at the airport. Airports have long been viewed as a nuisance by the people who live around them, and many citizens still feel that nothing much seems to have been done to improve this image, even though the FAA has spent millions of dollars to support airport purchases of noise-impacted lands around airports. Also, land use and community planners have not given enough attention to ways of integrating airports more closely with the communities they serve. In metropolitan areas airports have been typically surrounded by land uses such as manufacturing, auto body and equipment repair shops, and the inevitable motels and parking lots. In less-developed areas surrounding lands were usually devoted to agricultural or recreational uses, plus an occasional airport business park, many of which never quite seem to have gotten off the ground. More recently economic development officials, land use developers, and businesses have seen that development such as office parks, conference facilities, high-tech assembly plants, and consumer product distribution centers can benefit from the opportunities offered at local airports. Also it appears that airport executives are paying more attention to market forces and development opportunities on land adjacent to the airport as a means of increasing airport revenues and demonstrating the importance of airport facilities and services.

These land use observations are not intended as a criticism of airport operators, airport planners, land use planners, or government planning and zoning agencies. Land use planning is always a very complicated issue, and even more so around airports where there is a plethora of conflicting needs, interests, and governmental controls. Airport planners cannot change things overnight and should not expect to do so. Instead we should keep the big picture and the long-term future in mind in our day-to-day planning activities. Proper land use can only be accomplished one parcel at a time, but if it is done properly the long-term situation will improve. Given that the airport does not own most of the surrounding land, and at best has only minimal control over the type of development that takes place there, the best way to accomplish this is for airport planners (and the airport operator) to work closely with land use planners, particularly those with planning and zoning authority in the vicinity of the airport. It is also a good idea to coordinate with local business groups, especially real estate developers, to try to find optimal uses that will encourage a synergy between airports and surrounding land use activities.

To this end the American Planning Association (APA) has developed an "Airports in the Region" (AIR) initiative in response to what APA has called "a dearth of planning guidance on how airport commercial districts should be designed, engineered, and managed."[29] APA has also cited the need for policy guidance, planning and design standards, and recommendations for zoning and building ordinances around airports. The AIR initiative proposes to address the various socioeconomic and intergovernmental factors associated with airport and community development. Also, the Airport Cooperative Research Program (ACRP) has recently sponsored a study directed toward enhancing airport land use compatibility, which is in progress at this writing. The ACRP was established as part of the Transportation Research Board to undertake research and other technical activities in a variety of airport subject areas including design, construction, maintenance, operations, safety, security, policy, planning, human resources, and administration.

Hopefully the efforts of APA and ACRP will soon result in some definitive guidance in the areas of land use development and airport/land use compatibility. Until additional guidance is available, airport planners should keep a couple of points in mind. Land use around airports should not only be *compatible* with the airport, but also *complement* the airport and its services. Ideally there should be a synergy between the airport and its surrounding development. In some cases this may mean no more than agricultural or recreational uses, but these uses could also benefit the local community by preserving open space and helping to preserve air and water quality by providing needed gaps in what otherwise might be wall-to-wall development. In other cases business and industrial development might be accommodated that will help enhance airport usage and revenues as well as support economic growth in the community or region. Airport planners should work closely with local community planners and economic development agencies to determine what kinds of development will promote a synergistic relationship between the airport and its surrounding lands. Airport planners should also keep in mind that land use around airports occurs as a kind of continuum; the land surrounding the airport should be compatible with the

Table 2-4: Land Use Compatibility with Yearly Day-Night Average Sound Levels[30]

Land Use	Yearly Day-Night Average Sound Level (L_{dn}) in decibels					
	Below 65	65–70	70–75	75–80	80–85	Over 85
Residential						
Residential, other than mobile homes and transient lodgings	Y	N(1)	N(1)	N	N	N
Mobile home parks	Y	N	N	N	N	N
Transient lodgings	Y	N(1)	N(1)	N(1)	N	N
Public Use						
Schools	Y	N(1)	N(1)	N	N	N
Hospitals and nursing homes	Y	25	30	N	N	N
Churches, auditoriums, and concert halls	Y	25	30	N	N	N
Governmental services	Y	Y	25	30	N	N
Transportation	Y	Y	Y(2)	Y(3)	Y(4)	Y(4)
Parking	Y	Y	Y(2)	Y(3)	Y(4)	N
Commercial Use						
Offices, business and professional	Y	Y	25	30	N	N
Wholesale and retail – building materials, hardware, and farm equipment	Y	Y	Y(2)	Y(3)	Y(4)	N
Retail trade – general	Y	Y	25	30	N	N
Utilities	Y	Y	Y(2)	Y(3)	Y(4)	N
Communication	Y	Y	25	30	N	N
Manufacturing and Production						
Manufacturing – general	Y	Y	Y(2)	Y(3)	Y(4)	N
Photographic and optical	Y	Y	25	30	N	N
Agriculture (except livestock) and forestry	Y	Y(6)	Y(7)	Y(8)	Y(8)	Y(8)
Livestock farming and breeding	Y	Y(6)	Y(7)	N	N	N
Mining and fishing, resource production and extraction	Y	Y	Y	Y	Y	Y

continued next page

Land Use	Yearly Day-Night Average Sound Level (L_{dn}) in decibels					
	Below 65	65–70	70–75	75–80	80–85	Over 85
Recreational						
Outdoor sports arenas and spectator sports	Y	Y(5)	Y(5)	N	N	N
Outdoor music shells, amphitheaters	Y	N	N	N	N	N
Nature exhibits and zoos	Y	Y	N	N	N	N
Amusements, parks, resorts, and camps	Y	Y	Y	N	N	N
Golf courses, riding stables, and water recreation	Y	Y	25	30	N	N

Key:

Y (Yes) – Land use and related structures compatible without restrictions.

N (No) – Land use and related structures are not compatible and should be prohibited.

NLR – Noise Level Reduction (outdoor to indoor) to be achieved through incorporation of noise attenuation into the design and construction of the structure.

25, 30, or 35 – Land use and related structures generally compatible; measures to achieve NLR of 25, 30, or 35 decibels (dB) must be incorporated into design and construction of structure.

Notes:

1) *Where the community determines that residential or school uses must be allowed, measures to achieve outdoor to indoor Noise Level Reduction (NLR) of at least 25 dB and 30 dB should be incorporated into building codes and be considered in individual approvals. Normal residential construction can be expected to provide NLR of 20 dB, thus the reduction requirements are often stated as 5, 10, or 15 dB over standard construction and normally assume mechanical ventilation and closed windows year round. However, the use of NLR criteria will not eliminate outdoor noise problems.*

2) *Measures to achieve NLR of 25 dB must be incorporated into the design and construction of portions of these buildings where the public is received, office areas, noise-sensitive areas, or where the normal noise level is low.*

3) *Measures to achieve NLR of 30 dB must be incorporated into the design and construction of portions of these buildings where the public is received, office areas, noise-sensitive areas, or where the normal noise level is low.*

4) *Measures to achieve NLR of 35 dB must be incorporated into the design and construction of portions of these buildings where the public is received, office areas, noise-sensitive areas, or where the normal noise level is low.*

5) *Land use compatible, provided special sound reinforcement systems are installed.*

6) *Residential buildings require an NLR of 25.*

7) *Residential buildings require an NLR of 30.*

8) *Residential buildings not permitted.*

airport and also with the land uses beyond that. For example, studies may show that a manufacturing plant that gets critical parts and supplies by air, or that ships its products by air, would be an ideal use for a parcel of land adjacent to the airport. But if the plant activities generate a lot of noise, that land use may not be compatible with a residential community located adjacent to the plant. Also, airport planners and land use developers should work together with local transportation agencies to ensure that the surrounding roadway system will be able to accommodate the traffic associated with any new development. And finally, planners should always be conscious that airports are a part of a larger community, and should try to be a positive force for supporting economic development and maintaining a high quality of life.

In summary, always remember that an airport is comprised of several components, all of which complement each other, and all of which must work together to provide a safe, efficient, and convenient interface between air and ground transportation. The various airport components should be developed with a view to balancing the services provided by each. The runway system must work in sync with the taxiway system, and the taxiway system should be developed so that it supports runway activity and is in sync with the terminal gates, cargo ramps, and general aviation areas. The terminal must be able to accommodate and support the activity generated at the gates so that passengers and baggage flow smoothly through the various terminal functions. And the terminal roadway system should be developed so that it can accommodate the activity taking place at the terminal and is in sync with the airport roadway and transit access systems. Each airport component should be developed in balance with each of the other components. There is little sense in constructing a runway system that will handle 20 million passengers if the terminal can only handle 10 million. Similarly, a terminal and runway system that can handle 20 million passengers will be of little use if the ground access system can only support 10 million. At times during the process of airport expansion one component may get ahead of another. For example, a new parallel runway may increase the airport's capacity by 30 percent or more. This is fine as long as long-term plans call for future terminal and ground access development to balance the additional runway capacity.

And remember that this need for balance does not stop at the airport boundary. The airport should also be a good neighbor to the community it serves.

Endnotes

1. *Federal Aviation Regulations (FAR), Part 1, Definitions and Abbreviations*. Washington, D.C.: Federal Aviation Administration. Accessed February 2008, from http://www.airweb.faa.gov/Regulatory_and_Guidance_Library/rgFAR.nsf/0/7B29C0FFCE0C430A86256EDF00478339?OpenDocument

2. J.D. Power and Associates, *2008 North America Airport Satisfaction Study*^{SM}, press release, May 2008. Westlake Village, CA. Accessed June 2008, from http://www.jdpower.com/corporate/news/releases/pressrelease.aspx?ID=2008050

3. *Ibid.*

4. *Ibid.*

5. Travel Industry Association of America, *Multi-Billion-Dollar Economic Loss from Deteriorating Air Travel System Hits Small Businesses Hardest*, press release, June 26, 2008. Accessed August 2008, from http://tia.usdm.net/pressmedia/pressrec.asp?Item=905

6. *Airport Design*, AC 150/5300-13. Washington, D.C.: Federal Aviation Administration, 1989. Accessed April 2008, from http://www.faa.gov/airports_airtraffic/airports/resources/advisory_circulars/media/150-5300-13/150_5300_13.PDF

7. *Federal Aviation Regulations, Part 77, Objects Affecting Navigable Airspace*. Washington, D.C.: Federal Aviation Administration. Accessed April 2008, from http://www.airweb.faa.gov/Regulatory_and_Guidance_Library/rgFAR.nsf/MainFrame?OpenFrameSet

8. *Runway Length Requirements for Airport Design*, AC 150/5325-4B. Washington, D.C.: Federal Aviation Administration, July 1, 2005, p. 2. Accessed April 2008, from http://rgl.faa.gov/Regulatory_and_Guidance_Library/rgAdvisoryCircular.nsf/0/b5f123f1451fe9468625724100785f60/$FILE/150_5325_4b.pdf

9. *Ibid.*

10. *Federal Aviation Regulations, Part 91, Sec. 91.155*. Washington, D.C.: Federal Aviation Administration. Accessed May 2008, from http://rgl.faa.gov/REGULATORY_AND_GUIDANCE_LIBRARY/RGFAR.NSF/0/074608A2FA18B48A86256EEB006704EF?OpenDocument

11. *Instrument Procedures Handbook*. Washington, D.C.: Federal Aviation Administration. Accessed May 2008, from http://www.faa.gov/library/manuals/aviation/instrument_procedures_handbook/

12. *Aeronautical Information Manual*. Washington, D.C.: Federal Aviation Administration. Accessed May 2008, from http://www.faa.gov/airports_airtraffic/air_traffic/publications/atpubs/aim/Chap1/aim0101.html

13. *Federal Aviation Regulations, Part 91, Sec. 91.319*. Washington, D.C.: Federal Aviation Administration. Accessed May 2008, from http://www.faa.gov/airports_airtraffic/airports/airport_safety/part139_cert/media/part139_wcorrections.pdf

14   Federal Aviation Administration. Accessed July 2008, from http://www.awp.faa.gov/ops/awp600/runway/definitions.pdf

15   *Engineering Brief No. 75: Incorporation of Runway Incursion Prevention into Taxiway and Apron Design*, memorandum. Washington, D.C.: Federal Aviation Administration, November 2008. Accessed June 2008, from http://www.faa.gov/airports_airtraffic/airports/construction/engineering_briefs/media/EB_75.pdf

16   *Ibid.*, p. 2.

17   *Field Formulation of the National Plan of Integrated Airport Systems (NPIAS)*, FAA Order 5090.3C. Washington, D.C.: Federal Aviation Administration, December 4, 2000, p. 20. Accessed June 2008, from http://www.faa.gov/airports_airtraffic/airports/resources/publications/orders/media/planning_5090_3C.pdf

18   *Airport Design. Op cit.* Appendix 9, p. 141.

19   *Model Reviews, MIT Modeling Research Under NASA/AATT*. Massachusetts Institute of Technology. Accessed June 2008, from http://web.mit.edu/aeroastro/www/labs/AATT/reviews.html

20   *Airline On-Time Statistics*. Washington, D.C.: Bureau of Transportation Statistics (USDOT). Accessed May 2008, from http://www.bts.gov/programs/airline_information/airline_ontime_statistics/

21   TransSolutions, Inc., *TransSolutions' Team Selected to Lead Research Project for Airport Planning and Design*, press release, April 28, 2008. Fort Worth, TX.

22   Horonjeff, Robert, and Francis X. McKelvey, *Planning & Design of Airports*, 4th Edition. New York: McGraw-Hill, 1994, p. 431-432.

23   Wells, Alexander T., and Seth B. Young, *Airport Planning and Management*, 5th Edition. New York: McGraw-Hill, 2004, Chapter 6.

24   Poh, Eileen, *Airport Planning and Terminal Design*, presentation for the Strategic Airport Management Programme, April 9-13, 2007. Accessed May 2008, from http://clacsec.lima.icao.int/Reuniones/2007/Seminario-Chile/Presentations/PR07.pdf

25   Horonjeff. *Op cit.* Chapter 10.

26   J.D. Power and Associates. *Op cit.*

27   Poh. *Op cit.*

28   *Federal Aviation Regulations, Part 150, Airport Noise Compatibility Planning*. Washington, D.C.: Federal Aviation Administration. Accessed May 2008, from http://rgl.faa.gov/Regulatory_and_Guidance_Library/rgFAR.nsf/MainFrame?OpenFrameSet

29   *Higher Visions For Airports*. American Planning Association, Transportation Planning Division. Accessed May 2008, from http://www.apa-tpd.org/airports.html

30   *Federal Aviation Regulations, Part 150. Op cit.* Section A150.101.

CHAPTER 3

AIRPORT MANAGEMENT, OPERATIONS, AND FINANCE

Because airports are complex places, providing a variety of services with many specialized facilities, planners must have some understanding of how airports are owned, managed, operated, and financed. This chapter describes each of the key roles within an airport's management and operations staff and notes why they are important to airport planning. And because one of the most important aspects of a plan is whether or not it can be afforded, the chapter discusses the various airport funding sources at the federal, state, and local levels.

Background

The FAA prepares the National Plan of Integrated Airport Systems (NPIAS) every two years to provide Congress with a five-year estimate of airport development that is eligible for federal aid, as described later in this chapter. The NPIAS includes public-use airports that have been determined to be important to public transportation and contribute to the needs of civil aviation, national defense, and the U.S. Postal Service. The NPIAS is used by the FAA to manage and administer the Airport Improvement Program (AIP), which is the FAA's primary airport funding mechanism. The NPIAS is developed on the basis of plans and programs prepared by individual airport sponsors as part of airport master plans and other airport planning studies, as well as state and regional airport system plans, as discussed in Chapter 4: Strategic Planning.

Types of Airports

According to the FAA's 2008 Report to Congress, there were a total of 19,815 airports (including heliports and seaplane bases) in the United States and its territories.[1] The NPIAS airports—those eligible for federal aid—include 3,356 existing and 55 proposed airports. Of the grand total, 5,190 airports (26 percent) were open to the public; the remaining 14,625 were for private use only. Of the public-use airports, 4,150 are owned by a public agency. Most of these are owned by municipalities, others by counties or multi-county districts, and some by airport authorities. Private ownership accounted for 1,040 airports. Only 522 airports were classified by the FAA as *commercial service airports*, i.e., airports receiving scheduled passenger service and having 2,500 or more enplaned passengers per year. Of these commercial service airports, 383 (or 73 percent) have more than 10,000 enplaned passengers per year and are classified as *primary airports*. Primary airports receive an annual apportionment of at least $1 million in AIP funds (whenever the total AIP funding level is $3.2 billion or more), with the amount for each airport determined by the number of passengers enplaned at that airport. There is a little lag in enplanement figures to allow for data reporting and analysis; the airport apportionments for fiscal year 2008 were based on enplaned passengers in calendar year 2006. The NPIAS defines public and public-use airports as follows:

- **Public Airport:** any airport that is used or intended to be used for public purposes, under the control of a public agency, the landing area of which is publicly owned. (Section 47102(16) of Title 49 of the United States Code [USC])
- **Public-Use Airport:**
    - a public airport, or
    - a privately-owned airport used or intended to be used for public purposes that is a reliever airport or determined by the Secretary to have at least 2,500 passenger boardings each year and to receive scheduled passenger aircraft service. (Section 47102(17) of Title 49 of the USC)[2]

Airports are divided into two categories—commercial service and general aviation—that reflect the type of service provided to the community, as shown below.

- **Commercial Service Airports:** publicly-owned airports that enplane 2,500 or more passengers annually and receive scheduled passenger aircraft service. Commercial service airports are either:
    - **Primary** – enplaning more than 10,000 passengers annually, or
    - **Non-primary** – enplaning between 2,500 and 10,000 passengers annually.
- **General Aviation (GA) Airports:** not specifically defined; considered to be airports not classified as commercial service. Including:
    - **Reliever Airports** that are designated by the FAA as having the function of relieving congestion at a commercial service airport and providing more general aviation access to the overall community. Privately-owned airports may be identified as reliever airports.
    - **Privately-owned Public-use Airports** that enplane 2,500 or more passengers annually and receive scheduled passenger

service are also classified as general aviation because they do not meet the criteria for commercial service (i.e., are not publicly owned).

- **Other General Aviation Airports** that are largely intended to serve the needs of general aviation users (users who conduct nonmilitary operations not involving the carriage of passengers or cargo for hire or compensation).[3]

Primary airports are grouped into four categories: large, medium, and small hubs; and non-hubs; based on an airport's share of total U.S. passenger enplanements, as seen in Table 3-1. The 30 *large hub* airports each account for at least 1 percent of total U.S. enplanements, the 37 *medium hubs* each account for between 0.25 percent and 1 percent of the total, and the 72 *small hubs* enplane between 0.05 percent and 0.25 percent of the U.S. total. The 244 *non-hub* primary airports each account for less than 0.05 percent of the U.S. total, but enplane more than 10,000 passengers annually. It is interesting to note that the large hub airports alone accounted for 68.7 percent of the total U.S. passenger enplanements, and large and medium hubs combined accounted for 88.7 percent. In contrast, the 244 non-hub primary airports accounted for only 3 percent of the U.S. total. An additional 139 airports fall into the category of *non-primary commercial service* airports. These airports each enplane between 2,500 and 10,000 passengers annually and account for only 0.1 percent of the total. Additional data from the NPIAS regarding these airports are shown in Table 3-1. An explanation of the criteria for the designation of each of the airport categories can be found in FAA Order 5090.3C, *Field Formulation of the National Plan of Integrated Airport Systems (NPIAS)*.[4]

Table 3-1: Distribution of Airport Activity[5]

Number of Airports	Airport Type	Share of Enplanements	Share of Based Aircraft
30	Large Hub Primary	68.7	0.9
37	Medium Hub Primary	20.0	2.6
72	Small Hub Primary	8.1	4.3
244	Non-Hub Primary	3.0	10.9
139	Non-Primary Commercial Service	0.1	2.4
270	Relievers	0.0	28.2
2,564	General Aviation	0.0	40.8
3,356	Existing NPIAS Airports	99.9	89.8
16,459	Low Activity Landing Areas (Non-NPIAS)	0.1	10.2

Airport Ownership

The vast majority of airports that airport planners get involved with are those that are publicly owned; they are the airports where most of the facility improvements take place and they are generally the only ones that can afford to hire airport planning expertise. Public ownership takes several forms. Smaller airports, usually those serving general aviation aircraft, are owned by a local government agency, such as a city or county. As airports grow in size and volume of activity, and as the size of their geographic service or market area increases, they are more likely to be owned and operated by airport authorities. Some of the very largest airports are owned and operated by a port authority, an example being the Port Authority of New York and New Jersey which operates John F. Kennedy, LaGuardia, and Newark Liberty airports. State ownership of airports is not common. Of the major airports in the U.S., Baltimore/Washington International is owned by the State of Maryland and operated by the Maryland Aviation Administration, which is part of the Maryland Department of Transportation. Bradley International Airport in Windsor Locks, Connecticut, is owned by the state and operated by an agency of the Connecticut Department of Transportation. T.F. Green International Airport, in Providence, Rhode Island, used to be owned and operated by the state, but ownership was transferred several years ago to the Rhode Island Airport Corporation. Several other states including Alaska and Hawaii also own airports, but they are typically small facilities and most do not have scheduled airline service. Airports that are publicly owned have a distinct advantage in that they can be financially supported by revenues generated by a public agency and can benefit from the ability of the owning agency to issue bonds to help fund capital facility improvements. Publicly-owned airports can also be more closely integrated with other local transportation and land use development programs, although this often works better in theory than in practice.

Airport Oversight

Many publicly-owned airports are governed directly by an airport commission or a board of directors (and sometimes both), whose responsibilities vary from jurisdiction to jurisdiction. Airports that are owned and operated by an authority usually have a board of directors, whereas city- and county-owned airports usually have an airport commission. These groups are often staffed by political appointees. For example, a county-owned airport may be governed by a commission made up of several members from the county, plus a member or two from each of the political jurisdictions served by the airport, such as cities, towns, or townships. In some cases these individuals know next to nothing about airports and how they operate, in other cases they can be very astute and knowledgeable about aviation matters. The composition of most boards and commissions that I am aware of varies; they usually include individuals with varying degrees of experience, knowledge, and interest in aviation and airport matters. Airport privatization has been discussed actively off and on for over a decade (the FAA implemented an airport privatization program in 1996), but nothing much seems to have happened in that regard in the U.S. Under this concept the municipality usually retains ownership of the airport but enters into a contract with a private corporation to operate the facility. The way publicly-owned airports are actually operated seems to depend more on the size of the airport than it does on who owns it. As discussed in this chapter and in Chapter 5: Master Planning, Chapter 6: System Planning, and Chapter 9: Coordination and Communication, it is important to coordinate planning activities with the people who are going to have to make the facilities work once they are constructed. Therefore an airport planner should have a good understanding of the kinds of things that are done at airports and who is responsible for doing them. Large airports have complex management structures—usually with a sizeable support staff—and small airports have correspondingly smaller staffs, sometimes consisting solely of the airport manager.

Even though the size and complexity of the airport organization may vary, the basic functions are pretty much the same. Airports need to be maintained and kept operational; they need to be kept clean; they need to be run on a financially-sound basis; and they need to comply with federal, state, and local laws, rules, and regulations. Larger airports resemble small cities, and are typically organized like a city government. They have individuals and offices for planning, design, construction, and purchasing; along with finance, legal, operations, human resources, security, public relations, fire/rescue, and police departments.

Airports require maintenance departments to take care of day-to-day tasks such as cleaning, painting, pavement repairs, grounds keeping, snow and ice removal, and trash disposal. At small airports one person—the airport manager—may do all these jobs, and if he or she is lucky there may be an administrative assistant to help with the paperwork. If they are really lucky they may have someone to help with maintenance chores such as cutting the grass and plowing snow. Obviously, as an airport increases in size, more staff are needed to handle the additional work.

Airport Management and Operation

The following sections describe the functions of each of the offices or divisions involved in the management and operation of an airport. I have tried to point out those areas of responsibility that are particularly important to the airport planner, along with a brief explanation of why they are important and why planners must involve them in the planning process.

Management Staff

At the top of the airport organizational structure is the airport manager. This individual bears the overall responsibility for ensuring that the airport is operated in a safe and efficient manner, in conformance with all appropriate regulatory requirements. At larger airports the manager will have a staff to help with the work, and will usually be referred to as the airport director. At very large airports he will most likely be called the executive director, or something equally dignified. Whatever he (or she) is called, that is where the buck stops; the airport director is the person who takes credit for everything good that happens and bears the responsibility for everything that goes wrong. The director is the chief spokesperson and advocate for the airport. He promotes airport development and, in effect, "sells" airport improvement projects to the local airport commission, board of supervisors, or whoever else might have some say in airport expansion and funding approvals. He must also sell the project to the FAA to get AIP funds, and must ensure that the appropriate paperwork is completed properly and in a timely manner to be sent through the FAA grant application process.

Planners frequently work on "big picture" kinds of things that will determine where the airport is going in the long term, and how it will get there. Planners in effect draw a picture of what the airport will look like 10 or 20 years into the future and beyond. Therefore they must deal directly with the airport director and his key staff on a regular basis. To communicate effectively with the director, planners must understand the airport from his perspective. They must also see the airport as he sees it today, and they must understand the kinds of issues with which he must deal.

As noted above, the airport director is the person who has the last word on just about everything that happens at or to the airport. The airport director reports directly to the airport authority, board of directors, or commission, and one of his major functions is to prepare periodic reports on what is happening at the airport. Thus the director must be aware of and up-to-date on all issues concerning operations, maintenance, finance, development, tenant relations, marketing, and literally anything else that is going on at the airport. Airport management is obviously not a 9-to-5 job.

Whether a planner is a member of the airport's staff or is a consultant working for the airport, he should keep in mind that the director is a busy person and does not usually have the time to sit through long meetings or read thick reports. Information for the director's review and update should be kept concise and to the point. At larger airports the director has a staff who specialize in specific areas of airport operation and development, but they all report to the director and he must therefore have some knowledge in each of the subject areas, including operations, maintenance, planning, engineering, business management, accounting, human resources, marketing, and environmental responsibilities. The airport director should also have a thorough understanding of the airport user needs and characteristics, as well as the community's air travel needs. He should also understand the local economy and how the airport relates to and supports the local economy. And above all, a really good airport director will have vision and imagination—he will be able to see the airport as it exists today and how it will look 20 years from now and beyond.

Airport directors come in all sizes, shapes, and temperaments, and each has his own set of priorities and areas of special interest. Some are visionary; some are not. Some are focused on maintenance and operations issues, sometimes to the exclusion of everything else. Others are focused on the long-term development of facilities and/or services, leaving the day-to-day operation of the airport to their staff. Nearly all of the airport managers I have ever spoken with are focused on the financial bottom line. They want the airport to be able to show a profit and demonstrate that the airport is a vital part of the economy. Being an airport director obviously takes some courage, and some possess more than others. Some directors are reluctant to rock the boat so to speak when it comes to airport development. As long as the airport is clean and operating safely and efficiently, they are reluctant to buy into and promote ambitious and expensive long-term development plans. This seems to be especially true when the projects are potentially controversial, such as a new runway. Some directors seem to want to study everything to death and find some absolute *proof* that the proposed development is necessary and that the selected option is the best one, and that the future will occur exactly as forecast. Well, planning deals with the future and obviously there are no guarantees. When dealing with a reluctant or conservative airport director, planners should provide as much factual information as they can to support the need for and timing of the project, and they should present the information as clearly and as accurately as possible as they make a case for recommended plans. In a sense, planning is really half sales—if nobody buys into the plan a lot of time and money will be wasted. (This aspect of planning is discussed in more detail in Chapter 9: Coordination and Communication.)

To be an effective planner one must also be a perceptive strategist, and carefully consider the airport director's priorities and appetite for risk when presenting new plans. For example, if the analysis shows that a new parallel runway will be needed at some point in the future, and it is known that the director is wary of ambitious projects and won't support it, the runway project shouldn't be included in the final plan—or at least shouldn't be pushed. This is because one controversial project may turn the director off to the entire package. In these situations, if a planner is sure he is right, he should quietly be sure near-term development doesn't preclude that long-term option, making it possible to build the runway at some point in the future. After all, directors come and go and another director may come along who is more supportive.

Remember, though, that airport directors are usually a pretty savvy bunch and have a lot of experience. The better ones develop a feel for what works and what doesn't—a reluctant director could be right after all.

Operations Staff

The airport operations office (commonly referred to as Ops) is the organization that actually runs the airport day in and day out. Ops personnel ensure that the airport operates in accordance with FAA airport certification standards. They are responsible for all the operations-related aspects of the airport, and usually for safety and security as well, in coordination with fire and police agencies, and the Transportation Security Administration (TSA).

Operations staff conduct frequent and periodic inspections of the airport's runways, taxiways, and aircraft parking areas to monitor pavement condition and check for fuel and oil spills and foreign objects ranging from lost nuts and bolts to luggage that drops off baggage carts. Operations staff also monitor runway conditions during periods of inclement weather and are responsible for determining whether the runways should be closed because of icing, flooding, or other hazardous conditions. They verify that there are no obstructions to air navigation in the vicinity of the airport that would conflict with the safety of aircraft operations. Ops also regularly inspects circulation roadways, terminal buildings, and other support facilities. They develop, monitor, and enforce rules and procedures for landing, taxiing, parking, servicing, loading, and unloading aircraft, as well as for vehicular traffic on the airfield. Airport operations develops and enforces rules and procedures for airline operational activities and airline equipment usage and storage, including aircraft parking locations and aircraft boarding gate assignments. They also conduct regular inspections of all airfield and terminal area lighting, directional signage, and all other equipment that is used in aircraft operations and passenger and baggage processing. During periods of construction activity, Ops monitors the work to ensure safety and compliance with FAA regulations.

Planners should include Ops staff in their planning efforts from the earliest stages to ensure that the plan appropriately addresses the airport's operational needs. Ops should also be included in the development and evaluation of alternatives to ensure that they will be able to operate the airport safely and efficiently with the planned improvements in place.

Maintenance Staff
At many airports operations and maintenance functions are combined into one group, but at larger airports the responsibilities are divided and the maintenance group is assigned its own areas of responsibility. As an airport increases in size it also increases in the number of facilities and the complexity of operation, and it accordingly takes more people to keep the airport operational. Because operations and maintenance are really two separate functions, it is often more efficient to assign these responsibilities to two separate groups. For example, Ops notes that one of the taxiway lights has burnt out; maintenance replaces the bulb. Or during a periodic inspection Ops notes that a tree has grown to a height that may cause it to penetrate a runway approach surface; maintenance cuts the tree down. The maintenance staff make sure that all airport facilities stay functional and in good repair—from grass cutting and snow removal to washing windows and painting, from patching leaky roofs to patching cracked pavement, from fixing leaky faucets and blocked toilets to cleaning oil-water separators and vehicle wash racks. In addition to making sure that the airport's own facilities are maintained, the maintenance staff monitor and inspect all work done by airport tenants.

As with Ops staff, it is important for planners to involve maintenance in the planning process to get some understanding of what the maintenance group does at a particular airport, and to find out what their specific needs are. These include terminal support and storage space as well as support facilities located on the landside or the airside of the airport. For example, maintenance knows how many vehicles they need to park and how much area they need to store sand, salt, and other materials. Maintenance can help ensure that any planned facilities will not interfere with current operations and that new facilities are designed to be maintained efficiently. Including maintenance staff in the planning process will also help ensure efficient access routes to maintenance facilities that do not interfere with normal airport operations. Planners should also work with maintenance with respect to the materials used in construction, particularly in the terminal. It is important to make sure that the materials used can be maintained efficiently, and are locally available so that replacement of windows, tiles, furniture, etc., can be done cost-effectively.

Finance Staff

The finance and accounting group is responsible for fiscal planning and budget administration. At large airports this function is accomplished by airport staff who are trained in accounting, budgeting, and financial planning. At smaller county- or city-owned airports the finance and accounting functions are accomplished by the county or city department that handles that function for all agencies within that jurisdiction. This can be a problem at times because city and county finance departments are not always familiar with FAA rules and regulations for airports and airport funding. Most significantly, they are not familiar with the FAA's Grant Assurances, i.e., the assurances or guarantees the airport sponsor makes when he obtains federal funds for airport improvements. Particularly important is the federal restriction mandating that revenues generated at the airport remain at the airport; they cannot be used to fund other city or county projects or services. The finance group is responsible for basic finance functions such as accounts payable and receivable, auditing, and payroll. In addition the finance group is responsible for leasing airport property, developing rate structures, and negotiating tenant leases. At larger airports the leasing function is usually split off to a separate leasing, commercial management, or business management group.

Planners should work closely with the leasing staff to ensure that the facilities resulting from the plan will be leasable, i.e., located and configured such that they will be attractive to tenants and be able to function efficiently and profitably. For example, when planning a terminal expansion the planners should sit down with the people who will be responsible for leasing the space being planned. The gate locations, holdrooms, ticket counters, airline operations areas, and baggage makeup areas will be primarily determined by airline needs, but the size and location of other facilities, particularly food and retail concessions, should be determined in cooperation with the airport's commercial leasing staff. Planners should also work closely with finance to make sure the plan is affordable to begin with, and to help develop financing options. There is no sense in developing a plan if the airport can't afford to implement it.

Engineering Staff

Airport engineering and planning functions are often combined into one planning and engineering group because the staffs typically are not that large, especially at smaller airports. Unfortunately it also reflects the fact that many people do not understand the difference between engineering and planning. The engineering function includes designing facility improvements and monitoring facility design and construction projects. Some facility design work is done in-house, but most large or complicated projects are done by consultants under architectural and engineering (A&E) contracts. No matter who does the actual design, the airport engineer is responsible for ensuring that all design and construction activities conform to FAA requirements as well as local building and fire protection codes. Engineering develops standards for construction and design so that airport development follows a uniform theme; prepares or supervises facility design for all airport facility improvements; prepares construction plans (in coordination with airport operations); and ensures integrity of all airport construction, alteration, and installation programs.

Planners need to work closely with the airport's engineering staff to make sure that any planned airport improvements can actually be built at a reasonable cost and in a manner which conforms to overall airport standards. For example, it is not sufficient to locate a new cargo building or aircraft hangar, draw in the dimensional standards, add an access road and an employee parking lot, identify environmental issues, come up with a cost estimate, and call it done. To come up with a plan that is practical and a cost estimate that is accurate, planners also need to know whether utilities are located at or near the proposed site. If not, the cost estimate should include the cost of bringing needed utilities to the site, and these costs can be significant. Engineers can also give a good idea as to what kinds of soil conditions will be encountered at the proposed site. Soil conditions, which can range from soft, sandy layers to bedrock, have substantial implications for the cost and constructability of airport improvements.

Planners also need to coordinate with engineering to make sure that near-term projects are in sync with longer-term plans. For example, engineering could be designing a parking area for aircraft refueling or aircraft deicing vehicles, complete with spill containment and other environmental safeguards. At the same time, the planners are planning an expansion to an aircraft parking ramp that would take part of the area the engineers have decided to use for their vehicle parking facility. Small projects like this come up all the time, especially at larger airports, and they often originate as a request from airport maintenance or airport operations and go directly to engineering without going through an actual planning process. That is why the planning and engineering groups need to meet frequently to make sure each knows what the other is doing.

Planners also need to keep engineers informed about upcoming projects so that the engineers know what kinds of things they will be asked to design, and what the schedules are. Considerable lead time is necessary for engineering, and not just because they are engineers. It takes a significant amount of time to get the needed design funding in the airport's capital improvement program, and then to procure the necessary consultant services to get the design work and follow-on construction completed so that the new facility can come on-line when it is needed.

Planning Staff

The overall function of the planning group is to decide where the airport is going and determine how it will get there. Also, it often seems that everything that others don't want to do or don't know what to do with winds up as a planning responsibility. At most airports that have a separate planning staff, the group is responsible for ensuring that all plans, including the all-important ALP, are kept current and valid, and are prepared in conformance with all applicable FAA standards. Planning is usually responsible for the preparation of aviation demand forecasts, the airport's strategic plan, the Capital Improvement Program (CIP), federal and state grant applications, and for coordination with local transportation and planning and zoning agencies. The airport planning staff is also responsible for ensuring that they communicate regularly with the other appropriate airport groups, especially operations, maintenance, finance, engineering, and marketing. Regular communication ensures that planners are aware of what is going on, what is working, what is not working, and what each of the other groups has in mind for future programs and activities. This knowledge should help ensure that plans are practical, realistic, and responsive to needs and issues.

Environmental Staff

Airport environmental responsibilities cover two general areas of environmental interest: ensuring that day-to-day airport operations are in compliance with U.S. Environmental Protection Agency (EPA) and state regulations, and preparing documentation for airport improvements in compliance with the requirements of the National Environmental Policy Act of 1969 (NEPA). The day-to-day environmental aspects of airport operations are usually referred to as *environmental compliance*, and are often assigned to the airport operations or maintenance groups, although these functions are sometimes assigned to planning or engineering. Larger airports may have a separate environmental group that reports to the airport director. Responsibilities of the environmental compliance group include all aspects of keeping the airport operating in an environmentally-sensitive manner. This includes oversight of aircraft and runway deicing operations; outfall monitoring to ensure that surface runoff is not contaminated; hazardous materials storage, use, and disposal; and many other items. Planners need to work with the environmental compliance staff to find out what environmental requirements will have to be met, and especially what environmental requirements will have to be incorporated into the plan. For example, if a parking area for fuel trucks is being planned, planners need to know if fuel spill containment measures have to be included in the project, and if so, exactly what will be required. If a terminal expansion is being planned, the planners need to work with environmental compliance to find out whether aircraft gate deicing is needed, and if so, where the deicing fluid runoff should go and how it will have to be treated before it is discharged into the local waters. Items of this nature can be very expensive and this expense must be included in the project cost estimate generated during the planning process.

The NEPA documentation component of an airport's environmental responsibilities is usually assigned to the planning group, since NEPA documentation is required as part of the facility planning process. This aspect of airport environmental responsibilities includes the preparation of Environmental Impact Statements (EISs) (technically this is the responsibility of the FAA but the airport sponsor does most of the work, which then becomes a federal document), Environmental Assessments (EAs), and Categorical Exclusions (CEs). Guidance for preparing environmental documentation is set forth in FAA Order 1050.1E, *Policies and Procedures for Considering Environmental Impacts*,[6] and FAA Order 5050.4B, *National Environmental Policy Act (NEPA) Implementing Instructions for Airport Actions*.[7] The NEPA aspect of airport environmental responsibilities ensures that facility development is accomplished in a manner that avoids, minimizes, or mitigates the adverse effects of development on the environment.

Planners need to work very closely with the environmental staff, beginning with the day the planning study is conceived and continuing through any public meetings or hearings at the conclusion of the study. The environmental staff knows where the environmentally-sensitive resources are located, including forest stands, streams, wetlands, archeological sites, historic structures, etc. Working closely with the environmental staff throughout the planning process will ensure that planners are aware of the environmental requirements and the environmentally-sensitive areas. Knowing where the environmentally-sensitive areas are enables the planner to avoid them, and if they can't be avoided, to develop strategies to minimize and/or mitigate adverse impacts. Close cooperation also ensures that the environmental staff knows and understands exactly why each planned project is needed and exactly what it entails. Planners in turn must know exactly what kinds of environmental documentation are required. All this shared information is essential to the preparation of environmental documents. In fact, the lack of adequate information is often the reason why an environmental process takes so long. If the planning work is not accomplished and documented in sufficient detail, it means that additional planning work will be required as part of the environmental process, and that consumes additional time and money. Planning/environmental coordination is discussed in more detail in Chapter 5: Master Planning, and Chapter 8: Environmental Considerations.

Environmental groups also have the responsibility of making sure everyone knows what kinds of permits will be required, when they will be needed, and who will be responsible for getting them, before construction can begin on a project. Often this is left up to the contractor and can lead to delays in getting the project started and completed on time.

Most large airports have a separate office and staff devoted to aircraft noise monitoring and mitigation. This function is usually assigned to the planning group, but at some airports the noise office reports to the airport director. And of course, at smaller airports the noise office *is* the airport director. The noise office monitors aircraft noise levels on a monthly, quarterly, or annual basis, usually depending on the level of noise generated by aircraft operations. If appropriate, the noise office develops a noise abatement program to mitigate the impact of aircraft noise on surrounding communities. The noise office is usually also responsible for, or at least is a key player in, any land acquisition or residential soundproofing programs. The noise office staff is also responsible for handling citizens' noise complaints and attending meetings and briefings to provide detailed information on the airport operating environment.

Planners need to work closely with the noise staff to become aware of the noise sensitivities in the area surrounding the airport, especially when new runways are being considered, but also for taxiways, aircraft parking ramps, and engine runup pads. In short, any facility that can be expected to result in noise that will be apparent to the community should be coordinated with the noise staff. If a new runway will be subject to operational restrictions because of noise issues identified during the environmental analysis and public participation processes, that factor will obviously constrain the usefulness of the runway and may call its viability into question. Similarly, a runup pad that cannot be used during nighttime hours may not be worth building. Close coordination between planners and noise staff will help ensure that the final plan doesn't run into unpleasant surprises like these. In this regard, if the planners are going to speak to a community group or present a plan at a public hearing, they should be sure to bring along a noise expert. Noise questions and ensuing discussions can get complicated in a hurry, and it is valuable to have capable and knowledgeable support. The issue of aircraft noise in a public context is discussed in more detail in Chapter 9: Coordination and Communication.

Marketing and Communications Staff

Marketing and communications (sometimes known as public relations) functions are usually combined into one office at larger airports. At smaller airports they are usually combined into one person—again, the airport manager. The marketing component of an airport basically involves selling the airport and its services by encouraging new users and new services. One of their primary responsibilities is to identify airport and air service user needs and work to develop such service. At airports with scheduled air service the marketing group analyzes air trends and patterns in service demand, air service users, and user characteristics. They also prepare air service development plans to help obtain new or improved air services at the airport. Marketing staff typically conduct periodic customer satisfaction surveys; the resulting information is often useful to the planning group. The marketing group is also usually in charge of all public communications, including press releases, news media briefings, and responding to customer comments and complaints (although they usually refer noise complaints to the noise office). Part of their job is to keep the media and the general public informed of airport events and development programs. In effect they act as a clearinghouse to make sure everyone at the airport is on the same page. The public relations staff are also in charge of special events such as air shows, as well as the preparation of airport user guides and maps, information booths, airport Web sites, and related items.

Planners need to work closely with the marketing staff to ensure that planning and marketing are working toward common goals. In most cases planning and marketing go hand-in-hand; one can't be done successfully and effectively without the other. As a simple example, if the marketing group is working on a program to improve long-haul transcontinental or transoceanic air services, the marketing group should consult with the planners to make sure that the existing runways are long enough, or can be extended, to accommodate long-haul aircraft departures. Conversely, if the planners are working on alternative schemes to lengthen the runway, they should coordinate with the marketing group to see if the market (i.e., potential users) is there. Planners also need to coordinate with the public relations staff on all development programs; their skills are invaluable in determining the most effective ways to package information and identify relevant interest groups for the coordination and communication component of facility planning activities.

Human Resources Staff

The human resources office is primarily responsible for hiring, employing, and firing staff. They typically handle all recruitment, classification, training, and promotions, among other things. As with the finance group, large airports typically have their own human resources staff. Smaller airports usually rely on the city or county that owns the airport. Just as with a private corporation, the larger the airport, the larger the human resources staff, and the more complicated and bureaucratic the rules and procedures can become. If it is necessary for a human resources office to hire airport planning staff, the position's responsibilities should be specified *exactly* and *accurately*, along with the qualifications and experience a person must have to fill the position adequately.

In summary, a lot of things happen at airports and it takes a lot of different offices and personnel with a lot of different responsibilities to make them happen or to ensure that they happen the way they are supposed to. Planners need to coordinate with each of the offices to ensure that whatever they plan can be implemented, operated, and maintained to provide the maximum in safety and efficiency. If the other departments and offices involved in the operation of the airport are involved in the planning process—if they have the feeling that they have contributed something to the plan—they will have a tendency to regard it as "our plan," rather than a plan produced by the planning group, which would then be viewed by others at the airport as "their plan." Remember, planning is half sales, and involving the "customer" goes a long way toward making that sale and broadening the base of support for all types of plans.

Airport Finance

Unless you have a passion for accounting, discussions of airport financing tend to be very boring, and this one is probably no exception. Nevertheless, in order to do a good job, airport planners should have a clear understanding of how airports and airport improvements are financed. As discussed below, a substantial portion of the funding for airport capital improvements comes from the FAA; however, the local airport sponsor is responsible for the local share required to match an FAA grant, as well as all improvements not eligible for federal aid. The following presents some background and an overview of the various sources of airport improvement grants and project eligibility, as well as other airport revenue sources. It is particularly important to understand the federal funding mechanism and associated requirements. Remember: the best plan in the world will do no good if the airport sponsor can't afford to pay for it.

Airport expenses fall into two categories: capital and operating (usually referred to as operations and maintenance, or more simply, O&M). Capital expenses are those associated with the expansion or renovation/rehabilitation of airport facilities, including the construction of new runways or runway extensions, major runway overlays, terminal buildings, aircraft parking ramps, automobile parking facilities, cargo buildings, and airfield maintenance facilities, to name only a few. Capital expenses also include the acquisition of equipment such as snow removal and fire/rescue vehicles. O&M expenses are those associated with the daily costs of operating and maintaining the airport. O&M expenses include utilities (sewer, water, electricity, etc.), supplies (everything from toilet paper and light bulbs to runway deicing materials and paint), maintenance of airfield and landside pavements and vehicles, as well as airport employees' salaries.

Federal Funding

The capital costs of airport facility improvements are funded through a variety of sources, including federal and state grants, bonds, local tax revenues, and airport user fees. Most airport improvement funding comes from federal grants-in-aid, through the AIP, as noted above. The AIP provides grants to public agencies, and in some cases to private owners, for the planning and development of public-use airports that are included in the NPIAS and shown on an approved ALP.

Some background on federal airport funding is necessary here. Shortly after World War II the federal government implemented a grant-in-aid program to promote the development of a system of airports to meet the nation's air transportation needs. The first such program was called the Federal-Aid Airport Program (FAAP) and was authorized by the Federal Airport Act of 1946. Funds for this program were taken from the general program of the U.S. Treasury Department. This program was expanded under the Airport and Airway Development Act of 1970. This Act provided grants for airport development under the Airport Development Aid Program (ADAP) and for airport planning under the Planning Grant Program (PGP). This Act also created the Airport and Airway Trust Fund, which provided the funding support for ADAP and PGP, into which were deposited revenues from several aviation-user taxes on such items as airline fares, air freight, and aviation fuel. A brief summary of Trust Fund revenues for 2006 is shown in Table 3-2.

The current program, known as the Airport Improvement Program (AIP), was established by the Airport and Airway Improvement Act of 1982. Since then, the AIP has been amended several times, most recently with the passage of the Wendell H. Ford Aviation Investment and Reform Act for the 21st Century (AIR-21)[8] and the Vision 100 – Century of Aviation Reauthorization Act.[9] Funds obligated for the AIP are drawn from the Airport and Airway Trust Fund which is supported by user fees, fuel taxes, and other aviation-related revenue sources, as shown in Table 3-2. To be eligible for an AIP grant an airport must be included in the NPIAS. It can be publicly owned, or privately owned and designated by the FAA as a reliever, or privately owned with scheduled service and at least 2,500 annual enplanements. Recipients of AIP grants are referred to as *sponsors*. Of the 5,190 public-use airports noted above, the NPIAS identifies more than 3,300 that are significant to national air transportation and thus eligible to receive federal grants under the AIP. It includes estimates of the amount of AIP money needed over a five-year period to fund infrastructure development projects that will bring the system airports up to current design standards and add capacity to congested airports. According to the FAA:

> The description of eligible grant activities is described in the authorizing legislation and relates to capital items serving to develop and improve the airport in areas of safety, capacity, and noise compatibility. In addition to these basic principles, a sponsor must be legally, financially, and otherwise able to carry out the assurances and obligations contained in the project application and grant agreement.[10]

For large and medium primary hub airports, AIP grants cover 75 percent of eligible costs (80 percent for noise program implementation). For small and non-hub primary, non-primary commercial service, reliever, and general aviation airports, the grant covers 95 percent of eligible costs.[11] Because the demand for AIP funds always exceeds the availability, the FAA primarily distributes these funds on the basis of national priorities and objectives. Typically AIP funds are apportioned first to the major entitlement categories such as primary, cargo, and general aviation. These funds are distributed on the basis of entitlement formulas to primary airports based on enplanements and cargo, and to the states based on population. Funds remaining are assigned

Table 3-2: Aviation Excise Taxes – 2006[12]

Passenger		
Domestic Passenger Ticket Tax	Ad valorem tax	7.5% of ticket price
Domestic Flight Segment Tax	A flight leg consisting of one take-off and one landing by a flight	$3.30 per passenger (in CY 2006)
Passenger Ticket Tax for Rural Airports	Rural airport: <100K enplanements during second preceding CY, and either 1) not located within 75 miles of another airport with 100K+ enplanements, 2) is receiving essential air service subsidies, or 3) is not connected by paved roads to another airport	7.5% of ticket price segment fee does not apply
International Arrival & Departure Tax	Head tax assessed on passengers arriving or departing for foreign destinations (and U.S. territories) that are not subject to passenger ticket tax	$14.50 (in CY 2006)
Flights between continental U.S. and Alaska or Hawaii		$7.30 international facilities tax + applicable domestic tax rate (in CY 2006)
Frequent Flyer Tax	Ad valorem tax assessed on mileage awards (e.g., credit cards)	7.5% of value of miles
Freight/Mail		
Domestic Cargo/Mail		6.25% of amount paid for the transportation of property by air
Aviation Fuel		
General Aviation Fuel Tax		Aviation gasoline: $0.193/gallon Jet fuel: $0.218/gallon
Commercial Fuel Tax		$0.043/gallon

to a discretionary fund. Set-aside projects such as airport noise are funded first from the discretionary pot and the remaining discretionary funds are distributed according to a national prioritization formula developed by the FAA.

Not only must the airport be eligible to receive federal grants, but the projects to be funded must also meet specific eligibility criteria. Eligible projects are those which enhance airport safety, capacity, security, and address environmental concerns. AIP funds can be used on most airfield capital improvements except hangars, some portions of terminals, and non-aviation development. Professional consulting services that are associated with or necessary for eligible projects, such as planning, environmental analysis and documentation, and project design are also eligible for federal grants. In addition the FAA reviews the proposed projects against aviation demand at the airport to confirm that the improvements are justified. Proposed projects must also meet federal environmental requirements and follow the FAA guidelines for procurement. Projects related to day-to-day airport operations are typically not eligible for AIP funding. Operational costs such as salaries, maintenance services, supplies, and equipment are not eligible for AIP grants.

Table 3-3 lists some examples of typical projects that are eligible and ineligible for FAA funding under AIP. Table 3-4 shows the NPIAS funding by airport category and project development category. FAA Order 5100.38C, *AIP Handbook*, gives more detailed information about project eligibility.[13] It specifies the eligibility requirements, prohibitions, and environmental requirements for all kinds of projects, including planning; airfield construction and equipment; terminals, landside, and terminal access; land acquisition; and noise compatibility. The local FAA Airports District Office (ADO) should also be consulted to ensure that the interpretation of project eligibility is consistent with the FAA guidance. When applying for an FAA grant it should be understood that the FAA prefers to award grants for projects that are "ready to go." They want to know that if they give an airport a grant, work will commence on the project as soon as possible. Funds are too scarce to have them lying around waiting for a sponsor to get its act together. If the airport is not ready to start work in a reasonable amount of time, the FAA may withdraw the grant offer and allocate the funds to another airport.

The following conditions must also be met for the FAA to consider the project eligible for AIP funding.

- The project sponsorship requirements must be met.
- The project must be reasonably consistent with the plans of planning agencies for the development of the area in which the airport is located.
- Sufficient funds must be available for the local share, i.e., the portion of the project not covered by the AIP grant.
- The project must be completed without undue delay.
- The airport location must be included in the current version of the NPIAS.
- The project must involve more than $25,000 in AIP funds.
- The project must be depicted on a current airport layout plan approved by the FAA.[14]

Table 3-3: Typical Eligible and Ineligible Projects[15]

Eligible	Ineligible
Runway construction/rehabilitation	Maintenance equipment and vehicles
Taxiway construction/rehabilitation	Office and office equipment
Apron construction/rehabilitation	Fuel farms
Airfield lighting	Landscaping
Airfield signage	Artworks
Airfield drainage	Aircraft hangars
Land acquisition	Industrial park development
Weather observation stations (AWOS)	Marketing plans
NAVAIDs such as REILs and PAPIs	Training
Planning studies	Improvements for commercial enterprises
Environmental studies	General aviation terminal buildings
Safety area improvements	Automobile parking lots
Airport layout plans (ALPs)	Maintenance or repairs of buildings
Access roads only located on airport property	
Removing, lowering, moving, marking, and lighting hazards	

Notes:
REIL = Runway End Identifier Lights
PAPI = Precision Approach Path Indicator

A mechanism that is used to obtain an FAA funding commitment for major capacity improvements at primary and reliever airports over a period of time is the Letter of Intent (LOI). Under this mechanism an airport sponsor may notify the FAA that the airport intends to proceed with a project without federal funds and request that the FAA issue an LOI. The FAA is authorized to issue LOIs for specific airport development projects when current AIP or passenger facility charge (PFC) funds are not sufficient or available in a timely manner to meet a sponsor's need for a project. As stated in the FAA's Program Guidance Letter (PGL) on the subject:

> An LOI establishes a schedule of possible Discretionary AIP funding for multi-year capacity enhancement projects, subject to annual appropriations and availability of funds. A sponsor who has received an LOI may proceed with the project without waiting for individual AIP grants. The sponsor is assured that allowable costs related to the approved project remain eligible for reimbursement, subject to the payment schedule set forth in the LOI.[16]

Table 3-4: 2007 – 2011 NPIAS Costs by Airport Type and Project Category ($ millions)[17]

Project Category	Large Hub	Medium Hub	Small Hub	Non-Hub	Commercial Service	Reliever	GA	Total	Percent
Safety	457	290	174	692	46	65	161	1,885	3.8%
Security	386	166	59	66	22	43	224	966	1.9%
Reconstruction	2,484	1,106	988	1,360	367	863	2,441	9,609	19.4%
Standards	1,360	1,034	1,214	1,762	449	1,844	5,718	13,381	27.0%
Environment	1,166	607	320	199	1	7	123	2,423	4.9%
Capacity	5,729	1,432	396	189	16	414	458	8,634	17.4%
Terminal	5,393	2,009	813	675	50	29	145	9,114	18.4%
Access	994	508	155	124	27	110	183	2,101	4.2%
Other	41	14	35	33	11	23	61	218	0.4%
New Airports	--	--	--	--	--	--	--	1,305	2.6%
Total	**18,010**	**7,166**	**4,154**	**5,100**	**989**	**3,398**	**9,514**	**49,636**	--
Percent	36.3%	14.4%	8.4%	10.3%	2.0%	6.8%	19.2%	--	100%

Note: Above figures differ slightly from FAA original, reflecting corrected arithmetic.

Detailed guidance on the LOI process and requirements can be found in the cited Program Guidance Letter. Note also that this PGL updates the LOI information contained in the June 2005 AIP Handbook.

Another mechanism for obtaining AIP funding is the FAA's Block Grant Program. This program consolidates AIP funding to certain states for individual airport projects at selected locations. Under this program, states "…perform some AIP administrative functions traditionally accomplished by the FAA, such as preparation of airport grant information for sponsors, reviewing of the sponsor's requests, and accounting for program expenditures."[18] This program gives states some flexibility and authority with respect to the use of AIP funds. For example, states may allocate funds to certain airports based on a priority system developed as part of a statewide airport system plan. Details on eligibility requirements and grant application and administration procedures are set forth in the AIP Handbook.

An additional revenue source became available to airports with the passage of the Aviation Safety and Capacity Expansion Act of 1990. This Act authorized most airports with scheduled airline service to collect a *passenger facility charge* (PFC) on passengers enplaning at the local airport.[19] Airports may use these PFC fees to fund projects that enhance safety, security, or capacity; reduce noise; or increase air carrier competition, subject of course to FAA approval. The initial legislation authorized airports to collect $1, $2, or $3 for each enplaned passenger. Intermediate amounts such as $2.50 were not allowed. Subsequent legislation provided a further option for airports to collect $4 or $4.50 per enplanement. At this time, airports may apply a PFC of $1, $2, $3, $4, or $4.50. PFCs may only be charged on the first two segments of an air trip, or the first two segments on each leg of a round trip. For example, a passenger traveling from Philadelphia to Seattle with a connection in Detroit, and returning from Seattle to Philadelphia with a connection in Denver, would pay a PFC at Philadelphia and Detroit on the outbound flight and a PFC at Seattle and Denver on the return leg. The PFCs are collected by the airlines as part of the ticket purchase and remitted to the federal government for subsequent distribution to each airport charging the PFC. Specific guidance and procedures to be used by the FAA regarding PFC project eligibility are contained in FAA Order 5500.1, *Passenger Facility Charge*.[20] PFC project eligibility is generally similar to AIP eligibility requirements; detail on project eligibility is contained in Order 5500.1 as well as the *AIP Handbook* (Order 5100.38C). Also, as with anything federal, there is a catch: if a large or medium hub airport imposes a PFC, that airport's AIP entitlement funds are reduced by 75 percent of the expected PFC revenue or 75 percent of the enplaned passenger entitlement, whichever is less.

Grant Assurances

There are always strings attached when dealing with the federal government and airport aid is no exception. Federal funding carries with it certain obligations known fondly as *grant assurances*. Airport sponsors who accept an FAA grant offer must also accept the conditions and obligations associated with the grant. These obligations ensure that the airport sponsor will operate and maintain the airport in a safe and serviceable condition, will not grant exclusive rights, will mitigate airspace hazards, and will use airport revenues properly. Grant assurances appear either in the application for federal assistance and become part of the final grant offer, or in restrictive covenants to property deeds. The duration of these obligations depends on the type of recipient, the useful life of the facility being developed, and other conditions stipulated in the assurances.[21] Airport sponsors should review each grant agreement to make sure that they understand their obligations.

One of the most important of the assurances is that the airport sponsor must

> ...keep up-to-date at all times an airport layout plan of the airport showing 1) boundaries of the airport and all proposed additions thereto, together with the boundaries of all off-site areas owned or controlled by the sponsor for airport purposes and proposed additions thereto; 2) the location and nature of all existing and proposed airport facilities and structures (such as runways, taxiways, aprons, terminal buildings, hangars, and roads), including all proposed extensions and reductions of existing airport facilities; and 3) the location of all existing and proposed non-aviation areas and of all existing improvements thereon. Such airport lay-

out plans and each amendment, revision, or modification thereof shall be subject to the approval of the Secretary which approval shall be evidenced by the signature of a duly authorized representation of the Secretary on the face of the airport layout plan. The sponsor will not make or permit any changes of alterations in the airport or any of its facilities which are not in conformity with the airport layout plan as approved by the Secretary and which might, in the opinion of the Secretary, adversely affect the safety, utility, or efficiency of the airport.[22]

And further,

> ...if a change or alteration in the airport or the facilities is made which the Secretary determines adversely affects the safety, utility, or efficiency of any federally-owned, -leased, or -funded property on or off the airport and which is not in conformity with the airport layout plan as approved by the Secretary, the owner or operator will, if requested by the Secretary, 1) eliminate such adverse effect in a manner approved by the Secretary, or 2) bear all costs of relocating such property (or replacement thereof) to the level of safety, utility, efficiency, and cost of operation existing before the unapproved change in the airport or its facilities.[23]

Some explanation may be useful here. Quite often an airport sponsor may want to construct a facility improvement that is relatively inconsequential in the scheme of things, but will, if the FAA requirements are followed, result in what the sponsor might consider an inappropriate level of delay. For example, an airport sponsor may want to construct a small building (say something measuring about 1,000 square feet or less) for the storage of seasonal equipment, such as lawn mowers during the winter months. The building location will not interfere with airspace or other airport operations. The building will be constructed on land that has been previously disturbed and no tree clearing or other environmental disturbance is involved. Moreover, no federal funds are involved; the building will be constructed at the sponsor's expense. According to the grant assurance cited above, this shed is a modification that must be shown on the ALP and be approved by the FAA. This means that the sponsor must prepare the requisite number of ALPs and submit them to the FAA for distribution and review, all of which can take anywhere from 30 to 90 days, depending on the requirements and process followed by the local ADO. And because ALP approval is considered a federal action under NEPA, the FAA requires some sort of environmental documentation, which can take time and money to prepare, and time to review. In this case the sponsor may decide to go ahead and construct the building, and show it as an existing facility on the next ALP update. However, even though a small building such as this one may be inconsequential, constructing it without FAA ALP approval is, strictly speaking, a violation of the grant assurances. If the FAA chooses to go by the book, this action by the airport sponsor can jeopardize any federal funding for the airport. The bottom line here is that the airport sponsor should work closely with the FAA to see what

Chapter 3 – Airport Management, Operations, and Finance   85

types of projects (if any) are allowable as being too minor to require a separate ALP approval. Saving time may be a good thing, but not if it jeopardizes federal funding and the relationship between the airport sponsor and the ADO. It is necessary for the two to develop a good working relationship and level of trust to ensure that major projects will move through the FAA planning, environmental, and funding processes in a timely manner. Based on my experience, and that of others I have talked with, it is best not to take shortcuts or try to operate behind the FAA's back. As they used to say in the days of the Old West, "Don't tinkle in the waterhole."

One aspect of the FAA grant program that is a little troubling is related to grants for land purchased for noise compatibility. The following sponsor assurance applies to an FAA grant for such purposes.

> Title 49 USC Section 47107(c)(2)(A) provides that for land purchased under a grant for airport noise compatibility purposes, the airport owner will dispose of the land, when the land is no longer needed for such purposes, at fair-market value, at the earliest practicable time. Any disposal must assure that the land is reused compatibly with aircraft noise exposure levels.... Where possible, the FAA prefers the property to be reused for non-noise-sensitive development to provide a noise buffer around the airport to guard against potential new noncompatible land uses that could not be foreseen at the time the property was disposed. Further, the portion of the proceeds of such disposition that is proportionate to the United States' share of acquisition of such land will, at the discretion of the FAA acting on behalf of the Secretary of Transportation, 1) be repaid to the Airport and Airway Trust Fund, or 2) be reinvested in an approved noise compatibility project. Reinvestment of proceeds from the sale of noise land at the original airport is the option preferred by the FAA. See Section 3 of this chapter for more information on the use of proceeds from the sale of such land.[24]

Recognizing that land bought for noise compatibility purposes may be needed for airport development, the FAA also states:

> Land acquired for noise compatibility purposes may subsequently be redesignated as airport development land without any further certifications or adjustment in the federal share of the cost of acquisition, provided that the land being redesignated as airport development land is justified by a new or revised airport master plan. In addition to the justification, the land must be depicted on a new or revised airport layout plan, depicted as future development land, and unconditionally approved by the FAA.[25]

A potential problem with this is that an airport sponsor may not know if the land will be needed for airport development at some future time. I raised this point at a conference and the FAA representative said that any such land needed for airport development would be shown on the ALP. An ALP is supposed to show long-term development (20 years is generally considered "long term"). But a lot can change at an airport, and it can change very quickly. An ALP could easily become out-of-date in 5 or 10 years. Also, when we are thinking "big picture" about airport development we should be thinking about all the "maybes" that could come up beyond the 20 years usually considered in master planning. Clearly the FAA wants its money back so it can be reinvested in other noise compatibility projects, and clearly the FAA does not intend for this to become a land-banking program, but still, an airport sponsor would look pretty foolish if it acquired land (e.g., a residential community) for noise compatibility purposes and resold it to a developer for a compatible use (e.g., a Class A office park), and then had to turn around and buy it back for a new parallel runway because of some totally unexpected development (e.g., a cargo airline decides to establish a major sorting/distribution hub at the airport). In reality, this situation is not likely to arise, but it is a possibility, and I have been advised that the FAA is aware of this situation and is looking into it. Unless or until some further guidance comes out and new regulations are adopted, some caution—and a lot of forethought—should go into the decision to apply to the FAA for a land acquisition grant for noise compatibility purposes.

AIP funding also has two other sets of grant assurances: one applies to Planning Agency Sponsors[26] and the other to Non-Airport Sponsors Undertaking Noise Compatibility Program Projects.[27] Planning agency sponsors are typically state or regional planning agencies that obtain a grant to prepare an airport system plan. The planning agency sponsor assurances ensure that the project under grant is reasonably consistent with other existing local plans. They also ensure that the sponsor will comply with civil rights requirements and will not discriminate on the basis of race, color, national origin, or sex in the award and performance of any work done under the grant, and that the sponsor's accounting, auditing, and recordkeeping will conform to federal requirements. The noise compatibility program assurances apply to agencies that are not the airport sponsor (such as local planning agencies) implementing a noise compatibility program. The overall requirements concerning discrimination and accounting are virtually the same as for other grants; however, the noise program assurances also ensure that the non-airport sponsor will enact reasonable zoning laws to restrict the use of land surrounding the airport to uses which will be compatible with airport operations and not restrict airport operational activity. The assurances also require that land purchased for airport development or noise compatibility purposes will, when no longer needed for such purposes, be disposed of at fair market value, and that the federal share will be repaid in a timely manner.

An additional source of federal funds for airport development is the U.S. Department of Agriculture (USDA). Under its Rural Development Housing and Community Facilities Program, the USDA can make and guarantee loans for "essential community facilities in rural areas and towns of up to 20,000 in population."[28] Airports and airport hangars are listed as eligible projects under the USDA's Community Facilities Program.[29] The USDA's Rural Business

Enterprise Grants (RBEG) program "provides grants for rural projects that finance and facilitate development of small and emerging rural businesses" in rural areas, which are defined in this case as "any area other than a city or town that has a population of greater than 50,000 and the urbanized area contiguous and adjacent to such a city or town according to the latest decennial census."[30]

State and Local Funding

Many states also have airport grant programs that are structured in a manner similar to the federal AIP. Overall the sponsor and project eligibility requirements are at least very similar and in some cases identical. States usually cover about 50 percent of the nonfederal share of the eligible project costs. In addition, some states have programs to cover projects such as hangars or terminals that are not typically eligible for AIP funding. These programs can provide aid in the form of direct grants to airport sponsors or in the form of loans, which must be paid back on an agreed-upon schedule.

The remaining portion of the costs of AIP eligible projects and the costs of all noneligible facility improvements must be borne by the local airport sponsor, and may sometimes include private financial participation. This can be difficult for many airports, especially the smaller ones, and for the local government agency that owns the airport. In the past, airports were considered a public service, as part of the national multimodal transportation system. Increasingly, airports are now being expected to operate on a sound financial basis, in a business-like manner. Airport stakeholders, including airport users, funding and regulatory agencies, airport tenants, and on occasion the general taxpaying public, want to know how the airport is doing financially. They want to know if the airport is operating at a profit or a loss, what the revenue sources are, and where the money is being spent.

The local share required to match a federal (and/or state) grant can be raised through a variety of sources, including local taxes, general obligation bonds, revenue bonds, bank loans, and airport user fees. At smaller airports that do not generate sufficient revenues to support bond issues, the local share is usually taken from the local general tax fund. The general tax fund is the source of revenue used to cover local government expenses such as police and fire protection, local roadways, parks, and recreation facilities. They are not specifically related to or earmarked for the local airport.

During the 1970s a number of communities began levying *head taxes* or similar fees on passengers enplaning at their local airport to raise funds to help cover the local share needed to match federal and state grants, as well as to fund airport improvements not eligible for federal or state funding. The concept behind the head tax was similar to the PFC program discussed above. Unfortunately some communities saw this as a revenue source to help cover expenditures not related solely to the airport. Both the airport and airline industries became concerned about this issue, termed *revenue diversion*, almost to a level of paranoia. Industry lobbyists pressured Congress to get involved, based on the premise that airlines' and other users' rates and charges would have to be increased to make up for the revenues lost through diversion. This, they argued, would be an undue burden on interstate commerce. Thus current federal law (49 USC 47107) requires any report receiving an AIP grant to promise, as a grant assurance or condition, that all revenues generated by the airport will be spent on the capital or operating costs of that airport. This law prevents revenue diversion, i.e., using airport revenues to fund other local programs that have nothing to do with aviation. This helps ensure that revenues generated at the airport will be spent at the airport. Although many people argue the merits of this requirement, both pro and con, it does help ensure that airports retain their revenues for use in meeting their own expenses. The law also requires airports to charge *fair market value* for anyone leasing space at the airport, with the exception of aviation-related educational programs and aviation museums.[31] This helps ensure that airports are not pressured by local interests into leasing prime airport land, building, or office space at below-market rates to satisfy local special interests.

Historically, general obligation bonds have been issued by local governments to fund a variety of capital improvements, including airport projects as well as highways, parks, water supply and treatment facilities, sewage treatment plants, etc. These bonds are backed by the full faith and credit of the local community, thus they are considered a secure investment and thus carry a relatively low annual interest rate. However, each community has a statutory limit on the principal amount of general obligation bonds that can be outstanding at any one time. Therefore airport improvements must compete with the community's financing needs for other capital projects. Given this circumstance, general obligation bonds lose some of their attractiveness for airport funding. In the past airports relied quite heavily on general obligation bonds to fund facility improvements, since they were just about the only way for an airport to fund needed improvements in the absence of sufficient federal or state aid.

In recent years revenue bonds have become the preferred method of financing, especially at airports with a larger revenue base. Revenue bonds can be issued to cover a capital improvement (or capital improvement program) if it is estimated that the capital facility improvements will produce revenues in amounts equal to the principal, interest, and O&M costs over the term of the bond issue. Revenue bonds are usually backed only by the revenue-generating potential of the improvement being funded by the bond issues, but in some cases may be covered by the revenue-generating potential of the entire airport. Facilities that have a high revenue-generating potential, such as terminals and parking garages, are appropriate for revenue bond financing. Facilities with low revenue-generating potential, such as runways, taxiways, roadways, etc., are not typically financed with revenue bonds. Because revenue bonds are covered by a relatively limited revenue source (as opposed to the resources of the entire community) they carry a somewhat higher interest rate than general obligation bonds.

Bank loans may also sometimes be used to fund airport improvements, although the term of such loans is usually limited (three to five years is fairly common) and interest rates are generally higher than for bond issues. Bank loans can be used as something resembling the bridging loans that many home buyers use when they have to pay for a new home before they have sold their current residence. In the case of airports, bank loans can provide interim financing until a long-term borrowing mechanism is put in place.

Other state-specific financial support may be available for airport development. For example, the Commonwealth of Virginia has an interesting loan program that supplements the state's airport grants issued under its Airport Capital Program. This program is administered by the Virginia Resources Authority (VRA) to help publicly-owned airports (and other local government entities) finance airport improvement projects and equipment. According to VRA:

> Revolving loan funds provide below market rate loans that make projects more affordable and feasible. These funds are a permanent and perpetual source of funding for projects with specific designs for meeting a community need. "Seed Money" from federal and state sources capitalize the funds and the repayment of loans means that funds will be recycled into new loans and available as a sustainable source of financing.[32]

Under this program VRA partners with the Virginia Aviation Board (VAB) and the Virginia Department of Aviation to provide the loans, which are approved by both the VAB and VRA. VAB determines project appropriateness; VRA approves loans based on financial capability and availability of funding.[33] Under this loan program eligible projects include:

- Any airport-related capital project on an airport's approved layout plan including revenue producing projects.
- Local matching share of projects eligible for funding through other federal and state sources.
- Debt refinancing.[34]

Specific project examples include:

- hangars
- terminal buildings
- machinery and equipment
- lands and rights-in-land
- roadways
- parking facilities
- utilities
- fuel farms[35]

Airport revenues can also be used to provide the local share needed to match a federal or state grant, and to cover the costs of projects not eligible for such grants. However, especially at smaller airports, revenues usually are only sufficient to cover operating costs. Some airports have been able to arrange financing through long-term arrangements with tenants to cover some types of facility improvements. For example, an airport with scheduled air service may arrange with the airline or airlines to provide funds up front, and then allow the carriers to use the new space at a reduced rental or lease rate until the carriers' share is repaid. Similarly, smaller airports may use public/private partnering arrangements to obtain needed facility improvements. As an example, an airport may wish to build hangars to accommodate locally-based aircraft. The airport can arrange with a developer to build the hangar and arrange a long-term lease such that the developer gets the revenues from leasing the hangar space, minus a land rent and/or a small percentage of gross revenues. At the end of the lease, say 20 or 30 years, the hangar becomes the property of the airport. These kinds of arrangements are typically made for revenue-generating facilities, not the "operating" parts of the airport such as runways and taxiways.

Speaking of airport revenues, this is a good point at which to talk about some specific financial aspects of airport operation. Companies operating at an airport, such as airlines, food service and retail concessionaires, car rental agencies, fixed base operators, charter services, flight schools, aircraft repair services, freight handlers, etc., pay rent for or lease the space they occupy. In addition, depending on the particular agreement between the airport and the tenant, the airport may also receive a percentage of the tenant's gross revenues. This usually applies to concessionaires, hotel operators, and the like. Airports also usually charge aircraft landing fees, parking fees, and fuel flowage fees to generate revenue from companies that operate aircraft at the airport. Table 3-5 shows the various sources of revenues and expenses at large, medium, and small hub airports, as well as non-hubs. As such the data cover 510 commercial service airports, or about ten percent of the public-use airports in the U.S. Data for the remaining 4,680 airports, most of which serve general aviation exclusively, are unfortunately not available.

The FAA data show that airports, at least the commercial service airports included in the NPIAS analysis, operate at a profit. As shown in Table 3-5 the 510 commercial service airports had a net income of $3.6 billion in 2006. Also, according to the Air Transport Association (ATA):

> With the exception of a few small airports that receive subsidies from their municipality, U.S. airports are self-sustaining. The revenue collected from businesses, passengers, and shippers using the airport covers most of the operating expenses associated with operating the airport.[36]

The source of the ATA data supporting that statement is not provided, and experience has shown that while most airports may be able to generate enough in revenues to cover operating expenses, when capital costs are included airports operate at a net loss. In looking at the data in Table 3-5, grant receipts (primarily FAA AIP grants) accounted for approximately $2 billion of the airports' operating revenues. Looking even more closely, without the grant receipts small hubs would have had a net *loss* of $65 million, and non-hubs would have had a net *loss* of $214 million. Given that, of the 5,190 public-use airports in the U.S., only 3,411 of them are in the NPIAS and thus eligible for FAA funding, the overall airport financial picture doesn't seem to be all that rosy. In fact, the FAA's NPIAS Report to Congress states that:

> Non-hub primary and non-primary commercial service airports have limited incomes and generally do not give adequate operating surpluses to repay borrowed funds. As a result, small airports tend to rely heavily on grants to finance capital improvements.[37]

In terms of airport revenue sources, small airports generally have one account that covers all expenses for airside, terminal, and landside. At larger airports these components are usually broken out into cost centers. For example, airside costs cover runways, taxiways, and other aircraft operating areas, as well as obstruction clearing and other costs associated with aircraft operations. The costs include maintenance of existing facilities, including everything from pavement overlays to runway and taxiway lights. The airport typically sets landing fees and parking fees at a rate expected to cover all airside costs, including the airport sponsor's share of any improvements that are eligible for an AIP grant. The terminal area and other landside areas are usually combined into a landside cost center. Terminal maintenance and expansion costs are recovered through rental and lease rates set (typically on a square-foot basis) for ticket counters, holdrooms, baggage makeup areas, airline operations space, etc. Aircraft parking space is typically set at a monthly fee, but hangar space is more often rented on a square-footage basis. Cargo buildings and office space is similarly rented or leased based on the area occupied. Cost recovery for other landside areas such as access roads, public parking lots, etc., is a little more difficult to assess. Larger airports charge short- and long-term fees for public parking that are typically set to generate as much revenue as the market will bear. Parking revenues usually cover parking expenses, and any surplus revenue can be applied to other landside costs which cannot be directly tied to individual users, such as the costs of roadway maintenance and improvement.

There is a limit to how much airports can charge for these various items. Smaller airports may not charge for parking because they are trying to encourage people to use their local airport. A passenger boarding a commuter airline flight to a nearby airline hub usually pays more for his air trip than if he drove to the hub and boarded a direct flight there, even if he has to pay to park at the hub airport. Adding a parking fee at the local airport adds to the total cost of the passenger's trip and can encourage him to use the larger airport anyway, rather than fly local. But at large airports that do charge for parking, the customer doesn't very often have a choice…either pay the parking fee or take a cab or public transportation. Or walk. At some airports customers are known to park at nearby hotels and take the free hotel shuttle

Table 3-5: Airport Operating and Financial Summary 2006 ($millions)

Category	Large Hub $	Large Hub %	Medium Hub $	Medium Hub %	Small Hub $	Small Hub %	Non-Hub $	Non-Hub %	Total $	Total %
Aeronautical Operating Revenue	$	%	$	%	$	%	$	%	$	%
Landing Fees	1,932	15.4	523	12.8	146	7.6	62	4.1	2,663	13.3
Terminal Rents	2,339	18.7	555	13.6	197	10.3	68	4.5	3,159	15.7
Cargo and Hangar Rentals	252	2.0	79	1.9	51	2.7	50	3.3	432	2.2
Fixed Base Operator Revenue	33	0.3	36	0.9	23	1.2	32	2.1	124	0.6
Apron Charges/Tie Downs	52	0.4	39	1.0	20	1.0	9	0.6	120	0.6
Fuel Sales and Taxes	132	1.1	60	1.5	28	1.5	66	4.3	286	1.4
Other Aeronautical Fees	269	2.1	61	1.5	32	1.7	35	2.3	397	2.0
Total Aeronautical Operating Revenue	5,009	--	1,353	--	497	--	322	--	7,181	--
Non-Aeronautical Operating Revenue	$	%	$	%	$	%	$	%	$	%
Parking and Rental Car	2,296	18.3	1,057	25.8	440	23.0	153	10.0	3,946	19.7
Concessions	593	4.7	115	2.8	43	2.2	16	1.0	767	3.8
Terminal Rents	347	2.8	70	1.7	23	1.2	4	0.3	444	2.2
Land Rental and Non-Terminal	302	2.4	78	1.9	91	4.8	91	6.0	562	2.8
Other Non-Aeronautical Fees	548	4.4	85	2.1	41	2.1	30	2.0	704	3.5
Total Non-Aeronautical Operating Revenue	4,086	--	1,405	--	638	--	294	--	6,423	--
Other Revenue	$	%	$	%	$	%	$	%	$	%
Passenger Facility Charges	1,748	14.0	478	11.7	180	9.4	64	4.2	2,470	12.3
Grant Receipts	856	6.8	544	13.3	473	24.7	718	47.1	2,591	12.9
Interest	667	5.3	191	4.7	67	3.5	32	2.1	957	4.8
Other Non-Operating Revenue	164	1.3	124	3.0	60	3.1	95	6.2	443	2.2
Total Other Revenue	3,435	--	1,337	--	780	--	909	--	6,461	--
Total Airport Revenue	12,530	100.0	4,095	100.0	1,915	100.0	1,525	100.0	20,065	100.0

continued next page

Table 3-5 continued: Airport Operating and Financial Summary 2006 ($millions)

Category	Large Hub $	Large Hub %	Medium Hub $	Medium Hub %	Small Hub $	Small Hub %	Non-Hub $	Non-Hub %	Total $	Total %
Operating Expenses										
Personnel Compensation and Benefits	2,107	25.9	682	28.1	365	37.2	299	39.0	3,453	28.1
Contractual Services	1,559	19.2	557	23.0	170	17.3	103	13.4	2,389	19.4
Communications and Utilities	594	7.3	164	6.8	85	8.7	63	8.2	906	7.4
Supplies and Materials	472	5.8	70	2.9	49	5.0	46	6.0	637	5.2
Repairs and Maintenance	497	6.1	110	4.5	55	5.6	48	6.3	710	5.8
Insurance, Claims, and Settlements	150	1.8	43	1.8	26	2.7	27	3.5	246	2.0
Other	516	6.3	174	7.2	50	5.1	67	8.7	807	6.6
Total Operating Expenses	**5,895**	--	**1,800**	--	**800**	--	**653**	--	**9,148**	--
Non-Operating Expenses $	$	%	$	%	$	%	$	%	$	%
Interest Expense	2,145	26.4	495	20.4	151	15.4	45	5.9	2,836	23.1
Other	89	1.1	131	5.4	29	3.0	68	8.9	317	2.6
Total Non-Operating Expenses	**2,234**	--	**626**	--	**180**	--	**113**	--	**3,153**	--
Total Airport Expenses	**8,129**	**100.0**	**2,426**	**100.0**	**980**	**100.0**	**766**	**100.0**	**12,301**	**100.0**
Depreciation	2,480	--	881	--	439	--	402	--	4,202	--
NET AIRPORT INCOME	**1,921**	--	**788**	--	**496**	--	**357**	--	**3,562**	--

Source: Report to Congress. Op cit.

to the airport, but most airport patrons pay the tab. If the parking fees become outrageous the public will complain to their local elected officials or to the airport commission, or some other agency that has the clout to speak to airport management.

The same idea applies to hangar rents and landing fees at smaller airports. If an airport operator charges too much for hangar rents, landing fees, or fuel, the customer is likely to use another nearby airport. Although there usually aren't all that many airports to choose from, the flying public will react by relocating their operations to another airport, even if it means increasing the driving distance.

The bottom line is that most airports, especially those other than large and medium hubs, walk a pretty tight financial line. That is why it is important to make sure that when an airport development plan is prepared, a financial plan should be prepared along with it to make sure that the proposed development can actually be afforded. At the outset of any planning study, a planner should take the time to examine historical expense and revenue statements to get an idea of how much money the airport can reasonably afford to spend on airport improvements. There is little point in preparing an elaborate and expensive airport development program that the airport will not be able to afford.

In summary, for a plan to be effective it must consider and address the airport's needs. To identify the needs the planner must talk with the various offices and divisions that make the airport operate. For each airport being studied the planner must understand the organizational structure; how decisions are made and where the responsibilities lie. The planner must also have a good understanding of how the airport is financed—where the money comes from and where it goes—in order to prepare a viable financial plan to help ensure that the plan is implemented in a complete and timely manner.

Endnotes

1 *National Plan of Integrated Airport Systems, 2009-2013, Report to Congress.* Washington, D.C.: Federal Aviation Administration. Accessed January 2009, from http://www.faa.gov/airports_airtraffic/airports/planning_capacity/npias/reports/media/2009/npias_2009_narrative.pdf

2 *Field Formulation of the National Plan of Integrated Airport Systems (NPIAS),* FAA Order 5090.3C, p. 11. Accessed June 2008, from http://www.faa.gov/airports_airtraffic/airports/resources/publications/orders/media/planning_5090_3C.pdf

3 *Ibid.*

4 *Ibid.*, p. 20.

Chapter 3 – Airport Management, Operations, and Finance

5   *National Plan of Integrated Airport Systems. Op cit.* p. 6.

6   *Policies and Procedures for Considering Environmental Impacts*, FAA Order 1050.1E. Washington, D.C.: Federal Aviation Administration. Accessed July 2008, from http://www.faa.gov/regulations_policies/orders_notices/media/all1050-1e.pdf

7   *National Environmental Policy Act (NEPA) Implementing Instructions for Airport Actions*, FAA Order 5050.4B. Washington, D.C.: Federal Aviation Administration. Accessed July 2008, from http://www.faa.gov/airports_airtraffic/airports/resources/publications/orders/environmental_5050_4/

8   *Aviation Investment and Reform Act for the 21st Century (AIR 21)*, (HR 1000). Washington, D.C.: U.S. House of Representatives. Accessed May 2008, from http://thomas.loc.gov/cgi-bin/bdquery/z?d106:h.r.01000:

9   *Vision 100 – Century of Aviation Reauthorization Act*, (HR 2115), Public Law 108-176, Title III, Subchapter A, December 12, 2003. Washington, D.C.: U.S. House of Representatives. Accessed June 2008, from http://frwebgate.access.gpo.gov/cgi-bin/getdoc.cgi?dbname=108_cong_public_laws&docid=f:publ176.108.pdf

10 *Airport Improvement Program (AIP), Funding for Airport Planning and Development, Overview*. Washington, D.C.: Federal Aviation Administration. Accessed June 2008, from http://www.faa.gov/airports_airtraffic/airports/aip/overview/

11 *Ibid.*

12 *Current Aviation Excise Tax Structure*, Taxpayer Relief Act of 1997, Public Law 105-35. Accessed August 2007, from http://www.faa.gov/about/office_org/headquarters_offices/aep/aatf/media/Simplified_Tax_Table.xls

13 *Airport Improvement Program (AIP) Handbook*, FAA Order 5100.38C. Washington, D.C.: Federal Aviation Administration, June 2005. Accessed June 2008, from http://www.faa.gov/airports_airtraffic/airports/aip/aip_handbook/

14 *Airport Improvement Program Handbook. Op cit.* p. 27.

15 *Airport Improvement Program Overview. Op cit.*

16 *Program Guidance Letter 07-03 Revised and Updated Requirements for Letter of Intent (LOI) Requests*, November 20, 2006. Washington, D.C.: Federal Aviation Administration. Accessed May 2008, from http://www.faa.gov/airports_airtraffic/airports/aip/guidance_letters/media/pgl_07_03.pdf

17 *National Plan of Integrated Airport Systems. Op cit.* p. 63.

18 *Airport Improvement Program Handbook. Op cit.* p. 190.

19 *Aviation Safety and Capacity Expansion Act of 1990*, CIS-NO: 90-H643-3. Washington, D.C.: U.S. House of Representatives, Committee on Public Works and Transportation. Accessed April 2008, from http://thomas.loc.gov/cgi-bin/bdquery/z?d101:HR05170:@@@D&summ2=m&

20 *Passenger Facility Charge*, FAA Order 5500.1. Washington, D.C.: Federal Aviation Administration. Accessed August 2007, from http://www.faa.

gov/airports_airtraffic/airports/resources/publications/orders/media/PFC_55001.pdf

21. *Assurances, Airport Sponsors*. Washington, D.C.: Federal Aviation Administration, March 2005, p. 11, 12. Accessed May 2008, from http://www.faa.gov/airports_airtraffic/airports/aip/grant_assurances/media/airport_sponsor_assurances.pdf

22. *Ibid.*, p. 11.

23. *Ibid.*, p. 12.

24. *AIP Handbook. Op cit.* p. 141.

25. *Ibid.*, p. 146.

26. *Assurances, Airport Sponsors. Op cit.*

27. *Assurances, Non-Airport Sponsors Undertaking Noise Compatibility Program Projects*. Washington, D.C.: Federal Aviation Administration. Accessed May 2008, from http://www.faa.gov/airports_airtraffic/airports/aip/grant_assurances/media/nonairport_sponsor_assurances.pdf

28. U.S. Department of Agriculture, Rural Development Housing & Community Facilities Programs. Accessed June 2008, from http://www.rurdev.usda.gov/rhs/cf/brief_cp_direct.htm

29. U.S. Department of Agriculture, Rural Development Housing & Community Facilities Programs. Accessed June 2008, from http://www.rurdev.usda.gov/rhs/cf/essent_facil.htm

30. U.S. Department of Agriculture, Business and Cooperative Programs. Accessed June 2008, from http://www.rurdev.usda.gov/rbs/busp/rbeg.htm

31. *Federal Aviation Authorization Act of 1996*, House Report 104-714 – Part 1. Accessed April 2008, from http://thomas.loc.gov/cgi-bin/cpquery/?&sid=cp104v6n3H&refer=&r_n=hr714p1.104&db_id=104&item=&sel=TOC_134897&

32. Virginia Resources Authority, Revolving Loan Funds. Accessed June 2008, from http://virginiaresources.org/revolvingloan.shtml

33. Virginia Department of Aviation, State Funding Programs for Airports. Accessed June 2008, from http://www.doav.virginia.gov/Downloads/Airport_Grant_Program/Airport%20Program%20Manual/10%20Airports%20Revolving%20Fund.pdf

34. *Ibid.*

35. *Ibid.*

36. *The Airline Handbook – Online Version*. Washington, D.C.: Air Transport Association, 2001. Accessed February 2007, from http://members.airlines.org/about/d.aspx?nid=7951

37. *National Plan of Integrated Airport Systems. Op cit.* p. 39.

CHAPTER 4

STRATEGIC PLANNING

Planners live in a world of ideas and the development of the idea or the vision is the most important factor in the preparation of a sound airport plan and future development program. Ideas and alternative visions of the future and the airport's place in that future are best developed in the context of a strategic plan. A strategic plan presents a vision of the future, the airport's role in that future, and what has to be done to get there. Therefore a strategic plan should be the first step in the airport master planning process, because the strategic plan sets the stage for all follow-on airport development plans and programs. It represents the airport operator's prime opportunity to set the future for the airport.

Although strategic planning, or at least some serious strategic thinking, is the first step in any planning process, it is discussed here in a separate chapter because a strategic plan covers more than just the facility aspects of an airport, which are the primary focus of a master plan. This chapter explores the background and purpose of strategic planning and outlines the steps in an airport strategic planning context. It shows how and why a strategic plan should be the basis for follow-on activities such as master planning and marketing. It also discusses who should be involved in the development of the strategic plan and why each of the participants is important to a successful outcome.

What is a Strategic Plan?
A strategic plan is simply a look into the future, with a vision of how the airport sponsor or operator wants the airport to fit into that future and what has to be done to get it there.

The Overall Vision—for Various Possible Futures
Many in the airport industry believe that strategic planning is not possible in a field that is so dynamic and so susceptible to external factors that are beyond an airport's control. Among the external factors and uncertainties are

market forces, customer service expectations, environmental constraints, financial pressures, and competition for limited markets. But these factors are actually what make airport strategic planning even more important.

It may help to think of an airport as a boat—such as a sailboat or a small yacht. The boat is heading toward a planned destination, but suddenly the conditions change and the captain must decide whether to drift with the currents and tides or to try to take control and choose his new destination. He will need the proper tools and equipment to help steer a course to that destination, such as a rudder to help steer around all the rocks and shoals and currents. The rudder in the world of airport planning is, in effect, a strategic plan. The strategic plan will help guide the development of the airport through the shifting conditions and uncertainties and help maintain a steady course to achieve the desired vision of the airport's future. It follows that a strategic plan, or at least some serious strategic thinking, should be the first step in any airport planning or development program.

A strategic plan for an airport should set out the long-term expectations for airport growth and development, i.e., the "vision" for the airport's future. Ideally an airport strategic plan should include multiple visions for a variety of possible futures. Remember: what we expect to happen probably will not happen, or if it does it won't happen in the way we expect it to. In a way the vision can be thought of as, "What does the airport want to be when it grows up?" Will it be an international airport, or will it focus on domestic only? Will it be an air carrier airport or will it cater primarily or even exclusively to the general aviation community? If it is an air carrier airport, will it serve commuter and regional airlines, or will it cater more to the long-haul major carriers? If general aviation is the market, does the airport want to cater to the business and corporate crowd, or will it target the personal and recreational flying audience?

Goals, Objectives, Actions

A strategic plan is a simple statement of goals and objectives that lead to a series of actions. It documents the airport's goals, identifies the objectives that must be achieved to attain those goals, and follows up with a list of actions that must be taken to achieve those objectives. It includes a schedule or timetable and designates the individuals and/or agencies responsible for completing those actions.

In essence a strategic plan is very simple—it answers the following questions:

- Who are we?
- What do we do?
- Where do we want to go?
- How are we going to get there?
- Who is responsible?

A strategic plan presents the answers to these questions in a clear and organized manner, and in a series of logical and sequential steps. A strategic plan is not an academic exercise—although it can be made into one if desired (or if the people preparing the plan are not careful). Rather, it is a visioning process relying on the airport operator's and stakeholders' own knowledge and common sense.

In strategic planning language these questions are referred to as *mission*, *vision*, *goals*, and *objectives*. Strategic planning textbooks and workbooks also contain many other terms such as mission statements, values, guiding principles, strategies, tactics, action items, etc. Don't allow the strategic planning process to get caught up in the terminology. Strategic planning should be a simple, straightforward exercise, but it often seems to get complicated and bogged down with terminology and trivia. A lot of time can be wasted by arguing about the difference between a goal and an objective. The most important thing is to focus on where operator and stakeholders want the airport to go (the vision and goals) and what has to be done to get there (the objectives). As discussed in this book *Goals* are end-states that are part of the future vision. *Objectives* are the items that must be accomplished to achieve those goals, which should be stated so that they are in some way measurable or observable. *Action items* are specific actions that must be taken to achieve the objectives.

Comprehensive, Yet Focused

It is important to note that a good strategic plan is comprehensive and encompasses the entire airport—what it is, what it does, and how it is operated and managed—not just a single component such as airline service, concessions, or land use development.

A strategic plan can save the airport time and money by focusing on the most critical problems and issues and avoiding peripheral or minor issues. A strategic plan can improve an airport's efficiency by

- defining where the airport should be in the future and delineating what has to be done to get there,
- defining the steps that must be taken to achieve the airport's goals and identifying who is responsible for taking those steps, and
- helping to focus time and money on those areas that are critical to the airport's future.

A strategic plan helps keep the airport on an identified and agreed-upon course. Its goals should be flexible to allow for course adjustments to account for unexpected changes in the operating environment. A simple analogy: if you are vacationing in the mountains and decide you want to walk down to the lake to go fishing and find that a large tree has come down and is blocking your path, you find an alternative path to get to your ultimate goal, which is fishing in the lake. Or perhaps thunderstorms move in and you decide that you might want to change your goal of going fishing to a goal like sitting by the fireplace and sipping martinis.

At an airport, a goal might be to acquire some additional land to extend the runway safety area to meet FAA standards without losing runway length. But perhaps the airport's budget is not sufficient to cover the land acquisition cost, so it may be necessary to displace or relocate a runway threshold instead. In this case the goal is actually changing from meeting FAA standards without losing runway length, to simply meeting FAA standards, even though some runway must be lost. Another example of an alternative goal might be to extend a runway to allow jet transport aircraft being operated by a current airline to fly longer stage lengths with heavier loads. However, as the future unfolds, the local carrier may replace its jet transport aircraft with regional jets or with commuter aircraft that will not require a longer runway. Thus, the goal of extending the runway could be postponed until the need may arise at some point in the future.

The Planning Horizon

For airports, a strategic plan should establish a long-range vision for the airport that looks out 20 or 30 years and perhaps even longer. Focused attention should be given to the nearer term—a 5- to 10-year period is appropriate—but the long-term vision should be kept in mind throughout the strategic planning process. This is simply because it takes so long to accomplish many airport improvements. Consider a new runway or similar major project. Once the idea for a new runway is initially identified as part of a master plan, a substantial amount of detailed, site-specific planning must be accomplished, along with more detailed forecasting, and capacity analysis. Then the necessary environmental studies must be completed and appropriate approvals obtained, and then come the design and construction phases. Throughout this effort a considerable amount of time must also be spent in soliciting consultant services and selecting consulting firms and contractors to accomplish the necessary work. All this work can easily take 8 to 10 years to complete, and that is without adding time for lawsuits and other such unexpected events.

The Local Context

Strategic planning decisions are heavily influenced by local circumstances. For example, if the airport is located in the traffic shadow of a larger airport, expectations for growth may be limited. Philadelphia (PHL) is in the traffic shadow of New York's John F. Kennedy International (JFK) for international traffic, as are Baltimore/Washington International (BWI) and Washington Dulles International (IAD). JFK has so much international service that it is hard for other airports to develop viable nonstop international services on their own, particularly to a variety of destinations with a full range of price and schedule options. Because the volume of international traffic at JFK is so dense, carriers can offer much lower fares and more convenient schedules than at competing airports. Thus, much of the locally-originating Philadelphia, Baltimore, and Washington, D.C. traffic finds it more economical and convenient to fly out of JFK. Therefore, it would not be reasonable for a strategic plan for PHL, BWI, or IAD to state that the long-term vision for that airport is to become the premier east coast gateway to Europe. As another example, if an airport is located geographically at the fringe of the country, such as Miami, Boston, Seattle, or San Diego, it is not likely to be selected as a domestic hub airport for an airline, but will probably have a combination of point-to-point service and service to another airline hub city.

Identifying Funding, Supporters, and Opposition

In addition to establishing a vision for an airport, a strategic plan can help identify funding priorities and obtain support—especially political support—for future airport development. With a sound strategic plan, airport management should be able to review the airport's capital improvement program and identify a goal or objective associated with each line item. If a particular item does not support one of the airport's long-term goals, it may be given a lower funding priority, postponed, or even dropped from the program.

The FAA advisory circular on Airport Master Plans states that one of the factors that can drive the need for an airport planning study is the airport operator's strategic vision or business plan.[1] In fact federal funding may be available to cover the cost of preparing the strategic plan itself, if it is done as part of a master plan or other major facility improvement planning exercise. The airport sponsor should check with the local FAA Airports District Office (ADO) (or the FAA regional office in those regions that do not have ADOs) to determine whether the strategic plan is eligible for federal funding.

The strategic planning process can also help garner support for follow-on projects and programs, and can help build a solid team if all key elements of the airport are involved in the plan's development. This aspect is discussed further below, as part of the strategic planning process.

Strategic planning can also help identify potential areas of disagreement, contention, and possible opposition from airport stakeholders to some types of development.

Team-Building Opportunity

One of the most important (and often overlooked) side benefits of strategic planning is team building, i.e., ensuring that all airport employees have a sense of ownership of the plan. A strategic plan is often prepared as a *top-down* effort with little or no buy-in from those who will be responsible for implementing the plan by carrying out the objectives. This often turns out to be a fundamental flaw in the strategic planning process. Strategic planning documents are often something requested by the airport commission and then developed by top management with a consultant's help. They tend to be fairly boilerplate and/or all-encompassing without making the tough decisions and hard choices that really give a strategy the chance to work. If it means a change, how do people down the line cope? Are they expected to add the strategic plan recommendations to their existing responsibilities, in addition to all the other things they must accomplish? Or, will the staff be allowed to give priority to the strategic plan recommendations? If so, who will set the priorities to ensure that existing responsibilities are carried out, and that the strategic plan recommendations are implemented? Each group or division at the airport, and each individual within that group, should have a clear understanding of the airport's function, along with their role in making it function, both today and in the future. Large and complex organizations, such as the ones that manage and operate large airports, tend to become bureaucracies. The bureaucracy's rules and procedures tend to become more important than the mission—the overall sense of purpose or mission gets lost or obscured.

Whether an individual works in planning, design, construction, maintenance, marketing, operations, security, human resources, or finance, each person is crucial to a successfully-functioning organization. Quite often employees do not see themselves or their job in this larger context; a strategic plan is a means to convey this message. Accomplishing the strategic plan as a *bottom-up* exercise allows the staff to develop strategic planning goals and objectives in light of their day-to-day responsibilities. It will help ensure that the goals and objectives are achievable in a manner that is consistent with how the airport actually operates. In other words, it makes the strategic plan more realistic and attainable. To accomplish this, airport staff must be included in the process and their ideas and suggestions are valued. They must be able to see how their individual efforts contribute to the success of the plan and the future of the airport. Ideally strategic planning should include both top-down and bottom-up aspects; the top-down approach can provide direction and stability, while the bottom-up approach can provide practical considerations that add some reality to idealistic visions.

What a Strategic Plan is Not

A strategic plan is not a facility plan, a business plan, or an air service development or marketing plan. These kinds of plans should be done after the strategic plan because they should be based on the vision and goals established in the overall strategic plan. The follow-on plans are more detailed and more quantitative in nature, unlike a strategic plan's valid yet more conceptual approach. Each has its place in the future direction of the airport; however, it is the strategic plan that drives the need for these more focused studies.

For example, one of the goals identified in the strategic plan may be for the airport to develop facilities that are adequate to meet future needs and to ensure that all airport facilities meet current FAA design standards. Thus one of the supporting objectives for that goal would be to update the existing airport master plan. Facility plans are essentially master plans or airport layout plans and are primarily oriented toward specific airport facility improvements. A business plan is typically much more detailed than a strategic plan, and places more emphasis on the financial factors associated with airport development. Business plans also have a near-term focus—one to three years is most common. In a sense it may be helpful to think of a strategic plan as something that says what has to be done and a business plan is something that says how to do it and measures progress along the way.

A check of airport Web sites shows that many strategic plans that have been prepared for airports are really marketing plans or air service development plans. These plans focus on how to expand an airport's market, typically for scheduled air services, but also for increasing general aviation activity and expanding general aviation support services. Again, these plans should be prepared after the strategic plan, and should be based upon the vision and goals set forth in the strategic plan.

It is also important to remember that strategic plans are not strictly based on quantitative factors such as demand forecasts or airside capacity analyses. Rather, strategic plans are based on ideas and visions of the future. Remember: planning is thinking; when developing a plan thinking should come first and number-crunching should come later. Ideally, since the future usually turns out to be different from what we expect it to be, a strategic plan should consider alternative visions, typically called scenarios. Quantitative measures and analyses enter into the strategic planning process to some extent when alternative visions of the future are being evaluated later in the strategic planning process, and to a greater extent during master planning and business planning.

Also, strategic plans are not a consultant's vision of the airport's future; they should be developed by the key airport stakeholders—the people and organizations that have a direct interest or stake in the airport and its future. Consultants may assist in the process, but to be meaningful the vision and goals must originate with the stakeholders.

Avoid Fatal Flaws

It is important to note that a strategic plan is not perfect; remember that whenever we aim for perfection we often doom ourselves to failure because very few things in this world are truly perfect. In this regard, we often hear of strategic plans that fail. One of the main reasons for failure is the strategic planning process itself, as implied in the preceding paragraph. The world of aviation often changes too quickly and dramatically to allow us to envision the future with certainty. Thus strategic plans can fail because of faulty assumptions about the future. They can also fail because whoever was guiding the planning process allowed it to lose its focus and get off track. A firm hand is needed to keep the focus on the most critical issues at hand. Strategic plans can also fail because of poor group dynamics; one or two individuals simply do not work cooperatively, or try to dominate the discussions. On the other hand, the representative for a critical stakeholder group may be reluctant to express his views for fear of being wrong, or from being uncertain, i.e., unable to make a decision or focus on a particular topic. Also, an organization's capabilities may be overestimated. The strategic plan may be fine, but the staff or the organizational environment (i.e., bureaucracy) can't perform the way it should. Unforeseen delays on the part of other agencies or governmental action or inaction may delay the achievement of an objective, which in turn can delay the achievement of other objectives. Another reason why strategic plans can fail is sometimes referred to as "information overload." The plans try to do too much, focus on too many issues, and as a result wind up spinning wheels or spending an inordinate amount of time on trivial issues.

In short, to achieve success try to keep the strategic plan—and the process—simple, focused, and flexible.

The Strategic Planning Process

To help ensure success, the strategic planning process should be kept simple, straightforward, and focused on the issues. The strategic planning effort is normally managed by the airport planner (or planning department), assuming the airport is large enough and has enough staff to warrant a planning position. As pointed out in Chapter 3: Airport Management, Operations, and Finance, planners must coordinate closely with all components and divisions of the airport in order to develop an effective and viable plan. They must understand the mission or role of each component of the airport and how each component operates. Of course if the airport does not have an individual responsible for planning, management of the strategic plan normally becomes the responsibility of the airport director, possibly assisted by a planner employed by a consulting firm.

The first step in the strategic planning process is the establishment of a strategic planning management team, usually comprising key airport management staff, to provide overall direction and guidance for the strategic planning process. If the airport is expecting to have to address some complex technical issues, it may also be appropriate to add a representative or two from a consulting firm that is closely involved with the airport's development issues. For example, if the airport is surrounded by environmentally-sensitive areas, an environmental consulting firm might be a valuable addition to the team.

The strategic planning team will vary with the size of the airport; at a small general aviation airport the management team may consist of the airport manager and possibly an assistant. Regardless of the size of the team, it should be headed by the airport director or his designee, e.g., the airport planning director. The committee's responsibility is to guide the strategic planning process from the selection of participants through the initial inventories; the analysis of Strengths, Weaknesses, Opportunities, and Threats (the SWOT analysis); to the development of goals and objectives; and ultimately the final report. It is the management team's responsibility to select the stakeholder participants, provide all necessary airport background information, ensure that all work is done on schedule and is properly documented, and participate in the actual strategic planning process.

The strategic planning process itself is straightforward and consists of the following steps:

- Select a facilitator.
- Identify key stakeholders.
- Conduct a SWOT analysis.
- Develop the vision, goals, and objectives.
- Develop a monitoring and update process.
- Prepare and distribute the final plan.

Facilitator

The next step in the process is to select and retain the services of a facilitator, normally an outside consultant who specializes in this kind of work. This person assists the strategic plan management team by providing the necessary objectivity, focus, direction, and momentum to the strategic planning process. Bear in mind that the facilitator should not come up with the plan on behalf of the airport. The stakeholders do the planning; the facilitator is the guide. He (or she) provides organization for the planning process and structure for the plan itself. The facilitator should be someone who does not have a stake in the airport or in the community it serves. He should, however, be someone who is familiar with airports and their operation and regulation, i.e., someone who speaks the airport language. The facilitator should have the ability to tailor questions such that they accurately identify potential situations and pivotal directions unique to that particular airport. The facilitator should also establish a level of trust with the stakeholders, since some may resist sharing their thoughts candidly with a stranger. Other stakeholders may harbor the notion that a newcomer would be ineffective in understanding their concerns and effectively processing feedback into a useful plan. The familiarity factor must, however, be carefully monitored by the facilitator to ensure the optimum impartiality that is critical to a well-executed strategic plan. The facilitator in effect teaches the strategic planning process to the stakeholders. Since it is not possible even to write a letter by committee, let alone a strategic plan, the facilitator should be responsible for preparing all the plan documentation, including such tasks as recording meetings, translating the discussions into coherent documents, and preparing interim and final reports.

The facilitator will help collect the relevant information and sort through it to find key items that will lead to the development of a long-term vision and associated goals and objectives. At a large airport the facilitator may have several assistants from his firm. Their job will be to help with the legwork, including data gathering, interviewing, and report writing. A consultant can also add a strong element of objectivity that is essential to producing a viable document. The facilitator will guide group discussions and help ensure that the planning process focuses on key issues and areas of concern.

Throughout the strategic planning process it should be kept in mind that the goals and objectives should be locally-generated; after all, the airport belongs to the local stakeholders and it should go where they want it to go and become what they want it to become.

Stakeholders

Once the facilitator has been selected, the strategic planning team (possibly with the assistance of the facilitator) should identify the airport stakeholders and select the stakeholder representatives for the strategic planning process. These are people who have a direct stake in the future of the airport, or who represent organizations that have a similar key interest in airport development. The stakeholders will be responsible for setting the long-term vision for the plan, and will play a key role in the SWOT analysis and in developing goals and objectives. According to most strategic planning texts, the stakeholder group should number between eight and twelve people, although Bradford suggests that a group of six to eight people is the optimum.[2] With respect to larger airports, a group of fewer than eight may not be enough to represent all of the key entities that have an interest in the airport. Also, it is difficult to develop a group dynamic or synergy with a group of fewer than eight people. The individuals on the stakeholder group should be able to communicate their ideas without trying to dominate the process. It may be possible to have a group of more than a dozen people, but it is difficult to maintain the necessary focus in groups of 20 or 30 individuals. If the group is too large it can often result in rambling discussions and hangar stories which, although sometimes interesting, may not be a very productive use of time and resources.

For this reason it is important to have the facilitator lead the discussions; therefore, he should have a strong enough personality that he can keep the discussions focused without unduly constraining ideas and concepts. If it is necessary to establish a larger stakeholder group, e.g., to satisfy specific local concerns, it would be more efficient to break the larger group into smaller teams. It should also be kept in mind that adding more people to the stakeholder group does not necessarily mean adding more or different ideas or interests. The law of diminishing returns applies here and adding more people often winds up generating more of the same ideas.

The stakeholder group should consist of representatives of the following:

- Airport management and key staff, as well as individuals who sit on the airport commission or board of directors.

- Airport users such as airlines; airport tenants such as rental car companies and food, beverage, and other retail concessionaires; fixed base operators; flight schools; pilots who have aircraft based at the airport; etc.

- Local businesses, including companies that have aircraft based at the airport, chambers of commerce, and businesses that generate a lot of air travel, either via charter services or scheduled airlines.

- Local government agencies such as economic development agencies or commissions, planning and zoning agencies, and local elected officials.

If the airport is faced with politically-sensitive issues it may also be appropriate to add a representative or two from special interest groups, i.e., groups that may be directly affected by the development of the airport, in either a positive or negative way. It is also sometimes suggested that an FAA representative directly participate in the strategic planning process. I personally do not feel this is a good idea because the FAA is more of a regulatory agency than a direct airport user. The FAA should, however, be informed when a strategic plan is being prepared and should receive a copy of the draft plan for review and comment as appropriate. FAA guidance should also be solicited to help resolve complicated technical issues or issues related to FAA airport funding programs. And obviously the FAA should be closely involved in follow-on master plan studies, as discussed in Chapter 5: Master Planning.

Because it is not possible to include all of the individuals in these various airport components on the stakeholder group, the stakeholders should be people who can effectively represent their constituencies. For example, at a larger airport one or two individuals should be selected to represent tenants that have a business or service operation in the terminal. Similarly, one or two individuals should represent the various airlines serving the airport. These would usually (but not necessarily) be station managers, due to that position's comprehensive responsibility for operations, staff, customers, and facilities. In this case, it is wisest to include a representative from the busiest carrier serving the airport as well as one that typifies a carrier with an average flight level. Should the airport under study have a heavy schedule of international service, thought should be given to including a representative from one of its international carriers. It is particularly important to have airport staff, including engineering, maintenance, operations, and commercial management, represented on the stakeholder group, since these individuals will bear much of the responsibility for fulfilling the strategic plan's goals and carrying out the objectives. The stakeholders representing terminal tenants must be able to discuss the strategic planning process with their fellow tenants and get their ideas on the airport's future, as well as some input on its strengths, weaknesses, opportunities, and threats. The stakeholders representing airport staff should similarly be able to speak clearly on the ideas and concerns of the divisions they represent.

A strategic plan is far more likely to be successful if all the relevant groups, organizations, and individuals in the airport community have a role in its development. Soliciting their involvement can help it become "our plan" rather than "their plan," and consequently build support for future airport development. Their involvement can also help in team building by letting each group and individual know what his or her role is with respect to the operation and development of the airport. Ideally, the camaraderie and lines of communication established during the development of the strategic plan will help establish an effective, trusting workforce motivated to execute the plan.

Once the stakeholder group has been established, its first task should be to identify key issues and factors affecting the airport and its future. This is usually done as a group function, although it may also be appropriate to start the issues identification process by interviewing the key stakeholders individually. This allows each person to express his or her ideas without being influenced by a stronger personality or by peer pressure. Individual interviews can work at smaller airports, but they may be time-prohibitive at larger airports. The issues identification process should be somewhat structured, so that a strategic focus is maintained, but not so structured that the individuals cannot express their views, interests, and concerns. The discussions should bring out what each individual, as a representative of his group, expects or would like to see, both in terms of the airport and its development and operation and in terms of new or improved services and potential market area expansion. The discussions should encourage the stakeholders to state their expectations for future growth, not just for the airport, but for the agency, group, or constituency that he or she represents.

As part of the issues identification process, the stakeholder group should identify the geographical market served by the airport and what types of activities take place in the market area that need or benefit from the airport and its facilities and services. This not only helps to identify the traffic-generating power of the market, but also helps identify the types of airport facilities and services that are required. For example, resort communities may need scheduled air service to cities with large concentrations of people who will be traveling for vacation purposes. These travelers do not want to spend their vacation time getting from one point to another; they want to be there and have fun! Therefore, cities in the southern United States, Central America, and the Caribbean need nonstop air service to population concentrations in the Northeast, such as the Philadelphia-New York-Boston corridor, and the Chicago and Detroit area in the Upper Midwest. Similarly, a general aviation airport serving a resort community may need aircraft and passenger ground support facilities and services such as transient aircraft parking, charter aircraft services, etc. These are very simplified examples, but they illustrate the need to know the market and its travel characteristics, both existing and potential.

The stakeholders should also be intimately familiar with the physical setting of the airport and its environs. This includes a fairly simple inventory of the airport's physical facilities, including numbers of gates at the terminal, aircraft hangar and parking ramp capacities, types of instrument approaches, the number of public parking spaces, etc. The inventory should include a general assessment of the airport's physical growth potential. Are there physical or environmental features such as mountains, rivers, lakes, national parks, state wildlife refuges, etc., that would realistically constrain airport growth? Or are there cultural features such as large residential concentrations or manufacturing centers that may make physical expansion prohibitively expensive?

SWOT Analysis

Once the stakeholder group has reviewed and discussed the basic information about the airport and market area, the discussions about the airport and its future may begin. Together the stakeholders develop a future vision for the airport, or to be safe, alternative visions based upon alternative expectations of future events. The stakeholder sessions begin with generating ideas and potentials; these are the discussions of what the airport will be in the future. Also, at this point reality sets in and the stakeholders must also address the issue of what the airport *can* be, given existing and expected conditions and circumstances.

This is the point at which the identification of strengths, weaknesses, opportunities, and threats, i.e., the SWOT analysis, comes into play. The SWOT analysis is necessary to help focus strategic planning efforts on critical areas, and to help in the development of realistic and meaningful goals and objectives. These can be any number of things that the airport operator and the key stakeholders see as being important to the future of the airport.

The SWOT items discussed in the stakeholder sessions can and should cover any issues that are of concern to particular stakeholders, and can include both internal and external factors. These can range from a discussion of market area potentials, to the airport's customer services, to the airport's human resources staff or procurement processes. What is important is that the issues raised be ones that affect the operation and future development of the airport and the services it provides.

Among the strengths, for example, could be a strong airport management staff or dedicated workforce, or a vigorous local economy that has enough diversity to withstand economic slowdowns. Weaknesses could include such items as long-term airport tenant leases with unrealistically low terms, a local economy that is based on a single industry, or a poor ground transportation system. Opportunities can also vary widely from airport to airport, and can include such factors as a new industry with extensive travel or freight shipment needs, or a new airline or an existing airline that wants to expand its service at the airport. Threats could include anything from an airport procurement system that is inflexible and too time-consuming to respond to immediate needs, to a local industry that is about to close or relocate.

Strengths, weaknesses, opportunities, and threats typically include the following:

- Capital funding: Is it adequate to meet long-term needs? Is it consistent and dependable from year to year?
- Operating revenues: Does the airport have dependable revenue sources? Are operating revenues sufficient to cover operating expenses? Are revenue-generating opportunities constrained, or is there a possibility of adding new revenue sources? Is there a possibility of obtaining or improving scheduled air services? Are there opportunities for public/private partnering as a means to improve

the airport's financial picture? Are there opportunities for compatible business development on lands near or adjacent to the airport?
- Staff: Is there enough staff to operate the airport? Are they sufficiently trained and motivated? Does the airport have a problem attracting and retaining competent and experienced staff? Does the human resources system allow managers to hire the people needed to do the job? Is the salary structure competitive and adequate to attract and retain qualified people?
- Physical considerations: Are existing airport facilities, such as pavements, buildings, access roadways, etc., in good condition, or will repair and rehabilitation take a lot of the airport's budget in the foreseeable future? Does the runway have sufficient instrument landing aids and lighting? Is there room on airport property, or on adjacent property, for expansion? Is airport expansion constrained by adjacent land uses such as residential dwellings, schools, hospitals, parks, wildlife refuges? Is airport expansion constrained by physical features such as bodies of water, hills or mountains, or wetlands? Does the airport have adequate zoning protection?
- Institutional: Are the local governmental agencies supportive of the airport? Is there a potential for organized opposition to airport operations or expansion by citizens groups or environmental groups? Can the airport be directed and managed without undue influence from higher agencies that may have different goals?

Through the strategic planning process up to this point, the planning team should attempt to build consensus on each of the issues raised, including the SWOT analysis. It is unlikely that any group will achieve unanimous agreement on any complex issue. But having general concurrence on those items identified as key issues or focus areas will make the development of long-term goals and objectives a lot easier and help ensure that the results are more productive.

Goals and Objectives

Once the critical issues and possible futures have been identified and examined as part of the SWOT analysis, it is time to develop goals and objectives. Often airport operators or even the consultants participating in the exercise will want to start off the goal identification process with a mission statement for the airport. In effect, "This is who we are and what we do, or at least want to do." It has been my experience however, that while the concept of a mission statement is worthwhile, the resulting statements usually are not. Many are so broad and inspirational in nature that they wind up being in favor of everything from hard work and dedication, to motherhood and apple pie. For example, a mission statement for Wonderville Regional Airport might be simply:

"Our mission is to support Wonderville's aviation needs."

But then somebody says, "We don't just serve Wonderville, we serve the whole region!" So the mission statement becomes:

"Our mission is to support the aviation needs of the Wonderville region."

And then somebody says, "Well, we also support economic development." Thus:

"Our mission is to support the aviation needs and promote the economic viability of the Wonderville region."

And then somebody else says, "Don't forget that we want people to know that we place a priority on safety, and we operate efficiently in terms of both finances and customer services." So we now have:

"Our mission is to support the aviation needs and promote the economic viability of the Wonderville region in a safe and efficient manner."

Oops...don't forget the environment!

"Our mission is to support the aviation needs and promote the economic viability of the Wonderville region in a safe, efficient, and environmentally-friendly manner."

Oh, and what about our employees? After all, we couldn't operate without a good staff and we want them to know that they are important. Thus:

"Our mission is to support the aviation needs and promote the economic viability of the Wonderville region in a safe, efficient, and environmentally-friendly manner, and to maintain a skilled and motivated work force."

Almost any airport could be substituted for good old Wonderville Regional and it would smell as sweet. If a mission statement seems to be worthwhile as part of your planning process, go ahead and develop one, but personally I don't recommend spending a lot of time on it.

As noted above, goals should be thought of as statements about the end-state for the airport to achieve at a given point in time, and objectives are the steps in the process of getting there. For example, one goal could be that the airport will have direct, scheduled, daily air service to two major European destinations. Associated objectives could include contracting with an air service consultant to identify likely destination cities and air carriers, developing an incentive package to offer prospective carriers a break on rates and charges, and developing a business working group to add support to the airport's marketing efforts. Goals should be based on the issues and concerns developed earlier in the strategic planning process, and should be reasonably attainable, as noted above. If the airport lacks nonstop air service and the consensus is to increase the number of nonstop flights, the goal should be stated accordingly, and the objectives should state the things that must be done to increase the number of nonstop flights. It is important that these goals, in fact the strategic plan itself, be set in a defined, realistic time frame. Experts in the strategic planning field usually recommend a five-year target for both goals and objectives, even if the strategic plan includes a much longer time period into the future. Thus, if a strategic plan were being prepared in 2010, it might state the goal that by the year 2015 the airport will have direct service to two European destinations. The objectives would be structured such that by 2011 the necessary consultant services will have been procured, by 2012 the support of the local business community will have been appropriately mustered, and by 2013 an incentive package will have been prepared for prospective air carriers. It may be convenient and beneficial to key the strategic plan schedule to the airport's capital program cycle. Most airports use a five-year cycle, but some operate on a six- or seven-year capital program.

Most strategic planning experts suggest that the goals should be kept to a manageable number. Sometimes strategic plans fail because the agenda is too large and sets out too many things to be accomplished. As Bradford states, "It is better to identify 10 projects and complete them all than to identify 30 projects and merely get them all started."[3] It also helps if the goals are prioritized so that attention can be focused where it is needed. Typically goals related to safety have the highest priority at all airports. Goals that are related to increased capacity are also often given a high priority, followed by goals related to customer service, environmental compatibility, and cost-effectiveness. However, these relative priorities vary from airport to airport, depending upon local needs and conditions.

After the goals have been prepared and the steps or actions that need to be taken to achieve those goals have been identified, it is time to develop what are called performance measures, also sometimes known as benchmarks. This is the part that keeps the airport honest and usually offers the greatest challenge. Using the example noted above, the performance measures can be simply "yes" or "no," depending on whether a consultant has been hired and other stated items have been accomplished. Performance measures get a little tricky though, when stated in terms of increasing air passenger volumes or improving airport customer service. A goal can be to increase passenger traffic by 10 percent for the five-year period, but if the airport's major carrier goes bankrupt or the national economy goes into a recession, the goal will probably not be achieved, and these are really things that are outside the airport's control. Something like improving customer service is even more difficult because it is hard to measure progress. After all, the airport operator can't very well go around the terminal asking people if they are happy, or if they like it there, although some fairly sophisticated (and sometimes not so sophisticated) customer service surveys can be conducted to obtain this type of information. However, the results of customer service surveys are often hard to interpret because airport patrons often confuse airport functions and services with those of the airlines. Progress toward improved customer services can be measured by the number of complaints the airport receives, but as traffic increases, the number of complaints is likely to increase as well, so it might be more appropriate to consider a complaint rate. For example, five complaints per month per thousand enplaned passengers might be the end goal, and one of the objectives toward achieving this goal might be to reduce the complaint rate by one complaint per month each year for the next five years. But if improving customer service is to be a serious goal, one of the objectives might be to hire a specialized survey firm to conduct periodic surveys, or to make customer complaint forms more readily available (or to start using them if they aren't being used already). In that case an actual increase in complaints may be observed at first because people find it easier to complain than they have in the past. Problems can also be encountered if the complaints received are related to a particular airline or tenant—a restaurant for example. Many airports have standards of some sort for the quality and price of food served at a restaurant, but the airport does not control how the restaurant employees treat the customers. So if the number of complaints received is used as a measure of customer service, some way will have to be found to deal with complaints related to cancelled flights, expensive cab fares, or cold mashed potatoes at one of the airport's dining facilities.

Examples of goals, objectives, and action items are shown below, in a very simplified form. Remember that goals are end-states, objectives are things that must be accomplished to achieve the goal, and action items are specific tasks that must be accomplished to achieve the objective.

A. Goal: Make the airport self supporting

   1. Objective: Increase revenues

      - Action items:

         a. Examine existing rates and charges

         b. Look for new sources of revenue

         c. Consider public/private partnering

   2. Objective: Decrease expenses

      - Action items:

         a. Look for areas of waste

         b. Look for lower-cost solutions

B. Goal: Ensure airport meets all FAA standards

   1. Objective: Bring runway safety areas up to standard

      - Action items:

         a. Obtain consultant assistance

         b. Identify work needed

         c. Identify environmental impacts

       d. Develop cost estimates
       e. Prepare budget
       f. Secure funding
       g. Obtain environmental permits
       h. Hire contractor

2. Objective: Clear all FAR Part 77 obstructions
    - Action items:
        a. Survey surrounding area
        b. Identify obstructions
        c. Identify environmental impacts
        d. Obtain environmental permits
        e. Remove, mark, or light obstructions

Monitoring and Updating

Because all of the ideas and discussions on alternative visions, strengths, weaknesses, opportunities, threats, goals, and objectives cannot be documented by committee, it is the facilitator's responsibility to make an accurate record of the stakeholder discussions, synthesize them into a coherent document, and present the draft document to the stakeholder group for final discussion and approval. The strategic planning process should also identify an individual who will be responsible for monitoring the completion of each of the plan's objectives and the achievement of each of the goals, according to an identified and agreed-upon schedule. The monitoring process should also include external factors such as economic conditions, future security requirements, airline bankruptcies, and local business development factors that may necessitate changes to the plan's goals or objectives. In more extreme cases, external factors may require rethinking the ultimate vision for the airport.

The Final Plan

The strategic planning process should conclude with the preparation of a final strategic plan report that documents the planning process and participants, and includes a discussion of the airport's strengths, weaknesses, opportunities, and threats. The report should include clear statements of the airport's role and its vision for the future, along with the actions to be accomplished in the attainment of the future vision. The report should be candid and honest with respect to weaknesses and threats. Often airports are reluctant to discuss weaknesses, but if the vision is to be attained the plan should note how any weaknesses will be overcome, and how the threats will be confronted and addressed. The plan should also list all goals, objectives, and actions to be taken toward goal achievement, along with a clear documentation of who will be responsible for each objective or action. And finally, the plan should note which individual or group will be responsible for monitoring the performance of the plan and for keeping it up-to-date.

The final strategic plan report is usually shared with key stakeholders and participants in the planning process. A summary version of the final report should be prepared for a larger audience such as the general public, chambers of commerce, and legislative bodies. The summary report should present the future vision for the airport and a brief summary of the major actions to be taken to achieve that vision; it may even be appropriate to include milestones or target dates. The summary should also list the participants in the strategic planning process. This will demonstrate that the strategic plan does not simply reflect the desires of the airport operator, but rather establishes a vision for future airport development as identified by the airport stakeholders. Bear in mind that the summary report can be used as a marketing tool, so in that context it should "sizzle," both in content and appearance. It should be distributed to the entire airport community, including airport employees and tenants. It should also be distributed to local businesses, chambers of commerce, economic development agencies, elected officials, the general public, and perhaps most importantly, to potential new customers and service providers that the airport is trying to attract.

Finally, establishing a long-term vision for the airport and a strategic plan to achieve that vision is the key to a successful airport development program. A strategic plan should be the precursor to other planning efforts, since it defines the big picture and must be established and adopted in order to ensure that subsequent, more quantitative endeavors are both efficiently scoped and properly focused.

In summary, strategic planning is the key to a successful airport development program. Strategic plans can be prepared as standalone documents or as the first step in a comprehensive airport master plan study. A strategic plan can help organize thinking, set direction, and build support for future airport development. It can also help build a team and provide a focus for ongoing airport operations. A strategic plan should not be a long, drawn out, agonizing, and expensive document to prepare. It is the product of focused thinking and discussion, relying on knowledge of the airport, the community it serves, and plain old common sense.

Endnotes

1. *Airport Master Plans*, AC 150/5070-6B. Washington, D.C.: Federal Aviation Administration, 2005, p. 9.

2. Bradford, Robert W., J. Peter Duncan, and Brian Tarcy, *Simplified Strategic Planning*. Worcester, MA: Chandler House Press, 2000, p. 13.

3. *Ibid.*, p. 185.

CHAPTER 5

MASTER PLANNING

Virtually all airports have a master plan that identifies their long-term facility development program. Master planning is thus one of the most common types of planning with which airport planners are involved. The FAA provides explicit guidance on how a master plan should be prepared and what it should contain. This chapter describes and provides some context for the various elements involved in master planning. It notes how each of the elements fits into the planning process and provides some real-world guidance for developing an effective plan. The discussions in this chapter apply to other, smaller-scale or more specialized types of facility planning studies as well as master plans.

Background

A master plan is typically defined as a comprehensive study for the development of the airport. It usually presents near- (within five years), medium- (5 to 10 years), and long-term (10 or more years into the future) plans for new airport facilities and facility improvements.

Richard de Neufville describes the two methods most commonly followed when preparing airport master plans.[1] The first he calls "reactive" planning in that it represents one specific response to one specific expected future. He describes this traditional master planning process as "linear":

- Inventory existing conditions.
- Forecast future traffic.
- Determine facility requirements.
- Develop alternatives for comparison and evaluation.
- Select desired option.[2]

The second method de Neufville describes is "proactive" planning. With a proactive approach, planners determine what the airport's future *should* be and prepare a master plan based on that future. It sounds almost like, "Build it and they will come." In de Neufville's opinion master plans are inflexible because they focus on a single future and do not consider alternative futures. He maintains that airports will continue to develop master plans for the foreseeable future because they are a prerequisite for federal funding for airport improvements.

Actually though, the FAA does *not* require an airport to do a master plan—not for federal funding eligibility, nor for any other reason. What *is* required by the FAA is a current approved Airport Layout Plan. Keep in mind however, that changes to an ALP usually require some sort of narrative explanation of what is being proposed and why it is needed. For major ALP changes the master plan provides that narrative, so in this sense de Neufville is correct.

A Plan, Not a Blueprint

Master planning is not as cut-and-dried or as rigid as de Neufville implies. An ALP showing a 5-, 10-, and 20-year development program as documented in an airport master plan or other planning narrative simply enables the FAA to program funds to support the development program. Although there is often a tendency to regard this program as a blueprint for long-term development, especially among some in the FAA, things just aren't that simple. Conditions change and problems arise. As de Neufville states, "The forecast is always wrong."[3] What we expect to happen will probably not happen, particularly when we attempt to foresee conditions 10 and 20 years into the future. Thus a master plan must include an inherent flexibility.

Building in flexibility can be very difficult to do in the face of an uncertain future, especially because many people do not deal well with uncertainty. However, good planning demands it. Planners should always be thinking, "What if?" "What if the future is not what was expected?" Even the best plans cannot account for all contingencies, but they should be flexible enough to adapt to some change.

The master plan prepared for BWI Airport in 1987 provides an example of how conditions can change unexpectedly, and yet how development can still continue in an efficient and timely manner. When the BWI master plan study began in 1985, the airport had just been designated as a hub by Piedmont Airlines. Prior to that time BWI had been an O&D (origin-destination) airport, with annual volumes of under five million total passengers, only 10 percent of whom were connecting from one flight to another. During the course of the master plan study it was assumed that BWI would always be a hub airport. Aviation publications and the local newspapers were full of stories—complete with passenger forecasts—about how Piedmont was going to grow over the next 10 to 15 years. Although Maryland Aviation Administration (MAA) staff felt that Piedmont's growth projections were rather inflated, the master plan forecasts had to be based in part on the Piedmont projections, since they were public knowledge. It would have been difficult to justify forecasts that differed from the Piedmont forecasts that were seen in the newspapers by business leaders, elected officials, and the general public. The bulk of the master plan work effort focused on the airside—the

Chapter 5 – Master Planning

airport's runways and taxiways. At that time Piedmont was operating five connecting banks per day, with about 20 jet transport aircraft and 15 propeller-driven commuter aircraft. Compounding BWI's congestion problem was the fact that the airport's two primary jet runways intersected, requiring the sequencing of arrivals and departures and constraining capacity.

The master plan recommended that new runways and taxiways be constructed; however, it also included some *flexibility*, in the event that things did not come to pass as expected. Airport improvements would be linked to aviation activity levels rather than a calendar; if traffic did not grow as expected, improvements would be put on hold until needed. After the master plan was completed, MAA implemented an annual forecast review and update process to quantitatively monitor demand and reevaluate growth assumptions.

The master plan called for a near-term extension to the airport's general aviation runway. This would enable the runway to be used by commuter aircraft, thus separating prop aircraft from the faster-moving jet aircraft in the runway arrival streams, which greatly enhances overall capacity. The need for this improvement was clear, and the runway extension was completed in 1990, two-and-a-half years after the master plan was completed.

A new transport-category runway was also planned, with construction expected to begin in the mid-1990s. However, air traffic did not materialize as forecast in the master plan. US Airways acquired Piedmont in the late 1990s and began downsizing the BWI hub. Simultaneously, the national economy went into a recession. With growth stalled, MAA opted not to build the runway at that time. In fact, as of this writing the runway is still not built because, for several reasons, the number of aircraft operations has not increased, particularly during peak periods. Air traffic demand has not grown. When Southwest Airlines began service to BWI in 1993, it did not operate at BWI as a hub, with major connecting banks. Southwest spurred growth in origin-destination traffic rather than connecting traffic. So, even though passenger traffic has grown substantially over the past decade, the burden has been on the landside of the airport rather than the airside.

MAA has undertaken a new master plan study which will address long-term runway and taxiway needs, among other factors. This example illustrates one aspect of flexibility. Even though the master plan called for a new runway by the mid-1990s, it was not built because it was not needed.

An example from BWI where flexibility was not achieved was in the design of the terminal for the Piedmont hub operation, Concourse D. The concourse was designed to accommodate an airline hub operation. The concourse itself was wider than the terminal's other concourses in order to handle the large volumes of passengers running from one flight to another during the five peak connecting periods. The throat of the concourse—the point where the concourse joins the main terminal building—was not widened, because it was expected that the concourse would handle relatively few origin-destination passengers entering the concourse from the main terminal. For the same reason, the ticketing and baggage claim and makeup facilities were not expanded. These decisions seemed logical—connecting passengers usually have no reason to leave their concourse, and their bags are shifted from one flight to another on the ramp.

The problem arose when Southwest Airlines began to increase its BWI operation in the late 1990s. As other carriers also increased their flights, it became apparent that Concourse D would have to be used for airlines operating point-to-point services or services to their hub cities. Unfortunately this was difficult because the ticketing and baggage claim and makeup areas were undersized, and it turned out that the terminal itself could not be expanded without losing a couple of aircraft gate positions. Compounding these difficulties has been the need for additional passenger and baggage screening requirements as a result of the 9/11 tragedy, as noted in Chapter 3: Airport Management, Operations, and Finance.

Is It Worth It?
Some airport planners and airport operators occasionally question the need for airport master planning, which consumes significant time and money. Their opinion is that the airlines really determine what happens at an airport, so why spend all the time and money master planning? Why not put together a simple narrative along with an ALP that includes the best estimate of what might be needed in the foreseeable future and send it to the FAA? Then when the airlines come to the airport operator with a particular improvement (or set of improvements) that they would like to see, simply modify the ALP with another short narrative documenting why the airlines' request is valid.

Well, that is a pretty defeatist approach and it is not based on a valid premise. Airlines do not always get what they want—and quite often they get things they *don't* want. Yes, if a particular carrier is the dominant airline serving an airport and they say they need a new terminal, they could conceivably use political influence to advance such a project. For example, I know of one carrier that insisted on a runway extension so they could operate DC-9s on a particular route out of that airport. Although the planning and engineering analyses did not support the airline case, they succeeded in getting the runway extension. They got it just in time to handle their last DC-9 flight on that route. In fact, it was the last DC-9 they operated at that airport; their service was given to their commuter airline affiliate.

If the airport director is any good at all, and the planning staff and their supporting consultants are worth the money they are being paid, nobody should be able to dictate what happens at the airport other than the airport itself. It is true that there are exceptions but that does not mean it should be the rule. Moreover, if an airline, or any other tenant for that matter, demands some particular facility improvement, it is up to the planner to make sure that such an improvement does not preclude other airport facility development. It is true that money is sometimes wasted in the planning process, but good planners should make sure that they are getting (or giving) good value for each dollar spent.

The Master Planning Process

The FAA recently revised and updated its advisory circular on airport master plans. The new document, AC 150/5070-6B, *Airport Master Plans*, provides updated guidance to airport planners and is intended to be user-friendly and flexible enough to be used for small, general aviation airports as well as large, air carrier facilities.[4] The FAA emphasizes that the new Master Plan AC is a *process*, not a *cookbook*. The new version of the AC does a good job in reflecting current trends, issues, and best practices in airport planning, and does an excellent job of providing flexibility to allow an airport master plan to address the needs of a particular airport at a particular time, rather than presenting a standardized approach as the earlier version did. The guidance allows the study to be tailored to the particular needs of individual airports.

Remember: all airports are different. Or as somebody once told me, "If you've seen one airport, you've seen one airport." In this regard the AC states that, "…each master plan study must focus on the specific needs of the airport for which a plan is being prepared and the scope of a study must be tailored to the individual airport."[5] In this context studies that address major revisions to the existing airport layout plan (ALP) are considered "Master Plans," while studies that only focus on parts of the ALP are called "Master Plan Updates" or sometimes, "ALP Updates." The AC clearly points out that it is not always necessary to develop a master plan if changes and improvements are needed that do not affect the entire airport. For example, if an airport has runway and taxiway issues that are resulting in excessive aircraft delays, but the terminal, access roads, and parking facilities are performing adequately, a planning study can focus on those airside issues that are causing the problems. This focuses time and money where those resources are most needed.

The FAA plays an important role in any airport planning process and planners and airport operators should always keep the FAA informed on what is happening and why things are being done. For the most part the FAA is as eager to develop the airport as the airport operator. Most operators have indicated that the FAA is very supportive—as long as it can be demonstrated that the planned facility improvements are necessary and appropriate. With regard to master planning the FAA typically takes on the following responsibilities:

- Review and approve the master plan work scope.
- Review and approve the aviation demand forecasts.
- Review working papers.
- Play a role as a member of the project team.
- Participate in the public involvement process.
- Ensure internal FAA coordination.
- Ensure that the planned facilities are justified.

- Ensure that the facility requirements analysis is sufficient and can be defended in the Purpose and Need section of a follow-on environmental document.
- Review or conduct airspace studies.
- Ensure that the alternatives analysis is adequate for a follow-on environmental document.
- Review and approve site selection studies.
- Review and approve ALPs.

Although the importance of the FAA to the planning process is obvious from the above, the primary responsibility for completing airport master plans rests with the airport sponsor and their consultant. The FAA can help, but they should not be expected to do all the thinking or planning. Although virtually all airport master plans are prepared by consultants hired by the airport sponsor, airport operators and planners employed by an airport authority should always play a major role in the study. Airport input is especially important in developing the strategic vision that determines the future role of the airport. If the airport owner and planning staff do not establish this vision, the consultant will probably do it for them, and thus it is possible to wind up with the consultant's plan rather than an airport plan. This is often the case at general aviation airports whose staff do not have sufficient time to devote to a planning study or who are not knowledgeable about the planning process.

The AC describes the process that should be followed in the preparation of an airport master plan but it does not specify *how* to plan; rather it specifies the steps that must be taken to do the planning:

1. Pre-Planning
2. Public Involvement
3. Environmental Considerations
4. Existing Conditions
5. Aviation Forecasts
6. Facility Requirements
7. Alternatives Development and Evaluation
8. Airport Layout Plans
9. Facilities Implementation Plan
10. Financial Feasibility Analysis

Although these appear to be sequential steps in a linear planning process, good planning is not necessarily linear, and work on a number of these items can proceed simultaneously. For example, the Public Involvement element should be developed at the outset of the study and should continue until the study is complete. The Environmental Considerations should begin as soon as the scope of work is approved by the FAA, and should be considered in the Alternatives Development and Evaluation step. Work can begin on Public Involvement, Environmental Considerations, Existing Conditions, and Aviation Forecasts as soon as the federal grant is in place and the consultant receives Notice-to-Proceed.

Step 1: Pre-Planning

One of the first steps in the planning effort is to assemble the airport's planning team. The team typically should include planners, environmental specialists, and engineers, as well as other specialties that may be needed for the project. These specialists might include experts on airspace analysis and air traffic procedures, instrument approach procedure design, baggage systems, automobile parking, highway traffic analysis, etc., depending on the types of issues expected to be addressed in the study. The important thing is to make sure that the right people are available to do the planning work, and to make sure that they are qualified to handle their respective areas of responsibility. Although mentoring and teaching young planners requires on-the-job training (as discussed in Chapter 10: Mentoring, Managing, and Team Building) the experts should be proficient in their areas of expertise and should not be learning as they go.

The Master Plan AC includes coordination as part of Study Design (as discussed below), but some coordination during the Pre-Planning step will pay off in the long run. Specifically, the airport officials should coordinate with local planning and development officials to ensure consistency between community and airport planning and development efforts. Local elected officials should also be informed that a planning study will be taking place. They should not be blindsided; if they are it can make the real coordination work much harder. Even if the planning study is only just beginning, word somehow gets out and it is better to let key people know exactly what is going on in case they get hit with some question from a constituent or from someone from another agency.

It should also be remembered, both in the Pre-Planning step and throughout the study: there will be things the airport operator *wants*, things he *needs*, and things he can *afford*. If they are all the same things he will be in good shape. Unfortunately they are usually not the same and this can cause problems in the study, so it is imperative to keep some sense of realism through the study process, beginning in the Pre-Planning element. That can be difficult for planners, but it is necessary nonetheless.

According to the Master Plan AC, Pre-Planning involves the following stages:

  A. Initial Needs Determination

  B. Request for Qualifications and Consultant Selection

  C. Development of Study Design

  D. Negotiating Consultant Contracts

E. Application for Federal Funding

Stage A: Initial Needs Determination

The Initial Needs Determination might also be referred to as an identification of issues, or it should at least include the identification of issues that will be addressed in the study. It is important to note that the needs determination does not specify which facilities need to be improved; that information is developed in the Facility Requirements step described below. Rather, the needs determination is where the team identifies which facilities may be experiencing difficulties and need to be studied, as well as what kind or depth of planning study is appropriate. It is similar to the scoping process in environmental studies and the preparation of environmental documents. The issues identified guide the scope of the planning study to be undertaken, and help determine whether the situation requires a master plan or simply an ALP update. The needs determination is based in part on information developed in the strategic planning effort, in that the needs of the airport depend to a great extent on where the airport is going in the future. As stated in the AC, "The airport sponsor's strategic vision or business plan for the airport may drive the need for a planning study."[6]

The needs determination will also depend on any existing or expected deficiencies in the airport or the airport plan. The local FAA Airports District Office (ADO) should be consulted before deciding whether a master plan or an ALP update is appropriate. Their guidance is essential for determining both the content of and the process for the planning effort. For example, the needs determination will show whether the study should focus only on the need for a new runway, or for a runway extension, or for taxiway improvements alone, or whether it should focus on the whole airside of the airport, i.e., the runway/taxiway system in its entirety. If a particular runway or taxiway issue is all that really needs to be addressed, it is not likely that a complete master plan will be needed. But perhaps the needs determination shows that the airside is experiencing problems, and that the existing gates at the passenger terminal are overcrowded, and that there are also deficiencies in the ground access system, as well as a shortage of public parking facilities. In this case a full master plan study is appropriate.

The needs determination should also give some idea of the depth of the study to be undertaken. For example, serious terminal area congestion problems may be occurring on both the airside and at curbside, and some taxiway improvements may also be needed to accommodate the increased ground movement and maneuvering of aircraft. The curbside congestion problems may be due in part to a lack of adequate ground access capacity for private vehicles departing the terminal area once they have dropped off or picked up their passengers. In this example problems are occurring in all three airport components: airside, terminal, and landside. However, if the runway capacity is adequate to handle future demand, an in-depth study of the runway system is probably not needed; runway issues need only be considered as they relate to current or anticipated problems with the taxiway system.

As part of the needs determination process an initial determination should be made as to how much engineering should be done as part of the planning study. Some engineering and preliminary design work is usually necessary to develop reasonably accurate cost estimates. Engineering will also be needed to support the environmental analysis, at least in terms of defining limits of disturbance. Some people have estimated that the engineering work done during the planning process should be sufficient to get through 20 to 30 percent of the design phase. The level of engineering required will vary with the type and complexity of the individual facility improvements resulting from the planning process, but typically engineering will be needed to support the following activities:

- Define alternatives for analysis.
- Assess aeronautical safety and utility.
- Analyze environmental impacts.
- Inform the public and resource agencies.
- Identify potential environmental mitigation.
- Define order-of-magnitude project costs.

The needs determination should also consider whether the scale of the anticipated airport improvements will be to an extent that might require an Environmental Assessment (EA) or an Environmental Impact Statement (EIS). Consultation with FAA staff is essential at this point, prior to consultant selection, to determine when the procurement of consultant services for an environmental document should begin. Remember, if an EIS is required, the consultant must be selected by the FAA. The situation gets a little complicated if the potential environmental impacts may be severe enough to warrant an EA, and could possibly lead to an EIS. Early consultation with the FAA is particularly necessary in these cases to avoid losing time in the process that leads from planning through design and ultimate construction.

Stage B: Request for Qualifications and Consultant Selection

Once the issues have been identified and the scope of the planning effort has been determined, it is time to proceed to the Consultant Selection stage. The current edition of AC 150/5100-14, *Architectural, Engineering, and Planning Consultant Services for Airport Grant Projects*,[7] should be used for guidance in soliciting consultant services for airport planning studies. This publication provides a plethora of information on consultant selection including contract formats, methods of contracting, and allowable costs. Note that consultant selection for projects being funded by the FAA must be *qualifications-based*. As specified in the Consultant Selection AC:

> Qualifications-based procedures require that a contract for A/E services be awarded pursuant to a fair and open selection process based on the qualifications of the firms. The fees for such services

are established following selection of a firm through a negotiation process to determine a fair and reasonable price.[8]

The selection of a consultant to perform the work is usually accomplished by a consultant selection or consultant evaluation panel composed of three to five technically qualified individuals. Consultant selection is usually, although not always, done in a two-phase process. The first phase is the Request for Qualifications (RFQ). The sponsor advertises that he is looking for a consultant or consultant team to provide a range of services that are spelled out in the RFQ. The Qualifications Statement (or Quals Statement) submitted by prospective consultants is sometimes referred to as an Expression of Interest. Although it is called a statement it is really more than a simple statement of the consultant's interest in doing the work. It is a package of information that is prepared by the consultant that documents the firm's experience in performing the services requested. It identifies the key staff who will be working on the project and what their experience is in performing similar tasks on other airport planning projects. Thus it is important for the RFQ to state the study issues and objectives as clearly and completely as possible. The more information the consultant has, the more responsive he can be to the sponsor's request, both in terms of services and staff.

For example the RFQ should let the consultants know if the key issues will include airside capacity work, roadway access, terminal expansion, Part 77 issues, and/or other factors so the appropriate staff can be assigned. It is especially helpful, both for the consultant preparing the quals statement, and for the sponsor's review and evaluation, to identify the key staff positions that are expected to be working on the project. The key staff positions usually are listed as the Project Manager, Airport Planner, Airside Capacity Analyst, Aviation Demand Forecaster, Terminal Planner, Highway Traffic Planner, etc., depending on the issues to be studied. This makes it easier and more efficient for the evaluation process to then rate the proposed consultant team members assigned to the project on the basis of their experience at performing similar tasks at other airports or on other projects. From the sponsor's standpoint, it is important to note whether the project manager for a complex master plan study has managed similar master plan studies in the past. Similarly, he should note whether the forecaster proposed for a master plan at a major air carrier airport has experience in preparing air carrier demand forecasts. It is important to keep in mind here that the sponsor should ask for the kinds of staff people and specialists that he expects will be involved in the study. If the airport is not experiencing runway capacity issues, a specialist in airside capacity will probably not be needed for the planning study. Conversely, if ground access or terminal congestion issues have been identified, the RFQ should clearly state that a traffic planner or terminal planner should be part of the key staff proposed for the project.

The RFQ should also include the criteria that will be used to evaluate a consultant's quals statement. If quals statements will be evaluated on the basis of the experience of the firm and of the key staff, that should be made clear in the RFQ, along with the scoring and weighting procedure that will be used. After the quals statements have been received from the various interested consulting firms, the sponsor reviews and evaluates the candidate firms and selects those which are considered to be best qualified to perform the requested services. At this point the sponsor usually develops a "shortlist" of qualified firms and prepares a Request for Proposals (RFP).

For example, a sponsor may receive quals statements from eight or ten firms, and find that four or five of them have the greatest potential to perform the requested services. In some cases all interested firms may have the capability to do the job, but unless the selection panel is willing to review eight or ten detailed proposals, the final field should be limited to four or five best qualified candidates. These select few are thus "shortlisted."

If the project is devoted primarily or exclusively to highly-specialized work such as preparing a plan for a hydrant fueling system, there will probably not be very many firms that specialize in this area. In this case, since the field of potentially qualified candidates is limited, it would be appropriate to skip the RFQ phase and issue an RFP directly. In effect the entire field of potential applicants has been shortlisted. Skipping the RFQ phase can save a lot of time, but some care must be taken so that the sponsor doesn't wind up with a dozen detailed consultant proposals to review and evaluate.

When a shortlist has been prepared and the winners and losers have been notified, the sponsor prepares the RFP. This document requests much more detail about how the consultant will address the issues that will be studied as part of the planning effort. Often the RFP asks the consultants to prepare an outline of the study scope and schedule. This doesn't really seem to be fair to the consultant because the study scope is essentially the same as the Study Design, which is the next stage in the process after the consultant has been selected and involves a lot of interaction between the consultant and the sponsor, as discussed below. The consultant is not likely to get enough of an understanding of the project based on the information in the RFP to develop a worthwhile scope. It makes more sense to me to ask how the consultant will approach the study, based upon the RFP information. Also, there have been instances where a sponsor receives several scopes of services during the consultant selection phase, and then tries either to pick the best one or to combine them and use that as the final template to be used by the consultant ultimately selected. In this case a firm that prepares a good scope may wind up seeing it used by a competitor, and that doesn't seem fair.

Another question often asked in the RFP is how the consultant will manage the study. This is particularly important if it is a large, complex study, and the consultant team has a number of specialized subcontractors. The consultant proposal should specify who exactly will be in charge of the entire project, who will be responsible for each element, and how all of the various work activities will fit together. Lines of communication should be specified so that the sponsor will have one principal point of contact for the project. The RFP should also make clear who the principal point of contact will be for the sponsor.

Based on my own experience I think it is a good idea to have oral presentations as part of the RFP evaluation process for the shortlisted firms. At these orals, the sponsor can meet the various key staff who will be involved in the project, and gauge how they perform "under fire," so to speak. Although this is commonly done as a formal presentation by members of each consultant team, it can also be sufficient to hold a less formal interview with a question-and-answer session. My preference is to hold informal interviews and allow each consultant about 10 minutes to summarize his view of the study and to state *briefly* why he thinks his firm or team is the best qualified to do the job and the basic approach his team will follow in conducting the study. This short statement or summary can be followed by a question-and-answer session of about 20 minutes, where persons on the selection panel can seek clarification on any issues or questions they may have from reviewing the RFP.

Note that the FAA does not recommend that oral presentations be held until the shortlist has been developed.[9] Consultants usually put a lot of time and effort into these presentations and it does not seem fair to ask consultants to do all this work unless they have a serious chance at being selected. Also, sitting through all those presentations can be exhausting for the selection panel.

Generally speaking, the selection process should focus on the subject at hand and not digress into peripheral issues. Also, the process should be simple and straightforward, and should not involve inordinate expense on the part of the proposing firms. Obviously the complexity of the selection process is going to be directly related to the complexity of the study. However, the simpler the selection process, the sooner the firm can be selected and the sooner the study can begin. If an elaborate effort is called for in the consultant selection process, it may discourage some firms from proposing on the study, thereby limiting the field of potential firms. An elaborate process also can make it harder for the selection panel to make accurate and objective evaluations.

Although the proposal should include the consultant's approach to the project and a basic scope of work, a detailed, final scope of work should not be prepared until the selected consultant and the sponsor sit down together and review all the issues that may be involved in the study. Note that it is usually a good idea to have the ADO participate in that meeting to minimize the subsequent revisions to the draft scope required by the FAA.

With regard to timing, the entire consultant selection process can be done in as little as two or three months, or can take up to a year or more, depending on the complexity of the project, the sponsor's selection process, the time allowed for proposal preparation and evaluation, and the extent to which the sponsor's legal representative gets involved. Typically it takes about a month to prepare a package soliciting consultant services, assuming that the staff preparing the RFQ has other work to do at the same time. It also takes quite a while to schedule a meeting of the consultant evaluation and selection panel, so a meeting of this group should be scheduled as far in advance as possible. Ideally the consultant should be allowed at least two weeks (preferably three) to submit the quals statement. This will give the consultant adequate time to put together a team that is responsive to the work described in the RFQ. After the submissions have been received, it normally takes two to four weeks to evaluate the consultant qualifications and prepare a shortlist. Preparing the RFP will take about another month; for a complex project it could take longer, but this work can be done by airport staff during the RFQ process.

Shortlisted consultants should be given three or four weeks to put their proposals together, and another two to three weeks should be allowed for the selection committee to review the material. If oral interviews will be held with the shortlisted firms, they should be scheduled as soon as the firms have been shortlisted. Ideally, the selected firms should receive their selection notification and scheduled interview time in the same letter. The interviews should all be scheduled as closely together as possible, for example within a few days and definitely all within the same week. Within a week after that the consultant selection committee should meet to discuss the proposals and the interviews and complete the scoring. Depending on the level of bureaucracy in the airport's organization, it may take another week or two (or even longer in a large organization) to get all the appropriate administrative and legal concurrences, approvals, verifications, audits, and other nonsense out of the way. The winning and losing teams can then be notified accordingly.

The consulting team may include specialty subcontractors in areas such as airport fueling systems and financial planning, as well as environmental specialties such as wetlands identification, noise impact evaluation and mitigation, water quality investigation, etc. It has been my experience that these subcontractors are asked for their pertinent information for the quals statement submission, and unfortunately, on a good many occasions, they are never heard from again. Many times subcontractors are not even consulted for the preparation of the actual study proposal, and never get a copy of either the quals statement or the proposal. It is obviously good for the bottom line for the prime consultant to do as much of the work as they can with their own staff; however, this is not good business practice, and it is not fair to the subs or to the airport sponsor if they do not share the work. I remember talking with a consultant about needing a hydrant fuel system study and he said, "Oh yes, we have somebody who just did one of those at Airport X." Well, I didn't want somebody who did a hydrant fuel study at an airport once or twice, I wanted somebody who had done hydrant fuel studies at many airports—preferably somebody who does hydrant fueling studies all the time and who knows airport fueling issues inside out. On a number of occasions I have had to *demand* that the prime consultant assign a specific task to a subcontractor, or at least include the sub on the work for that task.

Unfortunately it often falls to the airport sponsor to ensure that prime consultants share meaningful work with a diverse, highly-qualified team of firms. Particularly for large projects, a prime consultant will assemble a team of subcontractors for submission and evaluation in the RFQ phase of the consultant selection process. Usually the team will include a minority or disadvantaged business enterprise (MBE or DBE) or two, as well as one or two smaller local firms. Unfortunately (and much to my continuing chagrin), the MBE/DBE firms are usually used for printing, graphics, public outreach, field surveys, highway traffic analysis, or sometimes a bit of civil engineering. They tend to be less involved in the heart of the planning effort. The sponsor should encourage the meaningful involvement of these smaller firms and then ensure that what was promised during the proposal phase is how the project is actually conducted.

A similar principle applies to the individuals participating on the project. Prior to selection, the sponsor should require a commitment from the prime contractor as to the level of involvement of key staff individuals (for the prime contractor and all subcontractors) on the project. Support staff is usually not as critical, but the personnel identified as key staff should actually be involved in executing the project. For example, if Ferdinand de Lesseps is listed in the RFP as the lead civil engineer, the sponsor's project manager should make sure that Mr. de Lesseps actually plays a key role in all civil engineering tasks in the project. He may not do all of the civil engineering, but he should be responsible for it and he should be able to brief the client on the status of any of the civil engineering tasks included in the project scope. Most contracts have a clause that states that the sponsor must approve of any changes or substitutions to the project staff, although this clause is not always enforced. Sometimes there are legitimate reasons for changes in personnel and that is perfectly understandable; however, some firms try to "bait-and-switch." The sponsor should not let them get away with it.

Stage C: Development of Study Design

Study Design really begins with the initial needs determination discussed above. Although the Master Plan AC discusses the scoping process as part of study design, scoping will also have begun earlier during the needs determination.

By the beginning of the study design stage the consultant will be on board and the expertise will be available to determine the detail of how the study will be conducted, which issues will need to be addressed, and the depth of analysis that will be required for each of the issues identified.

It is a very good idea to get the local ADO involved at this point, both for their technical expertise and because the airport sponsor will be asking them for a grant to do the study. Including FAA staff in the study design process helps ensure that they have a thorough understanding of what the airport is trying to do, why it is being done, and how it will be accomplished. FAA staff can also share their experiences at other airports that have addressed similar issues, and this information can be quite valuable. Note that a thorough, complete, and properly-prepared study design is critical because it forms the basis for the eventual cost estimate upon which an FAA planning grant is based—and it is virtually impossible to get a supplement to a planning grant, so the initial cost estimate must be accurate.

The AC lists some of the topics that are typically included in the Study Design stage. These include:

- Goals and Objectives
- Data Availability
- Forecast Horizons
- Environmental Considerations
- Schedules
- Deliverables
- Coordination and Public Involvement Program
- Budget

If it is anticipated that the plan will result in an action that may trigger the environmental process under NEPA, then FAA Order 5050.4B, *National Environmental Policy Act (NEPA) Implementing Instructions for Airport Actions*, should be consulted as soon as possible. It stresses the importance of developing the planning data necessary for NEPA purposes:

- an inventory of existing conditions and facilities,
- an airport layout plan (ALP) showing proposed development,
- planned project linkages versus independent utility,
- aircraft operation and enplanement (boarding passengers) forecasts,
- the design aircraft and fleet mix to accommodate those forecasts,
- the airport's existing capacity to accommodate those forecasts,
- facility requirements needed to accommodate those forecasts,
- timing and phasing of the projected necessary airport development,
- runway utilization and flight tracks, and
- an airspace analysis.[10]

Goals and Objectives
For the most part the goals and objectives should be based on the strategic plan as discussed earlier in the preceding chapter. Note, however, that you are now developing the goals and objectives for the *planning study*, which are not the same as the goals and objectives for the *airport* developed in the strategic plan. Even if the airport doesn't have a strategic plan, the airport operator, the key airport staff, and the planning team should at least do some strategic thinking before beginning any planning study. The planning study, whether it is a master plan or an ALP update, should help resolve most, if not all, of the facility-related issues raised in the strategic plan. As the study design is being developed, all of the issues raised during the needs determination should be discussed with the consultant and the FAA. As noted in the

AC, the study design should state why the study is being conducted, what issues will be addressed, and at what level of detail they will be addressed.

Data Availability

The level of effort required for a planning study will depend in large part on data availability. At this point the planning team should review the sources, accuracy, and completeness of the data that are available to address the issues at hand. If good data are not readily available the consultant will have to expend a considerable amount of time and money to collect it. Forecasts are usually the first item mentioned: they must be current and must be approved by the FAA. The FAA sets a general standard for forecasts through guidance materials, the forecast approval process, and comparisons of local forecasts with its Terminal Area Forecasts (TAF), as discussed below and in Chapter 7: Forecasting. However, the TAF may not sufficiently consider local factors or very recent trends. Also, more information is usually needed than is contained in the TAF, such as an estimate of originating passengers (to address some of the terminal capacity, ground access, curbside, and public parking issues, for example). If cargo facilities or activity are important at the airport and if cargo issues are to be addressed as part of the study, data on cargo movements will be needed, including cargo volumes and aircraft operations, including how much is carried in all-cargo flights versus carried as belly cargo on passenger flights. With the growth of integrated freight carriers such as FedEx, UPS, and others, the planner may need to know how much of the cargo passing through the airport is actually flown. A substantial portion of the cargo that passes through an airport cargo facility may actually be trucked in and trucked out. Also, published sources of cargo data are of questionable accuracy, to say the very least.

Another example of additional information needed for forecasting and other purposes in the planning process is economic data. The use of economic data in forecasting is also discussed in Chapter 7: Forecasting. At some point a Benefit-Cost Analysis may be required, as discussed in the Financial Feasibility Analysis step below. Economic benefit studies should also be performed to help support the airport's budget requests. In both cases some information will be needed on just what the airport contributes to the local economy in terms of direct and indirect jobs, income, and tax revenue.

In summary, much of the information needed for airport planning purposes, especially for the development of the forecasts, is not readily available. It can take a lot of time and effort to collect, sort, and/or analyze, so sufficient time and money should be allocated in the project schedule and budget.

Forecast Horizons

Determining forecast horizons is usually pretty straightforward. The Master Plan AC refers to forecast horizons of 5-, 10-, and 20-year time frames. As noted in Chapter 1: Overview of Airport Planning, some people feel that the emphasis should be on the near term, while others feel that 20 years does not go far enough into the future. Whatever is decided for forecast horizons,

Chapter 5 – Master Planning

they should be reasonable and realistic, and all study participants—especially the FAA—should agree with them. Remember that the 5- to 10- year period will probably be of most interest to the study because this period covers most airports' capital programs. But some consideration should be given to the distant future, i.e., beyond 20 years, even though most forecasts are notoriously inaccurate. This is usually done as part of strategic planning, but it is also important to consider possible future development when planning facilities that have a life of more than 20 years, such as terminal buildings, runways, highways, and the like. All planners should keep an eye to the future to keep from shooting themselves in the foot—putting a concourse where a runway will eventually be needed, and so on. After all, that is what planning is all about.

Environmental Considerations
It is critically important to identify environmental considerations as soon as possible in the study. Airport staff should already have an idea of what and where the airport's environmentally-sensitive areas are; these include wetlands, forests, historic structures, streams, etc. They should also know whether the airport has any issues with regard to air quality, water quality, and noise. If these factors are not known, somebody needs to find out about them in a hurry to avoid crippling delays later in the planning process.

The environmental aspects of planning are discussed below, and in Chapter 8: Environmental Considerations, but planners have to anticipate the nature and extent of potential environmental impacts as both the needs determination and the study design are being developed so that sufficient time and money can be allocated to prepare all necessary environmental documentation. There are federal environmental laws and regulations that may apply to airport development, including the Clean Air Act, Clean Water Act, and Endangered Species Act. Applicable state and local environmental regulations and requirements should also be reviewed to ensure that the planning team understands what kinds of documentation, permits, approvals, and other actions are required.

Clearly, an environmental specialist is an invaluable member of the planning team. This individual can provide guidance and expertise to:

- identify which federal, state, and local environmental regulations, requirements, and procedures apply to the planning study;
- identify environmental issues and environmentally-sensitive areas that should be considered in the planning process;
- help determine the adequacy of alternatives analysis with respect to follow-on environmental documentation;
- provide guidance on developing environmental overviews and similar narratives;
- assist in reviewing the planning work scope;

- assist in developing and conducting the outreach and public involvement efforts; and
- help decide whether the project justification is sufficient for the Purpose and Need portion of follow-on environmental documents.

Schedules
It sometimes seems that schedules, like laws, are made to be broken. This is especially true in planning. Planning involves turning over a lot of rocks, and one never knows when a Gila monster might be hiding under one of them. So be prepared. Having said that, the project schedule should really be managed the same as the cost: no slippage or overruns. The sponsor's project manager and the consultant's project manager should adopt a hard-nosed attitude about schedules—a slip here and a slip there can add up to trouble eventually.

To help ensure that the schedule is reasonable, the sponsor and the consultant should review the scope of work for the study and agree on a schedule and milestones. Milestones can be thought of as reporting points through the study. For example, the schedule may state that the inventory should be complete and an inventory report submitted by the end of the third month, and the forecasts should be ready for submission to the FAA by the end of the sixth month from the Notice-to-Proceed. The length of time required to do the study will vary with the complexity of the study. The schedule should reflect the amount of time it will take to accomplish each task, and should also allow for delays in collecting the data that was thought to be available, but really wasn't. It happens all the time, so be prepared for it. The schedule should also allow for review times for all study documents. This is especially true for any reports that will require FAA review. FAA district and regional offices have a lot of work to do and often don't have sufficient staffs to review all the reports and documents that are produced by all the airports for which they are responsible. Moreover, regulatory requirements have increased over the years without a corresponding increase in FAA staff. Although there is a lot of discussion about streamlining the environmental process, streamlining only applies to certain projects at specified airports. The best way to ensure timely reviews on the part of the FAA is to make sure that all study documentation is complete and accurate. It is also especially important in the development of the study schedule to note the milestones where FAA review and concurrence should be obtained. At these critical milestones work should not proceed until the FAA concurs with the work that has been done so far. If the work proceeds and the FAA is not satisfied with the earlier work, it will likely be necessary to go back and redo some things and that will take extra time and money. Once this schedule has been prepared and the study is underway, the sponsor should hold regular meetings with the consultant to make sure that the work is proceeding on schedule, as discussed in Chapter 10: Mentoring, Managing, and Team Building.

Chapter 5 – Master Planning

Deliverables
During the study design stage the sponsor, the consultant, and the FAA should agree on all of the study deliverables and the dates they are to be submitted. Deliverables include draft and final versions of study reports and drawings, as well as electronic files, models, or other items set forth in the scope of work. This will help the consultant prepare an accurate cost proposal and schedule, and will ensure that all parties know what they are going to get and what it will look like when they get it. As discussed in Chapter 10, if the sponsor is not getting the deliverables as promised, on time and of good quality, the sponsor and the consultant should get together and resolve the situation before things get worse.

It can't be emphasized enough that all parties—the sponsor, the consultant, and the FAA—should understand and agree to all study deliverables. Reaching this common understanding early on in the study will save a lot of time and anguish later on.

Coordination and Public Involvement Program
The coordination and public involvement program should be developed as soon as the overall scope of the study and extent of the issues have been identified and agreed upon. As with other aspects of the planning process, the nature of the program will vary with the complexity of the study and with the potential environmental impacts of the facility improvements recommended at the conclusion of the study. It is particularly important to remember that there are different "publics" and it should be determined early on how each of them will be involved in the study. The publics include airport tenants, airlines, environmental review agencies, various FAA offices (especially the ADO), elected officials, major airport users, businesses, and local residents. During the study design, a determination should be made as to how, to what extent, and at what point each of these publics will be involved, along with their roles and responsibilities. Note that these groups should be informed of their roles at the outset of the coordination process. All too often, especially at environmentally-sensitive airports, these groups tend to assume—and act like—they have an "approval" role rather than an advisory role.

The FAA has prepared a Community Involvement Manual that discusses the subject in general and provides specific guidance on various techniques. The manual recommends community involvement "…whenever public acceptance and understanding of an action or decision is necessary."[11] To me, that doesn't say a whole lot, but the manual goes on to state that community involvement is specifically required in the following cases:

- actions or projects involving the preparation of an environmental impact statement (EIS) or an environmental assessment (EA);
- noise compatibility studies conducted under FAR Part 150;
- planning studies including airport system plans and airport master plans; and

- facilities establishment, particularly if proposed navigational aids or other improvements could be interpreted as permitting or encouraging increased traffic or operations by larger or more noisy airplanes.[12]

Although the Master Plan AC combines coordination and public involvement, they are really two different things, as discussed in Chapter 9: Coordination and Communication. The coordination aspect typically includes working with other airport departments such as operations and maintenance as noted in Chapter 3: Airport Management, Operations, and Finance; airport stakeholders such as tenants and user groups; and with other government agencies at the federal, state, and local levels. Coordination with the other airport departments is especially important because it gives them a sense of participation and contribution, thus helping to make it "our plan" rather than "their plan" as dictated by the planning department. It is important to remember that *coordination* requires *communication*, and that communication is a two-way street. Airport sponsors must also incorporate local planning concerns and programs to help ensure consistency between airport and community planning and development efforts. Coordination allows the airport sponsor to state the airport's interests in land use planning and development as well as ground access, and it should also make the airport sponsor aware of how other agencies view these considerations, and also how they view the airport. This coordination effort is also a good time for the airport sponsor to emphasize to local officials the importance of zoning for airport-compatible land use, including height limitations, and other factors such as wildlife attractants, light sources, electronic emissions, etc.

Advance coordination with the various environmental review agencies gives the airport operator an opportunity to present the big picture regarding airport development. This provides a context for follow-on, individual facility-related actions that may come up for environmental review at some point in the future. One of the biggest concerns that has been expressed by the review agencies is that they often only get to review piecemeal actions and do not have a good grasp of what the airport might ultimately look like. Thus they have a tendency to be a little more critical (or picky) when reviewing environmental documents. Coordination with environmental agencies also gives the airport operator an opportunity to find out what the major environmental concerns or "hot buttons" are with respect to airport development. With this knowledge airport development can be planned with a view to avoiding or minimizing potential areas of conflict. In those areas where conflict cannot be avoided, the airport operator will have time to prepare and document the study findings accordingly.

Public involvement typically involves interacting with the general citizenry, especially those who are or may be affected by the operation and development of the airport. In the study design stage a determination should be made of the overall scope of the public involvement program, including which "publics" will be coordinated with and who will do the coordinating. Usually airport staff is involved in public outreach and coordination programs, but if consultant assistance is needed, sufficient time and money should be budgeted to cover all such aspects. Coordination and public involvement are discussed below in the Public Involvement step, and in more detail in Chapter 9: Coordination and Communication.

Budget

The preparation of the budget is the last step in the Study Design stage. This is a very critical step because, as noted above, once an FAA grant is issued, it is very difficult to get a supplemental grant. It is important to make sure that the schedule allows enough time for the consultant to do the work required, and that sufficient funds have been allocated for the successful completion of each study task. The consultant should prepare a budget and sit down with the sponsor and review each item so that both parties know what work is to be done, what the deliverables are, and how much each will cost. At this point the expected cost is compared with the sponsor's budget to make sure that sufficient funds are available. If not, the sponsor may be able to set aside additional funds, or the sponsor and the consultant should negotiate reductions in the cost or extent of the work to be done so that costs equal the study budget. If the scope of work or the nature of the deliverables has to be reduced to balance the budget, the FAA should be informed to ensure that the work and deliverables will still meet FAA requirements.

Stage D: Negotiating Consultant Contracts

When the study design is complete and agreed to by all parties, the sponsor must negotiate a contract with the consultant for the performance of the work identified in the scope. The Master Plan AC notes that a fixed-price (or lump sum) contract is usually preferred when the level of effort for the study can be predicted with comfortable accuracy. The AC goes on to point out that this type of contract is easiest to administer and can provide incentives for cost control and contract performance. Some state and local jurisdictions however, do not allow lump sum contracts; therefore a cost plus fixed fee or time and materials contract may be the appropriate mechanism. Cost plus contracts are also appropriate for studies where the level of effort is uncertain; remember that good planning often discovers new issues as the study progresses. In some cases the sponsor may want to add an on-call or task order contract to the package in order to allow the consultant to explore and resolve unforeseen issues during the course of the study. Study cost overruns and associated contractual agreements can be a problem if the sponsor receives an FAA grant for the study, because the FAA typically does not provide supplements to planning grants; rather, the FAA issues a new grant. To avoid complications the study design must be based on a complete assessment of the work to be done and must be reviewed with the ADO beforehand. Detailed guidance on consultant contracts is contained in AC 150/5100-14.[13]

Stage E: Application for Federal Funding

Most airport planning studies are accomplished with the assistance of an FAA planning grant. The Master Plan AC points out that for large and complex studies such as a master plan for a large airport, the sponsor may want to divide the planning study into phases and apply for a separate grant for each phase. The example used in the AC is to combine the early tasks such as the definition of issues, inventory, forecasts, and determination of facility requirements into one package for a federal grant application. The example goes on to say that the grant application for the second phase can be prepared when initial investigations and analyses have given the study team a better understanding of the scope and complexity of the issues to be addressed in the remainder of the study. Considering again that good planning is likely to uncover new issues, this seems a safe way to proceed. The important thing to remember is to involve the FAA in the study process as soon as possible to identify the best strategy for obtaining a grant and for determining the eligibility of the various study components for federal funds. Detailed guidance on the FAA grant application process, including project eligibility requirements and allowable costs, is contained in the *Airport Improvement Program Handbook*, FAA Order 5100.38C.[14] As noted in Chapter 3: Airport Management, Operations, and Finance, the FAA tends to award grants to projects that are ready to go, so make sure that all relevant information has been assembled and reviewed with the ADO. Delays to straighten out various details such as the study design, goals and objectives, schedules, etc., may result in an airport losing a grant, or at least having to wait for the next grant cycle.

Step 2: Public Involvement

Once the consultant team is under contract and has been issued a Notice-to-Proceed, a public involvement program should be established that identifies and documents the key issues of various individuals and agencies that may be affected by airport changes or improvements, including the general public. As noted above, a number of "publics" will be involved in the course of a study, and the way the planners work with them will vary based on their concerns and on the nature and complexity of the planning study.

Again, in a broad sense the publics may include airport tenants, airlines, environmental review agencies, various FAA offices, elected officials, major airport users, businesses, and local residents. But it is more useful (and more accurate for our purposes) to view the public as groups that do not have a direct stake in the airport. The study design stage will give an idea of which of these groups are likely to have an interest in the study. The study design stage should also have identified the approach to be used for public involvement, as well as the parties responsible for outreach and coordination. The AC provides some very good general guidance for public involvement techniques and tools, and it need not be repeated here. However, there are some particular factors that should be considered in developing a public involvement program.

First of all, it is helpful in the long run if the airport has an ongoing public outreach program in place. Some excellent guidance for public outreach is contained in a manual entitled *Partnering for Better Communities*, prepared by CH Planning for the Pennsylvania Department of Transportation. The manual "...is *not* intended to provide guidance for outreach *in conjunction with* airport planning, project development, or other activities in which public involvement is required...."[15] Rather, it provides guidance to airport operators "...in planning proactive public outreach programs to promote goodwill."[16] The Pennsylvania Bureau of Aviation "...has found that proactive outreach and a foundation of goodwill can substantially facilitate airport planning and project development."[17] Additional guidance on the various aspects of public involvement is contained in the FAA's Community Involvement Manual noted above. The subject of community outreach and communication is discussed further in this book in Chapter 9: Coordination and Communication.

For now, suffice it to say that if the airport sponsor has not been involved with the public, whether it is the local chamber of commerce, community associations, or elected officials, some problems may be encountered if the planning study is the first public contact. A level of trust is needed to ensure effective interaction with the public and this doesn't happen overnight; trust takes time to build. People will primarily want to know what is going to be built or changed and how these changes will affect them, particularly their quality of life and their property values. People will also want to know about a lot of things that have to do with the airport, but are not necessarily related to the study or even to any facility improvements that might result from the study. People will want to know all kinds of things, ranging from how to get cheap air fares, and who is responsible for lost luggage, to when the next air show will be held, and what the chances are of getting nonstop air service to such-and-such a city. The planning team may have to conduct an "Airports 101" program to educate people on what the airport management is and is not responsible for. For example, most people think the airport is responsible for air traffic control and sometimes they take a lot of convincing that this is really an FAA responsibility and that the FAA does not report to airport management. If the airport has an ongoing public outreach program this will not be much of a problem, but if such a program does not exist, a lot of time will have to be spent on some general education on airport basics before the study issues begin to be discussed. This will take time and money, and is often not thought of during the study design stage.

There seem to be two schools of thought on public involvement: one says that the public should be kept informed of any activities that may affect them or their quality of life; the other says that the public should only be involved if it is required by law. To me the latter approach is a recipe for disaster. Looking at airport planning from the perspective of the first point of view, people should know what is happening, why it is happening, and what, if any, impact it will have on them. It seems to me that keeping people, especially people who live near the airport, informed helps to promote the image of the airport as a good neighbor. Keeping people informed also gives them some idea of how the airport operates and why things happen the way they do. In this sense public involvement is like what some of the old-time politicians used to say about voting: do it early and do it often. On the other hand, there is also the thought that if people are going to be opposed to an airport or airport expansion project, they are going to be opposed no matter what they are told. This even applies to projects that may actually benefit citizens who live around the airport. For example, when the Maryland Aviation Administration proposed to construct a hiking/bicycling trail around BWI Airport, the neighbors were overwhelmingly supportive, but there actually were some residents who opposed even this project.

Regardless of which point of view is most appealing, there is something to be said for a proactive public involvement program. It lets people know what is going on and if they think it is going to affect them negatively they can try to stop the project. This is not necessarily a bad thing; it will let the planners know who is going to oppose the plan and on what grounds. This allows time to prepare and to perhaps reshape or refine plans. It also allows planners to focus specifically on issues that are of public concern and not spend a lot of time on those things that people don't seem to be too concerned about.

For example, an airport improvement program may include a terminal expansion, the construction of a new public parking lot, and the relocation of an existing airport access road, but not involve building a new runway or extending an existing runway. In this case people will probably not be too concerned about aircraft noise, but will instead be focused on increased highway traffic congestion and highway noise, and possibly air quality issues as well. Thus efforts can be focused on addressing their highway concerns rather than spending a lot of time and money analyzing aircraft noise impacts. Similarly, a group of citizens may be concerned about preserving forests and wetlands. If the improvement program is not expected to involve taking wetlands or cutting down a lot of trees, letting people know this early in the study will help defuse a potential source of opposition. Just make sure that people aren't told early on in the study that there will be no wetland impacts, only to come out with an environmental document some months later that shows six acres of wetlands being taken.

Since some form of public involvement is often required, and usually recommended, it might as well be done right. In this case "right" means being honest with the public, letting them know what is being done, and how it will affect them. Their comments and questions should be listened to and answered in a timely and truthful manner. Also, public involvement should not be a one-time thing. To function most effectively it should be part of an ongoing public outreach program.

Step 3: Environmental Considerations

At the outset I must state that I have always believed that it is possible to construct, operate, maintain, and expand an airport (or any other major facility) without trashing the environment. Specifically with respect to airport planning, the Master Plan AC states that planners should develop a "...clear understanding of the environmental requirements needed to move forward with each project in the recommended development program."[18] Based on my experience the most important thing to remember is that environmental considerations should take place as part of the planning process. For a long time planners prepared their plans and once the plan was complete they looked at the environmental impacts and prepared (or tried to prepare) the appropriate environmental documents. Considering that it often took years, sometimes decades, to get through the environmental approvals process, it seems that approach was a mistake.

Considering environmental issues as an integral part of the planning process provides the opportunity to avoid environmentally-sensitive areas, and to minimize or mitigate the impacts if such areas are involved. This seems to be implicit when the Master Plan AC states that, "Normally the environmental considerations should not be in a stand-alone chapter, but should be incorporated into the appropriate chapters such as existing conditions and alternatives development and evaluation."[19] The planning document should cover all aspects of planning to the level of detail required for the subsequent environmental document. However it should be kept in mind that the final report on the planning study is a planning document and *not* a NEPA document. According to the FAA, "The evaluation of potential impacts should only be done to the level necessary to evaluate and compare how each alternative would involve sensitive environmental resources."[20]

Remember: planning should be done in the planning phase, not later during the environmental phase. The project justification presented in the planning report should be sufficient to meet the requirements for the Purpose and Need portion of the environmental document; it should not be necessary to go back and do additional planning work to prepare a complete environmental document. This also applies to the selection and analysis of alternatives during the planning study. The planning report should document clearly why certain alternatives were dropped from further consideration in the planning process. If certain alternatives do not meet the Purpose and Need for the project, the planning report should note this and state why each of the rejected alternatives do not meet the desired planning goal. The required alternatives information should just be able to be lifted from the planning document and inserted into the environmental document—no further analysis should be needed. If additional work is needed the EIS process does provide opportunities to modify alternatives; however, this may delay the environmental process and cost more money. Thus, trying to take shortcuts usually doesn't make sense.

Appendix D of the Master Plan AC presents some invaluable guidance in considering environmental factors in airport planning and should be consulted prior to launching any airport planning activity. The Appendix recommends that an "...overview of environmentally-sensitive features of an airport...should be prepared as part of an airport master plan...[to] help an airport sponsor judge if the airport's environmental features affect day-to-day decisions as well as longer-term development strategies."[21] Appendix D also notes that such overviews should include readily available information such as

- items known from prior environmental and planning documents, and from the expertise of environmental professionals, community planners, and resource agencies;
- items that can be easily seen during a walking survey of the airport or off-airport area; and
- information from various types of available environmental resource maps of the airport area.[22]

It is also a good idea to note those items or issues that have public or political sensitivity. I have found such overviews to be a valuable resource in routine planning activities as well as in major planning studies. If properly prepared they present a useful summary of the airport's environmental conditions and resources.

With regard to additional environmental factors the Master Plan AC also notes that any federal, state, or local permits needed for each proposed project should be identified as part of the master plan study, including the

- Clean Water Act, Section 404 Dredge and Fill permit;
- air quality permit for on-site batch plants or other construction-related activities;
- local government construction permits;
- growth management permits;
- United States Fish and Wildlife Service, National Marine Fisheries Service opinions, or State Wildlife and Game Commission permits, if protected and endangered species could be impacted; and
- Clean Water Act, National Pollution Discharge Elimination System permits.[23]

During the master planning process it is often a good idea to identify any urgently-needed, near-term projects that will likely be recommended in the plan, and discuss with the FAA the possibility of beginning the environmental process for those projects before the master plan is completed. This will save time in constructing needed airport improvements, particularly safety-related improvements such as runway safety areas. In this case it will have to be verified that there are no cumulative impacts, and that the construction of these near-term projects will not predetermine the outcome for longer-term projects.

Remember that the NEPA process doesn't start during the planning study, but the planning study should anticipate the issues that the NEPA process will address and should provide the necessary background information and documentation accordingly. As Appendix D of the Master Plan AC states,

"The airport sponsor and FAA should always complete (and document) the following prior to commencing preparation of an EIS or EA:

- local aviation forecasts that are current and approved by the FAA;
- justification of the scope and timing of the project's planned facilities based on airport planning, operational requirements, and design standards;
- identification and consideration of all reasonable planning alternatives (within the sponsor's or FAA's jurisdiction), eliminating (and documenting) those not meeting the stated aeronautical need. If an alternative does potentially meet the aeronautical need, but is not considered reasonable, provide sufficient explanation as to why not; and
- tentative identification of studies or other information likely required for later federal action, as well as appropriate state and local agencies, Indian tribes, private persons, and organizations likely to have an interest in the project."[24]

All-in-all, if the guidance contained in the Master Plan AC is followed, and if the planning work is accomplished and documented properly, the subsequent NEPA process should not be as onerous and time-consuming as it seems to be in many cases today.

Step 4: Existing Conditions

The Existing Conditions step is an inventory of relevant data for use in subsequent plan elements. Typically, planners look at this as an inventory of existing airport facilities, chiefly with respect to number, type, and location. Wherever possible most inventory information should be presented in tabular or graphic representations versus long narratives. The following items or categories should be included in the collection of data describing existing conditions:

- history of the airport,
- physical facilities,
- environmental setting,
- socioeconomic and demographic data for the airport service area,
- historical aviation activity, and
- airport business affairs.

The inventory of physical facilities should include information on the number, size, type, and condition of the following:

- airfield/airspace;
- pavement;
- commercial passenger terminal facilities;
- general aviation facilities;

- cargo facilities;
- support facilities;
- access, circulation, and parking;
- utilities; and
- other (i.e., nonaeronautical uses).

Before beginning any data collection effort, the sponsor and consultant should review the study work scope to determine exactly what information will be required. There is no sense wasting time and money collecting information because someone thinks it might come in handy at some point in the future. Time and money can also be saved by using existing data to the extent possible, particularly data from published sources. Some caution is necessary here though, because the completeness and quality of the data available is not exactly the way it is described in some agencies' data summaries. Before deciding to use data from another source they should be realistically evaluated to be sure they will meet the study's needs. It should also be determined whether the political jurisdiction in which the airport is located has certain data requirements. For example, many states and localities require the use of population, income, or other socioeconomic data prepared by a designated state or local office, such as a state planning agency or regional planning commission.

Obviously an inventory of all the facilities in all these categories will not always be necessary; the inventory effort should be tailored to the issues that will be addressed and the work that will be done in the planning study. If the study is primarily focused on airside issues and facilities such as runways and taxiways, there is no need to do an exhaustive inventory of terminal or parking facilities, or ground access systems. The Master Plan AC presents a fairly complete description of the kinds of information that should be considered and collected in each of the above categories, and there is no need to repeat it here.

One item on the list can be particularly important: utilities. One frequent shortcoming in planning is that planners do not give enough attention to utility infrastructure, including electricity, water, gas, and sewage, as well as storm water collection and drainage, deicing materials runoff and treatment, and industrial waste disposal. These are especially important in planning because they either take up space, or add costs, or both. For example, the plan may include a new terminal expansion estimated to cost $25 million. At the conclusion of the planning study this cost will probably be put into the Capital Improvement Program, and sufficient funds will hopefully be budgeted to allow the eventual construction. However, in the design phase of a project, the engineers may find that the existing water supply is not adequate to accommodate the expected increase in water demand, with the addition of more drinking fountains, restrooms, and the water needs of any new concessionaires. Also, if the terminal addition is to include a fire suppression system, the existing water pressure may not support a sprinkler system. The electrical engineer may also find that the current power supply is not adequate to meet the increased heating and cooling needs, nor the needs associated with more lights, and airline ticketing and baggage support facilities and equipment. At that point it may be found that the actual cost of the new terminal addition is not the $25 million budgeted, but $32 million. By this time most people will forget that the initial planning cost was wrong, and instead are likely to blame the engineers or architects for not keeping the project within budget. Not only is it poor planning, it is just not fair to the engineers.

The AC has one drawback that is important to note and consider for the inventory phase of the planning study. The AC lists the types of facilities that should be inventoried, including the number and type of runways and taxiways; the number and type of aircraft hangars; and the number, size, and configuration of terminal facilities such as gates, passenger holdrooms, concessions, and so on. But it is also important to note the condition of these facilities, and whether they are capable of being expanded at their existing location.

For example, consider an airport that has five large corporate or community hangars and 120 general aviation T-hangars. During the inventory it should be noted whether these hangars are in good condition and can be expected to last another 10 or 20 years with minimal maintenance, or whether some of them have deteriorated to the point where they will have to be replaced within the next five years. One reason this is important is cost. If these hangars will have to be replaced, the replacement cost will have to be added to the capital program, along with the cost of additional hangars to meet an expected increase in demand. Another reason facility condition is important is that if most of the existing hangars are in poor condition and will have to be replaced, some thought may be given to rebuilding the hangar complex in a different, more efficient or more functional location. This is why it is also important to note whether the existing facilities can be expanded.

A cargo building example: say the buildings in the airport's existing air cargo complex range from fair to good, and none of them are likely to have to be replaced within the next 10 years at least. However, suppose the forecasts show that one or two new cargo buildings will be required in the future—one in the next five years, and one in the following five years. But unfortunately the existing cargo complex cannot be expanded to accommodate even one new building, let alone two. What happens now? The answer to that question of course depends on the particular circumstances at the airport under study, but the question emphasizes the need to look at more than just the number and type of buildings when doing an inventory of existing conditions. The history of the runway, taxiway, and apron/ramp pavements should also be included in the inventory; most of this information can be obtained by reviewing the FAA grant history.

The "Other" category under "physical facilities" also deserves special mention. The AC describes this as an inventory of nonaeronautical uses such as recreation areas, industrial parks, business parks, and the like. It is important not only to look at the current land uses, but also at local zoning ordinances and building codes, as well as local plans for use and development of the lands surrounding the airport. It should also be determined whether the surrounding land uses are compatible with both the current operation of the airport and the expected development of the airport in the future. This information can be obtained from local planning agencies, and these agencies should be kept involved through the course of the airport planning study. Another thing to remember is that land uses surrounding the airport are, in turn, surrounded by other land uses. It is important in airport land use planning to ensure that uses for lands around the airport should be compatible not only with the airport, but also with the other lands that adjoin them.

For example, an area adjacent to an airport may be impacted by aircraft noise, thus the airport planners can work with local planners to encourage noise-compatible development. Noise-compatible development could include establishing an industrial park that could also involve a synergy between the airport and an adjacent land use. However, if the land beyond the industrial area is used for residential purposes, an industrial park might not be such a good idea. Ideally land use around the airport should encourage a synergistic relationship with the airport, and with the other land uses beyond the immediate airport environs. This may be difficult, particularly in areas that are already intensely developed, but it is something that should be considered nonetheless.

The Existing Conditions step should also include an inventory of all environmental features, or what the AC calls the "environmental setting" of the airport and its surrounding lands. These include such features as wetlands, forests, historic structures and/or neighborhoods, as well as noise-sensitive features such as schools, hospitals, and churches, among others. The current edition of FAA Order 1050.1 contains a complete list of environmental categories that should be examined as part of an airport planning study (a similar list is shown in Chapter 8: Environmental Considerations). Not all of these items need to be included in the study; instead, planners should note whether there might be any impacts to any of those items. The study can then focus on those items which might be affected by current airport operations or future airport development.

The existing conditions survey should also include an inventory of airport users and their characteristics, as well as their wants and needs. Increasingly in airport planning we are becoming more responsive to customer satisfaction both as a driving element in the planning process and in the development of airport facilities. This is particularly true in the planning of terminals, public parking lots, and other customer service-oriented facilities. For example, passengers want convenient parking, which minimizes walking distances. Inside the terminal, passengers also want to minimize walking distances, and they also want convenient and easily-located restrooms and concessions such as food and beverage, and retail. The planner should also pay careful attention to the composition of the airport's passenger traffic—business versus discretionary travelers, connecting versus O&D—since each component has its own set of needs regarding airport terminal and access facilities. In the cargo sector it is important to note the volume of truck/plane movements versus truck/truck movements. Large volumes of trucked cargo can place significant and unique demands on ground access systems, and are also likely to require more truck parking and maneuvering areas, along with truck support facilities. As part of the user inventory, the local airport service area in terms of its geographical extent and socioeconomic characteristics should be defined and described. This is the area that generates the bulk of the airport's passenger traffic and based aircraft. Service area information, as well as data describing historical aviation activity at the airport, will be useful in the preparation of the aviation demand forecasts.

The final component of the existing conditions inventory is a fairly detailed summary of the airport's business affairs, and it should cover at least the last five years, and preferably longer. The information included in this component should describe the financial income and outgo for the airport, including all revenues, the revenue sources, and a list of both capital and operating expenses. It should also include all federal, state, and local grants received, the amount of each grant, and the project for which the grant was received. This information will be required as part of the Facilities Implementation Plan and the Financial Feasibility Analysis at the conclusion of the planning study. It will also be useful in the development of facility requirements.

Step 5: Aviation Forecasts

Forecasts of future aviation demand can be critical to the airport planning process and often provide the basis for making decisions about airport development. These projections are used to determine the need for new or expanded facilities. Forecasts of aviation demand for planning studies are typically prepared for near-, medium-, and long-term time frames (5, 10, and more than 10 years). The Master Plan AC lists those items for which forecasts must be prepared, as shown in Table 5.1. These items, including definitions and data sources, are discussed in detail in Chapter 7: Forecasting. The important point to be made here is that the FAA must approve the forecasts before they will provide any funding for follow-on facility improvements. General guidance for the preparation of aviation demand forecasts for airport planning studies is presented in Chapter 7 of the Master Plan AC; more detailed guidance is provided in the FAA report, *Forecasting Aviation Activity by Airport*.[25] Information on the FAA's forecast approval process and criteria are contained in an FAA memorandum, *Revision to Guidance on Review and Approval of Aviation Forecasts*.[26] An excellent summary of aviation demand forecasts, including uses of forecasts, methodologies, and data sources, can be found in a report entitled *Airport Aviation Activity Forecasting*, prepared for the Airport Cooperative Research Program (ACRP) of the Transportation Research Board.[27] Aviation demand forecasting is also discussed in detail in this book in Chapter 7: Forecasting.

Table 5-1: Aviation Demand Elements to be Forecast in Master Plan Studies[28]

Required	Included Where Appropriate
Operations (Annual)	
Itinerant	Domestic versus International
Air Carrier	Annual Instrument Approaches
Air Taxi and Commuter (Regional)	IFR versus VFR Operations
General Aviation	Air Cargo Aircraft Operations
Military	Touch-and-Go Operations (Training)
Local	Helicopter Operations
General Aviation	Average Load Factor
Military	Fuel Use
Passengers (Annual)	
Enplanements	Passenger and Cargo Data
Air Carrier	Domestic versus International
Commuter	General Aviation Passengers
Enplanements	Helicopter
Originating	Air Taxi
Connecting	Other
	Number of Student Pilots
	Number of Hours Flown
	Passenger and Cargo Data
Aircraft	
Based Aircraft	Average Seats per Aircraft
Aircraft Mix	
Critical Aircraft	

The FAA's Office of Policy and Plans prepares the TAF, as noted above, for the aviation demand elements shown in Table 5-2. The TAF forecasts are available for nearly all of the airports included in the NPIAS; the 2007-2025 TAF includes forecasts for 3,319 individual airports which are available on the FAA's TAF Web site.[29] Forecasts for airport planning studies must be sent to the ADO (or to the regional office if the region does not have an ADO) for review and approval. The ADO compares the forecasts prepared for individual planning studies with the TAF.

Table 5-2: TAF Forecast Elements

Forecast Elements
Enplanements:
Air Carrier
Commuter
Domestic
International
U.S. Flag
Foreign Flag
Aircraft Operations:
Itinerant
Air Carrier
Air Taxi and Commuter
General Aviation
Military
Local
General Aviation
Military
Based Aircraft
Operations per Based Aircraft Ratio

If the study forecasts do not meet the specific criteria stated in the Revision to Guidance memorandum, the ADO is required to send the forecasts to FAA Headquarters for review.[30] The primary criterion on this list is that the planning forecasts must be within 10 percent of the TAF five years into the future, and within 15 percent 10 years into the future.[31] Specifically, the Revision to Guidance memorandum states the following:

> Locally-developed forecasts for operations, based aircraft, and enplanements are considered consistent with FAA's Terminal Area Forecasts (TAF) if they meet the following criteria:
>
> *Large, Medium, and Small Hub Airports:*
> 1. Forecast differs by less than 10 percent in the 5-year forecast period and 15 percent in the 10-year period, or
> 2. Forecast activity levels do not affect the timing or scale of an airport project.
>
> *Other Commercial Service Airports:*
> 1. Forecast differs by less than 10 percent in the 5-year forecast period and 15 percent in the 10-year period, or

2. Forecast activity levels do not affect the timing or scale of an airport project, or

3. Forecast activity levels do not affect the role of the airport as defined in FAA Order 5090.3C, *Field Formulation of the National Plan of Integrated Airport Systems (NPIAS)*.

General Aviation and Reliever Airports:
Where the 5- or 10-year forecast exceeds 100,000 total annual operations or 100 based aircraft:

1. Forecast differs by less than 10 percent in the 5-year forecast period and 15 percent in the 10-year period, or

2. Forecast activity levels do not affect the timing or scale of an airport project, or

3. Forecast activity levels do not affect the role of the airport as defined in FAA Order 5090.3C, *Field Formulation of the National Plan of Integrated Airport Systems (NPIAS)*.

Where the 5- or 10-year forecast does not exceed 100,000 total annual operations or 100 based aircraft, then it does not need headquarters review, and should be provided for use in the annual update of the TAF. APO-110 may require additional information if the forecast exceeds normal expectations without adequate justification.[32]

Additionally the FAA states that forecasts should

- be realistic,
- be based on the latest available data,
- reflect the current conditions at the airport,
- be supported by information in the study, and
- provide an adequate justification for the airport planning and development.[33]

Over the years most of the forecasts I have prepared and have been aware of have been fairly close to the TAF. Any differences between the local airport forecast and the TAF were discussed with the FAA Office of Policy and Plans, seemingly to everyone's mutual satisfaction. More recently I have become aware of some disagreements between individual airports and the FAA's current forecast approval gurus in the Office of Planning and Programming. As far as I am aware the issues were worked out, but the whole process took a lot of time, paper shuffling, and money (forecast experts don't come cheap). In recent years I have been—and many other planners I have spoken with and worked with have been—inclined to just use the TAF as the base and add other essential forecast elements (such as originating passengers) not included in the TAF. This can certainly save a lot of time and money. However, this approach should be taken only after a careful review of the TAF for the airport under study. If it appears that some of the factors that are expected to influence aviation demand through the forecast period have not been considered in the TAF, it seems likely that new forecasts should be prepared.

For example, the TAF forecasts sometimes do not reflect peak period activity variations such as those taking place at small general aviation airports serving seasonal resorts. Also, for many small general aviation airports, the TAF shows no growth at all; it just extends the base year volume as a constant through the forecast period. In this regard it should be remembered that the TAF is prepared at FAA Headquarters and it is not clear just how much these forecasts incorporate information on local conditions that may affect aviation demand.

I once reviewed a draft TAF for BWI Airport and compared them with the forecasts my staff and I prepared. As strange as it may seem, the TAF and our own forecasts of total passengers and total aircraft operations were virtually identical—within one percent through the forecast period! However, the TAF assigned a much larger proportion of expected air passenger demand to commuter air carriers than was expected in our own forecasts. This was apparently based on BWI's history as a connecting hub for Piedmont Airlines and later, US Airways. What the TAF did not appear to consider was the fact that US Airways was abandoning its BWI hub, and that future growth would probably be coming from carriers that did not hub at BWI, and particularly from carriers that did not have commuter affiliates. We commented to the FAA on this point and never got a response; however, we noticed that the TAF prepared the following year had a much lower share of commuter airline activity.

The TAF does not include all of the aviation demand parameters typically needed in airport planning studies, such as the connecting passenger versus O&D passenger split, and cargo volumes, to name just two. Therefore some forecasts will have to be prepared as part of the planning study. Thus there is a choice of either accepting the TAF and using that information to develop the additional forecasts that will be needed, or of doing a complete set of aviation demand forecasts as part of the planning study. In this regard, and as discussed more completely in Chapter 7: Forecasting, the forecasts may not really be all that important because facilities are not built according to forecast demand; rather, they are built on the basis of need.

Step 6: Facility Requirements

The obvious purpose of an airport planning study is to determine what new facilities will be required in order to accommodate expected increases in aviation activity. Identifying those facility requirements involves assessing the ability of the existing airport—airside, landside, and terminal—to support the expected or forecast demand. In effect a capacity analysis is done for each airport component. Note also that some facility improvements are not based on capacity; they are required to meet an FAA airport standard, such as runway safety areas and runway/taxiway separations.

As part of facility requirements analysis, the master plan should define each problem and state clearly why the airport needs to solve it. This information is useful in helping planners to stay focused on the issues at hand, and it also feeds into the Purpose and Need section of the environmental document where the problem is stated, addressed, and the appropriate federal action is identified. Remember that the Facility Requirements step of a master plan is supposed to identify facilities that need to be improved and the extent to which they need to be improved. It should not include the development of alternatives—how the facilities could be improved. Further, the description or identification of the facility requirement should not be stated in such a way that locks the airport into a specific improvement.

The Master Plan AC lists a number of areas that should be considered in the facility requirements analysis, including:

- Airfield and Airspace (runways, taxiways, navigation and landing aids, airspace requirements)
- Passenger Terminal (gates, apron, terminal facilities, curbfront)
- General Aviation (aircraft hangars and tie-down areas, transient aircraft parking areas, terminal facilities)
- Air Cargo (integrated cargo, belly cargo, and all-cargo carriers; freight forwarders)
- Support Facilities (aircraft rescue and firefighting, airport maintenance, aircraft maintenance, fuel storage facilities, aircraft deicing)
- Ground Access, Circulation, and Parking Requirements (regional transportation network; on-airport circulation roadways; vehicle staging areas, including taxis, courtesy vans, charter buses, and rental cars; public parking; employee parking)
- Utilities (water, sanitary sewer, drainage and deicing, industrial waste, communications, power supply)
- Other (on-airport land uses)[34]

A capacity assessment is usually only required for those airport components that are under study. If the needs evaluation has determined that the runway/taxiway system is performing adequately, and the airport is not regularly experiencing aircraft operational delays, and undue increases in operational demand are not foreseen, it is probably not appropriate to spend the time and money to do an airside capacity analysis.

The AC suggests that the facility requirements analysis be documented in a separate chapter and that the chapter (and the study's executive summary report) include a summary of the individual facility requirements. This is so that the reader can easily see which facilities need to be improved without reading the entire chapter, in all its excruciating detail. It also suggests that the readability of the chapter can be improved by putting some of the technical detail in an appendix to the report, and states that the planner "... should avoid making the appendices a depository for unnecessary information, which can result in massive reports that may confuse and discourage the reader."[35] Sage advice indeed. Reading a planning report should not be like licking sandpaper.

The AC also notes that "Many of the significant improvements needed at an airport are actually driven by the demand level, not a time frame or a specific year."[36] In other words the airport improvement program should be tied to traffic volumes rather than years. Therefore, the planning study should identify the demand levels that will trigger the need for a new facility or the expansion of an existing facility. However, as noted several times elsewhere in this book (particularly in Chapter 7: Forecasting), most airport facilities are not constructed or improved because a forecast called for it; the improvements are made when the airport user (or users) say they need them—and say they would agree to the increases in rates and charges needed to pay for the improvement.

For example, a fixed base operator may need a new hangar and an associated aircraft parking ramp, along with increased space for customer automobile parking. Or an airline may say they need six new gates. Or the rental car companies say they need a new consolidated remote car rental facility. Now obviously these facilities aren't going to be built just because somebody says they want them; some evidence of need must be demonstrated as well. And of course a willingness and commitment to sign a lease must also be forthcoming. The point is that forecasts were likely useful in giving airport operators an idea of the impact that demand increases might have on airport facilities, and an idea of when such things might take place, but quite often these types of projects come up on rather short notice and have probably not been taken into consideration or quantified as part of the forecast process. Things do tend to happen quickly and unexpectedly at airports, regardless of what the FAA says about master plans and ALPs. Note that caution should be used in these cases; often an airport owner may be tempted to construct a new facility because he sees an opportunity for increasing revenues, whereas the space may be used more effectively in the long run for another aeronautical use. This emphasizes the need for a sound planning process, a viable ALP, and an airport owner who will stick with it.

Be wary of falling into a mechanical process or sequence of steps or occurrences (such as the old "inventory-forecast-alternatives-plan" sequence), without putting much thought into what is being planned or why it is being planned. We develop forecasts that show growth in demand, check the capacity of the existing facility to handle the expected demand, develop a program of alternative facility improvements, evaluate the alternatives, and recommend a facility expansion plan. We don't often spend much time considering whether the airport is following so-called "best management practices," i.e., using current facilities wisely and efficiently to get their maximum capacity before we implement a facility improvement. It is easy to get caught in this cycle without thinking of the needs of the people who use the airport, i.e., the stakeholders. That is why strategic planning, or at the very least, some serious strategic thinking, is so important.

We in the airport business often tend to think of airports as "ours." But airports do not belong to airport planners; they do not even belong to the airport managers. They belong to the communities they serve. The growth and development of any airport should be determined primarily by the community it serves. Conversely, the community must be willing to support and use the services provided by the airport. For example, a community may express a desire for scheduled nonstop air service to Chicago, but if the community does not support the service by using it, the service will not survive. Similarly, the community may want to have a longer runway to accommodate larger aircraft, but if the municipality does not provide the local share to match a federal or state grant, the runway will not be lengthened, master plan facility requirements analyses notwithstanding.

As a final thought on the development of facility requirements, the financial picture should always be kept in mind. The financial history of the airport should be reviewed and the revenue streams and expenses should be examined, along with the history of grants received. Before recommending an elaborate or extensive plan to improve facilities, the planner must have a pretty good idea of what the airport is likely to be able to afford. It makes no sense to prepare a set of facility requirements and lay out expansion alternatives for a program that the airport may not be able to implement based on its financial history. The only exception to this is if there is a stated desire and commitment to fund a major expansion program on the part of the airport sponsor, the FAA, and any other potential state or local funding agencies. If the airport sponsor can't afford to build the recommended plan, a lot of time and money will have been wasted.

Step 7: Alternatives Development and Evaluation

According to the Master Plan AC, this element of the planning study should identify options to meet projected facility requirements and alternative configurations for each major component. Bear in mind however that the facility requirements assessment is an unconstrained evaluation and not a feasibility assessment. Not all of the facility improvements identified will be able to be implemented, for a variety of reasons, and this often results in confusion among airport users and the general public.

The Alternatives Development and Evaluation step is the confluence of facility layout, operational requirements, environmental impacts, and financial considerations. The alternatives analysis should identify alternatives that the sponsor (usually with the help of the FAA) can execute to meet the need. The master plan process is really not intended to establish a single alternative, although the alternatives analysis may identify the sponsor's preferred alternative. Alternatives that do not meet the needs identified in the preceding planning work or are for some reason not feasible or prudent should be dismissed and documented, i.e., as to why they don't meet the need or why they are not feasible or prudent.

The alternatives should also include the "do nothing" option, often called the "null" alternative. The null alternative provides a good baseline against which other alternatives can be compared. All of the information leading to the development of alternatives, and their rejection, is needed for follow-on NEPA documentation. Remember, an alternative can't be discarded simply because someone doesn't like it.

The alternatives analysis includes the following components:

- Identification of alternative ways to address previously-identified facility requirements.
- Evaluation of the alternatives, individually and collectively, so that planners gain a thorough understanding of the strengths, weaknesses, and other implications of each.
- Selection of the recommended alternative.[37]

In developing alternatives, planners should pay particular attention to whether the alternative is justified, i.e., does it fulfill the purpose and meet the need that generated the study in the first place. If the alternative does not meet the purpose and need for the project, it is not really an alternative and should not be considered in the analysis. For example, if the overall purpose of a project is to bring a runway safety area up to FAA standards, and one of the alternatives has minimal environmental impacts but does not result in a safety area that is fully compliant with FAA standards, it is not really a viable alternative. One quick and easy test is to ask, "If we had to build this alternative, would we really do the project?" Sometimes the answer to this question is "No," and that alternative can be dropped from the study.

It is a good idea to include potentially-affected parties early on in the formulation of alternatives. When developing alternatives for a terminal expansion, for example, the planning team should get together with other groups at the airport that will be involved in the operation and maintenance of the new facility, such as the commercial management or leasing department who will be responsible for actually renting out the space when the project is finished. The airport operations office should also be involved to ensure that the gate and apron areas are laid out to conform to airport operating practices. And don't forget to include the airport maintenance staff who will have to maintain the facility for years to come. If the airport has an air traffic control tower it is important to consult with air traffic control staff to ensure that the airside operation of the new terminal provides for the safe and efficient movement of aircraft in the vicinity of the building. It is especially important to ensure that the alternatives do not generate shadows or blind spots on the apron, taxiways, or even the runways. Consultation with FAA air traffic personnel is particularly important when developing alternatives for airside improvements such as new or reconfigured runways and taxiways. Remember, air traffic control staff are responsible for ensuring the smooth, safe, and efficient flow of aircraft in and out of the airport, day by day, hour by hour, and minute by minute. If they get involved early in the alternatives development process it can help ensure that the resulting facility will be usable and will indeed enable the airport to handle more air traffic. This "screening" process can weed out those options that are not practical before spending too much time and money on detailed studies.

It is also important to pay close attention to the impact that an alternative for an improvement to one facility may have on alternatives for an improvement to another facility at that airport, particularly with respect to long-term growth. For example, an alternative for expanding the existing air cargo complex may preclude an alternative for lengthening a runway or for building a new runway in a particular location. Terminal expansions are particularly troublesome in this respect; often terminals are expanded or concourses added or extended in a manner that precludes the future development of smooth and efficient taxiway flows. This can be avoided by considering the long-term aspects of facility development alternatives.

The Master Plan AC states that the planner should "assess the expected performance of each alternative against a wide range of evaluation criteria, including its operational, environmental, and financial impacts."[38] It further states that "a recommended development alternative will emerge from this process and will be further refined in subsequent tasks."[39] It almost makes it sound like magic, but to be valuable it must be a rigorous process. In the past planners would identify alternatives, examine their benefits and costs, and determine which alternative best met the airport's needs at the most reasonable cost. Then they would turn the project over to whoever was doing the environmental documentation and declare their work finished. The people preparing the environmental documentation would then have to go back and review all the planning work that was done—including the work that was not properly documented, including alternatives that were considered and dropped without much analysis or discussion—in order to prepare an environmental document that would be acceptable to the FAA. As a result, the preparation of the environmental document took more time and cost more money than expected, and the blame was almost always placed on environmental requirements. In many (or perhaps most) cases this was unfair, and the fault rested with the planners who didn't do their jobs properly. Under the new planning guidance, environmental factors must be considered as the plan and the facility development alternatives are being developed.

The Master Plan AC provides some excellent guidance for ensuring a smooth transition from the planning study, or the planning phase of the project, to the environmental approval process. The emphasis here—and it cannot be emphasized too strongly—is to include enough information in the planning document to feed the Purpose and Need section of the environmental document, and to include a description of the alternatives considered and why one was selected and others were dropped. Many environmental documents are delayed because somebody has to go back and do some more planning. Thorough planning and clear communication in the planning document will save time and money. We have all heard stories of runways that took decades to build, and projects that should have been approved in months actually taking years. Many FAA staff have said that they have found that much of the delay in completing the environmental process is due to poor planning, and my own experience bears this out. Inadequate planning leaves gaps that must be filled in, and usually these gaps are uncovered during the environmental process.

For example, an airport may complete a planning study and move on to the environmental process only to find that the staff preparing the environmental document cannot find a project justification to put into the Purpose and Need section. The study is then delayed while the planners come up with the project justification. Then while this is going on the economy goes into a slump and the FAA comes out with a new set of aviation demand forecasts. When the project goes into the public review phase someone may notice that the forecasts used in the planning study are optimistic compared to the state of the economy and air traffic demand at that time. Thus they may call for a review of the forecasts, which could lead to a forecast revision. (Note that the forecast validation process doesn't usually change the need for the project, just the timing.) This process of questioning and reevaluation can take time, during which other elements of the planning study or environmental document, such as the wetlands determination, can become outdated. These kinds of issues, plus delays associated with the review of study documents add time, sometimes measured in months or years. And then somebody gets hit with a lawsuit and things really start getting delayed. To minimize or avoid these kinds of situations, planners need to understand the full scope of their job, focus on the task at hand, and do it correctly.

Although Purpose and Need is, strictly speaking, a part of the environmental document, not the planning document, the plan should state clearly *what the project is all about, why it is needed, and who will use it and benefit from it*. This is not just a matter of complying with an FAA planning requirement or guideline—it is just plain common sense. Putting Purpose and Need and similar information into the planning document clearly and concisely will make life a whole lot easier in the long run, whether trying to secure environmental approval or trying to convince an airport commission and the FAA to provide funding.

The FAA emphasizes the need to consult with the district and/or regional FAA environmental staff to help determine the degree of environmental analysis that might be needed in the planning study. This is particularly true for improvements that might be needed in the near future. For example, the master plan study will be recommending a number of airport improvements over the next 20 years. However, as soon as the ALP is approved, the airport will want to begin a project to bring the runway safety areas up to FAA standards. In this case the study will include much more detail on the environmental impacts associated with the safety area improvements than with the other longer-term projects. In addition to the Master Plan AC, the FAA recommends that planners consult Order 5050.4B, *National Environmental Policy Act (NEPA) Implementing Instructions for Airport Actions*; Order 1050.1E, *Policies and Procedures for Considering Environmental Impacts*; and AC 150/5300-13, *Airport Design*; to gain a better understanding of how the planning alternatives analysis fits into the overall project development process.

The financial component is another major factor in the development and evaluation of alternatives. Planners should always consider the costs associated with each of the facility improvement alternatives in light of the airport's revenues and federal and/or state financial aid prospects. If one of the alternatives under consideration is significantly more expensive than the others, the financial factor could kill the alternative. For example, I have always planned with the idealistic idea that if a project is a good one and meets the airport's needs, then that is the one to build. If the airport doesn't have the money, it can apply for additional aid, raise rates and charges, or hold off until sufficient funds become available so the project can be built. Trust me, this is not the way to go. Yes, there are ways to implement an expensive project—phasing the construction over time is one approach. However, as airport budgets become tighter and tighter, planners need to come up with alternatives that are financially feasible.

Two cost components should be examined as part of the financial component: construction costs and operations and maintenance (O&M) costs. Also, it may be possible to come up with the funds to build a facility, for example a terminal expansion, but will airlines and concessionaires be willing to rent the space so that the construction and O&M costs can be recovered? Airports are often accused (and perhaps are often guilty) of building architectural monuments when a simpler facility would work just as well. It is fine to build a masterpiece, but not if the rates and charges will be so high that no tenant will want to lease the space.

One final point with respect to the cost component of the alternatives evaluation: don't forget the null alternative. There are costs associated with doing nothing, i.e., making no facility improvements. Depending upon the particular project, they can include air travel delay costs, lost revenues, increased maintenance and/or operations costs, etc. For example, a consequence of not making improvements to a taxiway system could result in higher fuel costs (and exhaust emissions) by increasing aircraft taxi times and queuing times. They can be significant and should be as thoroughly documented as the cost factors for all of the other alternatives.

The Master Plan AC lays out an "alternatives analysis process planning hierarchy" that includes a primary analysis and a secondary analysis.[40] The primary analysis focuses on those facility improvements that require large areas of land and are considered a "functional whole." An example is a new runway and its associated taxiways. The secondary analysis addresses improvements that have more flexibility, presumably those that do not require large land areas, and for which there may be a number of alternative locations. The example used in the AC is an aircraft rescue and firefighting (ARFF) building. However, ARFF siting criteria are pretty specific in order to ensure minimum response times to various points on the runway system, so there really may not be as much flexibility as the FAA seems to think. In fact a key consider-

Chapter 5 – Master Planning 159

ation in developing and evaluating runway alternatives is the location of the ARFF building—that is why many large airports have more than one ARFF facility. The AC describes the alternatives analysis process in detail, complete with a sort of flow chart/wiring diagram to show how it is supposed to work. The AC states that the steps in the process are applicable to very large and complex projects, and that for many airport improvements (thankfully) "…some of the steps may not be applicable."[41]

The Master Plan AC states that the evaluation of alternatives "…should follow generally accepted planning practices, be replicable, consistently applied, and well documented."[42] This is pretty much common sense, but sometimes planners and airport operators try to sneak one through. Based on my experience, the rules should be followed; if they are not, something will likely turn around and bite you before it is all over. The AC sets out four categories for criteria to be used in evaluating project alternatives: *operational performance*, *best planning tenets and other factors*, *environmental factors*, and *fiscal factors*.

Operational Performance addresses how well the airport functions overall as a balanced system, and how the alternatives add to this performance. The AC recommends evaluating operational performance from the standpoint of *capacity*, *capability*, and *efficiency*. These are pretty much common sense, but sometimes, particularly on complex projects, it pays to lay them out objectively and evaluate each one separately. A group discussion can be helpful here; getting the views of a number of knowledgeable people can help ensure that all the bases have been covered and that the alternatives really are workable.

Capacity is a determination of how well, or to what extent, each alternative can accommodate projected volumes of activity. Capacity analyses can be applied to almost any aspect of airport operations, but are most commonly used for airside (i.e., runway and taxiway) performance, terminals, and ground access systems. Capacity analyses can be performed for runways and taxiways separately, or as a combined system, depending on the particular project circumstances. For example, if the airport has sufficient runway capacity but is experiencing operational delays, the capacity analysis might be focused on looking at taxiway issues. When planning a new runway, however, it is necessary to look at how well the runway would perform together with one or more supporting taxiway configurations. In this case there may be two or three different taxiway configurations that would work with the new runway; therefore, each taxiway alternative should be examined with respect to how it works in combination with the new runway. Runway and taxiway alternatives should also be examined with respect to how well they function in conjunction with the existing runway and taxiway systems.

The important thing is to examine the alternatives in the context of how they will actually be operating. Terminal capacity can be examined for the terminal building as a whole, but it is much more accurate to analyze each major component separately, including check-in, inbound and outbound baggage systems, passenger security screening, and baggage screening. Ground access similarly has a number of components including highways, public transportation systems, and public parking.

Airside capacity refers to the number of aircraft operations the airport's runways and taxiways can accommodate safely. Airside capacity studies are usually done as part of airport master plans, or when an airport is experiencing flight delays or is expected to experience delays in the foreseeable future. They should be done for both IFR and VFR conditions; quite often an airport will have sufficient VFR capacity but fall short during instrument conditions. Airside capacity studies can be complicated, because flight delays can be caused by a number of factors including the capability of the runway and taxiway system to accommodate the required level of air traffic, as well as weather, airspace congestion, and gate usage and availability. As discussed in Chapter 2: Airports, FAA AC 150/5060-5, *Airport Capacity and Delay*, provides guidance for determining airport capacity using manual calculations and a series of runway configuration diagrams. This methodology can be used for smaller airports, but at busier airports computer simulation modeling is usually employed. The primary models currently being used are The Airport Machine™, the Airport and Airspace Simulation Model (SIMMOD™), and the Total Airport and Airspace Modeler (TAAM™).

When considering airside capacity as part of the alternatives analysis it is important to examine the forecast fleet mix. If larger aircraft will be expected to enter the fleet at an airport it is possible that capacity may be reduced because the separation between arriving aircraft will have to be increased to account for wake turbulence. It is also possible that some parts of the airfield will not be able to be used by larger aircraft due to dimensional standards or weight limitations. For example, some taxiways may only be able to handle Design Group III aircraft; if Group IV aircraft are expected to be part of the future fleet mix, they will not be able to use these taxiways. Also, if smaller aircraft such as regional jets are expected to be added to the fleet, airfield capacity may actually increase, due to decreased aircraft separation requirements. A shift to regional jets in sufficient numbers may also warrant the analysis of a new runway specifically designed to handle those aircraft. But if that is the case, bear in mind that the airport may wind up handling fewer passengers by accommodating more small aircraft.

Thus it is important to remember that an airport operates as a system, with each component doing a specialized job, and all components needing to be in balance. Sometimes other quirky little things come up; for example, an airline moving into a proposed new terminal may decide to assign the new gates to its flights based on a baggage sort zone scheme. If this happens an arriving aircraft may not be able to use just any gate that happens to be open; the gate must be located in the appropriate baggage sort zone of the airline's portion of the terminal. Many air travelers complain that their flight had to wait on a taxiway for a gate to be available, but while they were waiting they could see unused gates. The point to all this is that a balance must be maintained between and among all airport components and this balance should be kept in mind when analyzing and evaluating alternatives.

Airspace usage can also be a significant contributor to aircraft delays, particularly in large metropolitan areas served by more than one airport. For example, through the 1980s and 1990s at BWI we often experienced aircraft departure delays due to the fact that all air traffic departing from BWI, National, and Dulles bound for airports in the Northeast were vectored over a common departure fix called the SWANN intersection, located on Maryland's Eastern Shore, about 50 miles east of BWI Airport. In order to obtain a five-mile in-trail aircraft separation over SWANN, BWI, National, and Dulles departures had to be sequenced, and during peak periods departing aircraft at all three airports had to hold, usually for short periods, on taxiways prior to departure. At BWI we had a shortage of taxi routes, so SWANN departures also held up aircraft bound for other parts of the country. The same situation occurred when northeastern cities such as Philadelphia, New York, and Boston experienced weather delays, which resulted in flights to those airports being held for a period of time on the ground at BWI, National, and Dulles. This particular issue was resolved through the construction of additional taxiways that provided a bypass capability so that aircraft destined for other parts of the country could have unobstructed runway access.

When analyzing alternatives from a capacity standpoint, make sure to understand the true root of the capacity problem—e.g., that flight delays are actually related to the airport's runway and taxiway configuration, and not due to a lack of gate space or airspace factors.

Capability is simply a question of whether the alternative will do the job it is supposed to do. For new runways or parking ramps the question is whether they will accommodate the design aircraft in the numbers projected. For terminals the question may be whether the holdrooms can accommodate the expected number of passengers, or whether there is enough concession space, or whether there are enough restrooms.

Efficiency is a measure of how well the alternatives perform under expected operational circumstances. Taxiway efficiency, for example, would consider the number of runway crossings and intersections with other taxiways. It would also consider taxi distances, although the proposed taxiway alternatives may reduce delays—one or two may result in longer taxi distances with higher overall taxi times. For terminals, efficiency considers the relative locations of restrooms, concessions, and other passenger support facilities with respect to the major flows or movements of both inbound and outbound passengers through the building. Efficiency in a terminal analysis might also consider relative passenger walking distances between connecting gates or other passenger support facilities. Operational safety is a key component of efficiency. Thus it is essential to have the appropriate FAA air traffic personnel review all plans for runway and taxiway improvements to ensure that they do not create situations that could present safety problems, particularly at night or in periods of inclement weather.

The AC also recommends consulting with the appropriate FAA office—usually the Air Traffic group—to assess the "aeronautical utility" of each of the alternatives. This is particularly critical for airside projects involving changes to runway or taxiway configurations. For example, when planning a new runway, particularly a parallel runway, it is necessary to ensure that an alternative does not have an approach or departure path that conflicts with one of the other existing runways at that airport or at another nearby airport. Discussions with FAA Air Traffic Control personnel are especially useful here, and should really begin when alternatives are being developed, as noted above.

Best Planning Tenets and Other Factors consists of a variety of factors that can influence how an alternative will function, both by itself and in concert with other airport components. Most of these factors are common sense, but it is often helpful to lay them out to make sure everything has been included. Remember: airport planning is easy—all you have to do is *think*. The only problem is, you have to think of *everything*. The AC lists a number of these practices or tenets that should apply to the evaluation of alternatives. Does the alternative:

- Conform to best practices for safety and security.
- Conform to the intent of applicable FAA design standards and other appropriate planning guidelines.
- Provide for the highest and best on- and off-airport land use.
- Allow for forecast growth throughout the planning period.
- Provide for growth beyond the forecast period, as applicable.
- Provide balance (typically capacity) between elements.
- Provide the flexibility to adjust to unforeseen changes.
- Conform to the airport sponsor's strategic vision.
- Conform to appropriate local, regional, and state transportation plans and other applicable plans.
- Prove technically feasible (limited site constraints).
- Appear socially and politically feasible.
- Satisfy user needs.[43]

Environmental Factors should also be considered in the evaluation of alternatives. As noted above, they should be considered during the development of alternatives as well; if potential environmental impacts are identified early on it can help the alternatives process move along more smoothly. If some of the alternatives have potentially significant environmental impacts, it is a good idea to have an alternative or two on the back burner, so to speak, in case the adverse environmental effects are significant enough to kill the project. Or, the mitigation costs associated with the alternatives may be so high that they might preclude the eventual construction of the facility. The

Chapter 5 – Master Planning

Master Plan AC does not specify exactly how to use environmental factors in the alternatives analysis, but it does recommend using the environmental impact categories contained in FAA Orders 1050.1 and 5050.4B as a guide. Appendix D of the AC also provides some very useful guidance for practices that can make the planning process and subsequent environmental analysis more efficient and effective. Most airport improvements will not affect very many of these categories; the ones typically encountered in most airport planning projects are noise, air quality, wetlands, and forests. As a general rule, the more complex a plan is, i.e., the more complex the projects that are included, the more detailed the environmental analysis will have to be. In complex studies it is always a good idea to have an environmental consultant on board, and if the impacts are significant enough to warrant an Environmental Assessment (EA) or an Environmental Impact Statement (EIS), make sure the consultant has successfully completed EAs and EISs at other *airports*, preferably on similar kinds of projects. Experience in preparing an EA for a highway improvement is not the same as an EA for an airport improvement, and dealing with the Federal Highway Administration requirements and procedures is not the same as dealing with the FAA requirements and procedures.

Many times consultants will create a matrix to show how each alternative compares with the other alternatives. These matrices are usually developed so alternatives can be compared objectively (at least in theory). Usually each evaluation factor will be assigned a weight, assuming for example that improving safety is two or three times as important as increasing capacity. Of course, assigning weights to different factors introduces an element of subjectivity. In fact some subjectivity is even involved in selecting the factors to be weighted. For example I have seen matrices that used "accessibility," "distance from terminal," and "convenience" as factors in evaluating alternative locations for public parking lots. In fact, they all really measure the same thing; to use all three is actually giving the accessibility/convenience factor a triple weight.

Also, rating according to factors such as "environmental" and "safety" can stir up a great deal of controversy. Many airport people, especially those dealing with operations, for example, don't think it is appropriate to compare safety to anything in terms of an alternatives evaluation. They typically don't think there is any such thing as "safer," either something is safe or it isn't, in that it either meets FAA standards or it doesn't. Thus including safety as one of the items in an evaluation matrix is usually not a good idea. After all, meeting safety requirements is really a part of the Purpose and Need for the project, and is not a negotiable option.

At some point in the study process questions will be raised about how the matrix was developed and the selection of factors and the weighting scheme will have to be explained and defended. Evaluation matrices may be a good way of summarizing project impacts, but they are generally not an analytical or evaluation tool.

The significance of Fiscal Factors is also obviously important in the evaluation of alternatives. The AC highlights the fact that "preparing rough cost estimates is a very effective way to compare alternatives and should be done in all alternatives analyses."[44] The term "rough cost estimates" is in a sense inappropriate because the estimates should not be all that rough; they usually wind up being an important part of successful budgeting and plan implementation. Planners usually like to talk about preparing "order-of-magnitude" costs as part of a planning study. During the planning phase it is difficult to prepare detailed and accurate cost estimates, because planning studies generally do not delve deeply enough into design and construction details to establish all the items that contribute to the actual cost of a project. If they did it wouldn't be planning, it would be design. However, because costs are so important the estimates should be as accurate and as thoroughly documented as possible. Bear in mind that the cost of a project includes more than just the construction of the facility; for example, it is not a good idea to say that a terminal expansion will cost approximately $25 million per gate, or that a surface automobile parking lot will cost $3,000 per space. All costs associated with bringing the facility on line, from planning all the way to building occupancy, must be included if cost estimates are to be accurate. For example, in addition to the actual cost of construction (sometimes referred to as the first cost), the cost estimate should also include the costs for design and construction management, infrastructure (such as site preparation, utilities, and access roadways), and environmental mitigation. If the new facility will also involve the relocation of current airport tenants, the relocation costs should be included. If the cost factor is important enough to be used to differentiate one alternative from another, it is important enough to be done right.

Cost estimates should be prepared in real or constant dollar costs, i.e., costs in terms of the year in which the planning study is conducted—2009 dollars, for example. Current dollars, i.e., dollars inflated to the year of construction, should not be used or shown in planning studies, with the possible exception of near-term projects that will be going directly into the CIP. For example, if a new cargo/office building is estimated to cost $500,000 in the base year of the study, but is not needed until 2020, inflating the cost at a fairly reasonable rate of three percent annually will yield a cost of $712,880 when it is needed 20 years in the future, or about 43 percent higher than the 2008 cost. If the costs for all of the projects, especially for facilities and improvements that won't be needed until 10 or 20 years in the future, are inflated to the year the facilities are to be constructed, the resulting cost estimates will be quite high and they may scare some people or cause them to question the accuracy of the cost estimates. Cost inflation factors are typically applied during the process of assembling the agency budget, and the budgeting people usually have their own inflation factors that are used for all items. If the master plan costs are used directly to develop the CIP the planners should check with the budgeting office to ensure that the appropriate inflation factors are used.

It doesn't seem as though much attention has been given to the concept of life-cycle costs in airport planning, and this could be especially critical in the evaluation of alternatives. Life-cycle costs are the combination of the initial and future costs associated with the construction and operation of a building over the expected life of the facility (or some other appropriate period of time). Instead, planners usually prepare cost estimates for facility improvements on the basis of what it will cost to construct the facility. Attention is rarely given to what it will cost to operate and maintain the facility through its useful life. It might be more useful and more effective if, instead of simply looking at a facility in terms of cost to design and build, airport operators would also consider operations, maintenance and repair, replacement, and disposal costs. Calculating life-cycle costs can be fairly expensive and time-consuming, but may pay off in the long run.

The cost factor is important for more than just comparing alternatives. The cost estimate developed during the planning phase is the cost estimate that will most likely be used in preparing the capital improvement program and will be the basis for applying for a grant from the FAA and from the state aviation department. As stated elsewhere in this book, if the planners grossly miscalculate the cost estimate and the actual construction cost of the project significantly exceeds the planning estimate, it will probably wind up getting a lot of public attention. But even more than a matter of public perception, it can reflect on the quality of the work and the professional competence of whoever prepared the cost estimates. It may make people wonder that if the consultants were so far in error on the cost estimates, how accurate were they on their estimate of the demand forecasts? The capacity estimates? The environmental impact estimates?

Sometimes the alternatives development and evaluation process can be made difficult by the fact that there simply *are* no alternatives, other than the "no build" option. For example, the plan may call for a new cargo building along with an associated ramp and taxiway connection. In many cases this will be an addition to an existing cargo complex. If so, there usually aren't too many options for locating a new building. The ramp will probably be located adjacent to the new building, and the taxiway extension will have to connect the new ramp to the existing taxiway system. The only alternatives in a case like this would be to locate the new building in another area, i.e., away from the existing cargo complex, or to relocate the entire complex. In this situation there may be alternatives, but they are really no-brainers. But from the standpoint of people reviewing environmental documents, they expect to see alternatives, because it says in their guidelines that the alternatives should be documented. In this case, rather than getting into a contest with the reviewers, which will take time and money, it is usually better to go ahead and document the alternatives; if they make no sense, document why they make no sense. This can be done without a lot of detailed environmental work; a simple discussion of why the new building, ramp, and taxiway connection are needed, who they will serve, and why they should be located where you propose should suffice. If a clear case can be made to support an action environmental reviewers will usually concur.

To summarize, the whole process of developing and evaluating alternatives can be described pretty simply: through the entire process planners should consider whether or not the alternative meets the need as identified in the facility requirements analysis, to what extent the alternatives have any environmental impacts and whether or not they can be mitigated, and whether or not the alternatives can be funded and financially supported.

Step 8: Airport Layout Plans
The Master Plan AC notes that the Airport Layout Plan is one of the key products of an airport planning study. Most planners and airport operators would say it is *the* key product, since it is the end product of the work done in the master planning process. The FAA approval of the ALP is the federal action that triggers the environmental process. Generally speaking, the ALP (sometimes referred to as the ALP set) is a set of drawings that provides a graphic representation of the long-term development plan for an airport in terms of the location and phasing of recommended facility improvements. Typically the term *Airport Layout Plan* is used when referring to the primary drawing in the set—the one that gets signed by the airport sponsor and the manager of the local ADO. Other drawings may also be included with the actual ALP, depending on the size and complexity of the individual airport and the projects involved.

To me the ALP is actually the most important document in the entire planning process because it is the official, signed representation of what the airport looks like now and what it will look like in the future. As noted in Chapter 3: Airport Management, Operations, and Finance, one of the grant assurances states that the airport will "…keep up-to-date at all times an airport layout plan…."[45] And as also noted in Chapter 3, the FAA will typically not provide funding for a project that is not included in a current, approved ALP. The Master Plan AC notes that an ALP typically remains current for five years, unless major changes are planned or actually constructed.

The AC provides guidance on what should be included on an ALP and in an ALP set. It includes the various drawings that may be required, as well as the type of information that should be shown on each drawing. The specific ALP guidance is not repeated here—requirements change from time to time, thus the current edition of the Master Plan AC should be used. Additional guidance on preparing ALPs is also contained in FAA Order 5100.38, *Airport Improvement Program Handbook*. Remember, preparing ALPs is not particle physics or brain surgery; the guidance is simple and straightforward, it just has to be followed and the work has to be double- and triple-checked. It is particularly important to check the dimensional standards, including runway and taxiway safety areas, runway protection zones, etc. These can easily be plotted incorrectly, particularly at large airports, and mistakes can be very easily overlooked. It is also important to check with the local ADO before preparing updated ALP drawings because specific ALP requirements, levels of detail, and associated checklists vary somewhat among ADOs and FAA regions.

One problem with ALPs is that so much information is typically required that the resulting drawings are so complicated and show so much detail that they are sometimes unusable. The resulting clutter also makes it harder to check the drawings for accuracy. Now that consultants use computer-aided design software to prepare ALP drawings, it is more common to generate a stripped-down drawing that shows only the details that are relevant to the purpose at hand. The FAA recommends developing standards for preparing computer-aided design drawings that include such things as line types and thicknesses, lettering styles, and file-naming conventions. The use of color on the drawings can also help in the identification and interpretation of the information shown on the ALP drawings, but unless some standards are applied, color can also make things a little more confusing.

The AC notes that geographic information systems (GIS) are useful in developing a complete and usable airport database. The FAA is reportedly considering the development of some sort of standardization, or at least some guidance, in this regard. GIS can be especially useful because it can link information shown on drawings to databases that provide a variety of useful information about each facility shown. For example the runways, taxiways, ramps, aprons, parking lots, and access and circulation roadways shown on the ALP can be linked to a database that contains information on the date that each of the pavements was constructed, the materials used, and the cost of the work, as well as the contractors who prepared the design and performed the construction. The complication that can arise is that many offices and departments at an airport may use different (and incompatible) GIS applications. Steps toward standardization would definitely help, but even if the FAA lays out some nationwide airport planning and design standards for GIS application, other groups at the airport, such as the commercial leasing office or the airport maintenance division, may not use these standards. Thus there is a potential for variation in GIS standards not only among airports, but within individual airports as well.

There is not much the planner can do about the lack of GIS standards except to be aware of it, and pay close attention to the information collected from, and input to, each airport's GIS framework.

Step 9: Facilities Implementation Plan

The Facilities Implementation Plan simply shows how and when the recommendations of the planning study will be implemented, and how much they will cost. The schedule for the improvements depends to a great extent on the levels of demand that trigger the need for expansion of existing facilities. The costs are those that were developed during the planning process—this is where they really become important. The implementation plan should at a minimum show the list of projects, the schedule for building the project, the project cost, and related projects that may be affected by or associated with each proposed project. The projects included in the facilities implementation plan should also be prioritized to guide local airport budget preparation and eventual FAA allocation. At larger airports and where a very complex development program is envisioned, the implementation plan should show a master schedule for project implementation and a more detailed coordination plan that includes key responsibilities and activities, particularly crucial decision points and major milestones. In effect the facilities implementation plan shows both the sponsor and the FAA how the planning recommendations will be implemented in conjunction with the daily operation of the airport. Strangely enough, even though it contains information that is obviously important, in 37 years of airport planning, I have never seen an actual document called a "Facilities Implementation Plan" and have never heard of an airport that had one. I have seen the components of such a plan, and I also recognize the importance of actually preparing *and following* such a plan.

The most obvious component is the airport's Capital Improvement Program (CIP), which is sometimes referred to as the Capital Improvement Plan. Typically the CIP is maintained by the airport sponsor and sets forth all of the airport planning and development projects. It is usually a five-year program, although some cover six or seven years, and once in a while somebody prepares a ten-year program, although anything beyond five or six years is usually pretty sketchy in the out years and is not very useful for the longer term. At BWI we had a six-year CIP and for the longer term we had a more general *Needs Assessment*. The Needs Assessment went out to at least 20 years and included everything we could think of that might come up and require major cash. It actually turned out to be a useful document for long-range programming purposes.

The CIP should include all capital costs, i.e., costs that are not directly related to operating or maintaining the airport. For example plowing snow and cutting grass are operations and maintenance (O&M) costs, but a runway or taxiway overlay is a capital cost. Similarly, building a new terminal or adding an addition to an existing building is a capital cost, whereas painting the existing terminal is an O&M cost. The FAA states that the CIP should include both items that are eligible for FAA funding as well as ineligible items. The eligible projects, or eligible portions of projects, are submitted to the ADO for inclusion in the FAA System of Airport Reporting (SOAR), and for the development of an FAA Airports Capital Improvement Plan (ACIP). The FAA prepares the ACIP by identifying the projects and costs, and then applying a priority system in conjunction with expected funding levels to determine which projects it will actually be able to fund.

It is particularly important to note that the CIP, and particularly the information submitted to the FAA, should include *all* capital improvements planned for the airport, including those which may not be eligible for federal funding. This means both the projects already in the CIP as well as any new projects arising from the planning study. Also, the documentation for each project should be complete and clearly understood by both the sponsor and the FAA.

Chapter 5 – Master Planning

The second component of a facility implementation plan is the part that says, "Next year we are going to do *this*, in two years we will do *these two things*, and the following year we will do *that*." It is simply a schedule of when each project is expected to be implemented, and is really a necessary ingredient of the CIP. The implementation plan is also used to identify what projects must be completed, what actions must be taken to complete the project, and in what sequence those actions must be executed. It is also helpful to identify who is responsible for each of the steps. For example, before building a terminal expansion, once the concept planning is complete, the proposed project must be put on the ALP and FAA approval must be obtained. Also, all the environmental documentation must be prepared and the necessary environmental approvals obtained. After the plan is complete and the FAA has approved the ALP, a federal grant will usually be requested and the necessary paperwork and associated documentation must be prepared.

Once the FAA has made a commitment for funding, the project must be designed and the necessary permits (e.g., storm water management and sediment and erosion control) must be obtained. Design usually begins when the environmental process is completed, or at least when the sponsor is sure that environmental approvals will be obtained. Usually some design work must be done to obtain enough information to secure the environmental permits and approvals. The extent of the design work depends primarily on the complexity of the project and the nature of the potential for environmental disturbance. For an EIS for example, 30 percent design is usually needed, but in any case sufficient design should be accomplished to show the limits of disturbance caused by the project and the construction activity. Once design is complete the construction contract is put out for bid and a contractor is selected.

When laying out the schedule and milestones for this series of events, time must be allowed for the review of all documents, including both environmental and design, and appropriate and realistic review times must be put into the schedule. Time must also be allowed for procurement of design and construction services. As this series of events is being developed, critical points or milestones must be identified in the environmental/design/construction process and expected completion dates must be specified. It is always important to remember that, in spite of all our best efforts, things happen that cause delays in implementing a project, and sometimes what appear to be minor delays can actually have a major effect on the project schedule. Remember, when considering construction schedules, especially at airports in the northern U.S. or other areas where construction is seasonal, a delay of a month or two in getting the necessary construction permits, or in procuring contractor services, can result in a loss of a construction season. In the northeastern U.S., major projects that involve a lot of earth work and concrete work do not start after mid-September. Work already underway may proceed, but contractors usually prefer to wait until spring before starting a major job. Along with the identification of the sequence of events and milestones, the offices or individuals who will be responsible for each item must also be identified. It is also a very good idea (and common sense) to include the responsible parties as the schedule is being developed so they can verify that they can actually do what they are supposed to do in the amount of time they are given to do it. This is also a very good way to make sure that everybody knows what they are supposed to do, when they are supposed to do it, and what everybody else is doing as well.

At larger airports this information is usually documented in some form, along with the appropriate workflow charts. Sometimes it may not all be in one document, but it is much more convenient and useful if all relevant information concerning airport capital facility improvements is shown in one place, and if all interested and affected parties are given a copy. It is also a good idea to remember to inform all parties, usually through a revised document, when schedules change. At smaller airports (and even at some larger ones) this information is often not written down—it resides in people's heads instead. In that case it is extremely important for the knowledgeable people to communicate completely and regularly. Overall, it is a lot safer and a lot more effective to actually prepare a Facilities Implementation Plan, as the FAA recommends, no matter how large or small the airport, or how complex the program.

Step 10: Financial Feasibility Analysis

The Financial Feasibility Analysis is really a verification of the fact that the airport sponsor can afford to implement the facility development program as planned. As noted earlier in this chapter, the sponsor and consultants should have a pretty good idea of the budgetary constraints and possibilities before the facilities improvement program is even developed. A thorough analysis of the airport's historical financial picture will guide the development of an affordable plan and implementation program. The Financial Feasibility Analysis should describe how the sponsor will finance the projects recommended in the planning study, including the amounts and sources of all project finances, and will thus demonstrate the financial feasibility of the program. Airport funding and financing are discussed in Chapter 3: Airport Management, Operations, and Finance.

The FAA requires that a Benefit-Cost Analysis (BCA) be prepared "…for projects that enhance capacity at an airport and will receive $5 million or more in AIP discretionary funds or are named in a Letter of Intent."[46] These BCAs can be completed as part of a master plan financial feasibility analysis, but they are more commonly done separately because they involve more detailed cost estimates and a higher degree of analysis than are usually prepared for most planning studies. Detailed FAA guidance for benefit-cost analyses is detailed in a report titled *Airports Benefit-Cost Analysis Guidance*.[47]

Something that is similar in a way to a BCA is an *economic impact analysis*. This is not mentioned in any planning guidance publication that I am aware of, but it is important nonetheless. This is not the same as the airport economic impact studies discussed in Chapter 2: Airports, but if they are properly done the data can be used as part of an economic impact assessment.

An economic impact analysis is a brief project-specific assessment of what a project means economically, i.e., what economic benefits will result if the sponsor builds the project? Just as planners have to prepare an assessment of some sort describing the environmental effects of a project, my personal opinion is that planners should also perform an assessment of the economic effects. This is a simple statement such as, "If we build these four new gates at the airport, we can expect to generate x new jobs, y in new annual revenues, z in new taxes, etc." Again: planning is half sales. People are more likely to accept a plan if they can see a good reason (or better yet, more than one reason) for it. Demonstrating the economic benefits of the plan can be an effective sales tool, particularly for the agencies responsible for coming up with the local share of project funds. This is not applicable for those projects that are intended to bring the airport up to current FAA facility standards, or for safety improvements, but it can be a good tool for those projects that are expected to generate revenues for the airport and for the community it serves.

As a final thought on financial feasibility, it is important to keep the customers' needs and desires in mind when considering the financial aspects of any airport improvement. Remember that the airline component of the airport's customer base will be opposed to just about anything that they feel will not benefit them directly (and sometimes exclusively). On the other hand, the airlines are the ones who wind up paying for a significant share of airport improvements, so their comments can't be simply discounted. To keep the airlines happy many airports take a "low cost" or "no frills" approach to facility development. But it is also important to consider the air passenger component of the airport customer base. At many (perhaps most) airports the so-called "high end" passengers are the ones who eventually share some of the cost burden. Thus if things are built on the cheap, some pretty influential customers may not be too happy and they will often find a way to make their dissatisfaction known.

To summarize the chapter, airport master planning (or any other kind of airport development planning) is complex and can be time-consuming and expensive. It usually involves a number of different airport components and airport users, as well as a range of airport management, operations, maintenance, environmental, and engineering staff. The Master Plan AC provides excellent guidance on how to conduct planning so that the methodologies and results will meet FAA criteria and will provide a solid basis for follow-on environmental studies and documentation. Unfortunately, even though the FAA does not intend the AC to be a "cookbook," many planning practitioners have a tendency to use it that way, especially at smaller airports. This should be avoided. Simply following the processes set forth in the Master Plan AC will not guarantee a good plan. Remember: planning is a world of ideas and these ideas come from the planner, not from a planning handbook.

Endnotes

1. de Neufville, Richard, and Amedeo Odoni, *Airport Systems Planning, Design, and Management.* New York: McGraw-Hill, 2003, Chapter 3.
2. *Ibid.*, p. 62.
3. *Ibid.*, p. 59.
4. *Airport Master Plans*, AC 150/5070-6B. Washington, D.C.: Federal Aviation Administration, 2005, title page.
5. *Ibid.*, p. 5.
6. *Ibid.*, p. 9.
7. *Architectural, Engineering, and Planning Consultant Services for Airport Grant Projects*, AC 150/5100-14. Washington, D.C.: Federal Aviation Administration, September 2005. Accessed April 2008, from http://rgl.faa.gov/Regulatory_and_Guidance_Library/rgAdvisoryCircular.nsf/0/87be820a72d12407862570a6006b4f29/$FILE/150-5100-14d.pdf
8. *Ibid.*, p. 5.
9. *Airport Master Plans. Op cit.* p. 10.
10. *National Environmental Policy Act (NEPA) Implementing Instructions for Airport Actions*, FAA Order 5050.4B. Washington, D.C.: Federal Aviation Administration, April 28, 2006, p. 5-3. Accessed July 2008, from http://www.faa.gov/airports_airtraffic/airports/resources/publications/orders/environmental_5050_4/media/chapter1.pdf
11. *Community Involvement Manual*, FAA-EE-90-03. Washington, D.C.: Federal Aviation Administration, Office of Environment and Energy, August 1990, p. 3.
12. *Ibid.*
13. *Architectural, Engineering, and Planning Consultant Services for Airport Grant Projects. Op cit.*
14. *Airport Improvement Program (AIP) Handbook*, FAA Order 5100.38C. Washington, D.C.: Federal Aviation Administration. Accessed June 2008, from http://www.faa.gov/airports_airtraffic/airports/aip/aip_handbook/
15. *Partnering for Better Communities*, Pub. 427 (01-02). CH Planning, for the Pennsylvania Department of Transportation, Bureau of Aviation. n.d., p. 1.
16. *Ibid.*
17. *Ibid.*
18. *Airport Master Plans. Op cit.* p. 5.
19. *Ibid.*, p. 23.
20. *Ibid.*, p. 24.
21. *Ibid.*, p. 120.
22. *Ibid.*

23 *Ibid.*, p. 25.

24 *Ibid.*, p. 14-15.

25 *Forecasting Aviation Activity by Airport*. Jenkintown, PA: GRA, 2001, incorporated for Federal Aviation Administration, Office of Aviation Policy and Plans, 2001. Accessed June 2008, from http://www.faa.gov/data_statistics/aviation_data_statistics/forecasting/media/af1.doc

26 *Revision to Guidance on Review and Approval of Aviation Forecasts*, memorandum. Washington, D.C.: Federal Aviation Administration, 2004. Accessed June 2008, from http://www.faa.gov/airports_airtraffic/airports/planning_capacity/media/approval_aviation_forecasts_2004.pdf

27 *Airport Aviation Activity Forecasting*. Washington, D.C.: Airport Cooperative Research Program, Transportation Research Board, 2007. Accessed June 2008, from http://onlinepubs.trb.org/onlinepubs/acrp/acrp_syn_002.pdf

28 *Airport Master Plans. Op cit.* p. 37.

29 *APO Terminal Area Forecast 2007*. Washington, D.C.: Federal Aviation Administration. Accessed July 2008, from http://tafpub.itworks-software.com/taf2007/default.asp

30 *Revision to Guidance. Op cit.*

31 *Ibid.*, p. 3.

32 *Ibid.*

33 *Field Formulation of the National Plan of Integrated Airport Systems (NPIAS)*, FAA Order 5090.3C. Washington, D.C.: Federal Aviation Administration, December 4, 2000, p. 19. Accessed June 2008, from http://www.faa.gov/airports_airtraffic/airports/resources/publications/orders/media/planning_5090_3C.pdf

34 *Airport Master Plans. Op cit.* Chapter 8.

35 *Ibid.*, p. 61.

36 *Ibid.*, p. 48.

37 *Ibid.*, p. 63.

38 *Ibid.*, p. 6.

39 *Ibid.*

40 *Ibid.*, p. 65.

41 *Ibid.*

42 *Ibid.*, p. 70.

43 *Ibid.*, p. 71.

44 *Ibid.*, p. 72.

45 *Assurances, Airport Sponsors*. Washington, D.C.: Federal Aviation Administration, March 2005, p. 11, 12. Accessed May 2008, from http://www.faa.gov/airports_airtraffic/airports/aip/grant_assurances/media/airport_sponsor_assurances.pdf

46 *Airport Master Plans. Op cit.* p. 95.

47 *Airports Benefit-Cost Analysis Guidance.* Washington, D.C.: Federal Aviation Administration, Office of Policy and Plans, 1999. Accessed December 2007, from http://www.faa.gov/airports_airtraffic/airports/aip/bc_analysis/media/faabca.pdf

CHAPTER 6

SYSTEM PLANNING

Airport system planning is a means of considering airports, and their functions and services, in the context of a larger area such as a region, a state, or the nation. It examines each airport and its planned development program with respect to other airports that provide both similar and complementary functions and services within the area under study. Airport system planning can provide an area-wide context for follow-on individual airport master plans. System plans are especially useful for determining how to allocate federal and state funds among a plethora of projects and airports according to an area-wide priority system. Airport system plans are usually conducted by state aviation authorities or regional planning agencies and thus allow state and regional planning officials to get a picture of airports in a broader context. This chapter explores the various components of airport system planning with a view to developing a useful and effective plan. It follows FAA system planning guidance and notes some practical aspects involved in each element of the system planning process.

Background

The FAA defines system planning in AC 150/5070-7, *The Airport System Planning Process*, as "…for planning purposes, information, and guidance to decide the extent, kind, location, and timing of airport development needed in a specific area to establish a viable, balanced, and integrated system of public-use airports."[1] The FAA goes on to state that, "The primary purpose of airport system planning is to study the performance and interaction of an entire aviation system to understand the interrelationship of the member airports."[2]

This AC was revised extensively in 2004 and is a significant departure from the "cookie cutter" approach (i.e., the same process applied to all types of system studies) previously used in airport system planning. Rather than using a standardized approach for all state and regional system planning, the new AC allows planners to tailor the planning process to meet specific needs. The new AC also emphasizes that system planning is a dynamic process, involving feedback from stakeholders throughout the effort. This is also true of any facility planning process, and is very important to the successful completion of any planning study.

The FAA states that the system plan should include all public-use airports including heliports and seaplane bases. This is a commendable goal, but including heliports can be time-consuming and expensive, and the end product may be as elusive as a basket of fog because most heliports require relatively little investment, and seem to come and go overnight. An exception might be in large urban areas where heliports are typically firmly established and play a significant role in the metropolitan airport system. For example, these facilities can accommodate police and rescue helicopters, and provide fuel and repair services for other helicopter operators, thereby relieving other airports from some helicopter activity.

The state aviation system plan should contain an inventory of how each airport is currently operating in terms of facilities, services, and demand levels. In system planning, as in all types of airport planning, the inventory should include the airport users and their needs and characteristics. Demand measurements should at minimum include passenger volumes and aircraft operations and fleet mix, including critical aircraft. The critical aircraft is the largest aircraft regularly using the airport; the FAA identifies regular use as at least 500 operations per year (one landing plus one take-off equals two operations).

A system plan also sets forth estimates of future demand levels and identifies the facility improvements needed for each airport to fulfill its system role. At a system level it is also important to note whether an airport has, or will need, paved runways, precision or nonprecision instrument approaches, runway and taxiway lighting, air traffic control services, passenger terminal facilities, fueling, public parking, and aircraft maintenance facilities, along with any other facilities that are critical to enabling an airport to fill its system role.

NPIAS

As noted in Chapter 3: Airport Management, Operations, and Finance, at the national planning level the FAA maintains the National Plan of Integrated Airport Systems, or NPIAS. Many people in the aviation community point out, however, that the NPIAS is a program, not a plan. Looking at the subject from a slightly different perspective, we can refer to Richard de Neufville, who states that the NPIAS "…is an uncoordinated collection of local wishes."[3] He quotes a former U.S. Secretary of Transportation as saying:

> Because the NPIAS is an aggregation of airport capital projects identified through the local planning process, rather than a spending plan, *no attempt is made to prioritize the projects* that comprise

the database *or to evaluate whether the benefits of specific development projects would exceed the costs.*[4] [italics is de Neufville's]

This statement does not seem to be entirely accurate. The NPIAS is used at the national level to get some idea, or order of magnitude, of what airport development costs might be over the next 10 to 20 years. The FAA uses a priority system for the distribution of airport improvement funds, "with highest priority given to safety, security, reconstruction, standards, and capacity, in that order."[5] This is apparently (at least in theory) used to guide the U.S. Department of Transportation (USDOT) budget that is submitted to Congress. It is not really clear that Congress actually uses this information when they appropriate funds for airports, but at least it sounds nice in theory. In fact, many people seem to feel that the NPIAS is not really a plan in this sense, but rather a program. But I believe it is correct to view the NPIAS as a plan— a plan that supports the FAA's Airport Improvement Program (AIP) as discussed in Chapter 3: Airport Management, Operations, and Finance.

The FAA System Planning AC specifically states, "Most of the data and analysis in the NPIAS is based upon an individual airport's master plans and its capital improvement plans (CIP), state and metropolitan airport system plans, and national forecasts."[6] The AC also notes that the state system plan includes airports that are important to a state's transportation system as well as airports that have a sufficient national interest to be incorporated into the NPIAS, and that one of the functions of a system plan is to identify airports that may meet NPIAS criteria but have not been so identified by the FAA. In other words there may be airports that serve a state or regional air transportation need but not a national air transportation need. The System Planning AC suggests that system planners should obtain a clear understanding of the NPIAS criteria as identified in FAA Order 5090.3C, *Field Formulation of the National Plan of Integrated Airport Systems (NPIAS).*[7] This Order contains a wealth of information related to the NPIAS and is well worth reading.

State Airport System Plans

In a sense a state system plan can be thought of as a mini-NPIAS. At the state level, broad planning is done in the form of airport system plans. The System Planning AC states that, "The primary purpose of airport system planning is to study the performance and interaction of an entire aviation system to understand the interrelationship of the member airports."[8] It further notes that the system plan can be for a metropolitan area, a state, or several bordering states, and that this effort involves examining the interaction of the airports with the aviation user requirement, economy, population, and surface transportation. As stated above, the AC also defines integrated airport system planning pursuant to federal law 49 USC 47102(8) as, "...developing for planning purposes, information, and guidance to decide the extent, kind, location, and timing of airport development needed in a specific area to establish a viable, balanced, and integrated system of public-use airports."[9] The AC also states that, "The overall goal of any airport system planning process is to ensure that the air transportation needs of a state or metropolitan area are adequately served by its system of airports, both now and in the future."[10]

In other words, system planning should address four basic questions:

1. Which airports are needed to meet current and future needs?
2. Why are they important, i.e., what is their system role?
3. How can the continued existence and viability of these airports be ensured?
4. What facility improvements do they need in order to meet their system role?

A statewide airport system plan lays out expected long-term development, i.e., facility improvements, for a selected set of airports identified as the state airport system, over the next 5, 10, and 20 years. Typically these airports are considered as serving an aviation function at a regional or statewide level. A system plan should also identify the role of each airport in the system. An airport's role considers such factors as whether it serves commercial airline traffic or whether it caters exclusively to the general aviation community. If it is exclusively a general aviation airport, the system role should consider whether it serves as a reliever for busy air carrier airports, and whether it primarily serves local business and recreational flying needs or whether it caters more to corporate aircraft. Also important is how the airport functions in terms of the services it provides. For example, many airports serve as gateways to major recreational areas, such as seashore resorts, skiing areas, or golfing centers.

Airport system planning has two potential weaknesses, which can render the plans fairly useless unless they are properly prepared. The first is that system plans imply that a number of airports in a given area function as a system. As de Neufville states, "Airports are integrated into airport systems. Each airport does not operate independently: it is part of one or more networks connecting other airports."[11] He goes on to describe different types of systems, such as geographical (regional, metropolitan, national, international) and functional (low fare, cargo).

Airports in general do indeed function as a system, similar to the telephone system. The telephone system enables you to call anyone you want who also happens to have a telephone. The more telephones there are, the more useful each one is. Airports are similar in that they enable people to fly from Point A to Point B, assuming that both points have an airport. Telephones function as a system insofar as they let people communicate directly, and airport systems function in a similar manner. An airport in Clearfield, Pennsylvania, lets someone fly to another airport in say, Allentown, Pennsylvania, or Salisbury, Maryland, or Boise, Idaho.

However, the role of the airport in Clearfield, Pennsylvania, has very little to do with the role of the airport in Erie, Pennsylvania, or the airport in Hazelton, Pennsylvania, or the role of most of the other airports in Pennsylvania.

At the state level, airports do not necessarily function as a system, in that there is not typically a strong interrelationship between individual airports. System planning makes more sense at the regional level because a region (which is typically smaller and anchored by one or more interrelated metropolitan areas, and may cross state lines) may contain one or more large air carrier airports, and one or more smaller, but well-equipped, general aviation reliever airports. Some areas also have additional general aviation airports that serve local business and recreational flying needs, but are not actually defined as relievers. These airports often don't interact with each other directly, but each airport does have a role in serving the region's air transportation needs.

The second, and potentially more critical, flaw in system planning is that airport system plans are often too broad in scope and too limited in depth to focus accurately on individual airport needs. A sound, valid airport improvement program is normally developed from an airport master plan. It is typically based on a detailed assessment of long-term airport needs, which is, in turn, based on a thorough analysis of airport market potential and traffic growth. It should also include an analysis of facility improvement alternatives and a detailed assessment of environmental considerations. Performing analyses at this level for a state system of 30 or 40 or more airports would take a great deal of time and money.

The AC lists a number of items that are appropriate for inclusion in a system plan study. The list includes such basic items as inventories, forecasts, capacity analyses, facility requirements, land use planning, environmental studies, cost estimates, and funding estimates. These are all valid items for airport planning studies, but system planning typically does not go into the level of detail or analysis normally required for some of these items. For example, in paragraph 409(d) the AC identifies a few of the various airfield and airspace simulation models for use in analyzing system-wide capacity issues. However, paragraph 507(b) notes that airfield capacity analysis is not normally required in system planning, and that airspace capacity is primarily an FAA function. Because of the level of detail of the data required for airfield and airspace capacity studies, these issues are usually far beyond the limited budgets typically available for system planning.

Similarly, environmental studies, land use compatibility analyses, and ground access studies are also data-hungry, and can usually only be covered in a general way in system planning. Detailed financial planning is also beyond the scope of system plans because the costs are typically broad-brush estimates, with the exception of those obtained from individual airport master plans. These broad-brush estimates are, however, sufficient for state and federal agencies to get an order-of-magnitude estimate of long-range airport system funding needs. In some cases it may be possible to obtain a grant under the continuous planning process to study some of these areas in detail, but they are usually covered as part of individual airport master plan studies.

Regional Airport System Plans

It seems to me that airport system planning done at the regional level is much more useful and effective than broader, statewide planning. In general, regions are typically more homogeneous in terms of socioeconomic, functional, and geographic factors than states. Also airports serving a region usually do function as a system and there are observable relationships between and among the various airports in a region that are not apparent at the statewide level. A region, particularly one that is based on a Metropolitan Statistical Area (MSA), includes at least one airport with scheduled air carrier service. If so, they usually have one or more airports that function as relievers for the air carrier airport. In addition, depending upon the region's population size and level of economic activity, they may have airports which accommodate only smaller single-engine or light twin-engine aircraft, as well as airports that cater to larger business aircraft and corporate jets. Some may also specialize by function, e.g., some may provide extensive flight training services while others accommodate aircraft servicing and repair. Establishing a regional system role for these airports can help provide a context or basis for airport master planning at each of the individual airports.

Ideally, regional airport system plans should be done by the planning agency responsible for transportation planning in the regional jurisdiction. In a metropolitan area, where higher air traffic volumes typically occur, system plans would logically be done by the metropolitan planning organization (MPO) or Council of Governments (COG). Note that MPOs were established by the federal government in the 1960s for urbanized areas with a population greater than 50,000. MPOs were specifically created to ensure that expenditures for transportation projects and programs were based on a continuing, cooperative, and comprehensive ("3-C") planning process. Federal funding for local transportation plans and facility improvements are channeled through the MPO planning and project development process. Because MPOs are made up of representatives from local governments and transportation authorities, they can provide effective sponsorship for regional airport system studies.

In other areas a regional planning board, commission, or council may have jurisdiction to plan on a region-wide basis. The System Planning AC states that:

> Airport system planning in areas that include large or medium hub airports (airports that have 0.25 percent or more of annual U.S. enplanements) can be conducted by a metropolitan or regional planning organization when that agency has the interest in and capability to conduct such planning.[12]

In reality, most regional planning agencies do not have staff with sufficient aviation planning expertise; also, they are usually more focused on other transportation modes such as highways and transit.

Some states have developed alternatives to broad-brush statewide system planning which appear to have been very successful. The State of New York, for example, prepares a statewide airport system plan that is a compilation of a number of regional airport system plans. Doing these studies at a regional level makes them more manageable, and allows a more detailed level of analysis and thus a more accurate and more useful plan. I understand that some states also receive federal system planning grants and use the money to prepare a series of mini airport master plans, the results of which are compiled into an airport system plan. I won't give any examples here, in case somebody in the federal bureaucracy considers this a misuse of system planning funds.

In any case, it may be appropriate to think of system plans as a compilation of master plan findings *and* a balancing of those findings to come up with a realistic assessment of area-wide aviation facility needs.

Regional airport system plans can also be prepared for multi-state areas, such as the plan completed in 2006 for the New England region. This study was sponsored by the New England Airport Coalition, a group of eleven airports with scheduled passenger service in the region. It was driven by capacity constraints at Boston Logan International Airport, the region's primary air carrier airport. The study focused on various alternative means for providing scheduled air services throughout the New England region. It provides an excellent example of how to look at an issue in a large-area context. The study provides

> …the foundations of a regional strategy for the air carrier airport system to support the needs of air passengers through 2020. Its underlying theme is to develop an airport system based upon the location of passengers and with adequate facilities to allow airlines to evolve the range of services that provide the best mix of efficiency, convenience, and reliability.[13]

Continuous Planning and Special Studies

The FAA's system planning program also provides for special studies that are relevant to an airport system analysis and that can be accomplished effectively within a statewide or regional system planning framework. According to the System Planning AC, special studies

> …may include, but are not limited to, air service, air cargo operations, standards reviews, safety area analyses, business jets access, satellite navigation and GPS, environmental or drainage inventories, surface access, economic impact, obstruction analysis or photogrammetry, general aviation security, multi-site acoustic aircraft counters, and pavement management.[14]

The FAA also notes that airport system planning may be appropriate under special circumstances or in unique situations. For example, when

> …airport sponsors do not…have the authority to study new airports as a means to supplement or replace capacity-constrained airports. They may have little interest in carrying out a study of a

new airport that they will not control, or even may consider as a potential competitor. However, special studies conducted as part of an airport system plan may be used in concert with master plans to evaluate airfield capacity alternatives for a metropolitan area. In these cases, the system plan can be used to examine the feasibility of building a new airport. In addition, system plans can be used to study transportation alternatives not within the jurisdiction of the airport sponsor, such as rail alternatives.

These special studies, as well as system plan updates, may be conducted as a continuous airport planning process. System plan study sponsors should develop a program for the continuing update of their airport system plans in light of changing conditions in the state or region. For example, the continuous planning process may be used to do periodic survey updates; do surveys or assessments of airport usage patterns, pavement conditions, and obstructions or potential hazards to air navigation; and account for changes in economic conditions such as new manufacturing facilities (or the loss thereof) or shifts in population patterns. Changing conditions should be monitored to ensure that the system plan remains valid and to determine whether plan updates are necessary.

The System Planning Process

AC 150/5070-7 sets forth the steps that should be followed in the system planning process at both the statewide and regional airport levels. The AC follows an overall planning process that is generally similar to the "inventory, forecast, plan, and test" process that is often taught in planning schools, and that is usually followed in preparing any plan, whether for airports or any other transportation facility. The steps in the airport system planning process noted by the FAA are:

1. Exploration of issues that impact aviation in the study area
2. Inventory of the current system
3. Identification of air transportation needs
4. Forecast of system demand
5. Consideration of alternative airport systems
6. Definition of airport roles and policy strategies
7. Recommendation of system changes, funding strategies, and airport development
8. Preparation of an implementation plan[15]

The System Planning AC does not describe exactly what is involved in each of these steps. To provide substance, some attention must be given to Chapter 5 of the AC, which describes the elements of an airport system plan report. These include:

Chapter 6 – System Planning

- Executive Summary
- Study Design
- State, Regional, and Local Airport Issues
- Activity Forecasts
- System Goals and Performance Measures
- Inventory of System Condition and Performance
- System Requirements
- Environmental Considerations
- Alternatives Analysis
- Public Consultation
- Intermodal Integration and Airport Access
- Identification of System of Airports
- Development Priorities and Justification
- Policy and Investigation Recommendations
- Recommended NPIAS Changes[16]

This list of contents can be used to guide the study process. Unfortunately the AC presents these as a sort of flow chart and seems to imply that the process is linear. As stated in Chapter 5: Master Planning, planning is not really a linear process—a number of these steps can be ongoing at the same time.

Because the AC system planning process outlined in Steps 1 through 8 is incomplete as noted above, I have added and adjusted a couple of steps. I have also added a description of what is included in each of the steps. The steps and descriptions shown below incorporate the system planning elements bulleted above.

A. Pre-Planning
B. Issues Identification
C. Study Design
D. System Inventory
E. System Goals and Performance Measures
F. System Demand Forecasts
G. Definition of Airport Roles
H. System Needs Identification
I. Alternative Systems Development
J. System Priorities
K. Recommended System Plan
L. Implementation Plan
M. Executive Summary

Step A: Pre-Planning

The airport system planning process should begin with some Pre-Planning activities, including the identification of study participants, selection of a consultant, and identification of issues. At the outset an agency desiring to sponsor and prepare an airport system plan should develop a list of key airport system stakeholders, i.e., agencies and individuals who have an interest in and/or are directly involved in the operation and use of the state or regional airport system. For a regional system plan this list would include the owners or operators of each airport in the region; major airport users or user groups; major businesses; local and regional planning, zoning, and economic development agencies; and the local FAA Airports District Office (ADO). A similar list could be developed for a state airport system plan, except rather than including all airports or all airport users or businesses in the state, it is advisable to include representatives from each type of group to reduce the list of study participants to a manageable size. A group of 10 to 15 individuals can usually adequately represent the various types of aviation system stakeholders and still be small enough to form a workable group that can be directly involved in the ongoing system planning study. This group could be thought of as a steering committee to guide the study effort and review draft reports and conclusions. A larger group of aviation system stakeholders could be established for more general and occasional coordination.

Early on in the system planning process the sponsoring agency should select a consulting firm to perform most of the system planning tasks, although consultant services can be supplemented with the sponsor's staff if they have sufficient expertise. The System Planning AC does not contain much in the way of useful information for selecting consultants; however, AC 150/5070-6B, *Airport Master Plans,* and AC 150/5100-14, *Architectural, Engineering, and Planning Consultant Services for Airport Grant Projects,* provide detailed information that is applicable to system planning. Consultant solicitation for airport system planning is generally similarly to that for master planning, discussed in Chapter 5. The consultant selected for a system planning study should have some airport system planning experience, either at the state or the regional level, although this is not always necessary. But the firm (or team of firms) should be able to demonstrate their understanding and have a working knowledge of FAA system planning requirements, aviation and airport development issues, and land use planning and zoning. It would also be a good idea to have a firm that has a good understanding of economic development issues, particularly at the local level, as well as a demonstrated understanding of the economic relationships between airports and the communities they serve.

Step B: Issues Identification

Once a working group of aviation system stakeholders has been established and a consultant has been selected, it is time to identify the issues that are affecting the operation and development of airports in the state or region under study. A good way to identify issues is to interview the owner or operator of each airport in the study area; however, this can be a time-consuming and expensive effort, and is usually not practical at the state system planning level. In this case the stakeholders should be able to provide a fairly comprehensive list of issues to be addressed in the study. Issues affecting the state or regional aviation system include such direct airport-related items as airport ownership, availability of land for expansion, degree of control of potential obstructions to air navigation, funding for capital improvements, airport revenues, airport function or role, and availability of scheduled air service. Other issues not directly under the control of the airport operator or the FAA include land use and zoning compatibility, environmental constraints, airspace considerations, and the degree to which the airport is accepted by the community. Community acceptance has two components: the first is whether the operation and development of the airport is accepted or opposed by the community living around the airport; the second is the degree to which the airport is viewed by local governing, funding, and planning and zoning agencies as an asset.

Step C: Study Design

The System Planning AC states, "The first element of a complex airport system planning effort should be a study design."[17] It also notes that the study design should be a comprehensive outline of what data will be collected, the methodologies to be used, and the output that is required. The AC states that the study design should "...include a detailed description of how, what, and when each element of the report will be completed."[18] I agree with the overall content of the AC's study design recommendations, but I don't agree that study design is the first element. In fact, the AC includes study design as an "element of an airport system plan report" but, although study design is a step in the system planning process, it is not included in a system plan report.

I recommend study design as the third step in the system planning process, because I don't think an accurate and useful study design can be prepared until the system plan goals and objectives and major issues have been identified, as noted in Steps A and B. The consultant and key stakeholders must prepare the study design in light of the issues that need to be addressed. The study design will guide the direction and the process to be followed by the consultant and other participants through the course of the study. Therefore it must set forth the goals and objectives for the study, i.e., it must state specifically what the final study products will be. The study design must also identify the data to be collected, along with the sources of the data, and the methodologies to be used for study analyses. Some of the topics that are typically considered and addressed in the study design phase include:

- Goals and Objectives
- Data Availability
- Forecast Horizons
- Environmental Considerations
- Schedules

- Deliverables
- Coordination and Public Involvement Program
- Budget

This list should also include a determination that should be made of which aviation facilities are to be included. For example, will the study deal only with airports, *per se*, or will it also cover heliports and/or seaplane bases? It should also determine the extent to which ground transportation and intermodal issues will be addressed. Some thought must also be given to how far the study will go in dealing with environmental, airspace, and land use compatibility issues, since they can be somewhat open-ended. Exploring these items in too much depth can result in gathering a lot of data that are not really needed at the system plan level, or in trying to address issues that are not appropriately dealt with in an aviation system plan. For example, a regional system plan being prepared for a metropolitan area that is experiencing high traffic volumes and airspace congestion should probably include some airspace modeling that would not normally be needed at the statewide planning level. Consultation with the local FAA ADO will be invaluable at this point. Careful consideration should be given to all of these items since they are all critical to determining the schedule and cost of the study.

A key item often overlooked in the early phases of a planning study is the availability of needed data. The study design should investigate the sources, completeness, accuracy, and availability of all the data that will be needed throughout the study. Especially important are data describing current and historical aircraft operations activity, population, and income, which will be used in preparing the forecasts, as well as financial data for each airport. The cost and time that will be needed to collect and examine the data for completeness should be reflected in the study schedule and cost. The consultant should put all this information together in the form of a work scope or scope of services, along with a schedule, including key milestones, deliverables, and cost.

It is also a very good idea to get the local ADO involved at this point, both for their technical expertise and because the study sponsor will be asking them for a grant to do the study. When FAA staff are involved in the development of the study design, they will have a thorough understanding of what work is intended to be done and how it will be accomplished. After the study design and associated cost are prepared the study sponsor must complete the necessary paperwork to obtain an FAA planning grant under the AIP. FAA Order 5100.38 provides guidance on the grant application process, and also identifies which elements or tasks in the planning process are eligible for federal aid. The local ADO should be consulted to ensure that the study scope and grant application can be approved in a timely manner.

Chapter 6 – System Planning

Step D: System Inventory

The System Inventory is usually the first major task in the study process. AC 150/5070-7 contains the following list of items typically considered in the inventory phase of a system planning study:

1. Airport physical characteristics
2. Airport activity levels
3. Environmental and land use considerations and applicable laws
4. Navigational aids
5. Local socioeconomic data
6. Airport financial data
7. Historical weather data
8. Surface transportation characteristics
9. Terminal airspace and airfield capacity

The inventory task should begin with identifying the airports that will be included in the study, regardless of whether they are privately or publicly owned, and regardless of whether they are open to the public or not. All airports in an area serve some aviation function and should be considered in the initial phases of a system planning study. For each airport in the study area, the inventory should note who owns the airport and whether or not it is open for public use. The obvious physical characteristics of each airport should also be inventoried. The most important of these are the number, configuration/location, and condition of runways, taxiways, aircraft parking and tie-down areas (both paved and unpaved), hangars, terminals, access roads, and public parking areas, as well as numbers and types of based aircraft and a count of aircraft operational activity. It is also especially important to note whether the airport facilities meet the design standards set forth in AC 150/5300-13 and the obstruction clearance requirements of FAR Part 77.

The next task is a review of the master plans prepared for each of the airports included in the system study. Master plans typically contain more detail than is needed at the system planning level, but it does save time and money to use existing data to the extent possible. Make sure however, that the master plan has been prepared recently and that the inventory data are still valid. A visit to the airport in question and/or an interview with the airport manager will usually determine if the master plan data are usable. Facility inventories for airport system plans typically don't have to include as much detail as for more detailed master plans and other facility planning efforts as described in Chapter 5. Bear in mind that system plans have a broad-brush or big-picture orientation, so it doesn't make much sense to visit individual airports and measure building square footages or count the exact number of spaces in the public parking areas. Also, the level of detail varies with the area included in the study; a regional system plan will typically require a more detailed inventory than a statewide system plan. The level of detail needed should be specified in the study design phase. Do not waste time and money by collecting information that is not needed for the study.

Obtaining accurate current and historical data on aircraft operational activity is difficult in system planning studies. Most of the airports included in the study will not have air traffic control towers—the operations count is usually the airport manager's guess. Some airport managers have a pretty good feel for this but others may tend to pad the count a little to make their airport seem busier than it really is. Various means are used to determine the number of aircraft operations at airports without air traffic control towers, including visual observations, pneumatic tubes and inductance loops (similar to the devices used to collect highway traffic volume data), and acoustical counters.

If the airport manager is going to be the source of the operations data, it is not a good idea to ask for an annual operations count. Who really knows the difference between 30,000 and 60,000 annual operations? Big numbers like that don't usually mean much to people. Ask the manager instead how many take-offs and landings the airport accommodates on a daily basis, preferably on a typical summer day and a typical winter day. Then the appropriate math can be done to come up with a number that may be a little more accurate than a big number that just pops out of the airport manager's head. Whatever the data source, it is a good idea to spend some time at the airport just to see what comes and goes during a given time period. This also gives planners an opportunity to talk with some of the local airport patrons to get their feel for how busy the airport is, what kinds of activities take place there, and what problems or issues they may be encountering.

At smaller airports the number of based aircraft can be a better indicator of overall "airport capacity" than the number of aircraft operations. The number of based aircraft determines how much area is needed for aircraft parking and hangar facilities—often a critical factor at small, space-constrained airports.

The number of transient aircraft is also an important factor in determining space requirements. The number of transient aircraft using an airport is a function of a number of factors, including the level of business activity that takes place in a community and the extent to which they use, or are served by, general aviation aircraft; the availability of specialized flight training services; and the extent of specialized FBO services. Even a good restaurant can attract visiting aircraft. An accurate and useful inventory of transient aircraft can be difficult at times. One method is to use an average, based on the airport manager's records and observations, supplemented by information provided by the FBO. However, an average number may not tell the full story, particularly at airports serving areas that have a lot of general aviation traffic associated with special events. For example, an airport serving a community that is home to a university with a high profile football or basketball team is likely to see a very high demand for transient aircraft parking and servicing during home games. These types of demand should not be ignored because they can be a highly significant source of revenue for the airport.

The system inventory should also pay close attention to environmental factors and features, as well as land use considerations. These are important because they could constrain future airport growth and development. Similar attention should be given to whatever laws, regulations, and other requirements control the environment within which the airports must operate. Again, the necessary level of detail should be considered. For a statewide or regional system plan it is not generally necessary to go out and inventory wetlands, forest stands, and streams; it is usually sufficient to know if such constraints exist and, if they do, if they are located such that they could constrain airport development. Most system plans do not deal with air and water quality issues unless there are indications that these are serious local issues.

Airspace and navigation aids should also be inventoried to the level of detail appropriate for the system study. For a statewide system plan airspace considerations generally do not play an important role, except in metropolitan areas, especially if the study will be addressing the need for general aviation reliever airports. Airspace capacity is usually of more interest in regional system studies; if airspace is seen to be a potential constraint it may be appropriate to involve FAA Air Traffic and Airway Facilities. Airway Facilities should also be involved if the system study will be addressing the need for new or improved navigation and landing aids.

All planning studies include an element devoted to an inventory of socio-economic data, but these data are rarely put to much use beyond aviation demand forecasts. Even then the data are sometimes there more to skew results to support preconceived ideas or generate desired forecast values. In other words, an analyst can examine some data items such as per capita income, total income, and disposable income, and select the value that produces the desired answer. And after all, they are all income measures and no one is likely to complain if income is used as an independent variable in forecasting aviation demand. Although it is not a professional thing to do, it is done much too often. Thus it is important to make sure that the socioeconomic data selected for use in the study actually say something about the study area, and if the data are used in forecasting, the intuitive relationship between any of the data and the propensity for air travel should be clearly explained.

The socioeconomic data typically regarded as relevant are population and income, which are often used (and misused) in aviation demand forecasting, as discussed in Chapter 7: Forecasting. Often the actual data values are not as important as historical and expected trends, particularly in population, income, and employment. Other socioeconomic factors relevant to aviation system development are measures of business and industrial growth, or other locally-important factors such as tourism and the development of recreation areas. The inventory phase is a good time to sit down with the state, regional, and/or local economic development agencies to see where they expect or would like economic growth to occur, and to find out what economic development plans and programs they have in place or are trying to implement.

Another key item to be included in the inventory phase is the ground access system serving each airport. It is not only important to note the key highway routes and conditions, but also whether the access roadway systems include directional signs telling people how to get to the airport. Based on my experience as a frequent airport visitor, most of our nation's airports are not clearly marked and not easily located. When driving I have found aeronautical charts to be as useful as highway maps when trying to find an airport, because the aeronautical charts show prominent landmarks such as bodies of water and hills, as well as man-made structures such as towers. These can help determine the location of a small airport pretty effectively. Highway signs to airports in rural areas are especially scarce, and those that exist are usually bullet-riddled. I know of one state highway director who refused to put airport signs along a state highway unless the airport received scheduled air service. In fact he didn't even know that the state had an official "airport system," believe it or not.

Airport financial data should also be included in the inventory, commensurate with the level of detail of the study. It is particularly important to know what kinds of funding sources are available for airport capital improvements, including federal, state, and local agencies and programs. Historical information should be collected on the number and amounts of federal and state airport improvement grants that have been awarded. Sometimes it may be useful to collect similar information for surrounding states or regions, in case a "fair share" argument may be raised. I have mixed feelings about collecting more information than that noted above at the system plan level. I am not sure that it is necessary to collect information on operating revenues for each airport in the system. An exception might be made in a case where the study wants to take a close look at how some airports seem to be more financially sound than others. In that case the work scope for the study should include an element for the documentation of the various revenue streams, if they are to be used as an example for other airports to follow.

Step E: System Goals and Performance Measures
According to the System Planning AC, System Goals and Performance Measures should be established at the outset of the planning process. The intent is to give state and local agencies and the FAA information that they can use in determining annual airport development needs. Ideally the system plan sponsor should be able to use these measures to ensure the implementation of a successful aviation system that meets user and community needs. Goals, objectives, and performance measures were discussed in detail in Chapter 4: Strategic Planning. The following summary gives some examples of how goals and performance measures fit into the system planning process.

Specific goals for a system plan report will depend on the characteristics of the study area and the functions or roles of the airports that serve that area. System planning goals are usually very broad because they are generally intended to apply to the entire study area. For example, a system goal might be to ensure that all population centers of 10,000 persons or more are within a 30-minute drive of a full-service airport, i.e., an airport that is open to the public and equipped to handle all-weather day/night aircraft operations. I have also seen system plans that stated that each county should have at least one such full-service airport. Some system plans set out a list of minimum facility requirements for each airport included in the state or regional system. For example, the plan may state that the system goal is for each system airport to have a minimum 5,000-foot paved, lighted runway, with a full parallel taxiway, and a nonprecision instrument approach, at minimum. Other facility standards might include a paved access road and public parking area, full-perimeter security fencing, paved aircraft parking and tie-down areas, a public restroom, etc.

A valuable goal is to state that all system airports shall meet FAA airport design standards as set forth in AC 150/5300-13, *Airport Design*, and shall comply with the obstruction standards set forth in FAR Part 77. In any event the goals set up for the system plan study should be thoroughly considered in terms of their usefulness and the feasibility of implementation. There is no sense in proposing a goal that won't be supported by the aviation community or that can't otherwise be met. The system analysis can be a useful tool in determining the feasibility of achieving goals.

The FAA also recommends developing performance measures that are tied to the system goals. In essence the performance measures are supposed to demonstrate whether or not the goals are being achieved. Properly used, the performance measures can help identify *why* any of the system goals are *not* being achieved. A simple example of a performance measure might be one that measures annually how many of the system airports meet the goals identified for the system.

To be successful, part of the system performance phase should also note the agency (or agencies) responsible for meeting each of the goals. This could be the airport operator, or the state, or the operator and the state working together—each entity could be responsible for individual components of achieving a goal.

Some goals, such as those related to land use compatibility, zoning, highway access, etc., may involve an "outside" agency such as local planning and zoning authorities, and highway or transportation departments. Therefore it is essential to involve these agencies as the goals are being developed to help ensure that they can be implemented in a timely manner.

Step F: System Demand Forecasts
The System Planning AC states that aviation Demand Forecasts define an airport's system role, help prioritize airport development, and determine air-

port reference codes (ARC). Aviation demand forecasting and the relevant FAA documents are discussed in detail in Chapter 7: Forecasting. This section summarizes some of the more significant aspects of forecasting at the airport system level.

To begin with I take exception to the commonly-held belief that aviation demand forecasts define the ARC for an airport. This may give the mistaken impression that the ARC is a function of the volume of aviation demand. As noted in Chapter 2: Airports, the ARC relates airport design criteria to the operational and physical characteristics of the aircraft expected to be operating at the airport. This is usually referred to as the *design aircraft*—the largest or most demanding aircraft expected to use the airport on a regular basis, regular being defined as 500 or more operations a year.

I also take exception to the notion that the demand forecasts define an airport's system role. The system role is in essence the *function* of the airport, and it is only partly related to the volume of aviation demand. For example, an airport's system role may be that of a general aviation reliever for a nearby air carrier airport. It may have a lower volume of activity than an airport located at a more remote location in the study area that does not have a reliever designation, but that does not make its role less significant. Conversely, an airport located outside a busy metropolitan area but which has a relatively high volume of aviation activity might be one that accommodates a high volume of flight training activity, or one that provides specialized aircraft or avionics installation or repair services—important activities but less vital to the overall airport system. In short, the airport role should be determined more by what the airport does than how busy it is.

System plan forecasts should include the number of annual and peak-hour aircraft operations, and whether the operations are local or itinerant. Local operations are those in which the aircraft takes off and lands at the same airport and the flight takes place within the local airport area, i.e., within three miles of the airport. It is also a good idea to identify the number or percent of operations that are "touch-and-go," i.e., flight training or practice operations where the aircraft makes an approach and touches down but does not make a full-stop landing. It is often important to know the volume of touch-and-go operations at airports that have capacity constraints, in that prohibition of touch-and-go operations, particularly during peak periods, is often suggested as a method of providing capacity relief.

Aviation demand forecasts should also include the number and type of based aircraft (sometimes called the fleet mix). The categories typically used are single-engine piston, multi-engine, turboprop/turbojet, and helicopter or rotorcraft. An estimate of glider and ultralight aircraft activity may also be important at some airports. The critical or design aircraft should also be identified through the forecast period. The critical aircraft is a key factor in airport design, as noted above. These components are usually sufficient for smaller airports in the system, but for larger airports forecasts should include separate projections for air carrier, commuter, general aviation, and military operations. At airports with scheduled air service, forecasts should also be provided for enplaned passengers and air cargo tonnage.

Forecasting aviation demand at the system level is a little tricky because if the forecast demand is for the study area as a whole, the problem then becomes one of assigning that demand to individual airports. On the other hand, a forecast done separately for each airport will usually be based, at least in part, on the historical volume of activity at that airport, and the forecast may not reflect a change in the system role of the airport. For example, the system may include a small general aviation airport that is designated to be improved significantly and become a reliever airport for a nearby air carrier facility. Also, the historical data for general aviation airports are usually not entirely complete or consistent and may therefore be inaccurate. The appropriate forecasting approach for each system plan should be based on the area under study, the study goals, the kinds and quality of information available, and other factors that may vary from state to state or region to region. Whatever approach is selected to forecast aviation demand, the methodology and underlying assumptions should be logical and clearly explained. This will help in obtaining FAA approval of the forecasts.

As noted above, demand forecasting for the general aviation component of system plans is made more difficult by the lack of accurate and consistent historical data on the volume of aircraft operations or number of aircraft based at any given airport. If planners do not have a good idea of what is going on today, they are going to have a hard time figuring out what will happen tomorrow. A good place to start is with a review of the forecasts for airports that have master plans. Their usefulness depends on when the master plan forecasts were prepared and the methodology used to prepare them. Another source for individual airport forecasts is the FAA's Terminal Area Forecast (TAF), discussed in more detail in Chapter 7: Forecasting. Unfortunately the TAF projections for small general aviation airports are usually flat line extensions of the base year activity volume; thus, they don't provide much insight into the growth potential. However, the FAA forecast approval requirement states that the forecasts must be within 10 percent of the TAF projection five years into the future, and within 15 percent 10 years into the future, as discussed in Chapter 5: Master Planning. Thus if an airport currently handles 60,000 aircraft operations a year and the TAF shows that number remaining constant through the forecast period, the 10 and 15 percent allowances still provide for an increase to 66,000 and 69,000 for the next 5 and 10 years respectively. For most general aviation airports at this activity level, that increase is probably adequate for planning purposes. But if the forecast developed for the master plan study shows a 5- or 10-year increase greater than the FAA allowance, the forecasts will have to be sent to the FAA for approval, as discussed in Chapter 5. The FAA has two publications that provide guidance in the preparation and approval of aviation demand forecasts. The first is a report entitled *Forecasting Aviation Activity by Airport*,[19] and the second is a memorandum entitled *Revision to Guidance on Review and Approval of Aviation Forecasts*.[20] The System Planning AC also states:

For general aviation and reliever airports where the five-year forecast is less than 100,000 total annual aircraft operations or 100 based aircraft, the forecast does not need FAA Headquarters review, and the data should be provided for use in the annual update of the TAF. APO-110 may require additional information if the forecast varies significantly from historical trends without adequate justification.[21]

Step G: Definition of Airport Roles

The AC lists the Definition of Airport Roles as a step in the system planning process, but combines it with policy strategies and places it *after* the needs identification and the forecasts. I think it is more accurate to define the role of each airport *before* the forecasts and needs identification. And unfortunately the AC doesn't contain much in the way of guidance or discussion of airport roles. It seems to me that the definition of an airport's role is often confused with its classification. As noted in Chapter 3: Airport Management, Operations, and Finance, the FAA classifies airports as primary commercial service, non-primary commercial service, reliever, or general aviation. Most state system plans I have seen also contain a similar classification for airports in the state. I know of at least one state system plan that includes three airport classification systems: the one used by the FAA, the one used by that state, and one developed especially for that system plan. But try as I might, I could not find any indication of how these classification systems were actually used in the study, aside from a designation placed beside each airport name. It seems entirely reasonable to have an airport classification system, and since the FAA's general aviation category probably covers about 90 percent of the airports in any state system plan, and in any state airport system for that matter, I can see where states would find it useful to have their own classification system that is a further refinement of the FAA's broad categories. The System Planning AC equates the FAA airport categories with airport roles. However, an airport's role in the state or regional transportation should be more than a category. It should reflect the *relationship* between the airport and the community, i.e., the airport's role should indicate what the airport does for the community and how important it is to the community. Virtually all of the FAA planning guidance I have seen and all the planning books I have read indicate that an airport's facility needs depend upon the number and type of aircraft it is expected to accommodate. Operational activity is a very important factor in the determination of facility needs, but it seems to me that the airport's role is an important factor also.

For example, say Airport A is located near a large metropolitan area and is projected to have a relatively high number of aircraft operations—100,000 to 150,000 a year. This airport is designated as a general aviation reliever and serves as a base for a couple of flight schools, so most of the operations are local and the number of transient aircraft using the airport for business or industrial flying is relatively small. There are several airports serving the metropolitan area, including one that accommodates scheduled air carrier activity. The air carrier airport has fully-instrumented, paved, lighted runways, and provides other support services such as food and beverage concessions, rental cars, and taxis. Businesses and corporations located in the area are more likely to base their aircraft at the well-equipped air carrier airport, and people flying into the area on business are also more likely to use that airport. The air carrier airport is also more likely to be used for air cargo and emergency medical flights. In this case the air carrier airport is the metropolitan area's key access to the national air transportation system. So although Airport A serves as a reliever for the air carrier facility, its primary customer base is the discretionary pilot flying for training or recreation, and most of the flight activity is likely to be in the daytime during good weather. Thus, although it may have a need for new or improved taxiways, or hangars and office buildings, it would not be expected to have a serious need for a precision instrument approach or a terminal building. The airport's role is a very important factor in determining facility improvement needs.

Now consider Airport B, which serves a small community in a more remote part of the state. It is only projected to accommodate 50,000 to 60,000 operations a year and does not have scheduled air carrier service. However, this airport is the only one within an hour's drive of the community and thus provides the only convenient access to the national air transportation system. It handles the community's business flying as well as recreational flying needs, and is the key access point for emergency medical services and high-priority parts and equipment delivery. Even though it has a much lower volume of aircraft operations, Airport B would seem to have a higher priority for an instrument landing system, a terminal building, and service facilities for transient aircraft than Airport A.

Note that in reality, because Airport A is designated by the FAA as a reliever, it has a better chance of securing federal airport improvement funds than does Airport B.

Step H: System Needs Identification

The System Needs Identification is a simple process of comparing capacity to demand. The inventory step says, "This is what we have to work with." The forecast step says, "This is what we are going to have to accommodate in the future." The needs identification says, "This is where we come up short." The needed airport facility improvements identified in the system planning process indicate the type, timing, and cost of airport development projects through the planning period. This is the information that typically goes into a Capital Improvement Program (CIP). Each airport has a CIP, as does each state. The System Planning AC states that a system plan

> ...provides a mechanism to assist in the preparation of an airport CIP for the facilities included in the plan, incorporating the objectives of the state and concentrating on funding priorities that are consistent with its aviation goals and policies. The state should rely, when possible, on the development and schedules recommended in individual airport master plans, because they are more detailed than those prepared in a system planning process.[22]

At this point one may wonder why anyone would bother to do a system plan, if the needs identification relies on information already available in individual airport master plans. But reading on in the AC it also notes:

> The state can evaluate an individual airport CIP and put those development items into the system plan that are consistent with its definition of airport roles, address identified aviation needs, and support realistic funding scenarios. In cases where no airport master plan exists or the plan is outdated, the state should develop airport capital improvement requirements for the facility using current planning methodologies and standards....[23]

The two quotes above make three key points: 1) the system plan's needs identification should use the facility requirements developed and contained in existing airport master plans, provided that the master plans are up-to-date, 2) system planning time and money should not be spent on identifying needs that are already available in airport master plan studies, unless some airports do not have useful master plans, and 3) the system plan's major role is not one of identifying system needs, but rather one of assembling individual airport needs into an aggregate set and developing a set of funding priorities (this aspect is discussed further below, in the System Priorities step).

As an example of the first and second points above, the System Planning AC indicates that a full-blown airfield capacity analysis is not normally required in system planning. Most of the airports in the system will be smaller general aviation facilities that typically do not have airside capacity problems. AC 150/5060-5, *Airport Capacity and Delay*, provides some fairly simple guidance for calculating airport capacity in terms of annual service volumes. Busier airports such as relievers that may have a capacity problem usually require a separate airport capacity study as part of the airport master planning process. Similarly, most of the airports in the state or regional airport system will not experience terminal crowding or capacity issues with access roadways or terminal curb space. For most airports the system plan recommendations might note such items as: the terminal building should be renovated and/or expanded to provide additional administration space or additional office space for a tenant, or the public parking area should be paved and the access road resurfaced. With small general aviation airports recommendations might include adding hangars or paving tie-down areas. In some cases it may be appropriate to recommend the removal of obstructions that would prohibit construction of a full parallel taxiway, to avoid having aircraft taxiing on the runway. These, however, are safety issues and are generally not related to the volume of activity taking place at the airport.

In fact, most of the airport improvements recommended in the system plan will involve improving the airport facilities to meet the airport design standards set forth in AC 150/5300-13 and the obstruction clearances set forth in FAR Part 77. The major exception would be in the case where an airport is recommended to be upgraded to fill a new role in the state or regional airport system. In this case more specific attention will have to be given to the needs identification, and some capacity studies may also be required.

Along with the identification of system needs or facility improvements, the system plan should also include an estimate of the cost of each of those improvements. Again, costs are best obtained from individual airport master plans, but if it becomes necessary to develop separate costs, general estimates will usually suffice at the system level. Costs should be presented in real dollar (present day) terms, as discussed in Chapter 5: Master Planning. Most state and regional transportation planning and programming agencies have their own cost inflators that they use in their CIPs. Bear in mind that most CIPs are only five- or six-year programs, so long-term projects won't even make it into the program for a while.

Step I: Alternative Systems Development

Once the system needs have been identified, the next step in the planning process is to develop alternative plans to meet those needs. Alternatives may include constructing new airports, expanding existing airports, or transferring some activity to another airport that has sufficient capacity. The AC also recommends a "do nothing" alternative. This option serves as a baseline for comparing alternatives and shows the consequences associated with not undertaking needed airport facility improvements. For example, the system plan might recommend the expansion of an airport to serve as a reliever for a nearby air carrier facility. This strategy will offer obvious benefits in terms of additional capacity and associated delay reduction, but it will also incur costs and probably some adverse environmental impacts. This alternative could then be compared with the "do nothing" alternative, which would show relative benefits in terms of cost and environmental impacts, but would indicate excessive operational delays and their associated costs.

In reality, many system planning studies do not seem to contain much in the way of alternatives. Airports are where they are and do what they do; the chances of building a new airport anywhere in the continental United States in this day and age are usually rather slim. Also, it is not likely to think that anyone at the state level will say that a certain type of activity should no longer take place at one of the existing airports and should instead be transferred to another existing airport. Most airports today operate—or at least try to operate—as businesses, and the government is not likely to meet with much success if it tries to interfere with someone's legitimate livelihood. Also, government intervention that is not safety-related could be construed as favoring one airport over another competing airport. The System Planning AC states that alternative plans should be developed, but doesn't really explain why or how. The AC suggests the following criteria to compare alternatives, but does not explain what they mean, how they should be measured or considered, or how they should be applied.[24] My interpretations of what these encompass are shown in parentheses.

- *Capital costs* (How much does the project cost?)
- *Aviation safety* (Does the project result in a safe aircraft operating environment?)
- *Airspace utilization* (Are aircraft operations in and out of an airport compatible with operations at other nearby airports, or will they cause airspace congestion that results in delays?)
- *Ability to address need* (Does the project satisfy a need and, if so, is it the best way to satisfy the need?)
- *Environmental impacts* (Does the project result in adverse environmental impacts and, if so, can they be minimized and/or mitigated?)
- *Delay and other operational costs* (Will this project reduce aircraft operating delay or other aircraft or airport operational costs?)
- *Consistency with local area comprehensive and transportation plans* (Is the project consistent with other plans, or does it result in a conflict?)
- *Land use availability and compatibility* (Is sufficient land available to accommodate the improvement, and is the proposed facility compatible with adjoining uses?)

These are important questions to ask in any facility planning study, but system plans do not usually contain enough detail or go into the required depth to come up with accurate and reliable answers. These are definitely the kinds of things that should be considered in airport planning and these and similar factors are discussed in detail in the previous chapter on master planning. However, they don't seem as though they would be very effective in comparing system alternatives.

One approach to system alternatives (or perhaps more correctly stated, getting around the issue of system alternatives) that makes some sense to me is to develop a system plan that is tiered, rather than to spend time trying to develop alternative systems. In this approach the "first tier" set of airports might consist of those that have scheduled air service, reliever airports, and airports that are identified as providing smaller cities with a link to the national air transportation system. This tier could be considered "essential" airports. If one of these airports were to close it would have a significant effect, especially an economic effect, on the community (or communities) the airport serves. These are the airports that the system could not do without because there is no replacement in that particular area.

The "second tier" of airports would consist of those that supplement the airports in the first tier. These might include busy general aviation airports that serve some community need, but are not the primary airport serving a given area, as well as airports that have some specialized function or offer some specialized service. Airports in this tier could be considered "important," meaning that they should be preserved and supported, but if one of them were to disappear, the services provided by that airport could be accommodated at another airport serving the same area. An example would be an airport that caters primarily to flight training, or that is the base for a firm that performs some sort of specialized aircraft or avionics repairs.

The "third tier" would then consist of all the other public-use airports in the state or region. These airports could be considered the "nice to haves" in that they serve an aviation function, but if they go away, another airport is readily available in the area that can accommodate the activities that would be displaced. This does not mean, however, that these airports should not be supported. They do serve an aviation function, and if several of them go out of business it is likely to have a serious impact on the airport system and access to the air transportation system.

A tiered approach can be very effective because it is based to a great extent on an airport's function. An airport's tiered ranking provides some justification for designating financial assistance, because the plan can state that, "We need to put some money into this airport because it does this, or because it serves that, and if the airport is not expanded or improved, or if it closes, we will have a hard time finding another airport to do this or that." Activity levels should of course also be considered—based aircraft and aircraft operations are always handy measures—but activity level alone does not tell the whole story. Airport function should be reflected in system development.

Step J: System Priorities

One problem with systems-level alternatives is that such an approach can imply that some airports may not be very important. In one way or another *all* airports are important, because they *all* serve an air transportation need, whether they are open to the public or for private use only. So it may help to take a step back and look at the bigger picture.

An airport system plan should provide information to state and local governments that will help them identify airport needs relative to other transportation needs. A system plan can help all agencies concerned with airports and their operation and use to have a voice in addressing airport issues. And, if done properly, a system plan can ensure that everybody's efforts are coordinated and generally compatible. Above all, the system plan should let policy- and decision-makers know *why* an airport is important, *why* public funds should be invested in the airport, and *what would happen* if the airport were not improved, or were allowed to disappear. Therefore some sort of priority designation should be developed as part of the system plan and its associated facility improvement recommendations and cost estimates. For a system plan to be of any value, it should contain a relative ranking of each airport's planned improvements compared with the same information for all other airports. With this information state and federal authorities can estimate how much money will be needed over time to make needed airport improvements. In theory they can also use the system plan to prioritize funding.

Unfortunately, it has been my experience that priority systems usually do not work or are misapplied. Quite often it is because the priority systems themselves are flawed, in that they do not provide accurate measures of relative need. This is understandable because priority systems are intended to be objective assessments, whereas determining relative priorities among airports competing for a limited amount of money can be quite subjective. Many planners prefer priority systems that use some sort of project evaluation matrix. These matrices can be a good thing in that they help individuals and agencies organize their thinking and focus on the most critical factors. The problem is, they can also create a deceiving illusion of objectivity. Someone can say, "Hey, this isn't my opinion, we were totally objective. We cranked the numbers through the system and this is what came out, and the numbers don't lie."

This implies that there is no personal opinion and no bias in the process. But there is bias. A person (or persons) selects the factors that go into the priority system to be measured, and this selection is often made on the basis of personal opinion. In a way this is good, because it brings experience and judgment into the picture, and experience is one of the most valuable tools we have. The problem comes in when we select only those things that can be measured, and more specifically, things for which data are readily available. As a result priority systems often include a measure of how busy an airport is, in terms of based aircraft and/or aircraft operations. For some airport improvements, those which increase capacity for example, activity levels are probably a good factor to consider. But this might also mean that projects at the busier airports will tend to be ranked higher priority than projects at smaller, less active airports—which may not be the best decision. If activity levels alone are considered, a project at an airport that accommodates a lot of flight training activity would be assigned a higher priority than a smaller airport that provides a community's only air access.

Similarly, a value for population is often included in a priority matrix; in this case a project at an airport serving a large community or more populous area will usually be ranked a higher priority than projects at airports serving small communities, again without regard to the need for air access. Great care must be taken in using a matrix to prioritize projects among competing airports.

Priority determination is made even more complex because some of the most important factors in determining a project's relative priority cannot be measured. Take safety improvements, for example. Almost everyone would agree that safety improvements should have the highest priority. But how can a value or numerical weight be put on safety? This has been handled in a number of different ways: one is to develop a numerical ranking scheme, usually weighted or adjusted so that all projects fall in a range of 1 to 10. In this case the safety projects would automatically be given a weight of 10.

Another approach is to say that safety projects will be funded first, and not be included in the priority ranking scheme. Whatever money is left over will be distributed among the non-safety projects according to their priority ranking. This seems quite reasonable, assuming the project budget is sufficient to complete all the safety projects, and hopefully have enough left over to do some other things. But this is not as straightforward as it sounds because there is no master list that defines what types of improvements are safety-related and what are not. After all, there is a safety aspect associated with almost any airport improvement. Suppose an airport needs money to clear obstructions to one of the runway approaches. And yet another airport needs money to extend a runway safety area to meet FAA standards, and another has a runway safety area that is long enough but does not quite meet the FAA's gradient standards for runway safety areas, and another wants to buy a snowplow, and still another has a taxiway that is only 35 feet wide but the FAA standard says it should be 50 feet. Is bringing an airport's facilities up to the appropriate FAA standard automatically a safety improvement? Is funding a snow broom for an airport that already has a plow more important than constructing an aircraft parking ramp for an airport that doesn't have enough space to park transient aircraft? Different FAA offices have different views on these issues, and the local airport funding agency may have an entirely different view of safety and project priorities. In at least one instance an aircraft overnight parking ramp was presented as a safety improvement because aircraft were being parked in a location that interfered with the line of sight from the control tower.

In most project priority ranking schemes, safety improvements come first, then projects that are intended to maintain operations, such as a runway or taxiway overlay that an airport needs to maintain its existing level of service (sometimes referred to as system preservation), then come projects that increase capacity. Everything else usually goes into a category called "other" or "nice to have." As an example of how the system can be played, suppose a small airport does not have a full parallel taxiway, and aircraft are frequently delayed while waiting for another aircraft to taxi to the runway threshold, turn, and take off. The airport could handle a lot more operations if it had a full parallel taxiway; thus it could be considered a capacity improvement. However, it could also be sold as a safety improvement, because it is really not safe to have aircraft taxiing on active runways.

Clearly, developing an accurate and unbiased project priority ranking scheme is not easy. But it is an essential part of system planning because, particularly at the state level, the agencies responsible for awarding airport development grants need some fairly objective justification for how funds are distributed.

Step K: Recommended System Plan

The final airport system plan—recommending system changes, policy strategies, funding strategies, and airport development—can be prepared following the identification of needed airport facility improvements, the evaluation of alternatives, and the identification of system project improvement priorities. For all facility improvements, the system plan should include a *phased implementation plan* (that is airport planner-speak for "schedule"), along with estimated facility improvement costs. The recommended facility improvements should be shown in 5-, 10-, and 20-year planning horizons. The final system plan should include recommended improvements at both existing and new airports. The existing and proposed roles of each airport to be included in the NPIAS should also be identified, and each airport included in the plan should have a service level and role based on the definitions contained in that document. Again the FAA NPIAS roles are: primary commercial service (large, medium, small, and non-hubs), non-primary commercial service, reliever, and general aviation. The plan should also include and clearly identify non-NPIAS airports. The NPIAS categories should be shown in the final plan even if other classification systems are used for the study. According to the AC, using the NPIAS role "...will establish a standard for uniformity in airport role definition that will help maximize the system benefits of airport investments, as well as ensure the rationalization of federal priorities across airport categories."[25] This means that it will make it easier for the FAA to understand the system plan's recommendations and to combine the results of one system plan with the results of other system plans to help them allocate federal funds according to some rational methodology.

As discussed above, many or most of the facility improvements recommended in the system plan will be based on the timing and sequence developed as part of a master plan study for each of the system airports that have a current master plan. Where master plan results are not available, or are not current, some facility improvements will be recommended on the basis of analyses done as part of the system plan study. It is very important at this point to review the sequencing of recommended improvements to ensure that the improvements at each airport follow a logical, balanced sequence—it makes no sense to add runway capacity when the terminal is already handling nearly as many passengers as it can, unless some corresponding terminal improvements are included. Or conversely, it makes no sense to add six new gates to a terminal complex when the runway/taxiway system is already at or near capacity. Also, any particular facility improvement should be constructed in a manner that is compatible with the day-to-day operation of an airport. An example is when the plan recommends the construction of a new aircraft parking ramp in the first five-year period of the plan, to be followed by the construction of a portion of taxiway that may require closing that ramp for a time. Normally details of this type are addressed in master plan studies, but sometimes people make mistakes; therefore a sequencing review is usually a good idea.

Typically the recommended system plan and improvement schedule are sent to the FAA for review and comment in draft form, and some adjustments are usually necessary before the final plan is approved and released for publication. Make sure sufficient time is provided in the study schedule for FAA review, because system plan recommendations can be complex and a lot of money may be riding on the outcome. For example, the FAA may concur with the facility improvements recommended by the plan, but sufficient federal funds may not be available in the time period for which they are being requested. Therefore the implementation plan schedule will have to be adjusted accordingly. System plan recommendations must be reviewed by both the local ADO and the appropriate FAA region. The managers of the FAA Regional Airports Divisions are responsible for making decisions with respect to entry and development inputs and revisions to the NPIAS, except for the recommendations for new commercial service airports. Recommendations for these airports must be approved by the Director of the FAA Office of Airport Planning and Programming at FAA Headquarters, before they can be included in the NPIAS.

As noted at the beginning of this chapter, any recommendations for NPIAS changes should be made according to the guidance set forth in FAA Order 5090.3C.

The draft system plan findings should also be reviewed by the state, regional, and local agencies that will have a stake in the outcome, and particularly by the agencies that will be responsible for implementing the plan's recommendations. A plan should not be prepared and sent off to the FAA for review and approval without getting the concurrence of these groups. FAA approval should not be solicited for a system plan that calls for the extension of a runway at a county-owned airport without making sure that the county is agreeable, supportive, and able to provide the local share to match an FAA grant in the time period it is requested. Similarly, the planners should know before they recommend a runway extension whether the county transportation or public works department has not already planned to construct some other facility such as a park-and-ride lot on that site.

Step L: Implementation Plan

Once the system plan has been accepted by the FAA, the final phase in the airport system planning process is the preparation of an Implementation Plan. The plan should include a comprehensive description of the improvements needed, the timing of the improvements, the levels and sources of funds required, and any special circumstances or approvals that might also be needed for plan implementation. As noted above, the system plan and its recommendations should be reviewed and approved by the agencies that will be responsible for implementing its individual components. It should be made very clear which agencies are responsible for which actions, how much money they will need to provide, and when their responsibilities kick in. Airport Improvement Program grants are made to airport sponsors, not state or regional planning agencies. If a county owns an airport for which the system plan recommends a runway extension, the county has to know, and agree to, a schedule for implementation. They have to know when they must begin the process of selecting a consultant to conduct an environmental analysis and prepare the appropriate NEPA documentation, selecting a consultant to design the project, and selecting a contractor for construction. And before these selection processes begin the county must budget the necessary funds and prepare the documentation to apply for a federal, and possibly state, airport improvement grant. The agency that prepared the system plan should be responsible for monitoring the various aspects of plan implementation.

The implementation plan should also contain any recommendations for changes to state, regional, or local policies to address aviation needs or to address any deficiencies that may come to light during the course of the study. These recommendations could include new funding mechanisms, new or revised land use and zoning controls, or regulatory changes. As an example, some states, particularly in the northeastern U.S., have something called "home rule," empowering cities, villages, boroughs, towns, townships, and other local governments to make their own decisions about issues such as zoning, within the overall guidance of the state and federal governments. This can lead to fragmented and uncoordinated decision-making if entities do not actively communicate. Situations arise wherein a county owns an airport that is located in a particular town (or township) and the town government's planning and zoning department is responsible for local land use controls. If the airport is to continue to grow and develop, the town must implement and enforce land use controls to prevent encroachment that could constrain further airport development, and in extreme cases could constrain current airport operations. In at least one instance a town planning and zoning board zoned the land around the airport (and in fact the airport itself!) for residential use. In another instance a school was constructed just off the end of the primary runway of an airport that had scheduled commuter air carrier service. In this case the threshold of the runway had to be relocated because the school penetrated the approach surface. Obviously there was the proverbial "failure to communicate" in both of these cases. Situations like these can sometimes be addressed and hopefully resolved as part of the system planning process, if local governments can be shown the value of the airport to the local community. This issue is discussed in more detail in Chapter 9: Coordination and Communication.

The implementation plan is also a good place to address organizational issues and recommend ways to enhance efficiency in implementing system plan recommendations, and ultimately help ensure continued operation and growth of the aviation system. For example, it may become obvious that a state aviation agency needs additional staff with experience in grant administration in order to allocate state airport improvement funds in a more timely manner. Or the agency may need additional inspectors to ensure that grant compliance requirements are being met by local airport sponsors. Obviously such recommendations would be developed with the collaboration and concurrence of the organization whose structure would be changed.

The implementation plan may also include recommendations for additional, more detailed studies associated with airport development in a given area. The system plan may show the need for, and recommend the development of, a reliever airport to serve a busy metropolitan area. This could be a recommendation for a new airport, but will more likely be a recommendation for substantial facility improvements at an existing general aviation airport. However, the additional traffic at the new reliever may result in increased airspace congestion and air traffic control issues. In this case the system plan could recommend that the FAA conduct an airspace capacity study to address any issues that may result from the increased activity. Similarly, a system plan study may note that one or two small communities exhibit the potential to support scheduled air service. In that case the system plan could recommend that a special air service analysis be conducted to address this issue on an area-wide basis.

Step M: Executive Summary

The Executive Summary is usually the last item produced, once all the study materials, findings, conclusions, and recommendations have been prepared. The AC notes that the executive summary should highlight the main elements and final recommendation of the system planning study, and that it should be made available to interested parties, particularly those outside the aviation industry to enable them to quickly review the study scope and major findings. The executive summary should be a quality document—professionally written and designed—since one of its main purposes will be to "sell" the system plan to the interested parties. Because this is the only system planning document that most decision-makers will read, it should include a brief statement on the purpose of the system plan study, along with the major findings and conclusions. It should also state specifically that the system plan and its recommendations should be implemented, i.e., it should make a strong case for investing public funds in airport improvements. Economic impacts are not listed in the System Planning AC as one of the study products, nor is an economic impact analysis listed as part of the study process. However, as noted in Chapter 5: Master Planning and Chapter 9: Coordination and Communication, communicating the economic benefits can be critical to the acceptance of the system plan. The agencies and individuals responsible for funding these improvements should be given enough information on economic benefits to provide a basis for committing the funds.

Agencies responsible for land use planning and zoning should also be given enough information to underscore the importance of airports in achieving the area's overall transportation and economic development goals. Bear in mind that the executive summary should be a relatively brief document; a booklet of 8 to 12 pages should be sufficient to contain all the pertinent information, without being daunting to the average reader. Typically outside agencies are not interested in detailed discussions of methodologies; if they want to know more they can always contact the agency that prepared the plan to get more information.

Additional Factors

Most planning work scopes include some items as steps in the planning process, or at least as discrete elements in a planning study, which are not, and should not be, considered separate elements. System plans are no exception; the System Planning AC notes three of these that are especially important: Environmental Considerations, Intermodal Integration and Airport Access, and Public Consultation.

Environmental Considerations

Environmental Considerations are usually included in a work scope as an item called *environmental analysis,* or something similar, with the implication that environmental analysis is a step in the planning process. But environmental factors and issues should be considered throughout the study, not just in one phase. Quite often planning reports include a chapter called environmental analysis, but if a planning study is conducted properly, environmental issues should be mentioned in almost every chapter. Projects should be planned with environmental considerations in mind. This particularly applies to facility plans as discussed in more detail in Chapter 5: Master Planning. At the system planning level environmental factors are not as detailed as they are in master planning or other site-specific facility planning. This is because facilities are not usually constructed on the basis of system plan recommendations. They are constructed on the basis of master plan recommendations as documented in detailed studies and shown on an Airport Layout Plan. Environmental documents are not normally a federal requirement for a state or regional system plan, although it should be noted that California is an exception, and other state laws vary, so environmental requirements should be investigated during the Pre-Planning step of a system plan study.

The System Planning AC notes that airport system plans do not normally include an investigation of environmental factors to the degree necessary to develop and evaluate individual airport master plan alternatives. For example, it is not usually necessary to conduct a field determination for wetlands or forest stands as part of a system plan study. But at the system planning level some consideration should be given to the major environmental features in the area of each of the airports included in the planning study. A system plan should note the existence of major wetlands in the vicinity of an airport if they could constrain development, along with other features such as parks, wildlife refuges, bodies of water, national monuments, and noise-sensitive land uses such as schools, hospitals, and residential areas. It should also be noted whether the airport is located in an air quality nonattainment area. The AC recommends that FAA Order 5050.4B, *National Environmental Policy Act (NEPA) Implementing Instructions for Airport Actions*, be consulted to help determine the level of environmental documentation that is needed for the system plan.

Because most of the projects included in system plan recommendations are taken from individual airport master plans, environmental considerations should have already been studied as part of the master plan process. As part of the inventory phase of the system plan study it is also a good idea to include a summary of the environmental factors associated with each airport that were identified as part of the master plan study for that airport. Also, since people sometimes overlook things, it is a good idea to review each of the master plans to make sure that environmental factors were considered in the planning process, and to identify any environmental issues that have the potential to constrain airport development. For system plan recommendations that are not taken from existing airport master plans, some environmental analysis should be undertaken as part of the process of identifying potential airport improvements.

For example, if the system plan identifies the need for a runway extension at an airport, the associated environmental analysis should note whether any environmental factors could preclude a runway extension, or at least reduce the options, both in terms of the length to which the runway could be extended and which end would be the best to extend. If a residential area or a wildlife refuge is located a mile or two from the end of one of the runways, it may be more appropriate to show the extension at the other end. The environmental factors that are important at the system plan level can usually be obtained from published sources, so field investigations are not normally required.

The environmental component of system plan studies can also be a good opportunity for the analysis of broad environmental issues leading to the development of area-wide goals and policies. For example, a regional system plan analysis of noise impacts, noise abatement, and land use controls can yield results that can be implemented on a region-wide basis.

Intermodal Integration and Airport Access

In 2005 the U.S. Government Accountability Office (GAO) submitted an excellent and comprehensive report to the U.S. House of Representatives that set forth potential strategies to redefine the role of the federal government in developing airport intermodal capabilities.[26] The report noted that the number of airline passengers at U.S. airports is expected to increase significantly in the future and that because most air travelers use cars to get to the airport, local cities can expect to face increased congestion on their airport access roadways. It also noted that the increased passenger traffic would further strain airport runway capacity. Together this congestion would result in delays that would have a number of adverse social and economic effects including "...wasting travelers' time and money, degrading air quality, slowing commerce, and increasing energy consumption."[27]

In 2007 the GAO submitted a follow-up report to the House concerning actions that the U.S. Department of Transportation (USDOT) could take to address barriers to intermodal development.[28] This report found that three primary barriers inhibit intermodal transportation:

- *Limited federal funding targeted toward intermodal projects.* Federal law generally ties transportation funding to a single mode, which limits the ability of state and local transportation planning agencies to use federal funds for intermodal projects. Although there are some federal programs under which intermodal projects can be funded, and one program that is specifically targeted for freight intermodal projects, all of the funds available through these programs have been congressionally-designated for specific projects.

- *Limited collaboration among stakeholders.* The [US]DOT's operating administrations and state and local transportation agencies are organized by mode—reflecting the structure of funding programs—resulting in an organizational structure that DOT's own assessments acknowledge can impede coordination between modes. In addition, collaboration between the public and private sector can be challenging; for example, some transportation officials told us that private-sector interests in airport, rail, and freight have historically not participated in the regional planning process.

- *Limited resources to evaluate intermodal projects.* Potential benefits of improving intermodal transportation, such as reduced congestion and improved air quality, are difficult for local planning agencies to measure and incorporate into analyses of regional transportation projects. In addition, it can be difficult to quantify benefits that are national, as opposed to local or regional. These barriers limit DOT's ability to fully implement the intermodal goal and impede state and local agencies' ability to plan, fund, and construct intermodal projects, which are inherently more complex than those involving one mode because of the variety of funding mechanisms and stakeholders involved and the difficulty in quantifying benefits.

With the passage of the Intermodal Surface Transportation Efficiency Act (ISTEA) in 1991, Congress established an Office of Intermodalism within US-DOT to maintain intermodal transportation data and to coordinate federal intermodal research. The Act also established a National Commission on Intermodal Transportation to

> …study the status of intermodal standardization, intermodal impacts on public works infrastructure, legal impediments to efficient intermodal transportation, financial issues, new technologies, problems in documenting intermodal transfers of freight, research and development needs, and the relationship of intermodal transportation to productivity.[29]

Intermodal issues are important to airport planners because an airport is part of a transportation system that includes highways, rail lines, and waterways. Airports should always be studied in the context of the overall transportation system, and the system plan should give some consideration to the interrelationships between and among the various modes. As the System Planning AC puts it, "Planners should focus on airports as an element of the larger transportation system that takes people and cargo from where they are to where they want to be."[30] The system plan should include a review of both the near- and long-range plans for other transportation modes, and should note where potential development of any of the other modes either complements or conflicts with the potential development of any of the system airports. An airport system plan, particularly a regional system plan, is an ideal place to identify these issues, because system planning involves coordination with other area-wide transportation agencies. The System Planning AC states:

The system plan needs to be coordinated with surface transportation planners to ensure that all airports in the system can be readily accessed by the population and businesses they serve; that surface access to larger primary airports is efficient, convenient, and cost-effective; that customers have a wide range of access choices; that travelers' special needs are met; and that additional truck traffic due to air cargo operations and its separation from passenger traffic is considered.[31]

The AC goes on to list some key questions that may be addressed in the system planning process, such as how an increase in airport traffic might result in a decrease in a highway level of service, or how the peaking characteristics of airport passenger and employee traffic might coincide with peaks in surface traffic through the day. In my opinion addressing these types of issues is a pretty tall order for a system plan because most of these factors require much more detailed analysis than is normally done at the system planning level. For example, most system plans do not include highway capacity studies, even for airport access roadways. For most of the airports included in system plans the major question is whether or not there is an access road, whether or not it is paved, and whether adequate directional signage is provided. If the system plan is being done at the regional level, and is sponsored by an MPO or regional planning agency, there is a much better chance of getting the data and expertise needed to give more detailed attention to ground access issues.

Remember that other transportation modes receive federal, state, and local funds just as airports do. Unlike the FAA however, the federal highway and transit agencies do not set project priorities—this is done by MPOs and state transportation agencies. Thus it is particularly important to coordinate closely with these agencies throughout the system study process. Some of these agencies may want to take an active role; others may be satisfied with the knowledge that an aviation system study is taking place. However, it is always a good idea to give all these groups the opportunity to participate to the degree they desire.

Also note that most discussions of intermodalism and intermodal transportation planning involve connections between transportation modes, such as airport/local rail system connections. But in a broader context intermodalism should also involve discussions of mode choice alternatives. In fact, the 2005 GAO report mentioned above noted that while 64 out of the 72 airports surveyed for the GAO study had direct connections to local bus systems, and 27 had direct connections to local rail systems, only 13 had a direct connection to an Amtrak station and only 12 had a direct connection to a nationwide bus station.[32]

Freight is often discussed in a truly intermodal context, and in fact that is the way freight systems typically operate. Much freight arrives at a U.S. port by ship, is then transported by train to an inland city, and is then delivered by truck to its local destination. For another way of looking at freight intermodalism, a shipper in Charleston, West Virginia, may want to send a package to St. Louis on a Monday for delivery the following Wednesday. The shipper is likely to contact one of the integrated carriers such as FedEx or UPS. The carrier will ensure that the package arrives in St. Louis at the required time, and will ship it by whichever mode (truck or plane) will meet the schedule at the lowest cost. The shipper and the recipient don't care how it gets there, just so it gets there on time.

Unfortunately for most travelers, mode choice in the United States seems to consist simply of personal auto for relatively short trips (typically trips taking less than about 1½ to 2 hours), and airplanes (either scheduled airline, charter, or general aviation) for longer trips. Rail service doesn't often enter into the picture, with the exception of a few city-pair markets, such as between New York City and Washington, D.C. Rail service in the U.S. is quite a contrast to rail travel in Europe and Japan. An article in the *International Herald Tribune* in 2007 noted that:

> High-speed trains are often the fastest way to travel between city centers in Europe, beating short-haul flights for journeys of up to 550 kilometers [about 342 miles].... At speeds of up to 320 kilometers an hour [just under 200 mph], the train certainly takes the strain; compared to airports, high-speed train stations are stress-free citadels of peace. [33]

Note that this hypothetical 342-mile trip would take about 1¾ hours at 200 mph and about 2 hours and 20 minutes at 150 mph. The article goes on to note that trains generally have the advantages of comfort, convenience, and cost when compared to airline travel. Rail does not involve the security hassles frequently encountered at major airports, and trains have larger seats with more legroom so that it is easier to relax or get some work done during the trip. Of course, conditions in Europe and Japan are quite different from the U.S. in that large cities are not as far apart. Let's face it: rail is not an alternative for people traveling between points such as Los Angeles and New York City, or Seattle and Atlanta. However, for people traveling between New York City and Washington, D.C., for example, rail service is quite attractive—especially for passengers originating in or destined to the city-center areas where driving a personal vehicle is a hassle, to say the least.

Unfortunately trains in the U.S. do not travel as fast as trains in Europe or Japan. Rail operating speeds in Europe and Japan generally range between 118 and 171 mph, as compared with 96 mph for Amtrak's Acela on its Washington, D.C. to New York City route and 66 mph on the New York City to Boston route.[34] Thus any given rail trip in the U.S. would take longer than a trip of a similar distance in Europe or Japan.

Also, a recent report prepared by the USDOT's Inspector General (IG) is critical of Amtrak's schedule performance, noting that Amtrak trains serving the Northeast Corridor (NEC) (Washington, D.C. to New York City to Boston) had an on-time performance of 88 percent for Acela service and 80 percent for other NEC trains. Note that these trains are dispatched by Amtrak and operate on Amtrak-owned track. By contrast, outside of the NEC almost all Amtrak trains operate on track owned, operated, and maintained by other railroads. In these other rail corridors Amtrak trains had an on-time performance of only 65 percent.[35] With regard to the causes of delays, the IG report notes that:

> Amtrak trains are delayed by 1) host railroad dispatching practices, some of which result in preference violations, 2) track maintenance practices and the resulting speed restrictions, 3) insufficient track capacity, and 4) external factors beyond the host railroads' control.[36]

Intercity rail service may seem peripheral to airports and airport planning, but airport planners should always remember that airports are one component of the overall transportation system. Our immediate job is planning airports, but our larger responsibilities include helping to ensure the safe and efficient movement of people and goods. Although it may be anathema to mention this in a book about airport planning, some trips made by air might be better made by rail. This particularly applies to trips of less than 300 miles between large population centers. Quite often the airports serving these large metropolitan areas have runway and airspace capacity constraints. Planners should ask whether it makes sense to use scarce runway capacity for relatively short-haul flights for which an alternative mode is available. This question bears some serious thinking, because it has shown up in environmental reviews for runway projects at large airports, and will likely show up with increasing frequency in the future, particularly if fuel costs continue to increase.

Public Consultation

The System Planning AC notes that, "The airport planning process should provide an opportunity for public participation, the extent of which should be commensurate with the scope of work."[37] It is always a good idea to involve the public in any planning study, whether it is system planning, master planning, or detailed facility planning. One consideration is that it is best to be forthright with accurate information because facilities projects will eventually be noticed by the public and media and people will want to know what is going on. And more importantly, if public involvement is done properly, it results in a better project and better cooperation by everyone involved in and affected by the work. Also, if any agencies or groups are going to be opposed to airport development, either at the broad system level or at the specific local level, it is good to know who will be opposing development, what kinds of development they will oppose, and why they will oppose it.

Certainly public involvement takes a lot of effort if done properly; it can be expensive, and it can seem as if only the disgruntled people show up for public meetings. Public consultation in the airport system planning process can be especially challenging because system planning is broad-brush in nature, and the projects recommended by system plan studies may not be built for a long time, if ever.

Techniques for dealing with the public, along with some thoughts on how to package and present the relevant information, are discussed in Chapter 9: Coordination and Communication. The most important thing to remember is that airports have several publics, and the planning process should include them all, at a level of detail commensurate with the level of interest each of the publics may have. Information about the plan should also be structured or packaged in a manner which each of the publics will understand and care about, given that each of the publics has a different level of knowledge about airports and how they operate.

Consider the various publics that may have an interest in airports and airport development, and what their level of interest might be in system-level planning. When airport planners think of the public, they usually think of the general public, or perhaps the citizens who live nearby and may be affected by the operation and development of the airport. The general public thinks in terms of tangible, fairly immediate projects, and less so about big-picture, regional, multimodal transportation strategies. Remember too, that many, perhaps most, of the projects recommended by an airport system plan will come from individual airport master plans, each of which will have to go through, or may have already gone through, a public involvement process. At the master plan or facility plan level of detail much information is available about the project, including environmental, socioeconomic, and other impacts. This type of information is not usually part of a system-level plan. So if the plan recommends a runway extension at a particular airport and people have questions about an increase in noise levels in their community, the answers will usually not be available unless this information has been documented in a master plan and/or its associated environmental study. In many cases the system plan may find that an airport needs a longer runway, and may even identify the particular runway to be extended and to what length, but additional study may be required before it is even known which end of the runway would be the best to extend. This type of analysis is not usually done at the system planning level.

Another "public" is the direct airport users such as airlines, air taxi or charter operators, flight schools, air freight handlers, aircraft maintenance and repair services, fixed base operators, concessionaires, and other individuals or organizations who operate at the airport. There are also those who use the services provided or available at the airport. This public is diverse and includes businesses and industries, air passengers, customers of chartered aircraft, freight shippers, pilots who rent aircraft, flight students, and people who just like to hang out at airports and watch the airplanes come and go and maybe buy a soda or a sandwich.

Realistically, most of the agencies and organizations in these groups are not likely to have much interest in system planning; their focus tends to be on the specific things that are happening, or may happen, at their local airport. The people who belong to or represent these groups have other things to do, and an airport system plan may not be at the top of their agenda. For example the airlines do not have sufficient technical staff to attend meetings and review study materials. An exception might be one of the general aviation user groups that might have an interest in preserving some of the existing airports, or designating an airport in a particularly busy metropolitan area as a reliever. Similarly, the air carriers do not usually participate in system planning studies unless there is a specific issue such as airport or airspace capacity to be dealt with. Normally air carrier participation would occur if a regional system plan recommends that the FAA undertake an airspace capacity study to address congestion and delay reduction strategies in a busy metropolitan area.

Other airport user groups may express interest in participating in a system planning study, but then lose that interest when they find out that the study will not result in a quick fix to a local situation. For example, a fixed base operator may be interested in getting some additional space to park aircraft, and when he finds that the system plan will make recommendations, but that additional planning and environmental study will be required at the local level, he will probably lose interest until the local airport picks it up on its list of things to do. Local businesses desiring improved freight or passenger services may also have some interest in participating in an airport system plan, but again it should be demonstrated how the study will directly affect them and what they do, otherwise it will be difficult to sustain their interest.

Another group consists of what are usually termed "industry groups" or "trade associations;" this group includes such diverse organizations as the Air Transport Association of America, the National Business Aircraft Association, and the Aircraft Owners and Pilots Association, and represents the interests of a broad spectrum of general aviation aircraft operators.

Still another group includes government agencies. They consist of entities who fund airport and other transportation improvements; federal, state, and local environmental agencies that review and approve airport improvement projects; agencies responsible for police and fire protection; and elected officials. Government agencies are the ones most likely to participate in an airport system plan because they are the ones with the funding and regulatory authority. Other transportation agencies will want to know what kinds of airport development are being proposed on an area-wide basis, to allow them an opportunity to coordinate surface transportation improvements with airport development. Agencies with the responsibility for funding airport improvements are also likely to get involved, for obvious reasons. Environmental review agencies may be skeptical at first unless the planners can demonstrate a genuine interest in identifying environmental issues; if these agencies see that their concerns will be recognized and taken into account during the study process, they will usually be happy to get involved. Local planning and zoning officials will probably want to be involved in the system planning process if they see that airport zoning is an issue to be addressed. Local elected officials are not likely to get involved, at least until the very end when the study is completed and the recommended plan is approved by the FAA and adopted by the study sponsor. Unfortunately their involvement may be more in opposition to development than in support.

It can be difficult to get people to attend meetings, review reports, and generally take an active role in system plan studies unless specific commitments are being discussed for specific airports or airport improvements. The key to successful public outreach is to present system planning information that is relevant to the various publics, in a manner that each of the publics can relate to and understand.

In a sense, public consultation at the system planning level can be viewed as being similar to the scoping process in environmental studies. It should begin by discussing broad issues that affect the airport system as a whole, and then narrowing the focus with a facility improvement plan that presents projects at individual airports. During the system planning process a good public outreach program can help identify both area-wide and local issues that may affect airport system development and operation. Planners can then focus on resolving these issues or at least defusing potential sources of contention. The importance of coordination and communication in general, and public outreach in particular, is discussed in detail in Chapter 9: Coordination and Communication.

A final factor to note with regard to system planning is that it is possible to introduce an element of bias into the planning process. This is true for other kinds of airport planning as well. We often start off by asking how we can make people realize how important the airport is to the community. But to be truly objective we should be asking how we can determine *objectively* whether or not the airport *is* important to the community. It is important to keep this in mind because this is often the way the question will be posed to airport advocates in any public, legislative, or financial review process.

Endnotes

1   *The Airport System Planning Process*, AC 150/5070-7. Washington, D.C.: Federal Aviation Administration, November 11, 2004, p. 1. Accessed June 2008, from http://www.faa.gov/airports_airtraffic/airports/resources/advisory_circulars/

2   *Ibid.*

3   de Neufville, Richard, and Amedeo Odoni, *Airport Systems Planning, Design, and Management*. New York: McGraw-Hill, 2003, p. 61.

4   *Ibid.*

5   *Airport Improvement Program (AIP) Handbook*, FAA Order 5100.38C. Washington, D.C.: Federal Aviation Administration, June 2005, p. 37.

Accessed June 2008, from http://www.faa.gov/airports_airtraffic/airports/aip/aip_handbook/

6. *The Airport System Planning Process. Op cit.* p. 16.

7. *Field Formulation of the National Plan of Integrated Airport Systems (NPIAS)*, FAA Order 5090.3C. Washington, D.C.: Federal Aviation Administration, December 4, 2000. Accessed June 2008, from http://www.faa.gov/airports_airtraffic/airports/resources/publications/orders/media/planning_5090_3C.pdf

8. *The Airport System Planning Process. Op cit.* p. 1.

9. *Ibid.*, p. 5.

10. *Ibid.*, p. 6.

11. de Neufville. *Op cit.* p. 65.

12. *The Airport System Planning Process. Op cit.* p. 13.

13. *New England Regional Airport System Plan*, n.d. New England Airport Coalition. Accessed March 2008, from http://www.faa.gov/airports_airtraffic/airports/regional_guidance/new_england/planning_capacity/airport_system_plan/

14. *The Airport System Planning Process. Op cit.* p. 28.

15. *Ibid.*, p. 2.

16. *Ibid.*, p. 45.

17. *Ibid.*, p. 46.

18. *Ibid.*

19. *Forecasting Aviation Activity by Airport.* Jenkintown, PA: GRA, 2001, incorporated for Federal Aviation Administration, Office of Aviation Policy and Plans, 2001. Accessed June 2008, from http://www.faa.gov/data_statistics/aviation_data_statistics/forecasting/media/af1.doc

20. *Revision to Guidance on Review and Approval of Aviation Forecasts*, memorandum. Washington, D.C.: Federal Aviation Administration, 2004. Accessed June 2008, from http://www.faa.gov/airports_airtraffic/airports/planning_capacity/media/approval_aviation_forecasts_2004.pdf

21. *The Airport System Planning Process. Op cit.* p. 51.

22. *Ibid.*, p. 19.

23. *Ibid.*

24. *Ibid.*, p. 54.

25. *Ibid.*, p. 55.

26. *Intermodal Transportation – Potential Strategies Would Redefine Federal Role in Developing Airport Intermodal Capabilities.* Washington, D.C.: U.S. Government Accountability Office, July 2005.

27. *Ibid.*, p. 1.

28. *Intermodal Transportation – DOT Could Take Further Actions to Address*

	Intermodal Barriers, GAO 07-718. Washington, D.C.: U.S. Government Accountability Office, July 2007. Accessed September 2008, from http://www.gao.gov/new.items/d07718.pdf
29	*Intermodal Surface Transportation Efficiency Act of 1991 – Summary.* Accessed September 2008, from http://ntl.bts.gov/DOCS/ste.html
30	*The Airport System Planning Process. Op cit.* p. 56.
31	*Ibid.*
32	*Intermodal Transportation*, 2005. *Op cit.* p. 3-4.
33	Collis, Roger. International Herald Tribune, July 26, 2007. Accessed January 2009, from http://www.iht.com/articles/2007/07/26/arts/trfreq27.php
34	Wendell Cox Consultancy, *The Public Purpose*. Belleville, IL. Accessed January 2009, from http://www.publicpurpose.com/ic-hsramtrak.htm
35	*Root Causes of Amtrak Train Delays*, Report Number CR-2008-076. Washington, D.C.: Federal Railroad Administration, September 8, 2008, p. ii. Accessed January 2009, from http://www.oig.dot.gov/StreamFile?file=/data/pdfdocs/Amtrak_Root_Causes_Final_Report_9_8_08_with_508_charts.pdf
36	*Ibid.*, p. iii.
37	*The Airport System Planning Process. Op cit.* p. 13, 57.

CHAPTER 7

FORECASTING

Forecasting is one of the most critical elements of the airport planning process. This chapter discusses the uses and importance of forecasts and provides some guidance for determining whether a forecast is reliable and acceptable for planning purposes. It lists the various aviation demand parameters that are typically included in the forecast process. A number of approaches and techniques for forecasting are also covered, along with appropriate data sources.

Why Do We Forecast?

Aviation demand forecasts are an important component of airport planning because they are used by the FAA to identify the need for capital projects that may qualify for funding under the Airport Improvement Program (AIP). In this sense many people feel that the forecast drives the plan. However, when doing airport planning, my opinion is that the ultimate plan, i.e., the picture of what the airport will look like in the future, is usually done in the strategic planning process. Even if a formal strategic plan is not prepared, somebody has a vision of how the airport should be expanded to meet future needs. This vision is not based on a forecast of air traffic demand volumes; rather it is arrived at by asking, "If this airport had to grow, how would it grow?" The forecasts are then used to give a more specific idea of when various airport components are likely to need to be constructed so that a capital improvement program can be prepared. In this sense the *vision* drives the *plan* and the *forecast* really drives the *program*. Most often in practice the facility is actually improved when someone demonstrates a need for it—and is willing to pay for it.

To provide some context regarding the importance of forecasts, it should be remembered that for most major airport improvements it usually takes at least five years to prepare and complete the plan—including the appropriate environmental documentation, obtaining the necessary FAA approvals, securing the funding, preparing the design, and constructing the facility. So a five-year projection is not very useful as far as airport facility planning goes. The time period most critical for facility planning purposes is the 5- to 10-year period. Anything beyond 10 years is really not much more than guessing. The FAA's Master Plan AC states that, "Short-term forecasts for up to five years are used to justify near-term development and support operational planning and environmental programs. Medium-term forecasts (a 6- to 10-year time frame) are typically used in planning capital improvements, and long-term forecasts (beyond 10 years) are helpful in general planning."[1] The problems with long-term forecasting are discussed later in this chapter, but first let's discuss some background information.

In facility planning, as noted above, people often regard the forecast as the key to the whole plan; if the forecasts are wrong the plan is thought to be wrong, or at least questionable. This is not necessarily correct however, when considered in terms of individual projects. True, long-term facility needs are determined on the basis of long-term forecasts. But think of how projects are actually built. New gates are not constructed because the forecast says new gates are needed; they are constructed because a carrier needs more gates to accommodate additional flights now, or in the near future. Similarly, most airports don't start construction on a new runway just because the forecasts say that aircraft operations will exceed the capacity of the existing runway system. Planning for a new runway may begin at any time it appears that there may be a capacity shortfall at some point in the future, but the environmental phase of the project usually does not start until the airport actually starts to experience delays—usually during the peak hour, and on a fairly regular basis.

Airport improvements such as terminals and runways are very expensive and, whether correctly or incorrectly, airport management is not likely to construct a major facility improvement based on speculation. For example, at BWI Airport, the master plan study completed in 1987 found that a new parallel transport-category runway would be needed by 1995. By 1990, however, it was clear that after US Airways acquired Piedmont Airlines, they were downsizing their BWI connecting hub operation, and that aircraft operations were not going to increase at the rate shown in the master plan forecasts. BWI management delayed plans for the new runway on the basis of revised forecasts and an updated capacity study which indicated that a new runway would not be needed for at least the next decade. Airport management continued to monitor the current and projected demand/capacity situation to ensure that a runway would be built when needed, but would not be constructed years before it was needed. BWI is currently addressing this issue as part of a new airport master plan study. The point is that the forecasts are an important part of facility planning, but they should not be the sole driver for developing a facility improvement program.

Although the forecast does not specify exactly when a particular facility should be improved, or exactly how large that facility should be, the forecast does provide enough documentation to support a phased, long-term plan for the development of the airport, generally referred to as a phased development program. This is where the forecasts get to be a bit more critical. The phased development program is presented to the local airport sponsor and submitted to the FAA, generally in the form of an Airport Layout Plan, plus a Capital Improvement Program (CIP), i.e., the budget. Local and federal authorities must have a reliable estimate of long-range airport improvement needs so they can ensure that sufficient funds will be available when needed. The forecast may show that a new parallel runway will be needed when aircraft operations reach an annual level of 300,000 take-offs and landings, and that level will likely be reached in 2020. What planners need to focus on here is not the year 2020, but rather the level of 300,000 operations. What the budgeting people need to know however, operating in the current year, is that they don't have to set aside money for the new runway in their current five-year CIP, nor do they have to request an immediate grant from the FAA. What they do have to be aware of is that there is a very, very expensive capital improvement on the horizon, and if they want to have that improvement completed and in operation by 2020, they will have to start budgeting so that funds will be available in about 2010 for the final planning, environmental studies, and design, and available for construction in about 2016 or 2017. If money is set aside for a facility improvement and it turns out that it is not needed when expected, the planning department (or the consultant) may look a little foolish. But if money is needed for a near-term improvement and it is not available, the entire airport will undoubtedly take some heat.

Even though some airport planners and airport operators have different views on the specific importance of forecasts, most agree that the forecast is an essential part of a successful planning exercise, and ultimately at least one of the keys to a successful plan. But what makes a good forecast? Obviously a good forecast is one that accurately projects future demand levels; however, there is no way of knowing if a forecast is accurate until the future happens, and by that time it may be too late to do anything but say, "Oops." Fortunately (or unfortunately at times), a forecast is considered "good" if it is accepted by the key people in the decision-making process. These people usually include the airport director and his or her executive staff, and the airport board or commission, among others. It could also be argued that a forecast is good if the FAA approves it, and as noted in Chapter 5: Master Planning, forecasts for airport planning studies must be approved by the FAA. In this sense "good" is not synonymous with "accurate," since FAA forecast experts are not usually the ones who review the submitted forecasts. But of course, if the FAA does not approve the forecast, that's bad.

The forecasting process can be simplified and the forecasts made more useful if the purpose is clearly identified and stated at the outset. Will the forecasts be used strictly for the development of long-term airport facility improvement plans, or will they also be used for other purposes, particularly with shorter time frames? Some of these other purposes include benefit-cost analyses, environmental analyses, noise compatibility studies, and serving as the basis for airport business contracts and leases, such as for rental cars, taxi and shuttle services, public parking, and food and retail concessions. Forecasts of landed weights are also used as the basis for the rates and charges set between the airport and the air carriers, such as landing fees. These types of contracts typically have a term of less than five years, although some may go further into the future. Therefore near-term forecasts are needed, and the airport planner is frequently called upon to provide them.

The forecast report of the Airport Cooperative Research Program (ACRP) of the Transportation Research Board states that, "The type and method of forecasting can depend importantly on the purpose for which the forecast is being made. For example, there may be sharp variations between forecasts used to support an annual budget versus a long-term facilities expansion."[2] Based on my own experience this dichotomy can be a little dangerous. Most information related to the development and operation of an airport is available to the public, and the public may pose some serious questions—"Do you guys know what you are doing?"—if they see two different forecasts for the same airport. For example an airport may prepare a forecast showing that a new runway is needed in the near future. Once the plan is completed the environmental phase begins, and if there has been a delay of a year or two (or more) from the start of the planning effort, a new, updated set of forecasts may be prepared for the environmental document. At that point the airport can be caught in a bind, basing the need for a new runway on one set of forecasts, and identifying and quantifying the environmental consequences on a revised set of forecasts. In this situation someone will have to provide a pretty clear explanation of why the forecasts are different, and what the differences mean, or the airport may wind up in court. Similarly, a forecast may show that the airport will grow to serve 10 million passengers by the year 2010, and a facility improvement plan and program may be developed accordingly. Shortly after planning begins, someone may see a newspaper article that says that the airport's marketing department has released projections showing the airport will handle 12 or 13 million passengers in 2010. If the people who control the funds, or review the environmental documents, see two sets of forecasts, somebody will again have some explaining to do. In this regard it is important that only one department at the airport is responsible for forecasting, and that this department coordinate and communicate with all other departments that use the forecasts. This may seem like a minor point, but it can save time, money, and aggravation in the long run. Also, to forestall potential criticism and avoid these kinds of embarrassments, it is often a good idea to prepare one set of forecasts to be used for all the purposes noted above.

Note that this does not mean *one forecast*. It means a *set of forecasts* that are developed using a consistent base under a consistent set of alternatives. For example, the forecast exercise could develop a forecast under a high-growth scenario that is based on an optimistic outlook regarding the factors that influence aviation demand. This forecast would be *unconstrained* by capacity limitations, assuming that facilities and services will be available to accommodate the expected growth. This forecast is typically used for master plans and other long-range facility plans. Another forecast could be developed under a less optimistic or low-growth scenario regarding the air travel market, and it could also include some capacity constraints if appropriate.

This less optimistic forecast could be used for financial planning, benefit-cost analyses, and revenue bond issues. The high-growth scenario provides a target or series of targets for long-range planning, saying that if things grow according to expectations, or even a little ahead of expectations, these are the areas that will reach capacity at certain specified times. The resulting plan would be timed to provide the necessary facilities to increase capacity when and where needed. The low-growth forecast shows the downside—the potential consequences (primarily financial) of overbuilding or building too far in advance of when facilities are needed.

A problem that frequently arises when one set of forecasts is used for a variety of near-term and long-term purposes is that aviation demand can change very quickly from year to year. Most of the forecast methodologies discussed below rely on a fairly long period of historical data, which has a tendency to dampen these near-term fluctuations, or at least put them into a long-term context. But this can be a problem for near-term forecasts, such as those used for tenant leases and financial analyses. This is why many people prepare long-range forecasts for planning purposes and short-range forecasts for near-term uses. But in this regard it should be kept in mind that long-term forecasts are exactly that—long-term. The forecasts can be updated each year based upon another year's worth of data without necessarily changing the long-term numbers. The forecasts for the next five years, or even a little more, can be updated to connect with the long-term forecasts at some point 5 or 10 years into the future. This allows more accurate forecasting for near-term needs without redoing a complete set of long-term forecasts. In fact it is a good idea to monitor actual traffic growth (and air service changes) each year and conduct an annual forecast review. This review should result in a determination as to whether the near-term component of the forecasts is still valid or whether it needs to be adjusted. It can also give some indication as to whether the underlying assumptions for the long-term component are still valid. For example, an economic downturn usually results in a decline in growth for a year or two, followed by recovery to historical levels. But in the event of a traffic decline due to a loss of air service, as happens when a carrier severely cuts back or even ceases all service to a city, it might be a good idea to do some reevaluation and possibly even consider a complete forecast revision.

What Should We Look For in a Forecast?

To begin with it should be noted that most people are either afraid of numbers or easily confused by them. People either freeze or their eyes glaze over when the subject of mathematics arises, or when data tables are handed out. Planners do not need a Ph.D. in Econometrics, but they do need a basic grasp of the mathematical processes related to forecasting. It is also frequently up to planners to communicate the complex forecasting processes and interpret the results in ways that are meaningful and useful for general audiences.

It seems that sometime during the 1960s the world started becoming more quantitative. Planners, along with most other professionals, surveyed and measured everything they could. If a recommendation or a plan didn't have a set of numbers associated with it, it was regarded as simplistic, based on subjective assumptions or personal opinions, and therefore unacceptable. Conversely, if a recommendation did have a number associated with it, it had a tendency to be considered accurate and thus accepted. Moreover, it seemed like the more numbers we had and the more things we measured the better, especially if a few letters (preferably from the Greek alphabet) were mixed in. Not much thought seemed to be given to where the numbers came from, or more importantly, whether the numbers made sense or were tied to some underlying logic.

As an example, I once attended a forecast briefing by a consultant who was preparing passenger forecasts for all airports served by commercial air carriers in the state. The consultant used a multiple regression analysis (this methodology is discussed in more detail below) that included population, per capita income, air fares, jet fuel prices, and intercity bus fares(!). The client representatives were somewhat surprised at the addition of bus fares and questioned the fact. The consultant's initial response was that there was at least a theoretical relationship between bus fares and air passenger traffic in that if bus fares increased with respect to air fares, passengers would have a greater tendency to fly rather than take a bus. After considerable discussion the consultant conceded that adding bus fares to the forecast equation increased the degree of correlation, even though the logic might be a little shaky because buses and airplanes did not generally compete for the same component of the travel market. The net result was that the bus fare component was deleted and the forecast project was completed, but the consultant had lost the confidence of the client, the forecasts were subsequently discarded, and another group was hired to prepare new forecasts. The point is that no matter which methodology is used, the forecaster must be able to explain the resulting projections in a manner that is logical and makes sense to the people who will be expected to use them or approve them.

Thus some thought should be given as to what makes a good forecast. The key factors most commonly given would almost always include accuracy and consistency. Unfortunately, accuracy cannot really be evaluated until the future happens, but there are some guideposts that can be used along the way, as discussed below. The FAA has published a report entitled *Forecasting Aviation Activity by Airport*[3] that provides guidance for people who prepare forecasts, as well as those who use forecasts. The report aims to promote consistency in the preparation of aviation demand forecasts and includes two appendices that would be useful when submitting forecasts to the FAA for approval. Also, FAA Order 5090.3C, *Field Formulation of the National Plan of Integrated Airport Systems (NPIAS)*,[4] prepared in 2008 states that forecasts should

- be realistic,
- be based on the latest available data,

- reflect the current conditions at the airport,
- be supported by information in the study, and
- provide an adequate justification for the airport planning and development.[5]

These are obviously important, but experience suggests looking at three additional factors when preparing a forecast or evaluating an existing forecast:

- Simplicity
- Consistency
- Logic

Simplicity doesn't necessarily mean that the methodology must be simple, but rather that the explanation must be simple. Forecasters should not try to fool people and should not pretend to know more than they really do. Remember, there is nothing certain about a forecast, so don't pretend there is. The forecasting process, methodology, and underlying assumptions must be clear and presented in a manner that is understandable to the client or audience. In other words, don't use smoke and mirrors and don't try to baffle anyone with ambiguities. In this regard the methodology should be readily explainable and easily understood. In the case of a regression analysis (discussed below), the relationship between the dependent variable and the independent variable or variables may be statistically valid but not logical. The problem is that if the forecast methodology is not logical, or if a complicated statistical explanation is involved, the forecasts may not be believed or accepted by the executive decision-makers, as noted in the earlier example. Again, most people are frightened by numbers and are easily confused when information is presented in numerical terms. When confronted by someone trained in econometrics or statistics, nonmathematical audiences can be snowed or intimidated by complex mathematical jargon or statistical theory. To be effective a forecaster must be able to clearly explain the process and methodology to audiences such as legislative officials, airport commissioners, and the general public.

Consistency has two components: internal and external. Internal consistency, i.e., internal to the airport under study, covers such factors as consistency with previous forecasts, with other current forecasts, and with other related activities at the airport under study. Determining consistency with previous airport forecasts, as well as with other current airport forecasts, involves looking at projected traffic volumes, growth rates, and underlying assumptions. If the current forecast differs markedly from previous forecasts, the difference should be explained and any changes justified. For example, if the forecast shows a sharp increase in traffic volumes, it may be because a new carrier recently started service, and this service may not have been anticipated in previous forecasts. This scenario would need to be explained in order for the forecast figures to make sense. Conversely, previous forecasts may have anticipated introduction of service by a new carrier or expansion of service by an existing carrier, but that new service never materialized;

moreover, it now appears that significant service improvements are not forthcoming in the foreseeable future. This scenario would logically explain a substantial drop in projected volumes.

Consistency with other related activities can easily be overlooked, or not considered to be significant with respect to future growth projections. For example, an airport marketing group may be launching a program that is expected to result in improved air services, which in turn would result in higher traffic growth than might otherwise be forecast. A major facility expansion or rehabilitation could also have the effect of hindering traffic growth in the near term. This situation may arise when an airport begins a major rehabilitation of airport access or circulation roadways, resulting in inordinate ground traffic congestion with commensurate delay and customer aggravation. In this circumstance passengers may either choose to travel by another mode or via a nearby airport for the duration of the construction activity. Although this may be an unusual circumstance, and may have only a finite duration, a major construction program could take several years to complete, and could adversely affect near-term traffic growth. Thus, such activities should be considered in the forecast process.

Logic is based upon professional judgment, both on the part of the forecaster and the audience. For example, at BWI Airport, we used to make what we considered a logical assumption about the future air traffic growth, in that over the long term, say beyond 10 years, BWI would grow at a rate lower than that projected by the FAA for the U.S. as a whole. There were two reasons for this assumption: BWI is located in the northeastern section of the country, which is not one of the nation's fastest growing areas, and BWI serves an area also served by two other competing airports, Washington National and Washington Dulles. Counting Philadelphia, the area has four airports whose service areas overlap. Over the near term, e.g., 5 or 10 years, BWI grew at a rate above the national average—first when Piedmont Airlines began using BWI as a connecting hub, then when Southwest began low-cost service. These service improvements resulted in rapid traffic growth, but we did not think it was logical to assume that this kind of growth could go on forever. Our forecasts thus reflected potential changes in our air service pattern.

Logic is also important in choosing the particular methodology to be used to prepare the forecast. If the socioeconomic data are not reliable or sufficient, an elaborate econometric model should not be used. Similarly, forecasters should avoid using independent variables that don't have an obvious relationship to the propensity for air travel. As discussed below, a model may be statistically valid, but it won't do much good if the audience doesn't believe it or see some logic behind what is going on inside the model.

What Do We Forecast?

The basic aviation demand parameters typically included in airport planning studies are summarized in Table 5-1 of Chapter 5 as part of the discussion on airport master plans, and are described in detail below. These parameters primarily include air passenger volumes and aircraft operations, as well as annual air cargo tonnage and the number of general aviation aircraft based at the airport. Additional parameters may be forecast, based on the specific needs of the study; they are usually derived from passenger or operations forecast totals.

Even though forecasts are commonly presented in terms of annual volumes, most airport facilities, such as runways and taxiways, terminal facilities, access roadways, etc., are planned on the basis of their expected throughput during peak periods, thus the peak period forecasts are especially important. Airports are not planned for the busiest period they will ever experience throughout the year. If they were, airport improvement projects would be prohibitively expensive and the facility would go unused throughout most of the year. Instead, annual forecasts are translated into forecasts for peak periods. As the ACRP report *Airport Aviation Activity Forecasting* states, "…depending on the situation, the appropriate measure of peak activity may refer to seasonal, monthly, daily, and/or time-of-day demands."[6] According to AC 150/5360-13, "The Average Day/Peak Month (ADPM) represents the most common method of converting planning statistics to a daily and ultimately to an hourly demand baseline."[7] The peak month can be identified from existing data; most airports and the FAA maintain passenger and aircraft operations data by month and by year. The peak month percentage of the annual total is derived by dividing the monthly volume by the annual total. If traffic were distributed evenly throughout the year, each month would have just over 8.3 percent of the annual traffic. Peak month percentages generally fall between 9.5 and 10.5 percent of the annual total, but this can vary widely among airports (such as those serving seasonal vacation areas), so data specific to the airport under study should be used. It is also a good idea to check back 5 or 10 years to see if the peak month percentage for the base year is consistent with the historical data. For future years the peak month percentage of the annual total for the base year can be applied to forecast annual totals to develop an estimate of peak month activity in future years. Some subjectivity can be involved here—the peak month ratio may be subject to change if some change in the nature of air travel demand is expected.

The average day volume is easily derived at this point by dividing the peak month total by the number of days in the month. If a quick estimate or approximation of peak day volume is needed, the annual total can be simply divided by 300, and the result will at least be in the ball park. Some adjustment may be necessary to account for unusual circumstances at the airport, such as extreme peaking on weekend days.

Developing a peak hour estimate (sometimes referred to as the busy hour) can be a little more difficult. If passenger traffic were evenly distributed throughout the day, assuming a 16-hour operational day, each hour would account for 6.25 percent of the daily total. But according to the Terminal Planning AC, "An airport may have peak hour operations as high as 12 to 20 percent of daily total operations."[8] For the most part the busier an airport is, the smaller the ratio of peak hour activity to the daily total. At most airports with control towers, the air traffic staff keep an hourly record of aircraft operations, and are sometimes willing to share the data, if approached properly. Getting historical peak period operations data is a little more difficult because hourly records are not always kept, at least not in an easily retrievable form (or location). Data sources are discussed in more detail below.

The most serious difficulties arise when trying to determine peak hour passenger volumes, which are needed for planning terminal, roadway, and parking facility improvements. One way to develop a peak hour passenger estimate is to multiply the number of aircraft operations by the average number of passengers per operation. This will only be an approximation however, because aircraft usually operate during peak periods with higher load factors than during off-peak periods. Using an average number of passengers per operation is likely to result in a passenger volume estimate which is much too low. An alternative is to multiply the number of peak hour operations by a number of passengers assuming high load factors, but this is still an approximation. The Terminal Planning AC includes a few graphs that can be used to calculate peak activity; unfortunately the graphs contain the notation:

> CAUTION: NOT TO BE USED FOR DESIGN OR ANALYSIS. FOR USE IN OBTAINING ORDER-OF-MAGNITUDE ESTIMATES PRIOR TO IN-DEPTH ANALYSIS.[9]

The in-depth analysis referred to typically involves a fairly detailed process that includes identifying the individual aircraft types and seating capacities (by airline). In this regard it should be kept in mind that at busy airports the airlines tend to operate larger equipment during peak periods than during off-peak periods. This information can be supplemented with actual on-site surveys, i.e., having some survey staff persons count the number of people entering and leaving passenger boarding areas. Often this is difficult to do because of the variations in terminal configurations, and it should also be kept in mind that passengers may arrive very early to make sure they can actually get on the flight for which they have made a reservation. Theoretically it should be possible to get data on the number of passengers passing through security checkpoints, both hourly and daily. The security staff probably record these volumes, but I have never heard of this information being used in any large-scale planning effort. Having said all that, if accurate information is needed it is probably a good idea to use a couple of different methodologies and compare the results.

Passengers

Air passengers consist of three components: enplaning, originating, and connecting. Enplaned passengers are obviously passengers who are boarding an aircraft. They consist of two types: originating passengers (those who are boarding an aircraft on the first leg of an air trip), and connecting passengers (those who are passing through the airport in order to connect from one flight to another as part of an air trip). Air passenger data for scheduled and nonscheduled operations are compiled by USDOT and maintained by the Department's Bureau of Transportation Statistics (BTS). Complete information on all the BTS databases is available on the BTS Web site.[10] The enplaned passenger data are obtained from various reporting forms filed by the airlines and include Schedule T-100 for U.S. domestic and international enplanements, Form 298C, and Schedule T-1 for most commuter enplanements. Originating passenger data (usually referred to as O&D data) are obtained from a continuous 10 percent Origin-Destination Ticket Sample (DB-1). It should be noted that the O&D data are not always precise because some air trips may involve circuitous routings, possibly taking more than one day and possibly even involving a change of mode to get to a destination. In such cases the exact trip origin may be difficult to determine. For airport planning purposes, however, such trips may be considered exceptions and the O&D sample may be used with confidence as a reliable estimate of locally-originating air passengers.

The passenger data are reasonably accurate and useful at larger airports, but they can be a problem at smaller airports where a significant portion of the air passenger traffic is accommodated by commuter airlines. As the ACRP forecast report states:

> Of particular concern for airport planners and forecasters are the co-mingling of air taxi and commuter and regional operations, as well as the distinction between air carrier and commuter activity. The FAA definition of "air taxi" refers to carriers that operate aircraft with 60 or fewer seats or a cargo payload capacity of less than 18,000 pounds, and carry passengers on an on-demand basis only (charter service) and/or carry cargo or mail on either a scheduled or charter basis. "Commuter" operators as defined by the [US]DOT are those with scheduled passenger service (five or more round trips per week on at least one route according to published flight schedules) while utilizing aircraft of 60 or fewer seats. Air taxi carriers are governed under Part 135 and commuter carriers are governed under Part 121 of the Federal Aviation Regulations.
>
> In terms of airport planning and use, the co-mingling between air taxi and commuter makes little operational sense. The more relevant distinction would be between scheduled and nonscheduled service, which has a primary influence on the type of facilities that must be provided (e.g., terminal services).
>
> For this reason, for airport planners it would be useful to distinguish between air taxi (nonscheduled) operations and commuter (scheduled) operations.
>
> Both commuter and air carrier operations involve scheduled service; the primary distinction is only in terms of the size of the aircraft used. The distinction between air carrier and commuter (regional) operations is becoming even more blurred as commuter markets are served more and more by larger regional jet air-

craft with between 60 and 90 seats. This has been accompanied by changes in carriers' scope clauses with their pilot unions that specify the size of the aircraft that must be flown by union pilots. Recent relaxation of these clauses has allowed carriers' regional affiliates to fly these larger aircraft. Today, the categorization of commuter operations as referring to scheduled service with aircraft of 60 or fewer seats is rather arbitrary and does not correspond with the observed patterns of flying. Nevertheless, as with the commuter/air taxi co-mingling issue, it is important that forecasts that are to be reviewed and subject to FAA approval meet the necessary requirements regarding user group distinctions.[11]

At small airports where air taxi operations are significant, air taxi enplanements are reported to the FAA on Form 1800-31.[12] Unfortunately this is a voluntary form and it includes only scheduled and nonscheduled passengers by city; the number of operations and aircraft type are not included.

Most large airports also maintain their own historical databases on air passenger enplanements and this information is often available on the airport's Web site. The accuracy and completeness of this information varies, since each airport can be expected to have its own way of doing things, and quite often the numbers are provided by the local airline station managers. Even if USDOT data are used in the forecast process, it is a good idea to check those numbers against the local airport records. If there are any significant differences, an explanation should be forthcoming to ensure that the forecasts are based on correct data. Also, this information is usually available to the public and the difference between the airport's data and USDOT data can lead to some embarrassing questions. For example, "Why should we trust your forecast for 10 years from now, when you don't even know how many passengers used the airport last year?"

The aviation demand forecasts should also include a forecast of originating passengers, particularly if the forecasts will be used for terminal, roadway, or public parking plans. Although the FAA Forecast Report states that enplaned passenger forecasts are necessary to "...determine the size of the terminal, the number of gates, and other elements of airport infrastructure,"[13] most terminal facilities are used only by passengers arriving at the airport by ground transportation. Enplaned passengers include these originating passengers, but also include connecting passengers, i.e., people using the airport to connect from one flight to another. These connecting passengers do not use local access roadways, parking lots, ticket lobbies, or baggage claim areas, to name a few examples. If the forecasts only include enplaned passengers, it will be necessary to calculate the number of connecting passengers by using a connecting factor (connecting passengers as a percent of the total) to come up with a number of originating passengers. Connecting factors can be derived by subtracting the originating passenger total (obtained from the O&D survey noted above) from the enplaned passenger total and dividing by the enplaned passenger total. Conversely, if a bottom-up or originating passenger forecast is being prepared, as described below, it will be necessary to add an estimate of connecting passengers to come up with a total enplaned passenger forecast.

The FAA notes that forecasts should include average seats per aircraft and average load factor in order to come up with an estimate of the number of gates that will be needed. Although this can work if reliable data on aircraft fleet mix, seating capacities, and load factors are available, it is easier, and a lot more reliable, to use a factor called enplanements per departure. This value is obtained by dividing the total number of enplaning passengers by the total number of air carrier departures. This method gets the same thing in the end, i.e., the average number of passengers departing on each flight. Average enplanements per departure should be calculated separately for domestic and international passengers, and for air carrier and commuter carriers. The enplanements per departure value works well because aircraft seating varies among carriers for any given type of aircraft, and although an average can be used, it adds a little more accuracy and credibility if the forecasts are based on actual data. Average load factors are also a problem because this information can cause confusion. Average load factors can be calculated for groups of carriers such as domestic, international, and commuter, or for each individual carrier. If data for individual carriers are desired it must be determined whether the need is for a system load factor, i.e., for all that carrier's routes taken together, or if it is a route load factor, i.e., the load factor on any particular one of that carrier's routes. To calculate how many people are departing on each flight, or how many flights it will take to carry out so many thousand or so many million people, the enplanements per departure statistic does the trick. This information is available for each airport served by air carriers or commuters from the air passenger databases identified above.

Air Cargo

Air freight and air mail data (combined referred to as air cargo) can be obtained from the Schedule T-100 and T-1 sources used for air passenger enplanements. Unfortunately this information does not provide a very accurate picture of the cargo that passes through an airport because a significant portion of the cargo is trucked in, sorted and reloaded onto other trucks, and then trucked to its destination, never being transported by air. The size of an airport's cargo facility is determined by the total amount of cargo moving through the airport, regardless of mode. Particularly with the rise of integrated carriers such as FedEx and UPS, cargo has become truly intermodal. The specific nature and quantity of this activity can vary significantly from airport to airport, thus planners should speak directly with each of the major cargo handlers at an airport to find out exactly what (and how much) is going on. Needless to say, historical cargo data are virtually nonexistent.

One other point to be aware of is that such cargo data as are available are often reported in pounds. Cargo forecasts are usually prepared in terms of tons and this usually means short tons—a short ton being equal to 2,000 pounds.

Sometimes cargo data are reported in metric tons (also shown as tonnes), one metric ton being equivalent to 1,000 kilograms or 2,204.6 pounds.

Aircraft Operations

The primary source for aircraft operations data (take-offs and landings) is the FAA's Air Traffic Activity Data System (ATADS). This information is comprised of data collected by FAA Air Traffic Control Towers, FAA Contract Towers, and Air Route Air Traffic Control Centers. It can be accessed at the FAA Terminal Area Forecast (TAF) Web site.[14] It is available for individual airports and includes annual and monthly counts of aircraft operations, instrument operations, and instrument approaches by user category including air carrier, commuter, air taxi, general aviation, and military. Instrument Operations include arrivals, departures, and overflights conducted by an FAA approach control facility for aircraft with an Instrument Flight Rules (IFR) flight plan or special Visual Flight Rules (VFR) procedures. They also contain operations where a terminal control facility provides IFR aircraft separation. Instrument Approaches are a subset of instrument operations; they are approaches conducted by aircraft actually making an instrument approach to a runway. General Aviation and Military operations are further divided into local and itinerant operations. Local operations include aircraft operating in the local airport traffic pattern or within sight of the tower, aircraft known to be departing to or arriving from local practice or flight training areas, and aircraft executing practice instrument approaches at the airport. Itinerant operations essentially consist of all aircraft operations not classified as local, primarily aircraft traveling from one airport to another.

Historical data on aircraft operations at non-towered airports may be obtained from the TAF Web site noted above for airports included in the NPIAS. For other airports this information is available on the FAA's Airport Master Record, Form 5010. As the name implies, this form is filled out annually; unfortunately the data are often of questionable accuracy. For an extreme example of inaccuracy, I saw Form 5010s for an airport that showed 50 based twin-engine aircraft over a period of about five years. When an actual site inspection was conducted as part of an airport system planning study it was found that the only based aircraft was a badly damaged airframe behind a dilapidated hangar. The only other sign that this was an airport were the remnants of some large Xs that were visible on fragments of what had once been a runway.

For a less egregious but more common example of inaccuracy, the form asks for the number of annual operations, but that is a hard number to estimate unless accurate records are kept by airport management. Some airport operators do not understand that an operation can be either a take-off or a landing and that an aircraft that lands and takes off again actually generates two operations. Also, most small airports do not have the time or the staff to record each take-off or landing. Consider as an example the difference between 25,000, 50,000, or 75,000 annual operations. Does anybody really have a concept of what those numbers mean? But dividing those annual estimates by 365 to come up with average daily estimates of 70, 137, or 205 operations per day are numbers that local airport management can relate to and visualize. It is always a good idea to discuss average daily operations volumes (for both weekdays and weekend days) to help gain some idea of how accurate the annual estimates on the Form 5010 might be. Also, Form 5010 data are usually available for the current year only; neither the forms nor the data seem to be retained on a consistent basis. Regarding Form 5010 data, the FAA also notes that, "Some Regional Airports Offices have prepared variations of these forms and instructions for use by airports in their regions. Before completing a form, please check with the appropriate Regional or District Office to determine which form you should use."[15] Note that private corporations also provide 5010 data, including MyAFD.com (http://www.myafd.com/airport/hgr), AirNav.com (http://airnav.com/), and GCR & Associates (www.gcr1.com/5010WEB).

At airports with flight schools the school operator can usually provide detail on its component of operational activity. Other sources of operations data for non-towered airports have been used with reasonably acceptable results. These include various forms of counting such as human counting; pneumatic, electromagnetic, or acoustical machine counts; and more recently, video counts. A video counting system called FlightRev™, distributed and operated by Vector Airport Solutions (http://vector-us.com/) is advertised to capture more traffic than any other system available to general aviation airports. Video counts have an additional benefit in that they show the actual aircraft so the results yield not only the number of aircraft operations, but also an accurate documentation of aircraft types, regardless of weather, lighting conditions, or time of day. It should be kept in mind however that if counts other than the 5010 data are used as part of the planning process, they must be documented and explained, and must be accepted by the local ADO. On occasion ADOs do not accept alternative counts and there does not appear to be any clear or consistent rationale for this. Therefore, before embarking on an alternative counting methodology it is a good idea to check with the ADO and get their concurrence beforehand.

Based Aircraft

The number of aircraft based at an airport is also an important parameter to be forecast because it influences the need for hangars and contributes to the need for fueling, maintenance, and other facilities. The current number of based aircraft can usually be obtained from the airport manager, especially at general aviation airports, but a lengthy historical data series may not always be available. Data on the number of based aircraft can also be obtained from the TAF for airports included in the NPIAS. This information is obtained from the Form 5010 discussed above. Some additional based aircraft information may be obtained from other methods or sources such as fixed base operators; if the aircraft is parked on their ramp or purchases fuel from them they usually keep a record of the financial transaction.

Fleet Mix

The aircraft fleet mix, i.e., the number of operations by aircraft type or category, is needed for the load factor and gate use analyses, and it is essential for airside capacity studies and noise analyses. Unfortunately the data are often not very accurate, especially at general aviation airports. Data on air carrier operations by aircraft type can be obtained from the Schedule T-100 noted above, and from the *Official Airline Guide* (http://www.oagaviation.com/). Fleet mix data for air carrier, commuter, and general aviation operations at large airports may also be obtained from the aircraft noise monitoring systems. Fleet mix data for general aviation airports, and for general aviation activity at air carrier airports, are much more difficult to obtain. Site surveys are often conducted at general aviation airports, but this requires establishing a statistically reliable sampling period, and care must be taken to sample weekdays and weekend days separately, since the fleet composition can vary. The video count system noted above can also provide accurate fleet mix information. Sometimes the based aircraft fleet composition is used to estimate the operational fleet mix. This method is not always accurate because the airplanes based at an airport are not necessarily the ones that do most of the flying. For example, 80 or 90 percent of the based aircraft may be single-engine piston aircraft used for personal or recreational flying; however, they may account for a much smaller portion of the flight activity, especially on weekdays. During the week the airport may be used more often by aircraft flying for business or corporate flight activity using larger, more sophisticated aircraft.

Socioeconomic Data

Socioeconomic data are essential to regression analyses and other forms of econometric modeling. Regardless of the forecast methodology used it is a good idea to include some socioeconomic background and data to provide some context for the forecasts and for the airport as a whole. The most relevant socioeconomic data relate to population, income (disposable, per capita, and total income are commonly available), and employment (total and white-collar are both available). Historical data on these socioeconomic indicators are usually available from the U.S. Department of Commerce's Bureau of the Census, as well as local, regional, and state sources. Projections may also be available from these sources for some of the indicators. In fact, many jurisdictions mandate the use of these projections for all forecasting efforts (although this requirement seems to be ignored in most airport planning studies). Historical and forecast socioeconomic data are also available from commercial sources, some of which are listed below:

- DRI McGraw-Hill, Inc. (www.dri.mcgraw-hill.com)
- NPA Data Services, Inc. (www.npadata.com)
- Regional Financial Associates (www.rfa.com)
- WEFA, Inc. (www.wefa.com)
- Woods and Poole (www.woodsandpoole.com)

Forecast Methodologies

Sometimes it seems that there are as many aviation demand forecasting methodologies as there are people who make their living doing aviation demand forecasts. In all cases forecasting is essentially guesswork, because no one really knows what the future will bring. It is always good to remember that no matter what we think the future will be, it will probably be something else—and probably something we haven't even thought of. Or as de Neufville so eloquently puts it, "The forecast is always wrong."[16] It must be clearly understood that for the purposes of this discussion the terms "forecast" and "projection" are used interchangeably. Purists (purity being a relative and highly subjective term) may argue that there is a difference, but I could never follow those discussions. In my experience both terms mean the same thing: a guess.

The FAA Forecasting Report cited above describes seven methods for aviation demand forecasting:

- Regression and Trend Analysis
- Share Analysis
- Exponential Smoothing
- Comparison With Other Airports
- Survey Techniques
- Cohort Analysis
- Choice and Distribution Models

Wells and Young summarize forecasting methodologies rather nicely, dividing them into two categories: Qualitative Methods and Quantitative Methods.[17] Under qualitative methods they list Jury of Executive Opinion, Sales Force Composite, Consumer Market Survey, and the Delphi Method. Quantitative Methods are rather usefully divided into two categories: Time Series or Trend Analysis Models, and Causal Models. Qualitative methods, which may also be termed *subjective* methods, tend to be based on the knowledge, experience, and judgment of the forecaster, and do not rely strictly or exclusively on historical data. Quantitative methods, or as they are sometimes called, *objective* methods, rely on numerical data describing past aviation activity at the airport or in the region under study.

Wells and Young note that quantitative methods are strictly objective and do not directly consider judgment on the part of the forecaster. But this is not quite true because historical data, in terms of market development, growth rates, air services patterns, and the number and type of carriers serving the airport, often provide the background upon which subjective or judgmental forecasts are based. The particular set of historical data used—and the historical time period selected—are based on the judgment of the forecaster. Also, the selection of the particular quantitative technique or model and the selection of the specific independent variables used in econometric models can be quite subjective. An example of how a seemingly objective forecast methodology can be "tweaked" is shown below in the Trend Analysis section of the discussion of Quantitative Methods. In any event the methodology used to prepare the forecasts should be appropriate to the quality of the historical data available. Using a sophisticated forecasting model with poor quality data will result in poor quality forecasts.

Qualitative Methods

The *Jury of Executive Opinion* typically relies on the experience and judgment of the airport administration and key management staff, and may also include major airport tenants and other key airport stakeholders. Remember to strike a balance here, because increasing the number of participants to broaden the range of experience and insight runs the risk of adding a few who don't have all that much relevant experience or especially keen insight. And it is not a wise idea to "stack the deck" by selecting only those who share one particular view of the world and its future.

The *Sales Force Composite* method is very similar, except that the participants are typically restricted to airport employees, or the employees of firms such as airlines, rental car companies, concessionaires, etc., who work directly at the airport. Conversely, the *Consumer Market Survey* method relies upon the airport's customers, such as air passengers, cargo shippers, and other businesses located at or around the airport. The theory is that these participants will form the base of future aeronautical demand, therefore, they should have some insight into future travel patterns and demand levels. Based on my limited experience with this approach, all I can say here is, "Good Luck."

The *Delphi Method* was originally developed by marketing types in the private sector. As described by Wells and Young, a group of experts is selected and each individual is sent a questionnaire. The experts operate independently and each expert is not even supposed to know who the other experts are. This assures independence and avoids internal influences. The process is typically an interactive one, in that all responses and supporting arguments and opinions are collected and then shared with the group. After a few iterations a consensus develops (hopefully) and a collective future vision appears.

Although Wells and Young do not indicate the types of questions asked and the opinions solicited in the qualitative methods described above, they typically include such items as total annual passengers, cargo volumes, and aircraft operations, as well as expected annual growth rates for each demand component. It is also desirable to try to identify new carriers, markets, or types of service, as well as shifts in the concentrations of aviation demand within the airport's market area; an example might be a shift in local trip origins or destinations from a downtown area to a major suburb or two. Opinions regarding the nature of future demand are relevant. This might include an assessment of the area's potential for developing nonbusiness or tourist-related air travel, or a potential shift from heavy air cargo shipments associated with local manufacturers to smaller, high-priority shipments associated with integrated carriers such as FedEx and UPS.

Quantitative Methods

Although a number of quantitative forecasting techniques are available, it is important to note that they all involve an extrapolation of past events in one way or another. Sometimes this is merely a relatively simple linear extrapolation of historical data—Wells and Young refer to this as a Time Series Model. At other times an attempt is made to establish a historical relationship between an air traffic measure and one or more independent factors, and then apply the historical relationship into the future—Wells and Young refer to this as a Causal Model.

Regression Analysis, also referred to as correlation analysis or correlation technique, attempts to determine the existence and strength of a relationship between two or more variables. This method is probably the most common forecasting technique. A more complete explanation of regression analysis can be found in any good statistics text—a simple review will suffice for the purposes of this book. Simple regression is a method for determining the existence of a linear or straight-line relationship between two variables, one of which is referred to as the dependent variable and the other as the independent variable. Most regression analyses are based on the assumption that the relationship between the two variables is linear, although nonlinear models are sometimes used. When a linear regression technique is used for aviation demand forecasting, the total number of enplaned passengers is the dependent variable and another measure, population for example, is the independent variable. The implication here is that variations in enplaned passengers *depend* on variations in population, although this is something of an oversimplification, as discussed further below. Multiple regression is a method for determining the existence of a linear relationship between one (dependent) variable and a number of other (independent) variables. A simple regression equation takes the form $Y = a+bX$, where "Y" is the dependent variable, "X" is the independent variable, "a" is the Y intercept, or constant, and "b" is the slope or regression coefficient. The dependent variable for our purposes is the measure of aviation demand we are trying to forecast, such as total enplaned passengers. The independent variable is a measure of a factor that we assume is somehow related to the dependent variable. Simply stated, the values for "a" and "b" are most commonly determined using the *least squares* method. The least squares technique is used to fit a line to a group of points such that the sum of the squared deviations of each point from the line is minimized. The line then represents an average, i.e., predicted, relationship between the variables "X" and "Y." The value for "a" determines the point at which the regression line meets the Y or vertical axis; the value for "b" determines the slope of the regression line.

The strength of a hypothesized relationship is indicated by the correlation coefficient "r"—the value of this coefficient varies between -1.00 and +1.00. A positive sign indicates that the dependent variable "X" increases with an increase in the dependent variable "Y." A negative sign indicates a decrease in "X" with an increase in "Y." The higher the value of "r," the closer the individual points are to the regression line; a lower "r" value indicates that the data points are more widely scattered or separated from the regression line. An "r" value of zero means that there is no correlation between the dependent and independent variables. The coefficient of determination, denoted as "r^2," is calculated by squaring the correlation coefficient. The coefficient of determination indicates the proportion of variation in "X" that is associated with a variation in "Y." For example, an "r" value of 0.94 yields an "r^2" of 0.88, that is, 88 percent of the variation in "X" is associated with, *but not explained by*, a variation in "Y." It must be clearly understood that *correlation* is not *causation*. In spite of the Wells and Young reference to causal models, a regression analysis identifies an association between a dependent variable, such as passenger enplanements, and an independent variable, such as population. This may seem a bit fussy, since people travel and thereby generate passenger enplanements; however, a lot of people do not fly. Thus, the existence of a large number of people does not necessarily imply a large number of air trips, or in fact, any air trips. Regression analysis shows a statistical relationship, but not a cause-and-effect relationship.

Figures 7-1 and 7-2 illustrate a simple linear regression graph. Figure 7-1 shows a set of data points in which the variation in the "Y" values is closely related to the variation in the "X" values, having an "r" of 0.92 and an "r^2" of 0.84. Figure 7-2 illustrates a weaker relationship between the "X" and "Y" values, with the data points more widely scattered from the trend line. The data in Figure 7-2 have an "r" of 0.63 and an "r^2" of 0.39.

Multiple regression analysis implies the same type of linear statistical relationship between variables, except that multiple regression identifies the relationship between a dependent variable—again typically enplaned passengers—and two or more independent variables. Among the most common measures used as independent variables in aviation demand forecasting are population, per capita or disposable income, employment (particularly white-collar employment), and a measure of average air fares or yield. In this instance the technique is often referred to as an econometric model. The correlation coefficient in a multiple regression analysis is noted as "R" and the coefficient of determination as "R^2."

One of the problems associated with using a regression analysis, either simple or multiple, is that both the dependent and independent variables may be more closely related to some other factor than to each other. For example, passengers and population both typically increase over time, thus the strength of the regression relationship between passengers and population may be more a function of the time variable. Also, population and income are often used as independent variables in a multiple regression equation. Population and income may be so closely related to each other, and to time, that it unduly influences the strength of their relationship with the dependent variable, passengers.

Chapter 7 – Forecasting

Figure 7-1: Strong Correlation

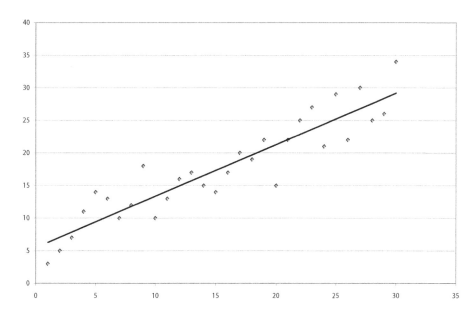

Figure 7-2: Weak Correlation

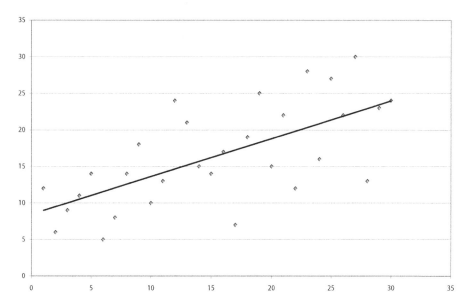

Another factor to consider when using any sort of econometric or multiple regression model is that it may not be a good idea to use enplaned passengers as the dependent variable. Some consideration should be given to using originating passengers instead. As noted above, an estimate of originating passengers is needed for determining future requirements for many terminal facilities as well as access and parking facilities. The difference between total enplanements and total originations is the connecting passenger component. It does not seem reasonable to postulate that an airport's connecting traffic is a function of local factors such as population, income, employment, or even air fares. This is a situation where the relationship may be statistically valid, but the underlying assumption does not pass the intuitive logic test.

Originating passengers are often used in "bottom-up" forecasts. For example, a region or metropolitan area may be divided into zones and a separate forecast developed for each zone, with the resulting zonal forecasts aggregated to provide an airport total. Or separate forecasts may be developed for each route to a major destination city and the resulting city-pair totals aggregated for an airport total.

The use of regression analysis in aviation demand forecasting implicitly assumes that the relationship between air travel and socioeconomic indicators in the past will continue to hold in the future. This may or may not be true, and that fact should be kept in mind. Regression analysis also seems to assume that the independent socioeconomic variable or variables are more easily or reliably projected than the dependent variable. For example, a multiple regression analysis that relates enplaned passengers to total population and per capita income assumes that population and income may be forecast more reliably than passenger volumes could be using some other method. But as the noted economist John Kenneth Galbraith is reported to have said, "The only function of economic forecasting is to make astrology look respectable."[18]

Note that the parameters used as independent variables should be ones for which forecasts are readily and reliably available, such as population and income. Aviation fuel prices are often used as independent variables, but they may not be regarded as trustworthy, given the volatility in the oil industry.

Although regression analysis is a sound forecasting technique because it considers a number of different factors that may influence air travel demand, and regression analysis appears to be completely objective, it can be misused to provide some preconceived or desired forecast result. This can be done by cherry-picking the independent variables that give the most desired result, and/or by selecting a historical time series that does the same thing. The time series aspect is illustrated by the BWI example discussed in the following section.

A *Trend Analysis or Time Series Model* is a form of regression analysis (using time as the independent variable) and is probably the most widely used forecasting technique—it is certainly the easiest to apply. It is simply a matter of projecting a series of historical data into the future. A trend analysis can be as simple as drawing a line through a series of historical data points on a graph and extending that line into the future. A trend analysis can also be used in a simple linear regression model, as described above, where the change in the dependent variable is associated with the independent variable, time. It is often used when a quick estimate is needed, e.g., when somebody asks for a projection just before a meeting. Also, it is fairly certain that a trend analysis will be used to evaluate a forecast, no matter which methodology is used to prepare it. Trust me, in any meeting at which forecasts are discussed somebody will sneak a ruler or scale out of his pocket and align the little historical data points to see if the trend line matches the projection laboriously derived from a sophisticated multivariate econometric model. In these cases the forecaster may be inclined to throw something at him.

An example of how to use (or misuse) an apparently simple and theoretically objective time series analysis to obtain the desired forecast results is illustrated in Figure 7-3. This is a graph of a simple linear trend of air passenger growth at BWI Airport. Analysis of the historical data from 1985 through 2005 indicates that the average annual growth rate was 4.2 percent. Applying that rate through the next 20 years shows that by the year 2025 the airport will handle 44.9 million total passengers. This is fairly straightforward, assuming that traffic will grow over the next 20 years as it has in the past 20 years. However, if the historical period begins in 1980 instead of 1985, the resulting forecasts are quite different. Historical growth over this 25-year period averaged 7.1 percent; applying that figure to the future yields 77.8 million passengers by 2025.

Little tricks like this are often used in forecasting, and who could argue with the logic of using as long a historical period for which data are available? Although this example uses a simple linear projection of growth rates, it should be easy to see how other supposedly objective analyses could be crafted to give the desired answer. If a linear regression or even a multiple regression analysis were to be applied to the historical data, a similar discrepancy would result. Typically a regression analysis would use a population measure, or population and income for a multiple regression analysis, but the results would differ between a 20-year and a 23-year historical period, because population and income in the Baltimore area did not grow significantly between 1980 and 1985. The big increase in air passenger traffic during those three years was due to the establishment of a connecting hub at BWI.

Share Analysis or Market Share Model is another type of quantitative technique occasionally used to forecast aviation demand. This is a technique that simply looks at an individual airport's share of a larger unit, such as a regional, state, or even national total. For example, the total number of aircraft based at an airport could be projected as a share of a regional or state total. Because this method uses a forecast for a larger unit to develop projections for a smaller unit, it is often referred to as a "top-down" model. This technique implicitly assumes a relationship between a particular airport and

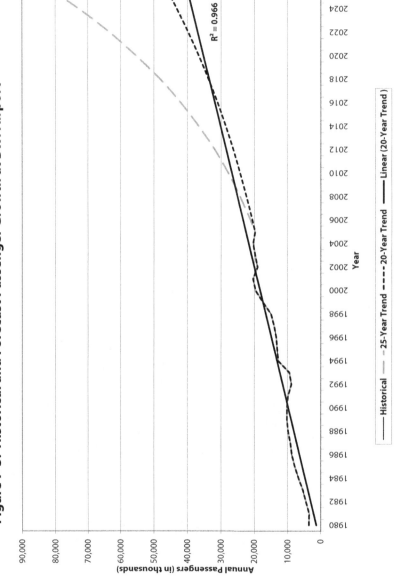

Figure 7-3: Historical and Forecast Passenger Growth at BWI Airport

the larger aggregate total and that this relationship will continue through the forecast period. It also assumes (or hopes) that the forecast for the larger entity is accurate. Note also that the assumption that an airport's share of a larger total will remain constant through the forecast period also implicitly assumes that the airport will grow at the same rate as the larger entity. Although this assumption may be valid at the regional or state level, it may be tenuous at the national level. The assumption that an airport's share of the nation's total passenger enplanements will remain constant (or increase or decrease) through the forecast period ignores numerous other factors that influence aviation demand at the local or regional level. On the other hand, a simple share analysis is often a good check on the reasonableness of a forecast developed using another methodology.

Exponential Smoothing is a variation of a trend analysis that gives more weight to more recent data and less weight to earlier data. According to the FAA Forecast Report, this technique is sometimes used to prepare near-term forecasts. A similar smoothing variation is a *moving average* method. This technique is sometimes used when data vary significantly from year to year. In that case the first data point can be obtained by averaging the first, second, and third years of data; the second point by averaging the second, third, and fourth years; the third point by averaging the third, fourth, and fifth years, and so on. To me this appears to be something that people do when they don't like the historical data, or when the historical data do not support a preconceived conclusion. In order to get the answer they want, they tend to mess around a little with the data. This is my opinion only, based on my experience in reviewing various forecasts over the years—I'm sure statisticians and modelers would disagree. But keep in mind that the client or somebody in the audience may feel the same way I do about these techniques, and the forecaster may be called on it, so he should be prepared to defend his forecasts and methodology.

Comparison With Other Airports is a method that involves comparing growth at the airport in question with growth at a few other, similar airports. The airports selected should have similar traffic volumes and service characteristics. For example, forecasts for passenger enplanements at Greater Buffalo International would not be compared with passenger growth projections at Miami, San Diego, Atlanta, or Chicago O'Hare. Instead, airports such as Indianapolis, Cleveland, or Pittsburgh may be more appropriate. Similarly, an airport that is heavily served by a low-cost carrier like Southwest should not be compared with airports that are predominantly served by the mainline carriers such as American, United, or Delta. This technique would be useful at an airport that is about to obtain new service from a low-cost carrier, in comparison with the growth that actually occurred at airports that had a similar experience, such as BWI or Providence, Rhode Island.

The FAA Forecast Report lists *Survey Techniques* as a possible methodology for preparing aviation demand forecasts in situations where information about local trip origin and destination points is available for a subsequent analysis of local travel patterns. This method does not appear to be commonly used as an aviation demand forecasting technique but it has been used to help develop base data and assumptions for use with other forecasting methodologies.

Cohort Analysis is also listed in the FAA Forecast Report. This is a method for preparing forecasts for separate groups within an overall demand framework. For example, if a forecast of total enplaned passengers is being prepared for a particular airport, a separate projection for traffic in certain city pairs may also be desired and would be developed using a cohort analysis. This is not so much a forecast methodology as it is a way of handling or analyzing the data. Once the traffic demand for an airport is broken into separate units or cohorts, one of the other forecast methodologies noted herein can be used to prepare the actual traffic projections. Typically this is done as part of a bottom-up forecast process.

A number of relatively sophisticated *Choice and Distribution Models* are sometimes used in air traffic demand forecasting. Usually these models are used to forecast traffic in city-pair markets, although the individual city-pair forecasts can be aggregated to come up with an airport total. These models are usually based on some form of the Gravity Model, which was developed by Isaac Newton as a means of determining the force of attraction between two planetary bodies, such as the Earth and the Moon. A gravity model takes the form $I_{ab} = P_a P_b / d_{ab}$, where "I" is the force of attraction between two bodies, "a" and "b;" "P_a" is the mass of body "a;" "P_b" is the mass of body "b;" and "d_{ab}" is the distance between bodies "a" and "b." To make it a little more relevant, assume that body "a" is the city of Baltimore and body "b" is the city of Cleveland. The masses of each city, "P_a" and "P_b," may be measured by the population of each city. Or perhaps the accuracy of the model can be improved by using a segment of the total population that is likely to travel by air, for example white-collar employment or population over the age of 15 or 21 or whatever. And the distance between the city pairs can actually be the distance between the cities; for aviation demand forecasting purposes it can be the direct airline mileage between the city pairs, although travel cost is usually considered a more appropriate surrogate for mileage as a distance measure. Because this technique involves forecasting based on small units and aggregating the individual results to a grand total for the airport, it is known as a "bottom-up" model, as opposed to the "top-down" model noted above. Years ago this model was used to forecast highway traffic between city pairs, and still is, in a modified and more sophisticated form. Gravity model forecasts have been used in instances where a city is divided into zones, and traffic between each of these zones and a number of destination cities is analyzed and projected separately. In the few examples with which I am familiar, the models were very successful in generating revenue for the consultants doing the forecast modeling, but did not fare very well at forecasting future air traffic at the airports under study. In each case the models drastically under-projected future traffic volumes; unfortunately nobody stayed around long enough to find out why. Nonetheless, this type of model is good grist for the master's thesis mill, and perhaps someday success may be realized in a real-world situation.

The methodologies described above are typically used for forecasting passenger demand and related growth at larger airports. Forecasting for general aviation airports does not usually involve such sophisticated forecasting methodologies; this is primarily because the historical data are not very reliable. Some of the smaller airports that are equipped with air traffic control towers are likely to have a fairly reliable data base to work with, but most general aviation airports are not tower-equipped and the forecasts must be based on data from Form 5010, or another similarly questionable source. Using sophisticated forecasting methodologies at small airports is akin to putting calipers on butter. As stated above, the forecast methodology should be consistent with the quality of the historical data available. The best policy is to keep the forecast as simple as possible and explain the methodology clearly, with an emphasis on the underlying logic.

Planning studies at general aviation airports often use a methodology that uses an operations per based aircraft ratio. This ratio is obtained by dividing the total number of operations by the total number of based aircraft. The ratio is then applied to the independently-developed forecast of based aircraft to obtain forecasts of aircraft operations. If desired the operations can be divided into local and itinerant and a separate ratio can be developed for each. Note that this is a mathematical ratio only—it does not mean that the operations are actually carried out by the aircraft based at the airport. Because this ratio can vary significantly from airport to airport, it should be developed separately for the individual airport under study. If accurate information is not available for that airport it is appropriate to use ratios for other, similar airports—preferably ones located in the same region or area. It is particularly helpful if one of these airports has a control tower where accurate historical operations data are available.

How Can We Tell if the Forecast is Good?

As noted above, one way to tell if a forecast is good is whether the FAA approves it. However, some additional thought is necessary to ensure that the forecast will provide a solid base for further planning. Although most guidance on the subject of forecasting does not emphasize this, anyone reviewing forecasts should be able to verify that the methodology, the underlying assumptions, and the resulting forecasts make sense. The forecasts prepared for an airport planning study should include documentation that explains how the forecasts were prepared, along with the underlying assumptions. If an airport operator receives a set of forecasts prepared by a consultant he should make sure this documentation is also provided. Many (perhaps most) forecasts are based on a regression or multiple regression (or correlation) approach. As noted above, this methodology implies that the behavior of the dependent variable (typically air passengers) is related to (or is a function of) the behavior of one or more independent variables, such as population, an income measure, perhaps air fares, fuel prices, etc. Remember that correlation is not causation, i.e., the equation says that the growth in passengers is related to the growth in population, income, etc., but is not necessarily caused by it. The first question to ask then is whether the relationship is logical. Reasons should be given for the selection of each of the independent variables, along with an explanation of how each of the variables is related to aviation demand—not just statistically but also logically.

How can we determine if a forecast is good and is appropriate for later use in determining future facility requirements? One way to establish a comfort factor is to use two, or perhaps even three, different forecast methodologies. If a regression analysis or econometric model has been used, it would be appropriate to do a simple linear trend analysis to see if it yields similar results. This can be as simple as drawing a straight line through the historical data points (just like the guy in the forecast presentation example).

Historical and projected growth rates should also be examined for the total passenger and total operations forecasts as well as for each of the components. If passenger enplanements have been growing at a fairly steady rate of 3.5 percent for the past 20 years and the forecast calls for an increase to an average of 4.2 percent for the next 20 years, some explanation should be provided. Beware also of abrupt changes in growth rates. For example, demand may have been growing at the 3.5 percent average rate through the historical period, but the past few years show a lower rate of 2.5 or 3.0 percent. This should be noted and discussed in the forecast report. If the forecasts revert to the long-term 3.5 percent rate in the near-term years of the forecast period, some explanation should be provided.

Yet another simple check against a regression analysis or trend analysis is the share analysis. In this case the results of the regression forecast can be checked as a percentage of the national total. The FAA produces annual forecasts of total U.S. domestic and international passenger traffic which should be used as a basis for a share comparison of local airport forecasts. If the locally-prepared forecasts show a significant increase or decrease in an airport's share of the national total it doesn't necessarily mean that the forecasts are wrong or even suspect, but a clear and logical explanation of the change in share should be provided.

It is also good practice to compare the separate components of the forecasts. For example, a projection of total enplaned passengers can be divided by an estimated or projected enplaning load factor, i.e., passengers per departure, to obtain a forecast of airline departures. A projection of airline departures can be prepared independently and compared with the values calculated from the enplaned passenger forecast. This is a very good check because the average number of annual enplanements per departure at most airports usually increases at a rather slow and steady rate. Again, a marked change in the forecast of enplanements per departure may not be incorrect, but some explanation should be given. An example might be a shift from air carrier service with large aircraft to commuter service with smaller aircraft. Another useful check on the passenger forecasts at large airports is to compare the historical and projected share of international passengers as a percent of the enplaned passenger total. If international traffic has historically accounted for about 10 percent of the total and the forecast shows this proportion growing to 15 or 20 percent, the assumptions should be checked. This is not to say that such a change could not occur, rather it suggests that a very good explanation should be provided to explain the shift. The same comparison should be made for the commuter share of the total enplaned passenger volume. If a mainline air carrier is shifting some of its short-haul service to a commuter operator, the forecasts should show an increase in the commuter share of the total. Similarly, if a carrier is de-emphasizing or "downsizing" its hub operations at an airport, the commuter share would be expected to decline through the forecast period, unless there is a good reason for assuming otherwise.

Other relevant and useful comparisons may be made for aircraft operations forecasts. Aircraft operations are usually projected separately for air carriers, commuters, air taxi, general aviation, and military. Note whether the projected shares for each of these components are consistent with historical record, and if they are not, make sure there is a good explanation for any changes. If the commuter share of aircraft operations is expected to increase relative to air carrier operations, some explanation or justification is necessary. Also make sure that the increase in the commuter share of operations is accompanied by a corresponding increase in the commuter share of enplaned passengers. If not, some explanation is needed.

As a final note on forecasting, we tend to forget, or perhaps it is more accurate to say we tend to discount, the human aspects of judgment and experience. All the things we have seen and learned over the years must count for something. After preparing aviation demand forecasts for several years, a good forecaster develops a sense or feeling that the forecasts and their underlying methodologies and assumptions make sense. Another way of saying this is that a good forecaster develops a feel for the accuracy or appropriateness (or conversely, inaccuracy or inappropriateness) of the forecast results. This feeling can't be measured and it is not likely to hold up in court, as the expression goes, but it should not be discounted.

Endnotes

1. *Airport Master Plans*, AC 150/5070-6B. Washington, D.C.: Federal Aviation Administration, 2005, p. 37.

2. *Airport Aviation Activity Forecasting*. Washington, D.C.: Airport Cooperative Research Program, Transportation Research Board, 2007, p. 1. Accessed June 2008, from http://onlinepubs.trb.org/onlinepubs/acrp/acrp_syn_002.pdf

3. *Forecasting Aviation Activity by Airport*. Jenkintown, PA: GRA, 2001, incorporated for Federal Aviation Administration, Office of Aviation Policy and Plans, 2001. Accessed June 2008, from http://www.faa.gov/data_statistics/aviation_data_statistics/forecasting/media/af1.doc

4. *Field Formulation of the National Plan of Integrated Airport Systems (NPIAS)*, FAA Order 5090.3C. Washington, D.C.: Federal Aviation Administration, December 4, 2000. Accessed June 2008, from http://www.faa.gov/airports_airtraffic/airports/resources/publications/orders/media/planning_5090_3C.pdf

5. *Ibid.*, p. 19.

6. *Airport Aviation Activity Forecasting. Op cit.* p. 1.

7. *Planning and Design Guidelines for Airport Terminal Facilities*, AC 150/5360-13. Washington, D.C.: Federal Aviation Administration, 1994, p. 7.

8. *Ibid.*

9. *Ibid.*, p. 10-11.

10. http://www.bts.gov

11. *Airport Aviation Activity Forecasting. Op cit.* p. 5-6.

12. http://forms.faa.gov/forms/faa1800-31.pdf

13. *Forecasting Aviation Activity by Airport. Op cit.* p. 3.

14. http://tafpub.itworks-software.com/taf2007/LoginPage.asp

15. http://www.faa.gov/airports_airtraffic/airports/resources/forms/index.cfm?sect=airportmaster

16. de Neufville, Richard, and Amedeo Odoni, *Airport Systems Planning, Design, and Management*. New York: McGraw-Hill, 2003, p. 70.

17. Wells, Alexander T., and Seth B. Young, *Airport Planning and Management*, 5th Edition. New York: McGraw-Hill, 2004.

18. Galbraith, John Kenneth, as quoted in *The New York Times*, March 15, 2009.

CHAPTER 8

ENVIRONMENTAL CONSIDERATIONS

The environmental component is one of the most critical elements of the airport planning process. Airport planners are not normally environmental specialists and do not need to know the details of environmental regulation. However, planners should have some familiarity with the environmental regulatory process and with some of the key attributes of environmental resources that could be impacted by airport development. This will help develop airport plans that avoid or minimize adverse environmental impacts. Unlike some of the other elements of the planning process, the environmental analysis and supporting documentation must be prepared in accordance with strict guidelines and regulations, with very little allowance for flexibility. Consideration of these requirements as part of the planning process is a good way to help ensure that airport plans are workable. This chapter outlines the major factors involved in the environmental component of airport planning and references the federal documents that are the primary source of environmental guidance. It also discusses the overall concept behind the environmental requirements and includes a discussion of sustainability and how airports can become "greener." The chapter approaches the environmental analysis in the context of something that should be done for the sake of a cleaner planet, not from the standpoint of how to avoid or shortcut the environmental process.

Background

As discussed in Chapter 2, airports include a variety of facilities and services that can be regarded in some sense as an intrusion into a larger community. Undoubtedly airports have beneficial impacts on the communities they serve, but they can also have adverse impacts on the surrounding cultural and physical (or natural) environments. These adverse impacts result both from the physical presence of the airport and its facilities and from its associated aircraft and ground vehicular activities. Airport construction, operation, and maintenance activities, as well as associated ground access systems and vehicles, generate noise, contribute to air and water pollution, disturb groundwater and surface runoff patterns, and eliminate large areas of wetlands and vegetation. If proper procedures are followed, it is possible to build and operate an airport, or any other major facility, that avoids or minimizes impacts to the environment. Environmental regulations and guidelines that try to minimize the impact of potentially disruptive activities are based primarily on the National Environmental Policy Act of 1969 (NEPA). This law states that all agencies of the federal government shall

> ...include in every recommendation or report on proposals for legislation and other major federal actions significantly affecting the quality of the human environment, a detailed statement by the responsible official on:
>
> - the environmental impact of the proposed action,
> - any adverse environmental effects which cannot be avoided should the proposal be implemented,
> - alternatives to the proposed action,
> - the relationship between local short-term uses of man's environment and the maintenance and enhancement of long-term productivity, and
> - any irreversible and irretrievable commitments of resources which would be involved in the proposed action should it be implemented.[1]

The NEPA legislation also created the Council on Environmental Quality (CEQ), which is assigned the task of ensuring that federal agencies meet their NEPA obligations.

It is important to understand that airport sponsors own and operate public-use airports in the U.S. It is therefore the sponsor's responsibility to determine when, where, and what kind of development is needed to meet the airport's role and fulfill its functions. The sponsor is also responsible for constructing new facilities, along with operating and maintaining the airport. Because these are the sponsor's responsibilities, not the FAA's, sponsors may perform all these functions and activities (for the most part) without obtaining federal environmental approvals under NEPA, although state and local environmental approvals may be required. NEPA provisions come into play when the sponsor requests FAA approval of the ALP and/or requests federal

Chapter 8 – Environmental Considerations

aid to accomplish any of the projects. Approving the ALP and awarding airport improvement grants are federal actions under NEPA and a federal action is what triggers the NEPA process. These and other federal actions listed in Order 5050.4B, paragraph 9(g) are:

- Conditional, unconditional, or mixed approval of federal funding for airport planning and development projects, including separate funding of plans and specifications for those projects.
- Conditional, unconditional, or mixed approval of a location for a new, public-use airport.
- Conditional, unconditional, or mixed approval of a first-time or changed airport layout plan (ALP).
- Authorizing an airport sponsor to impose and use Passenger Facility Charges (PFC).
- Conditional, unconditional, or mixed approval of an airport sponsor's request under 49 USC Section 47125, to use or transfer federally-owned land to carry out an action under 49 USC Chapter 471, Subchapter I, at a public-use airport or to support the airport's operations.
- Conditional, unconditional, or mixed approval of an airport sponsor's request to release airport land from a federally-obligated, public-use airport when the land would be used for nonaeronautical purposes.
- Conditional, unconditional, or mixed approval of the use of a facility as a public-use airport when the facility becomes available under the Surplus Property Act.
- Approving noise compatibility programs under 14 CFR Part 150.
- Approving an airport sponsor to restrict the use of Stage 3 aircraft at public-use airports under 14 CFR Part 161.
- Issuing a Part 139 certification.
- Conditional, unconditional, or mixed approval of funding for measures in an FAA-approved Wildlife Hazard Management Plan or approving ALP changes to accommodate those measures.[2]

The FAA has published the following three documents that translate these NEPA requirements and CEQ regulations into guidelines for environmental analysis in the context of various FAA functions and responsibilities including air traffic control, airway facilities, and safety (among others), as well as airports:

- FAA Order 1050.1E, *Policies and Procedures for Considering Environmental Impacts*
- FAA Order 5050.4B, *National Environmental Policy Act (NEPA) Implementing Instructions for Airport Actions*
- *Environmental Desk Reference for Airport Actions*

These documents are the primary source for the information needed to determine when an environmental analysis is needed, the type of analysis to be done, the factors to be included, and the type and level of documentation required to obtain FAA approval. All three of these documents are available on the FAA Web site and, because environmental laws, regulations, and associated criteria change from time to time, the latest versions of the documents should be consulted prior to undertaking any airport development project.

FAA Order 1050.1E identifies FAA policies and procedures to ensure that the agency complies with the provisions of CEQ regulations implementing NEPA.[3] This Order provides guidelines for all FAA actions, including "…grants, loans, contracts, leases, construction, research activities, rulemaking and regulatory actions, certifications, licensing, permits, plans submitted to the FAA that require FAA approval, and legislation proposed by the FAA."[4] Appendix A of Order 1050.1E also lists 18 potential environmental impact categories as noted further below. For each of these potential impact categories the Order lists the major applicable federal statute(s), regulations, executive orders, and guidance, as well as the agencies responsible for oversight.

Order 1050.1E also specifically states that the FAA can use the NEPA process to give appropriate consideration to specific environmental concerns by

- describing the agency's underlying purpose and need for taking action;
- identifying reasonable alternatives to the proposed action (must include the no action alternative);
- rigorously analyzing the reasonable foreseeable direct, indirect, and cumulative environmental impacts of the proposed action and alternatives;
- providing for public disclosure and comment and a mechanism for responding to public comments;
- providing the basis for informed selection of the preferred alternative;
- identifying and evaluating measures to mitigate adverse effects of the preferred alternative and ensuring that appropriate measures are implemented; and
- facilitating compliance with applicable environmental laws, regulations, and executive orders.[5]

FAA Order 5050.4B supplements Order 1050.1E and provides guidance for the FAA Office of Airports (ARP) and others with regard to evaluating NEPA requirements for airport actions that fall under the FAA's authority. The ARP is responsible for identifying major federal actions involving the public-use airports and for analyzing the environmental effects of each action as well as its alternatives. Order 5050.4B provides extremely valuable guidance with respect to the type and level of environmental analysis required for airport projects, including comprehensive explanations of Environmental Assessment (EA) and Environmental Impact Statement (EIS) processes, documentation requirements, and approvals, as listed below.

- To airport sponsors on proposed projects that may be categorically excluded.
- To airport sponsors, their environmental consultants, and other interested parties about preparing EAs for proposed airport projects and how the FAA will determine if the EAs are acceptable and if a Finding of No Significant Impact (FONSI) is appropriate for those projects.
- About the process the ARP must complete for airport projects having impacts that require the FAA (the ARP) to prepare EISs and issue Records of Decision.[6]

Order 5050.4B also lists the planning information necessary for the NEPA process.[7] As noted in Chapter 5: Master Planning, if the planning information is not in a complete and usable form the environmental analysis will have to be delayed until the necessary information is obtained, resulting in a loss of time and money. It is also important to begin considering environmental factors, including potential areas of environmental impact, as early as possible in the planning process. If an environmental issue is lurking somewhere, it must be addressed in order to obtain federal approval for the project. Delaying any environmental analysis in hopes that the problem will go away or that the regulations will change is simply delaying the inevitable. It will save a lot of time and effort in the long run if the issues are identified up front and addressed as part of the planning process. Also, if there is any question as to the adequacy of the information in the planning documents, they should be sent to the FAA for review prior to the commencement of the environmental documentation. The need for complete and accurate information is very clearly stated in Order 5050.4B:

> Airport planning information is the backbone of a proposed airport action. As noted earlier, it is critical to complete the NEPA process efficiently and effectively. ARP airport planners are responsible for reviewing the sponsor's proposed actions and alternatives for consistency with FAA's airport planning and design standards. Those planners approve only projects meeting those standards, unless they determine the projects warrant modifications to those standards. The Purpose and Need is developed during the NEPA process after considering FAA's statutory mission and the sponsor's goals and objectives. Among other uses, planning information helps the sponsor or the ARP during the NEPA process to
>
> - define the airport sponsor's proposed project,
> - describe the Purpose and Need and identify reasonable alternatives to address the Purpose and Need,

- provide analyses of potential environmental impacts the proposed project and its reasonable alternatives could cause, and
- develop the full scope of reasonably foreseeable airport development that is critical to the federal action's cumulative impact analysis.[8]

The *Environmental Desk Reference for Airport Actions* (Desk Reference) is a compendium that provides guidance on special purpose laws affecting airports. Specifically it includes federal laws, regulations, executive orders, and departmental orders, as defined in paragraph 9(t) of Order 5050.4B, that are not specifically included in NEPA. The Desk Reference describes ways to evaluate potential environmental impacts of a proposed airport action and its alternatives. It also provides information on mitigation measures. The Desk Reference contains a separate chapter on each of 23 potential environmental impact categories. These categories cover the same material as the 18 categories listed in Appendix A of Order 1050.1 because some of the latter categories have been subdivided to provide more detail. Each chapter includes the significant threshold for that category as well as the applicable statutes and implementing regulations, summary descriptions, and the oversight agency for each. For many of the categories the Desk Reference contains more information on how to evaluate that category than Order 1050.1E, because airport development often disturbs more physical area and involves more environmental categories than do other FAA actions. Note also that the Desk Reference clearly points out that, "When citing a legal requirement, the responsible FAA official or other user should cite the law, order, or regulation specifying the requirement, not the summary or description in the Desk Reference."[9]

The 23 potential environmental impact categories are:

1. Air Quality
2. Biotic Resources
3. Coastal Barriers
4. Coastal Zone Management and Visual Effects
5. Compatible Land Use
6. Construction Impacts
7. Section 4(f) Resources
8. Federally-listed Endangered or Threatened Species
9. Energy Supplies, Natural Resources, and Sustainable Design
10. Environmental Justice
11. Farmlands
12. Flood plains
13. Hazardous Materials
14. Historic Properties
15. Induced Socioeconomic Impacts
16. Light Emissions
17. Noise
18. Social Impacts
19. Solid Waste
20. Water Quality
21. Wetlands
22. Wild and Scenic Rivers
23. Cumulative Impacts

The NEPA Process

As noted above, pursuant to NEPA legislation and CEQ regulations, the FAA is responsible for ensuring that airport development plans take into account their potential impact on the environment. The FAA accomplishes this through three levels of NEPA review as identified in Order 1050.1E: Categorical Exclusions (CEs), Environmental Assessments (EAs), and Environmental Impact Statements (EISs). Each of these is discussed in the following paragraphs. Responsibility for approving environmental documents and findings typically rests with the FAA Regional Administrator or Regional Airports Division Manager, who is identified in FAA documents as the "approving FAA official" or sometimes the "responsible FAA official." Specific FAA staff responsibilities are set forth in Order 1100.154A, *Delegations of Authority*.[10] Before any airport action (as identified in Order 5050.4B) can be approved, "The responsible FAA official must clearly identify potential environmental impacts the proposed action and its alternatives may cause. Based on the proposed airport project and its environmental effects, the responsible FAA official decides if the federal action qualifies as a categorical exclusion or if an environmental assessment (EA) or an environmental impact statement (EIS) is required."[11]

As stated in Chapter 5: Master Planning, the environmental process can be facilitated if airport planners start working with environmental specialists (including FAA staff) at the outset of the planning process. These specialists can offer advice regarding sensitive environmental resources on and near the airport, and help planners develop alternatives that reduce or even eliminate adverse environmental impacts.

Categorical Exclusions

Categorical exclusions apply to actions which are determined to not have a significant effect on the environment. The responsibility for determining whether an action can be categorically excluded rests with the FAA. Chapter 3 of Order 1050.1E contains detailed guidance regarding actions which may normally be categorically excluded, and Chapter 6 of Order 5050.4B provides this detail specifically with respect to airport actions. Tables 6-1 and 6-2 of 5050.4B present specific detail on airport actions that would normally be categorically excluded (Table 6-1), and those that would not (Table 6-2). Note however that Order 1050.1E also states that:

> Some actions that would normally be categorically excluded could require additional environmental analysis to determine the appropriate NEPA documentation. A determination of whether a proposed action that is normally categorically excluded requires an EA or EIS depends on whether the proposed action involves extraordinary circumstances.[12]

These circumstances are presented in detail in Chapter 3 of Order 1050.1E, and include such things as adverse impacts on air or water quality; cultural resources covered under the National Historic Preservation Act; natural, ecological, or scenic resources; impacts that cause a division or disruption of an established community; or an increase in congestion from surface transportation. The important point is that there is often some subjectivity involved with respect to whether an action is categorically excluded. Also, an action at one airport may be categorically excluded while the same action at another airport is not. This is not necessarily due to individual interpretation on the part of FAA staff; the same project at the second airport could involve an extraordinary circumstance referenced above. If a situation appears questionable, the issues should be resolved in consultation with the FAA before any assumptions are made.

Environmental Assessments

An EA is basically a document prepared by the airport sponsor that describes a proposed action's potential or expected environmental impacts. It is the responsible FAA official's duty to notify the airport sponsor that an EA must be prepared when

- the official determines that extraordinary circumstances applicable to a normally categorically excluded action suggest an EA is needed, or
- the action is not listed in Chapter 6, Tables 6-1 or 6-2 [of Order 5050.4B] and, therefore, normally requires an EA at a minimum.[13]

A detailed list of actions that normally require an EA, along with helpful explanatory guidance, are provided in Chapter 7 of Order 5050.4B.

The airport sponsor normally selects a qualified environmental consultant to prepare the EA. The FAA's role is to advise and assist the sponsor during the preparation of the EA. However, if it is expected that the proposed action or project could have significant impacts that could not be mitigated below applicable significance thresholds, it is advisable for the FAA to select the consultant. This will save time in the long run because if the impacts are significant it will trigger an EIS, and the FAA is responsible for selecting the consultant for an EIS.[14]

The specific purpose of an EA is to determine whether a proposed project, or any alternatives to the proposed project, may have the potential to have a significant effect on the environment and to document what those effects might be and what efforts can be made to mitigate those effects. During the preparation of an EA planners should coordinate with the environmental resource agencies and the affected community to ensure that the document addresses the issues of significant concern. Public hearings are not normally required as part of the EA process unless the FAA determines that a hearing is warranted, considering the following factors:

- There is environmental controversy concerning the proposed action or substantial interest in holding the hearing.
- Or, another agency with jurisdiction over the action has requested a public hearing and has supported its request with reasons why a hearing would be helpful.[15]

Order 5050.4B also includes detailed guidance on the format and content of an EA, as summarized in the following list.

- The EA Cover Sheet
- Purpose and Need
- The Proposed Action
- Alternatives
- Affected Environment
- Environmental Consequences
- Mitigation
- Cumulative Impact Analysis
- Agencies and People Consulted[16]

The Order also notes that, ideally, the EA should consist of no more than 15 pages that summarize the most important facts and conclusions related to the proposed action.[17] Although this may be difficult for complex projects or projects with extensive environmental impacts, the Order notes that technical documents, correspondence, and other related materials can be incorporated by reference or attached as appendices to the EA.

When the EA is completed the FAA reviews the document, the public comments, and other related materials. This ensures that the potential for a conflict of interest on the part of the airport sponsor does not impair the objectivity of the document. If the EA does not satisfy FAA requirements the sponsor must correct any deficiencies and resubmit the document.

An EA is typically good for three years; after that time the document must be reviewed to ensure that the information is still accurate and valid. This includes the proposed action and its alternatives, as well as the environmental resources. Anything that has changed must be updated and properly documented. If the EA indicates that the project will have no significant environmental impacts, the responsible FAA official may issue a Finding Of No Significant Impact (FONSI), which documents in writing the basis for the FAA's decision. If the proposed action or project incorporates mitigation measures that are intended to avoid, eliminate, or reduce anticipated impacts, the FONSI must include the appropriate mitigation measures. It is important to note that the FONSI does *not* represent the FAA's decision to implement the proposed project. FAA project approvals depend on a number of other factors, the most significant of which is usually funding availability.

Environmental Impact Statements

If an EA shows that the adverse impacts of the proposed action or actions would meet or exceed the significance threshold for an environmental resource, or that mitigation would not reduce the impact below the significance threshold, the FAA is required to prepare an EIS to provide additional and more detailed evaluations of the action and its alternatives. According to Order 5050.4B the responsible FAA official should begin to prepare an EIS when

- the proposed action normally requires an EIS (see paragraph 903) [of Order 5050.4B],
- an EA indicates that the approving FAA official cannot issue a FONSI because the proposed action is likely to cause significant environmental effects that cannot be mitigated below significance thresholds, or
- ARP experience shows an action addressed in an EA would cause significant environmental impacts.[18]

Note that the EIS is an FAA document. If consultant assistance is needed the FAA must select the consultant—that is not the sponsor's responsibility. However, the airport sponsor normally funds the consultant's work through third-party contracts under the guidelines set forth in paragraph 204 and Appendix B of Order 1050.1E.[19] The sponsor is also required to provide the FAA and the consultant with the necessary planning and environmental information and supporting studies. This includes the EA materials if an EA has been prepared and if the information is not more than three years old.

According to federal procurement policy, "…procurements may not be awarded to contractors who have unacceptable actual or potential organizational conflicts of interest" in the proposed action or project.[20] A potential conflict of interest would arise if the contractor selected to prepare an EA were also selected to perform the final design work, if the final design is part of the construction contract for the project. Sometimes this can create problems in selecting a consultant for a major project such as a new runway at a large airport. Many of the large airport consulting firms have expertise in planning, environmental analysis, facility design, and construction management. A firm may be reluctant to bid on an EIS contract if that firm would be precluded from doing the final design work or providing construction management and inspection services. [This could happen in a case where design and construction management was part of the EIS contract. A conflict of interest could exist when the contractor is selected to do both an EIS and follow-on work. A conflict of interest would not ordinarily exist if the contractor is selected to do only an EIS, completes its contract, and then is selected competitively for follow-on work.] Note also that the FAA may select a contractor to prepare both an EA and preliminary design work provided that the design work is conceptual in nature.[21]

Another problem can occur if the FAA and the sponsor feel that additional planning work is needed prior to the start of a NEPA process, particularly an EIS. If the FAA and the sponsor agree that the consultant selected to prepare the EIS has the capability to perform the additional planning work, the delay should be minimal. The potential for project delay increases when the sponsor wants its own planning/design firm to perform the additional work, and at that point turns the project over to the FAA for review by the EIS contractor. This eventuality should be given some thought prior to the beginning of the planning work so that sufficient reserve funds can be included in the project budget.

After completing an EIS, the FAA prepares a Record of Decision (ROD) that explains the rationale for their selection of a preferred alternative. Regardless of the document prepared, the NEPA process leads to a final FAA decision to approve or not approve a proposed airport action.[22] As noted above regarding a FONSI, the issuance of a ROD does *not* represent the FAA's decision to implement the proposed project. Note also that an EIS ROD is usually only valid for five years, and must then be reaffirmed.

Environmental Streamlining

In 2001 the President signed Executive Order 13274, *Environmental Stewardship and Transportation Infrastructure Project Reviews*, which instructed executive departments and agencies of the U.S. Government to "…promote environmental stewardship in the nation's transportation system and expedite environmental reviews of high-priority transportation infrastructure projects…for relevant permits or other approvals."[23] In 2003 the U.S. Congress passed the Vision 100 – Century of Aviation Reauthorization Act, Title III of which specifically applied streamlining to aviation projects.[24] At the time many in the airport community felt that these actions meant that the NEPA environmental process would be short-circuited and that environmental analyses were not going to be as rigorous as in the past. Airport projects would be able to move ahead without extensive environmental reviews. But that is not what environmental streamlining was about. Specifically, the Act states that:

> The Secretary of Transportation shall develop and implement an expedited and coordinated environmental review process for airport capacity enhancement projects at congested airports, aviation safety projects, and aviation security projects, that:
>
> 1) provides for better coordination among the federal, regional, state, and local agencies concerned with the preparation of environmental impact statements or environmental assessments under the National Environmental Policy Act of 1969;
>
> 2) provides that all environmental reviews, analyses, opinions, permits, licenses, and approvals that must be issued or made by a federal agency or airport sponsor for such a project will be conducted concurrently, to the maximum extent practicable; and
>
> 3) provides that any environmental review, analysis, opinion, permit, license, or approval that must be issued or made by a federal agency or airport sponsor for such a project will be completed within a time period established by the Secretary, in cooperation with the agencies identified under subsection (d) with respect to the project.[25]

It makes no mention of diluting the quality or rigor of the environmental analysis, nor does it eliminate any steps in the NEPA process.

Note that the Act does not apply to all airport projects; it only applies to "airport capacity projects at congested airports, aviation safety projects, and aviation security projects."[26] The airport capacity projects are limited to those at congested airports—"congested" being defined as "an airport that accounted for at least 1 percent of all delayed aircraft operations in the nation, and is an airport listed in Table 1 of FAA's *Airport Capacity Benchmark Report 2001.*" With regard to the quality of environmental analyses, FAA Order 5050.4B states that the:

> ...ARP will adhere to the high standards of environmental review described in Order 1050.1E and [Order 5050.4B] for projects subject to environmental streamlining under Vision 100. ARP will comply with all environmental requirements, maintain the environmental process' integrity, and respect the environmental responsibilities of other agencies.[27]

Order 5050.4B also notes that all parties must work cooperatively to "set and achieve milestones and deadlines to address a plan's resultant environmental effects, and work to protect the environment."[28] The parties in this case include the FAA; the airport sponsor/operator; other federal, state, and local government agencies (including environmental resource agencies); and communities. The Order also states that the ARP will use the streamlining process to

- give priority review to certain projects,
- promote public review and comment,
- manage timelines during the review process,
- improve and expedite interagency coordination,
- reduce undue delays, and
- stress quality and accountability.[29]

In practice by most accounts the streamlining process seems to be working well, due to the emphasis on cooperation and adhering to milestones and deadlines. The streamlining process generally involves a task force approach with the agencies noted above. In the event that task force members are unable to resolve a particular issue, procedures have been established to go up the chain of command in each agency, and to set a deadline for the issue to be resolved. Also, once an agency has signed off on a component of the environmental analysis it is typically not revisited.

Environmental Practice

Overview
As noted elsewhere in this book (and in many of the FAA publications cited herein), the environmental process can go a lot more smoothly and in a

timely manner if the proper amount of planning is done before the environmental process begins. For example, it is essential that the planning work is sufficient to provide the basis for the Purpose and Need section of the environmental document. If it doesn't, Planning hasn't done its job. It will also help if the planning process includes enough design work to identify the limits of disturbance. In this case it pays to be conservative on the estimates, i.e., overestimate the areas and resources that will be impacted by the project or action. If the necessary environmental permits are based on this worst-case scenario, the rest of the environmental process will go a lot more smoothly.

Speaking of permits, the environmental documentation should be prepared with the long-term development program in mind, and the permits should be sought accordingly. This will reduce the possibility of unpleasant surprises during the environmental process. Remember that permits can be revised or modified. Even if a particular expansion project is temporarily inactive, the permits should still be kept active so that the project can move ahead expeditiously when the time is right.

Time and money can be saved in both the environmental and planning processes by preparing and maintaining environmental resource inventories. A resource inventory usually consists of a report or reference book that contains all the known information, data, maps, drawings, and photographs relating to a resource category. It can also include copies of correspondence between the airport and each resource agency. At large airports a separate resource inventory can be prepared for most of the 23 natural environmental resource categories listed in Order 5050.4B. Such categories as construction impacts and cumulative impacts, and others that are more project-specific in nature, will usually not warrant a resource inventory. Separate resource inventories should be prepared and maintained for major categories that are likely to be affected by most airport development activities. These include noise, air quality, water quality, forests, wetlands, and historic properties. At smaller airports with less of an environmental footprint, many of the resource categories can be combined in one or two volumes. A resource inventory should be available to planners so plans can be developed in a manner that avoids environmentally-sensitive areas or minimizes the potential environmental impacts. The resource inventories should be kept current or at least revised and updated periodically as conditions change.

It is also good practice for airport planners to meet with environmental resource agencies regularly, particularly throughout the planning and design process, to show them what is being planned, why it is being planned, and what the potential impacts might be. It is very important to show that planners are committed to minimizing environmental impacts throughout the planning process.

Often the resource agencies receive plans, reports, and other documentation to review concerning a particular project or set of projects. If the materials involve master plans, the reviewers can usually get a fairly complete idea of the overall context of the airport and its future needs. If the study materials are related to specific projects, however, it may be difficult for the resource agency reviewers to get a feel for the big picture. Periodic meetings help give the resource agencies a better understanding of what is happening and why, thus minimizing questions and project delays. Periodic meetings with resource agencies also help planners and airport operators get a better understanding of the environmental issues and concerns at and around the airport. For example if deforestation and loss of wetlands due to increasing development around the airport has been an ongoing concern, a plan can be developed that avoids or minimizes the clearing of trees and wetlands. These efforts during the planning process can be emphasized in the planning and environmental documentation. If nothing else this helps build good will because such efforts are appreciated by the environmental resource agencies. Also, being aware of the issues up front helps develop a better plan and a smoother environmental review process.

The environmental process can also go more smoothly if airports maintain an open dialogue with elected officials and neighboring communities. The subject of community outreach and its various programs and benefits are discussed in detail in Chapter 9: Coordination and Communication. The same ideas that apply to environmental resources and coordination with the resource agencies also apply to community coordination. If planners are aware of community issues, concerns, and potential areas of conflict, plans can be developed that minimize those kinds of impacts. At the very least planners will know what the issues are so they can be prepared to respond to community comments in the public involvement phase of the project.

Of the 23 environmental impact categories listed in the Desk Reference, five are most commonly encountered in airport planning, and must be addressed in detail in most environmental documents: noise, air quality, water quality, wetlands, and cumulative impacts. These categories also seem to have caused the most problems in the NEPA process documentation. Hazardous materials and environmental justice (i.e., one community receiving a disproportionate share of impacts) can also be significant, depending on the project and the location of the airport. The others listed in the Desk Reference are usually rather easy to address or are encountered only occasionally. Some, such as coastal barriers and wild and scenic rivers, typically only affect certain airports or airports in unique locations. Each of the impact categories is discussed in detail in the Desk Reference, but some background and summary information is presented below for the five most common categories.

Noise
Noise is normally defined as sound that is "…unpleasant, unexpected, or undesired".[30] This means that noise is often a relative thing and is therefore sometimes difficult to analyze objectively. Unfortunately it is also the most significant environmental impact associated with airports. The vast majority of airport noise is that generated by aircraft arriving at and departing from the airport, but residents living close to the airport are also affected by air-

craft ground movements and engine run-ups as part of aircraft maintenance activities. Vehicle traffic from airport access roads can also be a problem, and on occasion people living around the airport can be affected by noise associated with construction activities. The noise issue seems to have improved dramatically since the 1970s, primarily as a result of the mandated phase-out of noisier Stage 2 aircraft and the introduction and widespread use of quieter Stage 3 aircraft. The FAA's land acquisition and relocation programs for residential areas and soundproofing programs for residences and public buildings have also been highly effective. Chapter 17 of the Desk Reference contains an excellent description of noise analysis as it relates to airport environmental requirements, including measurement techniques, significance thresholds, and statutory requirements. The major elements are summarized in the following paragraphs.

Aircraft noise is normally measured using a metric known as the Day-Night Average Sound Level (DNL), formerly (and still occasionally) shown as L_{dn}. This measure is required by the FAA in all airport noise studies, although Chapter 17 of the Desk Reference notes some unique or specialized occasions when other metrics may be applied. The DNL metric is a summary of the 24-hour average sound level in decibels (dB) and is derived from the total aircraft operations during a 24-hour period on an average operational day. Significantly, DNL adds a 10 dB noise penalty to aircraft operation occurring during nighttime hours (10 p.m. to 7 a.m.) to account for the fact that people are more sensitive to noise during that period.

Airport actions or development projects that could cause noise impacts beyond the airport boundaries include

- new or extended runways and taxiways;
- navigational aid (NAVAID) installation;
- land purchased for airport-related uses;
- substantial amounts of airport construction or demolition activities;
- substantial changes in aircraft operations involving numbers of aircraft, aircraft types, new or revised approach or departure profiles or tracks; and
- new or relocated airport access roadways.[31]

The Desk Reference cites specific actions for which the FAA *must* conduct a noise analysis, as listed below. Note that a noise analysis is typically not required for airport actions whose DNL 65 dB contour lies entirely within airport boundaries.[32]

1. **General aviation-related actions.** Projects that would involve more than:

    a. 90,000 annual (247 average daily operations) piston-powered aircraft operations in Approach Categories A through D (i.e., landing speed < 166 knots), or

b. 700 annual jet-powered aircraft operations (about 2 average daily operations) during the period the environmental document covers.

Note: These levels of piston-powered or jet-powered general aviation operations have been shown to produce a DNL 60 dB contour less than 1.1 square miles in area and extending no more than 12,500 feet from the start of take-off roll. The resulting maximum DNL 65 dB contour would be 0.5 square mile and would not extend more than 10,000 feet from the start of take-off roll. The Cessna Citation 500 and other jet aircraft producing noise levels less than or equal to the Beech Baron 58P may be counted as propeller aircraft, not jets.

2. **Actions involving a new airport location, a new runway, a major runway extension, or runway strengthening.** A noise analysis is needed for these projects when they would:

   a. serve Airplane Design Groups I and II, if forecast operations exceed those noted in Section 3.b(1) of this chapter [Desk Reference];

   b. serve Airplane Design Groups III through VI;

   c. be highly controversial because of noise; or

   d. would serve special aircraft (e.g., helicopters) and those aircraft would fly over noise-sensitive areas.

3. **Actions at existing heliports or airports.** A noise analysis is needed at these facilities when forecasted helicopter operations for the period the analysis covers would exceed 10 operations per day (annual basis) and hover times would exceed 2 minutes.

Note: Helicopter operations typically cause a DNL 60 dB contour having an area less than 0.10 square mile and not extending more than 1,000 feet from the helicopter pad. This finding applies to Sikorsky S-70 models having a maximum gross take-off weight of 20,244 pounds, or any other helicopter of less weight or causing equal or lower noise levels.[33]

Airport noise analysis is a fairly rigorous process that must follow FAA guidance to be acceptable to the FAA. Specifically, the FAA requires the use of the Integrated Noise Model (INM) to generate noise contours used to estimate long-term effects based on average annual input data. Note that the INM is modified from time to time, so the latest version should be used. The aviation demand forecasts must be consistent with the FAA's Terminal Area Forecast, as noted in Chapter 5: Master Planning. Note also that the EIS process often can extend over several years and quite often an opponent of the project may claim that the forecast prepared at the beginning of the study is not current. If the FAA supports this line of thinking, new forecasts may have to be prepared. Thus a lot of care and consideration should be taken in the preparation of the forecasts for the EIS. The time frames for the noise analysis must be consistent with those used for other environmental impact categories in the NEPA document, and are typically consistent with the time frames for the master plan or other airport planning study. The Desk Reference notes the following time frame requirements for noise contours:

- the existing condition (normally the last 12 consecutive months of available data);
- the future year without the proposed project (i.e., no action/no build alternative);
- the future year of anticipated project implementation (project opening year); and
- another future year, normally, 5 to 10 years beyond the projected year of project implementation. In some cases, this may be the outer year of an airport sponsor's master plan. Additional time frames may be desirable for a particular project.[34]

The Desk Reference also notes the following contours that should normally be generated as part of the noise analysis:

- the existing DNL 65, 70, and 75 dB contours;
- the future DNL 65, 70, and 75 dB contours without the proposed action (i.e., the no action/no build alternative);
- the future DNL 65, 70, and 75 dB contours for the proposed action; and
- the future DNL 65, 70, and 75 dB contours for each reasonable alternative.

The FAA has established that the noise impact is significant if "…an action, compared to the no action alternative for the same time frame, would cause noise-sensitive areas located at or above DNL 65 dB to experience a noise increase of at least 1.5 DNL dB."[35] Thus, an increase from DNL 63.5 dB to DNL 65 dB, for example, is a significant impact. The Desk Reference also notes that supplemental noise studies may be appropriate for certain land uses such as national parks, national wildlife refuges, and historic sites, where a quiet setting is an important part of the general ambience.

Some airport improvements have the potential to cause surface transportation noise impacts. These include new, expanded, or realigned access roads, or other roadway projects that would increase vehicular activity or increased vehicle speeds. Construction activities can also generate higher noise levels—including blasting, demolition, construction equipment, and trucks hauling materials to or removing debris and refuse from the site. In these cases a noise analysis should be conducted using the Federal Highway Administration's (FHWA's) *Procedures for Abatement of Highway Traffic Noise and Construction Noise* (23 CFR Part 772).[36]

Even though the primary noise impact is caused by aircraft, the courts have determined that aircraft operators are not responsible for any impacts caused by aircraft noise. Rather, the courts have determined that the legal liability associated with aircraft noise is the responsibility of the airport sponsor. However, airport restrictions adopted by the airport must be nondiscriminatory and must not be a burden to interstate commerce. For example, a prohibition on jet aircraft operations would be discriminatory because some jet aircraft are quieter than some turboprop aircraft. In that case the aircraft noise limit must be based on a particular noise level that would apply to all aircraft exceeding that level, regardless of whether they are jet or turboprop. Airport noise restrictions must also be supported by the process set forth in Part 150 (Airport Noise Compatibility Planning) or Part 158 (Notice and Approval of Airport Noise and Access Restrictions) of the Federal Aviation Regulations.

Rules in the area of aircraft noise abatement are sometimes imprecise and must therefore be reviewed by the FAA on a case-by-case basis. And finally, aircraft noise restrictions or noise abatement programs must not compromise safety, or in any way interfere with the FAA's control of aircraft in navigable airspace. Some of the noise abatement and noise impact reduction programs that airports have used successfully are:

- take-off and landing procedures to reduce noise;
- preferential runway use that avoids or minimizes flights over noise-sensitive areas;
- construction of sound or noise barriers and soundproofing of buildings;
- acquisition of residential dwellings and relocation of occupants;
- soundproofing of residential dwellings and office buildings within noise-impacted areas;
- acquisition of land and land interests such as navigation easements, air rights, and development rights to ensure non-noise-sensitive land uses;
- curfews, either for the entire airport or for specified runways; and
- denial of airport use or specific runway use to aircraft types generating noise levels above specified levels.

The restrictions involving aircraft and airport operations should be used carefully and in cooperation with the various offices within the FAA (e.g., Airports, Air Traffic). Closing runways during specified hours, restricting runway use to certain types of aircraft, and establishing specified aircraft flight paths can reduce the capacity of the airport. Thus the overall effect of any of these kinds of restrictions should be examined from a capacity standpoint. For example, a proposed runway that will have several restrictions with regard to aircraft type and operating hours may not provide the needed additional capacity, and therefore may not be worth the investment.

Although airport noise impacts have been reduced over the past two decades—primarily due to quieter aircraft engines and FAA land acquisition and soundproofing programs—noise is likely to remain a problem for the foreseeable future. It does not appear that aircraft engines will be getting significantly quieter any time soon, but aircraft operations will undoubtedly increase, thus increasing the frequency of overflights. The extent of this impact will vary from airport to airport, but in some cases the area covered by the DNL 65 dB contour may increase. Areas that are now outside the DNL 65 dB contour, and thus suitable for residential development, could fall within the contour 10 or 15 years in the future. In that case homes in these areas will have to be purchased or soundproofed. Airport planners should keep this possibility in mind if the long-term airport development outlook calls for significant traffic increases and new or expanded supporting facilities. Close and candid coordination with local planning and zoning officials would be very useful in this regard.

Air Quality

Air quality must be considered as part of the NEPA process associated with airport expansion plans and programs. People living near airports often report seeing engine exhaust emissions, and also complain frequently that aircraft emissions have put a layer of soot on their home, car, swimming pool, child, or what have you. The various sources of emissions that contribute to the reduction in air quality around airports include vehicular sources such as aircraft engines, baggage tugs, maintenance vehicles, shuttle buses, trucks, cars, etc., operating on or adjacent to the airport. Other airport emission sources include power plants and generators, aircraft ground power equipment, fuel storage facilities and fueling operations, construction equipment, and other activities such as deicing and paving. With respect to aircraft, the FAA states that

> …about 10 percent of aircraft emissions of all types, except hydrocarbons and CO [carbon monoxide], are produced during airport ground level operations and during landing and take-off. The bulk of aircraft emissions (90 percent) occur at higher altitudes. For hydrocarbons and CO, the split is closer to 30 percent ground level emissions and 70 percent at higher altitudes.[37]

Recognizing that air pollution poses a danger to public health, the U.S. Congress enacted the Clean Air Act of 1970, established the Environmental Protection Agency (EPA), and gave it the primary responsibility for carrying out the provisions of the law. In 1990 the Act was significantly revised and expanded, and a number of minor changes have been added since then. Under the Clean Air Act, the EPA sets limits on certain air pollutants, including limits on how much can be in the air anywhere in the United States. State and local agencies have been given the lead responsibility in carrying out the provisions of the Act. Among their responsibilities are monitoring air quality and inspecting facilities under their jurisdictions, as well as enforcing Clean Air Act regulations. States are also required to develop EPA-approved

State Implementation Plans (SIP). A SIP is a collection of the regulations, programs, and policies that show how the state will achieve or maintain the National Ambient Air Quality Standards (NAAQS) within time frames set under the Clean Air Act.

The pollutants or "criteria" for which the EPA has established NAAQS under the Clean Air Act are carbon monoxide (CO), lead (Pb), nitrogen dioxide (NO_2), ozone (O_3), particulate matter (PM) for both PM10 and PM2.5, and sulfur dioxide (SO_2). Each of these is summarized below, based on information obtained from the Clean Air Trust Web site, which is an excellent source for air quality information (http://www.cleanairtrust.org/lead.html).

About 60 percent of *carbon monoxide* (CO) nationwide is produced by motor vehicle sources, although it may be much higher in cities. Other CO sources include industrial processes, nontransportation fuel combustion, and wildfires. Carbon monoxide reduces the amount of oxygen delivered to the body's organs and tissues. Excessive CO can result in visual impairment, reduced work capacity, reduced manual dexterity, poor learning ability, and difficulty in performing complex tasks.

It is interesting to note that motor vehicles used to be the largest source of *lead* (Pb) pollution. But since leaded gasoline has been phased out for motor vehicles, lead emissions have decreased by about 98 percent. Metal processing is now the most significant source of atmospheric lead, with the highest concentrations found in the vicinity of smelters and battery manufacturers. Atmospheric pollution from Pb is generally minimal around airports and is normally not a major concern. Lead may cause neurological impairments and may also result in lowered IQ and learning problems for children.

The major sources of *nitrogen dioxide* (NO_2) are cars, trucks, and electric power plants. Another concern is that NO_2 can be transformed in the atmosphere to ozone or fine particulate soot, e.g., PM2.5. Exposure to NO_2 is associated with respiratory infection. Nitrogen oxides also help form acid rain and can contribute to explosive algae growth which can deplete oxygen in bodies of water such as lakes and bays.

Ozone (O_3) is formed by the reaction of volatile organic compounds (VOCs) and nitrogen oxides (NOx) in the presence of heat and sunlight. VOCs are emitted by a variety of sources, including motor vehicles, chemical plants, refineries, and other factories. NOx are emitted by motor vehicles, electric power plants, and other combustion sources. In the upper atmosphere O_3 reflects heat but at lower altitudes it is the main component of smog and is considered to be the most widespread air pollutant. It is a powerful respiratory irritant and can also reduce the body's resistance to infection. Ozone is considered to be especially dangerous for children, the elderly, people with chronic lung and heart disease, and people who exercise outdoors.

Particulate matter (PM) is a general term for the mixture of solid particles and liquid droplets in the air, some of which are large enough to be visible as smoke or soot. Fine particulates are referred to as PM2.5 (having an aerodynamic diameter less than or equal to 2.5 micrometers) and larger particulates as PM10 (diameter less than or equal to 10 micrometers). Fine particulates are produced by motor vehicles, coal-burning electric power plants, and factories, as well as residential fireplaces and wood stoves. Larger particulates come largely from windblown dust, vehicles traveling on unpaved roads, and crushing and grinding operations. Some particles are emitted directly from their sources (e.g., smokestacks and automobile tailpipes); in other cases fine particulates are formed by the interaction of gases such as sulfur oxides and nitrogen oxides with other compounds in the air. Fine particles can irritate and damage the lungs and cause breathing problems, particularly in people with asthma or other lung or heart disease. Particulates in the form of soot are a major cause of reduced visibility and can also damage paints and building materials.

Sulfur dioxide (SO_2) is produced by the combustion of fuel, especially fuels containing sulfur such as coal and oil. High concentrations of SO_2 can result in breathing problems for asthmatic children and adults who are active outdoors. In conjunction with particulate matter SO_2 has been associated with respiratory illness, alterations in the lungs' defenses, and aggravation of existing cardiovascular disease. Sulfur dioxide and nitrogen oxides are the major precursors of acid rain, which has acidified soils, lakes, and streams; accelerated corrosion of buildings and monuments; and reduced visibility. Sulfur dioxide also is a major precursor of fine particulate soot, which poses a significant health threat as noted above.

As part of the SIP, states are responsible for designating attainment, nonattainment, or maintenance areas for each of the criteria pollutants. Specifically:

- An attainment area is a geographical area where the levels of all criteria air pollutants meet the NAAQS.

- A nonattainment area is a geographic area where the concentration of one or more of the criteria air pollutants is higher than the NAAQS. It is not uncommon for an area to have acceptable levels of five criteria pollutants but an unacceptable level for another.

- A maintenance area is an area previously designated "nonattainment" but redesignated as a "maintenance" area because air pollution levels have improved above levels that would place the area in nonattainment status.[38]

In nonattainment areas and maintenance areas an air quality analysis is normally conducted as part of the NEPA process to determine whether project emissions would potentially have a significant air quality impact, i.e., would result in levels of air pollution that would exceed the NAAQS. In attainment areas an air quality analysis may still be necessary, depending on the size of the airport and the nature of the project. Pursuant to the Clean Air Act federal agencies may not fund or approve activities that do not conform to the SIP established for a nonattainment or maintenance area. The specific details and requirements for air quality analyses can be quite complex and the Desk Reference should be consulted when it is expected that an air quality analysis may be required. Putting it simply, a general conformity determination compares emissions resulting from a proposed action with the emissions associated with the no build alternative "...to calculate the total net emissions of each criteria air pollutant and its precursors that a proposed action will cause."[39] Note also that the air quality analysis must consider the impacts associated with construction of the project as well as its operation.

Airports only have a few ways of demonstrating conformity with air quality requirements:

- documenting that planned emission increases are included in the existing SIP;
- persuading the state to include the emission increases in the SIP; or
- offsetting or mitigating emission increases from the project, provided the offsets are for the *entire* action, not just an incremental amount to attain levels below *de minimis* standards.[40]

Because air quality can be a significant issue, airports should become actively involved in their state's SIP process and make sure the SIP includes accurate emissions information and forecasts for the airport. As one of the environmental resource inventories noted above, airports should conduct a complete emissions inventory, prepare compliance assessments, and prepare a plan for meeting applicable compliance deadlines. It has also been recommended that, "Where possible airports should work with local regulators to develop a program allowing the banking of emission reduction credits to offset future development, and make the community and regulators aware of these reductions."[41]

Airport staff should also meet with the individuals who prepare the SIP to ensure that all emissions sources are properly documented and that actions taken by the airport to reduce emissions are counted as offsets as part of the airport's air quality analysis. For example, many larger airports have off-site parking lots and remote rental car facilities. If a state or metropolitan planning organization is preparing an emissions inventory, they may count these airport shuttle buses as part of that inventory. And when the airport does an emissions inventory as part of an air quality analysis, the same vehicles may be counted again, resulting in double counting. Proper coordination will ensure that such double counting does not occur. Similarly, the airport may purchase cleaner-burning shuttle buses such as compressed natural gas (CNG) vehicles which will offset the increases in pollutants associated with expected airport traffic in future years. The airport sponsor should ensure that the airport is credited with this offset.

The air quality impacts associated with airport development and operations can be reduced or mitigated by improving the efficiency of airport operations. For example, more efficient aircraft taxi operations, which minimize the total time and distance aircraft are burning fuel on airport property, will reduce the volume of pollutants from engine operations. Widening airport roadways can often result in lower emissions levels because vehicles do not spend as much time stopped due to roadway congestion. The use of mass transit systems, rather than private automobiles, for travel to and from the airport by passengers and employees will contribute to reduced emissions generated from automobile use. For example, an air quality improvement plan can include a component to develop a public advertising campaign encouraging passengers and employees to use transit. Planners can develop an estimate of how many people (and how many vehicle trips) can be diverted to transit, which can then be used to develop an emissions reduction estimate. A similar program can be developed to encourage airport and airline employees to carpool.

In addition to purchasing cleaner-burning shuttle buses as mentioned above, airports can purchase cleaner-burning aircraft ground support equipment and maintenance vehicles to reduce the air pollution burden. The FAA provides financial support through AIP and PFC funding under its Voluntary Airport Low Emissions Program (VALE). The goal of this program is to reduce airport ground emissions at commercial service airports located in designated air quality nonattainment and maintenance areas. VALE allows airport sponsors to use AIP and PFC funds "…to finance low emission vehicles, refueling and recharging stations, gate electrification, and other airport air quality improvements."[42] Airport improvements that provide preconditioned air and electric power to operate aircraft systems at terminal gates can reduce the air quality burden by replacing ground power equipment, which is notoriously fuel-inefficient. Similarly, installing aircraft hydrant fueling systems can reduce air pollution resulting both from fueling operations and from fuel trucks. Although these improvements can be expensive, they can result in long-term savings both in pollution reduction and in dollars.

Water Quality

When widespread airport construction began to take place in the early 1930s, airports were built on relatively large and fairly level areas, primarily to reduce costs and avoid obstacles to aircraft operations. In most cases those areas were located near bodies of water such as rivers, lakes, and bays. In fact many airports were built on flood plains. For example, as the story goes, Lunken Field (now known as Cincinnati Municipal Airport) was built so close to the Ohio River that flooding was a frequent occurrence, leading to the nickname "Sunken Lunken." Many airports were built adjacent to bodies of water so they could serve seaplanes as well as conventional aircraft. Day-to-day airport operational activities and new construction can be major contributors to water pollution unless suitable containment and/or treatment facilities are provided. Sources of water pollution at airports are sewage from airport facilities such as terminals and offices, and industrial discharges and wastes such as fuel spills. Degradation of surface waters can also be caused when high temperature water is discharged from airport power-generating facilities. Contaminated runoff from vehicle wash facilities, fueling facilities, and aircraft and airfield deicing operations also contribute to the discharge of pollutants into surrounding waters. Airports also contain large areas of impervious surfaces, i.e., primarily paved surfaces such as runways and taxiways, aircraft parking ramps, apron areas, vehicle access and circulation roadways, as well as rooftops and sidewalks. These materials seal surfaces so that precipitation and meltwater cannot penetrate the soil. Soils compacted by intense development may also be highly impervious. Occasionally residents near airports complain of flooded basements due to the runoff from an airport's paved surfaces. It should also be kept in mind that when precipitation or meltwater flows off of an airport's paved surfaces, it takes a significant portion of the surface contaminants, such as deicing fluids and spilled fuel, with it into adjacent waterways. Today airports are struggling with programs to maintain stream flows and groundwater recharge areas and to reduce the impacts of flooding and sedimentation.

In order to curtail the degradation of the nation's waters, in 1972 Congress enacted the Federal Water Pollution Control Act, commonly referred to as the Clean Water Act (CWA). The Act was strengthened by the Clean Water Act of 1977 and the Water Quality Act of 1987. The objectives of the Act are to reduce direct pollutant discharges into waterways, finance municipal wastewater treatment facilities, and manage polluted runoff, with the broader goal of restoring and maintaining the chemical, physical, and biological integrity of the nation's waters so that they can support "...the protection and propagation of fish, shellfish, and wildlife and recreation in and on the water."[43] Various regulations under the Act require airports to prevent the discharge of contaminated runoff into drainage systems that empty into adjacent streams, lakes, rivers, and other bodies of water unless a permit is obtained from the EPA or another designated agency. For the most part permitting and certification authority has been delegated to the states, thus airport sponsors must coordinate with the appropriate state agency responsible for water quality.

Because construction and operations and maintenance activities at airports can have adverse effects on water quality, the FAA must evaluate project-related discharges "...having the potential to affect navigable waterways, municipal drinking water supplies, important sole-source aquifers, or protected groundwater supplies"[44] that can come from "...both point and non-point sources."[45] According to federal law:

> Navigable waters of the United States are those waters that are subject to the ebb and flow of the tide and/or are presently used, or have been used in the past, or may be susceptible for use to transport interstate or foreign commerce. A determination of navigability, once made, applies laterally over the entire surface of the water body, and is not extinguished by later actions or events which impede or destroy navigable capacity.[46]

> The term "point source" means any discernible, confined, and discrete conveyance, including but not limited to any pipe, ditch, channel, tunnel, conduit, well, discrete fissure, container, rolling stock, concentrated animal feeding operation, or vessel or other floating craft, from which pollutants are or may be discharged.

Non-point source (NPS) pollution, unlike pollution from industrial and sewage treatment plants, comes from many diffuse sources. NPS pollution is caused by rainfall or snowmelt moving over and through the ground. As the runoff moves, it picks up and carries away natural and human-made pollutants, finally depositing them into lakes, rivers, wetlands, coastal waters, and even our underground sources of drinking water. These pollutants include

- excess fertilizers, herbicides, and insecticides from agricultural lands and residential areas;
- oil, grease, and toxic chemicals from urban runoff and energy production;
- sediment from improperly managed construction sites, crop and forest lands, and eroding stream banks;
- salt from irrigation practices and acid drainage from abandoned mines; and
- bacteria and nutrients from livestock, pet wastes, and faulty septic systems.[47]

A number of permits, certifications, and other forms of approval are required in order to construct airport facilities and to operate and maintain airports on a day-to-day basis. The two most common are Water Quality Certification and the National Pollutant Discharge Elimination System (NPDES) permit, as described in Chapter 20 of the Desk Reference. Airports must prepare Stormwater Pollution Prevention Plans (SWPPP) to protect water quality primarily during construction activities[48] (note that SWPPP requirements vary from state to state), and Spill Prevention, Control and Countermeasure (SPCC) Plans. SPCC Plans ensure that facilities include containment and other measures that would prevent oil spills from reaching navigable waters.[49] The FAA must review water quality documentation to ensure that the necessary approvals have been obtained and that the proposed project will not adversely impact water quality.

If the project has the potential to exceed water quality standards that could not be mitigated, or the necessary permits could not be obtained, it is considered to represent a significant water quality impact. Mitigation measures normally involve programs for treating contaminated water from point sources before it is discharged into nearby waterways, and maintaining appropriate safeguards during airport construction activities. Airports should consider both the quantity and quality of infiltration in their storm water management plans. It should not be just a matter of controlling quantity of runoff, but also of finding ways to make sure that the runoff is as clean as possible. In this regard it should be remembered that forests and other vegetation are very effective in improving water quality.

It can be assumed that there would be no significant impacts on water quality "...when the environmental document and appropriate consultation demonstrate that water quality standards can be met, no special water quality problem exists, and no difficulty is anticipated in obtaining permits...."[50]

Wetlands

To many people the term wetland is just another name for a swamp—home to snakes and bugs and other unpleasant creatures. But for regulatory purposes under the Clean Water Act, wetlands are

> ...those areas that are inundated or saturated by surface or groundwater at a frequency and duration sufficient to support, and that under normal circumstances do support, a prevalence of vegetation typically adapted for life in saturated soil conditions. Wetlands generally include swamps, marshes, bogs, and similar areas.[51]

But wetlands do more than provide habitat for myriad plants and animals; they help absorb floodwaters and excessive runoff during periods of heavy precipitation or snowmelt. Wetlands also absorb excess nutrients, sediment, and other pollutants before they reach rivers, lakes, and other bodies of water.

Because airports are generally fairly uniform in topography (flat), and often located in low-lying areas as noted above, wetlands may be found in many places on the airfield and surrounding areas. It should also be noted that drainage ditches, swales, and other low-lying areas can turn into wetlands, given a couple of years of above-average precipitation. Therefore airport operators should ensure that such areas are properly mowed and maintained to avoid excess water accumulations. In some cases permits may be issued by the agency responsible for wetlands and water quality to allow maintenance in these potentially sensitive areas. And almost any construction that takes place on an airport has the potential to affect a wetland area or areas. More specifically, an airport action is considered to affect a wetland if it

- requires building a structure, facility, or other development in a wetland;
- requires dredging, filling, draining, channelizing, diking, impounding, or other direct effects on a wetland;
- requires disturbing the water table of an area in which a wetland is located; or
- indirectly affects a wetland because it impacts areas upstream or downstream of the wetland or it introduces secondary development that would affect a wetland.[52]

Wetlands are included as waters of the United States as defined above for purposes of the Clean Water Act. This is because wetlands can improve water quality by filtering runoff and recycling nutrients. Section 404 of the Clean Water Act assigns the responsibility for regulating dredging and filling activities that would affect wetlands to the Secretary of the Army, acting through the U.S. Army Corps of Engineers. In this context wetlands consist of two types: jurisdictional and nonjurisdictional. According to the CWA, jurisdictional wetlands are those connected or adjacent to navigable waters as defined above. Filling or dredging in these areas requires a permit from the Corps. Nonjurisdictional wetlands do not involve navigable waters and activities in these areas do not require Corps approval, i.e., they are not within the jurisdiction of the Corps. Note also that some states have assumed the Corps' responsibilities in this regard; the regional Corps office should be contacted to confirm the responsible agency.

As part of the environmental review process the FAA needs certain information to determine whether the proposed action or development would have a significant effect on wetlands. The environmental document should note whether wetlands will be affected by the proposed action, verify that there are no feasible alternatives, and confirm that measures will be taken to minimize any adverse effects. According to the Desk Reference, "If the proposed action would affect a wetland, and no practicable alternative that avoids the wetland exists, the environmental document must provide the following information:

1. A description of the location, types, and extent of wetlands the action and its alternatives would affect. Contact the U.S. Fish and Wildlife Service, Corps, or state or local agencies responsible for wetlands in the affected area for information, if needed.

2. A description of potential impacts on the following wetland resources as appropriate:

    a. water quality;

    b. water supply and the capability to recharge that supply;

    c. surface or subsurface water flows;

    d. levels of siltation or sedimentation;

    e. the biotic community; or

    f. the effects of storm hazards, floods, or the ability to store storm runoff or storm flows."[53]

Because wetlands are so critical and can affect mammals, fish, and other marine creatures, as well as agricultural resources, several federal agencies may also have some jurisdiction over wetlands, depending on their type, location, and specific attributes. These include the EPA, U.S. Fish and Wildlife Service, National Marine Fisheries Service, and Natural Resource Conservation Service. State wetland or water quality and wildlife agencies may also be involved, depending on the location of the airport. These agencies should be identified and consulted with, beginning as soon as the planners become aware of potential wetland impacts. Their assistance can help avoid or minimize wetland disturbance. Correspondence with these agencies should be part of the environmental document, usually as either an appendix or reference.

Although the FAA does not have a specific wetland mitigation requirement, each of the agencies noted above may have some specific requirements for the mitigation or replacement of wetlands. Mitigation techniques and procedures typically involve runoff controls during and after construction, where runoff is treated to ensure that contaminants do not reach wetland areas. Wetlands that are severely impacted usually have to be replaced, and this can be a problem in the highly-developed areas normally found around airports. It is especially a problem due to the fact that most regulations require the replacement of a wetland in the same watershed. Also, depending on the quality of the wetland and the specific requirements of some state agencies, replacement is often done on a 1:1 basis (i.e., an acre of wetland must be replaced for each acre taken), although replacement ratios of 2:1 or 3:1 may be required. Replacing wetlands can be done either by constructing a new wetland or by preserving an existing wetland that may be taken by other development. For example, an airport could buy four acres of wetlands on a nearby property that has the potential of being sold to a real estate developer, and guarantee to preserve that acreage in perpetuity. As noted above, coordination is essential with each federal and state agency that has some authority or responsibility with regard to wetlands.

Cumulative Impacts

Cumulative impacts are sometimes difficult to assess properly, in part because they include not only FAA actions (as defined above) but also the actions of others. And in addition to present actions, past and future actions must be considered as well. According to the EPA:

> Cumulative impacts result when the effects of an action are added to or interact with other effects in a particular place and within a particular time. It is the combination of these effects, and any resulting environmental degradation, that should be the focus of cumulative impact analysis.[54]

It is important to understand that it is not just the specific environmental effects of the proposed action, but also the effects of other actions on the same environmental resource. For example, a new addition to an airport terminal may have an effect on water quality that is determined not to be significant. However, when the water quality effects of the new terminal are combined with the water quality effects associated with a new cargo building and associated aircraft and truck parking areas, the impact may be significant. And if a new office complex is to be constructed adjacent to the airport by another party (a public agency or a private party), the impacts of that development must be considered as well. Overall, planners should avoid "segmentation" as a way to get something built without conducting a rigorous analysis.

The Desk Reference provides some guidance for determining the parameters for a cumulative impact analysis.

1. Where? This is a "specific geographic area." It is that geographical area containing environmental resources that the proposed action would affect. Consultation with resource agencies in the affected area is important when defining this area.

2. When? This is a "designated time period." Typically, it is the cycle during which the project is expected to affect a resource, ecosystem, or human community. The FAA or the sponsor should determine this time period after consulting with agencies having knowledge of other actions in the area that the proposed action would affect.

3. What? These are the actions considered in a proposed project's cumulative impact analysis. They include the proposed FAA action and past, present, and reasonably foreseeable future actions of the FAA *and/or* other entities or individuals.[55]

As a general rule, if a project is in the CIP then it is usually considered as "reasonably foreseeable," but if it is only included in the long-range period of a master plan it is not. One would think that the terms "specific geographic area" and "designated time period" would narrow things down a bit—unfortunately they don't. Also the significance threshold will vary depending on the specific resource affected, thereby adding another potentially complicating factor. Mitigation measures will also vary with the affected resource, as determined by the agency with jurisdiction over that resource. Obviously, consultation with the appropriate resource agencies is necessary to come up with some specifications and limits. And again, this consultation should begin as soon in the planning process as the potentially impacted resources can be identified.

The bottom line is that the FAA does not have a specific cumulative impacts requirement of its own; the FAA makes a cumulative impact determination based on the specifications and permits that the sponsor has obtained from the appropriate resource agencies. If the resource agency (or agencies) with jurisdiction where the airport is located find the cumulative impact(s) to be significant and the proposed mitigation inadequate, the FAA may not approve the action. The FAA's particular requirement is that all this information has to be addressed and verified in the appropriate NEPA document.

Sustainability

The NEPA process seems to be working well to prevent environmental degradation associated with airport planning and development. However, the NEPA process applies primarily to federal actions, most of which are associated with new construction or expansion of existing facilities. But the day-to-day operation of airports also generates some significant environmental impacts, most of which are not covered by the NEPA process. Remember that airports, unlike such facilities as office buildings and schools, operate on a 24/7 basis. Airports need to keep HVAC, fueling, lighting, and other services going around the clock. In some ways this makes it more difficult to implement energy-saving and pollution-reducing strategies, but on the other hand the results can be much more beneficial because airports consume so much in the way of resources.

Many in the airport community feel that airports can and should adopt a more proactive approach to environmental issues, specifically focused on improving environmental quality rather than just maintaining it. Many also feel that airports should have some environmental goals and objectives of their own, beyond simple conformance with FAA and NEPA regulations. Many airport operators and aviation organizations such as the Airport Operators Council International, American Association of Airport Executives, and Airport Consultants Council are actively promoting sustainability in airport operations. Table 8-1 lists some environmentally-friendly projects and the airports that are implementing them at this writing.

Sustainability at airports begins with the will and desire to improve environmental quality, and that is where airport planning comes into the picture. As emphasized in Chapter 2: Airports and Chapter 4: Strategic Planning, airport planners who are employed by airports are the people who have the most involvement with all aspects of the operation and development of an airport, both now and in the future. And because planners are also the ones who are responsible for developing an airport strategic plan, they should promote goals for environmental stewardship and sustainability for all aspects of the operation and future development of the airport. Establishing these goals as part of the airport's strategic plan promotes the integration of environmental programs into airport operations. One of the main goals should be the establishment of an airport sustainability program, complete with sustainability goals and objectives.

One of the first steps in a sustainability program, once the goals and objectives have been established, is the development of benchmarks to measure progress toward the desired objectives. A number of airports have adopted environmental benchmarks, including auditing and inspection programs, which are documented in periodic reports that are available to the public. Boston Logan International Airport, for example, produces an Environmental Status and Planning Report (ESPR) every five years, and Environmental Data Reports (EDRs) in the interim years.[56] These reports measure and report progress toward achieving environmental goals. They should be made available to the appropriate environmental resource agencies and the general public because they have a right to know what effect the airport has on the environment, what the airport's environmental goals are, and what efforts the airport is making toward environmental sustainability. Although some may cringe at the thought of making all this information available to the public, providing the public with accurate information can assist in resolving misunderstandings and in gaining acceptance for airport development projects. These documents can also be an excellent resource in any subsequent EIS process, and may be used as a reference document in an EIS in lieu of having to produce new data.

Table 8-1: Green Projects and Some of the Airports That are Adopting Them

Project	Airports
Alternative energy production: Solar, wind, geothermal	San Jose, Boston, Fresno, Denver, San Francisco, New York JFK, Portland (Oregon), Chicago O'Hare, Oakland
Ground power systems at gates: Electrical connections, piped-in preconditioned air, underground jet fueling	Denver, San Francisco, Minneapolis-St. Paul, Boston, San Jose, New York JFK, Stewart International (New Windsor, NY), Detroit, Portland (Oregon)
Alternative fuel shuttles and taxis: Compressed natural gas (CNG), hybrid, biodiesel	San Jose, Boston, Seattle, Phoenix, Dallas/Fort Worth, Milwaukee, Albuquerque, Nashville, Las Vegas, Fort Lauderdale, Portland (Oregon), Denver, San Francisco, Kansas City, Chicago O'Hare, Chicago Midway
Water conservation: Low-flow toilets, drip irrigation	San Jose, Atlanta, Boston, Seattle, Nashville, Fort Lauderdale, Miami, Portland (Oregon), Dallas/Fort Worth
In-house recycling: Food, trash, newspaper, deicing fluids, building materials	San Jose, Atlanta, Seattle, Denver, Albuquerque, Nashville, Minneapolis-St. Paul, Philadelphia, Las Vegas, Phoenix, Fort Lauderdale, Detroit, Miami, Indianapolis, Portland (Oregon), Kansas City
Light-color roof: For sunlight reflection	Boston, Nashville, Atlanta, Dallas/Fort Worth, Chicago O'Hare
Lighting: Automated dimmer switch, more efficient fixtures, solar lighting, light-emitting diode (LED) runway lights	Albuquerque, Boston, Stewart International (New Windsor, NY), San Jose, Nashville, Fort Lauderdale, Detroit, Miami, Indianapolis, Seattle, Minneapolis-St. Paul, Chicago O'Hare, Chicago Midway, Dallas/Fort Worth
Landscaping: Native plants, less grass lawn, goats and sheep for weed control, recycled mulch	San Jose, Seattle, Boston, Nashville, Phoenix, Indianapolis

Source: USA TODAY research[57]

The benchmark aspect of an environmental program not only marks progress toward goal achievement, but also provides some feedback to program managers to enable them to see which policies, programs, and actions have been most effective. Ongoing environmental monitoring should also include periodic reviews of federal, state, and local laws, regulations, and procedures to make sure that the airport is and remains in compliance.

An initial baseline assessment of environmental resources must be made so that the airport can get an accurate picture of its environmental status, including noise, air quality, water quality, and other factors as noted below. Much of the information contained in the baseline assessment can be obtained from the environmental resource plans described above. Airport efforts to identify and take positive steps toward a cleaner environment typically focus on several parameters, discussed in the following section. Much of this information is based on an informative and thought-provoking article in the magazine, *Airport Consulting*.[58]

Noise
The most common and widespread airport environmental impact is noise, as discussed above. A number of larger airports have prepared noise contour maps showing the extent of noise impacts and have acquired and implemented noise monitoring systems to track flight activity. The monitoring systems record such information as flight paths, overflight frequencies, time of day, and type of aircraft. They can also help in affirming the results of the DNL modeling for an airport. Performance measures for noise impacts could include such items as the number of noise complaints received, and the number of people and noise-sensitive land uses affected. Associated mitigation programs might include aircraft operations curfews, noise-preferential runway systems, residential soundproofing programs, land acquisition programs, and homeowner assistance programs to help those people who wish to sell their homes and relocate to other areas.

Air Quality
Most air pollution at airports results from vehicle emissions, although power plants and generators, and fuel storage facilities and fueling operations also contribute to emissions. Air quality monitoring systems can be installed at various locations on and around the airport. They can identify various pollutants and their quantities, and lead to the establishment of benchmarks and the implementation of measures to reduce potentially harmful air quality emissions. These measures can include such things as vapor recovery systems for fueling airport vehicles. These systems use specialized pumps to capture vapors that would otherwise be released into the atmosphere. As noted in the discussion of air quality above, airports can also purchase cleaner-burning shuttle buses and ground support and maintenance vehicles to reduce the air pollution burden. Terminal gate improvements that provide preconditioned air and electric power to operate aircraft systems also reduce the amount of pollutants released into the air. Vehicle painting also releases noxious fumes into the air—this can be drastically reduced by

constructing paint booths that have adequate ventilation and filtering systems. A change to non-carbon burning energy sources can also reduce the air quality burden significantly.

Water Consumption and Quality

Airports consume large quantities of water, primarily in the terminal building for restrooms, food preparation, and other passenger services. Water is also used to wash airport vehicles such as shuttle buses and cargo delivery trucks. Water consumption can be monitored and reported in terms of gallons per passenger, and this measure can be used to set the appropriate benchmarks to gauge progress toward reducing water consumption. Water-saving measures include the installation of low-flow restroom fixtures and the use of recycled water for vehicle washing and irrigation.

Airport activities also result in the potential for releasing contaminated water into drainage systems, which then flows into streams, rivers, and other bodies of water. Prime examples are aircraft and runway deicing fluids, and dirty wastewater that results from vehicle wash facilities. Pollution and sedimentation can also result from airport construction activities. Water quality monitoring can be measured at outfalls where the discharged or runoff water leaves airport property. As with water consumption, benchmarks can be set to measure progress toward improving water quality. To improve water quality many airports are switching from urea to less-harmful sodium acetate for pavement deicing. At large airports one of the most effective measures to improve water quality is the designation of specific areas for aircraft deicing, along with the installation of aircraft deicing fluid recovery and containment/treatment systems. The recovered deicing fluids can be recycled for use in other products. The installation of oil-water separators in vehicle wash areas and the adoption of construction techniques that minimize runoff and sedimentation can also play a significant role in improving water quality.

Waste and Recycling

The amount of waste materials produced by airports and airlines can be mind-boggling. According to the Natural Resources Defense Council:

> The U.S. airline industry discards enough aluminum cans each year to build 58 Boeing 747 airplanes, and the airline industry discarded 9,000 tons of plastic in 2004 and enough newspapers and magazines to fill a football field to a depth of more than 230 feet.[59]

According to another source, in 2006 over 1,500 tons of airline solid waste was recycled at one large airport, and an additional 1,600 tons was diverted to landfills or incinerators.[60] The trash produced by airlines typically includes food and drink containers, uneaten food, and reading matter. In addition to the trash that is removed from airplanes, airports generate waste consisting primarily of the same materials. Waste can be monitored, reported, and benchmarked in terms of the amount of waste produced per passenger per day. Airport waste is generated by food and beverage concessions, offices, restrooms, and cargo and maintenance areas. Of these waste materials, paper, cardboard, aluminum cans, and plastic bottles can be recycled, and in fact are recycled in many cities and communities as part of established recycling programs. Airport recycling can be done in two different ways, although some airports use a combination of both. Some airports use a common recycling system in which the airport operator contracts with one waste management company to handle all waste materials, both those generated by the airport and those generated by the airlines. Under the other alternative each airline and each tenant executes an independent contract with its own waste management contractor.

Encouraging the use of recycled materials at airports and establishing appropriate benchmarks is another way to promote recycling. For example an airport operator can require all airport offices to use recycled materials such as paper for letters and reports. Airports can also promote recycling by using recycled materials to the extent feasible in airport construction projects. An example is the use of combustion by-products such as coal ash as fill material. Some pavements (primarily light duty) can be constructed with a paving material using recycled glass as part of the aggregate. Also, recycled paving materials such as portland cement concrete, asphalt concrete, stabilized base materials, and aggregates can be used to construct new pavement for airport access and circulation roadways and parking areas.

Energy Consumption

As noted above, airports operate all day, every day, and thus use an enormous amount of energy. Most lights, both in the terminal and on the airfield, are on nearly all day. Passenger services such as restrooms and food service facilities need hot water—again, all day. Energy use can be monitored and reported in terms of the energy used per passenger per day, and appropriate goals and benchmarks can be established to promote a reduction in energy use, and a switch to cleaner and/or renewable forms of energy production. Many airport activities can be operated on wind or solar power because they are large and relatively shade-free areas. Solar collection panels can be installed on rooftops and open areas such as parking lots. The use of wind power at airports may be a problem because wind power is generated by wind towers, and towers are not desirable around airports where they may constitute an obstruction to air navigation. However, Boston Logan has constructed 20 wind towers that are only six feet high and are expected to generate about 100,000 kilowatt-hours annually.[61] Wind-generated power can also be obtained from off-site power generation sources. Solar power is currently being used at a number of airports, particularly for airport passenger and cargo terminals. For example, FedEx installed a solar power system at its Oakland, California, facility that provides up to 80 percent of the hub facility's peak energy demand. In the first two years of operation the system generated more than 2 billion kilowatt hours of energy, saving 342 tons of carbon dioxide from being emitted into the atmosphere.[62] The excess energy produced by solar power systems can be transferred to local power grids for use elsewhere.

A reduction in energy consumption can also be achieved through some of the ground transportation measures discussed below.

Ground Transportation

Programs to improve ground transportation efficiency can achieve benefits in reduced energy consumption and in improving air quality. Because one of the biggest energy consumers—and air polluters—is the automobile, airport environmental performance monitoring should include base values on the numbers of passengers and employees arriving at the airport by car. Airports can offer incentive programs to encourage passengers to use transit to get to and from the airport—an example is to offer coupons that will cover all or part of the transit fare. A similar program can encourage employees to use transit. Airport operators and businesses and other employers in the vicinity of the airport can encourage employees to carpool or vanpool by sponsoring a program to coordinate ridesharing. Such a program could match employee trip origins, destinations, and work schedules to help employees find rides to work.

Aircraft ground support equipment and airport maintenance vehicles also consume significant quantities of gasoline and diesel fuel and are notoriously inefficient in the use of that fuel. Exhaust fumes contain high levels of contaminants, reducing air quality. Switching to terminal-based power systems and acquiring vehicles that use alternative fuels can help the airport's sustainability program. Rental car and parking lot shuttle buses, and shuttles to area hotels and motels also add to energy consumption and the air quality burden. Shared or common-use shuttles for rental cars and motels can result in significant improvements in both.

Buildings

Many airports are now constructing new buildings such as terminals, hangars, and cargo buildings with sustainability in mind. While no airport-specific guidelines have been established regarding sustainable design, many airports are constructing projects that conform to Leadership in Energy and Environmental Design (LEED) building standards. The LEED Green Building Rating System standards have been established by the U.S. Green Building Council to promote sustainability. Four levels of LEED certification—Certified, Silver, Gold, and Platinum—are based on state-of-the-art strategies in five areas: sustainable site development, water savings, energy efficiency, materials and resources selection, and indoor environmental quality.[63] At this writing twenty-three airports have constructed LEED-certified buildings.[64] Although constructing buildings to LEED standards may cost a little more initially, these so-called "green buildings" have the potential to reduce long-term costs of energy and utilities. That is one of the reasons planners should use life-cycle costing when preparing cost estimates as discussed in Chapter 5: Master Planning. Constructing buildings that promote sustainability sets a good example that shows the community that the airport cares about the environment and is trying to be a good neighbor.

Community Relations

As mentioned throughout this book, and emphasized in Chapter 9: Coordination and Communication, airports are part of a larger community and it is essential that airports be a good neighbor. With respect to environmental issues and sustainability, airports have two avenues to demonstrate their environmental awareness: actions and information. The actions include constructing projects that conform to environmental standards, reduce negative environmental impacts, and promote sustainability. Airports can also construct facilities and sponsor programs that benefit residents of the surrounding communities. A number of airports have constructed bike trails around the airport perimeter; these can be used by airport employees as a transportation facility and by the community as a recreational facility. They are most effective when linked with other local bike trail systems. Although some airport officials raise security concerns whenever bike trails are mentioned, these trails can enhance security by opening up secluded areas around the airport perimeter, making observation and monitoring easier by security patrols. Airports can also use vacant land that must be kept clear of obstructions to build parks, playgrounds, athletic facilities, and recreational open space areas. Some care must be taken here, however. The trails and parks may be considered protected properties under section 4(f) of the Department of Transportation Act (DOT Act) of 1966; thus difficulties may arise if the airport needs to reclaim these areas for airport expansion.

As another kind of action, many airports sponsor educational initiatives such as public tours and programs dealing with various airport-related subject areas; they should include outreach dealing with the relationship between the environment and airport operations. For example, airports that construct LEED buildings should give public tours describing the various aspects of sustainability inherent in the projects. The general public and local contractors and business leaders could gain the benefit of an airport's firsthand experience at green building construction, as well as other environmental programs such as alternative-fueled vehicles and aircraft deicing fluid recovery systems. Airports can also establish scholarship funds and attend (or sponsor) career fairs for local schools.

The information aspect of community relations can be an important and effective tool in gaining community support for the airport as well as for reducing opposition to airport operations and development. This aspect is also explained in detail in Chapter 9: Coordination and Communication. Airports should keep the community informed about various environmental programs that help reduce negative environmental impacts. Periodic "environmental report cards" should be made available to the public and to the news media, reporting on steps the airport has taken to improve environmental quality. Airport information programs should also stress that the airport is an important part of the community in that it provides jobs for residents, and obtains goods and services from local businesses. Above all, airports should provide the public with accurate and timely information that demonstrates the fact that airports are concerned about environmental issues and are taking positive steps to maintain a high level of operations and quality services while promoting a sustainable environment.

Endnotes

1 *The National Environmental Policy Act of 1969*, Pub. L. 91-190. Washington, D.C.: U.S. Congress. Accessed July 2008, from http://www.nepa.gov/nepa/regs/nepa/nepaeqia.htm

2 *National Environmental Policy Act (NEPA) Implementing Instructions for Airport Actions*, FAA Order 5050.4B. Washington, D.C.: Federal Aviation Administration, April 28, 2006, Chapter 1, p. 5-6. Accessed July 2008, from http://www.faa.gov/airports_airtraffic/airports/resources/publications/orders/environmental_5050_4/media/chapter1.pdf

3 *Policies and Procedures for Considering Environmental Impacts*, FAA Order 1050.1E, CHG 1. Washington, D.C.: Federal Aviation Administration, March 20, 2006, p. 1-1. Accessed July 2008, from http://rgl.faa.gov/regulatory_and_guidance_library/rgorders.nsf/0/2bb5c3876ba31261862571810047a403!OpenDocument&Click=

4 *Ibid.*, p. 2-2.

5 *Ibid.*, p. 2-1.

6 FAA Order 5050.4B. *Op cit.* p. 3.

7 *Ibid.*, p. 5-3.

8 *Ibid.*

9 *Environmental Desk Reference for Airport Actions*. Washington, D.C.: Federal Aviation Administration, Office of Airports, October 2007, Introduction. http://www.faa.gov/airports_airtraffic/airports/environmental/environmental_desk_ref/

10 *Delegations of Authority*, FAA Order 1100.154A. Washington, D.C.: Federal Aviation Administration, June 12, 1990. Accessed July 2008, from http://rgl.faa.gov/Regulatory_and_Guidance_Library/rgOrders.nsf/0/5b3290986c1763598625717f0051c024/$FILE/1100.154a.pdf

11 FAA Order 5050.4B. *Op cit.* p. 5-1.

12 FAA Order 1050.1E. *Op cit.* p. 3-3.

13 FAA Order 5050.4B. *Op cit.* p. 5-6.

14 *Ibid.*, p. 7-3.

15 *Ibid.*, p. 4-2.

16	*Ibid.*, p. 7-5 through 7-11.
17	*Ibid.*, p. 7-1.
18	*Ibid.*, p. 5-6, 5-7.
19	FAA Order 1050.1E. *Op cit.* p. 2-5, 2-6.
20	*Ibid.*, p. 2-5.
21	*Ibid.*, p. 2-5.
22	*Ibid.*, Introduction, p. 2, 3.
23	*Environmental Stewardship and Transportation Infrastructure Project Reviews*, Executive Order 13274. Executive Order Implementation. Washington, D.C.: U.S. Department of Transportation, September 18, 2002. Accessed July 2008, from http://www.dot.gov/execorder/13274/eo13274/index.htm
24	*Vision 100 – Century of Aviation Reauthorization Act*, (HR 2115), Public Law 108-176, Title III, Subchapter A, December 12, 2003. Washington, D.C.: U.S. House of Representatives. Accessed June 2008, from http://frwebgate.access.gpo.gov/cgi-bin/getdoc.cgi?dbname=108_cong_public_laws&docid=f:publ176.108.pdf
25	*Ibid.*
26	FAA Order 5050.4B. *Op cit.* p. 15-1.
27	*Ibid.*, p. 2.
28	*Ibid.*, p. 1.
29	*Ibid.*
30	*Webster's II New Riverside University Dictionary*. Boston: Houghton-Mifflin, 1998.
31	*Desk Reference. Op cit.* Chapter 17, p. 4.
32	*Ibid.*
33	*Ibid.*, p. 5.
34	*Ibid.*, p. 9.
35	*Ibid.*, p. 13.
36	*Procedures for Abatement of Highway Traffic Noise and Construction Noise* (23 CFR Part 772). Washington, D.C.: Federal Highway Administration. Accessed July 2008, from http://www.fhwa.dot.gov/hep/23cfr772.htm
37	*Aviation & Emissions – A Primer*. Washington, D.C.: Federal Aviation Administration, Office of Environment and Energy, January 2005. Accessed July 2008, from http://www.faa.gov/regulations_policies/policy_guidance/envir_policy/media/aeprimer.pdf
38	*Desk Reference. Op cit.* Chapter 1, p. 1.
39	*Ibid.*, p. 4.
40	*Ibid.*, p. 18.

Chapter 8 – Environmental Considerations

41 Pehrson, John R., "Air Quality Regulations Compliance: Act Now," *Airport Magazine*, September/October 2005, AAAE Service Corporation, Inc., Alexandria, VA.

42 Voluntary Airport Low Emissions Program (VALE). Washington, D.C.: Federal Aviation Administration. Accessed July 2008, from http://www.faa.gov/airports_airtraffic/airports/environmental/vale/

43 *Introduction to the Clean Water Act*. Washington, D.C.: U.S. Environmental Protection Agency. Accessed August 2008, from http://www.epa.gov/watertrain/cwa/

44 *Desk Reference. Op cit.* Chapter 20, p. 1.

45 *Ibid.*

46 *Definition of Navigable Waters of the U.S.* (33 CFR Part 329). http://www.usace.army.mil/cw/cecwo/reg/33cfr329.htm#329.4

47 *Polluted Runoff (Nonpoint Source Pollution)*. Washington, D. C.: U.S. Environmental Protection Agency. Accessed August 2008, from http://www.epa.gov/owow/NPS/MMGI/Chapter1/ch1-1.html

48 *Stormwater Program National Pollutant Discharge Elimination System (NPDES)*. Washington, D.C.: U.S. Environmental Protection Agency. Accessed August 2008, from http://cfpub.epa.gov/npdes/home.cfm?program_id=6

49 *Spill Prevention, Control and Countermeasure Plans (SPCC)*. Washington, D.C.: U.S. Environmental Protection Agency. Accessed August 2008, from http://www.epa.gov/region5/oil/plan/spcc.html

50 *Desk Reference. Op cit.* Chapter 20, p. 5.

51 *Wetlands Definitions*. Washington, D.C.: U.S. Environmental Protection Agency. Accessed August 2008, from http://www.epa.gov/owow/wetlands/what/definitions.html

52 *Desk Reference. Op cit.* Chapter 21, p. 3.

53 *Ibid.*, p. 8, 9.

54 *Consideration Of Cumulative Impacts In EPA Review of NEPA Documents*. U.S. Environmental Protection Agency, May 1999. Accessed August 2008, from http://www.epa.gov/compliance/resources/policies/nepa/cumulative.pdf

55 *Desk Reference. Op cit.* Chapter 23, p. 4.

56 Massport, Logan Airport. Airport Programs, Environmental. Accessed August 2008, from http://www.massport.com/LOGAN/airpo_envir_data.html

57 Yu, Roger, "Airports Go for Green with Eco-friendly Efforts," *USA Today*, September 18, 2008. Accessed September 2008, from http://www.usatoday.com/travel/flights/2008-09-16-green-airports_N.htm

58 Lurie, Carol, and Sarah Townsend, "How Do Airports Stack Up?," *Airport Consulting*, Winter 2007/2008, Airport Consultants Council, Alexandria, VA.

59 Atkin, Peter, *Trash Landings – How Airlines and Airports Can Clean Up Their Recycling Programs*. National Resources Defense Council, December 2006.

	Accessed September 2008, from http://www.nrdc.org/cities/recycling/airline/airline.pdf
60	Airport Recycling Specialists, home page. Accessed August 2008, from http://www.airportrecycling.com/
61	Yu, Roger. *Op cit.*
62	Elgun, Serdar Z., M. Issapour, Y. Dathatri, and A. Filios, *Retrofitting Airports by Harnessing The Sun's Energy*, (n.d.) presentation at Farmingdale State College, State University of New York, Solar Energy Center. Accessed September 2008, from http://www.faa.gov/airports_airtraffic/airports/regional_guidance/eastern/airports_news_events/hershey/media_08/airportdesign.ppt#256,1,Slide 1
63	U.S. Green Building Council. Accessed August 2008, from http://www.usgbc.org/
64	U.S. Green Building Council. Accessed August 2008, from http://www.usgbc.org/LEED/Project/RegisteredProjectList.aspx

CHAPTER 9

COORDINATION AND COMMUNICATION

Coordination and communication are a fundamental part of planning. Airport planners cannot work in a vacuum. An exchange of ideas between and among other key airport stakeholders can help produce a plan that is well thought out, soundly based, and implementable. This chapter discusses the need for and benefits of coordination as well as the need for clear communication in the coordination process. The discussion includes all groups that may have some interest in the operation and development of airports, including other internal airport groups, key airport stakeholders, local governmental agencies, special interest groups, and elected officials, to name a few. The chapter includes a discussion of the reasons for opposition to airport development plans, along with some thought on how to mitigate or lessen the impact of the opposition. Public involvement is a generally required component of planning studies, and can be most effective in the context of an overall public outreach program. The various attributes of public involvement and public outreach are discussed in some detail. Just as successful coordination depends on effective communication, successful communication depends on the quality of oral and written presentation. The chapter concludes with some guidance on preparing and delivering oral presentations, and preparing written materials including reports and summary brochures. Specific attention is given to speaking, writing, and preparing and using visual aids.

Coordination

Coordination is interwoven with nearly everything an effective airport planner does. When the planning starts, it is necessary to coordinate with just about every group involved in the operation of the airport, including maintenance, operations, marketing, and engineering. It is also important to remember to coordinate with groups such as the FAA air traffic control staff, airlines, cargo operators, rental car companies, concessionaires, fixed base operators, pilots' groups, and fire and police protection agencies, to name a few. It is also essential to coordinate with other state and local planning agencies, environmental review agencies, and government officials.

The FAA's Master Plan AC lists "Coordination and Public Involvement" as one of the steps in the Pre-Planning process.[1] This is unfortunate for two reasons. First, coordination should not be considered as a "step" in the planning process, because that implies that it is a discrete activity—"First you do this, then you do that, and then you coordinate…." But as noted in the planning chapters of this book, planning is not a linear or strictly step-by-step process, and coordination should continue throughout the planning effort as a natural exchange—rather like breathing. Coordination includes all groups involved with the operation of the airport: user groups and tenants; other transportation, planning, and environmental agencies; elected officials; and the general public.

Second, *public involvement* is part of the coordination process, but usually refers more specifically to coordination with the general public, especially those living and/or operating businesses near the airport, as well as those who will be directly affected by the future development of the airport. Public involvement usually takes place at specific points in the planning process, as discussed below. *Public outreach* is sometimes regarded as synonymous with coordination and public involvement but it is actually slightly different. This section of the chapter deals specifically with coordination; public involvement and public outreach are discussed separately in the second section of this chapter.

The Planner's Role

Plan coordination is best led by planners. They should be the ones who deal directly with all parties, including airport stakeholders, tenants, elected officials, other government agencies, the general public, and special interest groups. Thus planners must know what to present and what to discuss, and equally important, they should know what kinds of information they are responsible for—and what level of detail they should leave to other professionals such as traffic engineers.

Ideally coordination should be conducted by planners directly employed by the airport, but if the in-house staff is not large enough or does not have the expertise to address all the issues adequately, consultant assistance should be obtained. For complex projects it may also be appropriate to hire a consultant to help set up the coordination program, particularly for those aspects dealing with public involvement. A number of reputable firms have extensive expertise in this area and their assistance in setting up the overall coordination program and assisting in public hearings and meetings can be invaluable.

Coordination in one sense means letting people know what is going on—what is being done, who is doing it, and why. Too often this is done so that planners can check off the appropriate box, for example to meet federal requirements. However, if done properly, coordination means communication. It is a two-way street. Planners must not only tell people what they are doing, but also ask for their input to make sure that the resulting plan meets their needs.

Listen First, Plan Later

This broad, two-way involvement should start at the very beginning of the planning process. All stakeholders should be informed that a planning study is beginning, whether it is a comprehensive master plan or a smaller-scale plan for the development of the terminal area or a cargo facility. This applies to planning studies at large airports as well as small, general aviation airports, although the scale of the coordination effort is typically much smaller as the airport decreases in size and the issues become less complex.

It is really not a good idea to complete the planning process and then announce to airport operations, or the marketing or leasing people, "Look what I have for you!" Or even to tell them that a plan has been prepared and now their comments and suggestions are being solicited. It is much more effective to go to each of the key stakeholders, including operations, marketing, leasing, the major tenants or tenant groups, and tell them why the plan is being done in the first place, and ask if they have any issues they would like to see addressed as part of the planning study and/or in the final plan.

For example, there are situations where the planners lay out a concept for an expanded terminal and present it to the leasing people, who are then told, "This is the space you are going to have for concessions." It is similarly presented to the affected airlines, who are told, "This is the ticket counter, baggage makeup, holdroom, and operations space you are going to have to work with." As you might imagine, this approach doesn't work very well. The leasing people should be involved up front to find out how much space they think they will need for concessions, and the airlines should be involved up front to find out what their space requirements are. Of course, most of the time they will ask for much more than can be reasonably provided while keeping the plan functional and affordable. But even if they can't get everything they want, this is a good way to determine what kinds of things are most important to them. Giving them some input to the planning process for the facilities they will ultimately occupy is common sense and good business.

Sometimes dealing with these groups can be difficult. For example, it is often frustrating to talk with the airport operations, or maintenance, or leasing staff because they can give an impression of being unable to see the long-term benefit of the plans you are developing. In these cases you should remember that these staff members are focused on today's issues and solving a slew of immediate problems, so it can be hard for them to make the jump to "what if" or "what might be." As a planner it is your job to make your concepts and plans, your interpretation of future issues and solutions, real for them. You have to put things in terms they can understand and relate to. This is in no way intended to be demeaning or to imply that they have no imagination or aren't very bright; it just means that operating an airport day-to-day in a fast-paced environment is hard work and does not leave a lot of time for contemplating the future. That is why talking with these people early on in the planning process is so essential, and why it is so important to find out how they think and what they think about.

Building Support for the Plan

As noted elsewhere in this book, in a sense half of the art (or science) of planning is selling. People aren't going to buy into a plan and accept its commitments unless they are convinced that it is highly beneficial. Part of the planner's job is to prepare the plan; the other part is to identify the reasons why people should accept it. The best plan in the world will be of no use if it is not accepted, particularly by the airport's key stakeholders.

As far as airport planning is concerned, the key stakeholders are most likely to include the airport's engineering, construction, operations, maintenance, commercial or business management, and capital programming and financial groups, as well as the local FAA air traffic control staff. Stakeholders also include the executive management staff and whatever exists in terms of an airport board or airport commission. As discussed in Chapter 3: Airport Management, Operations, and Finance, other stakeholders include the airlines, miscellaneous airport tenants, cargo operators, fixed base operators, and other airport user groups. These people all have different interests, some of which may overlap, and they will all have their own thoughts of where the airport should be headed in the future.

Selling the plan begins with getting these interest groups involved up front, at the outset of the planning process. That is why key airport stakeholders should be included in the development of the strategic plan, which will provide the basis for follow-on planning work. Incorporating the views and suggestions of the key stakeholders, beginning with strategic planning and continuing through master planning and detailed facility planning, helps develop the idea of "our plan" versus "their plan." The more that people feel they have a hand in developing a plan, the better the chances that they will support it.

Launching the Discussion

As noted above, discussions with any of the airport operating or user groups should begin with a description of what type of plan is being developed and why. Using the terminal planning example above, these groups should be told that a terminal planning study is being undertaken and that it will look at the existing terminal, how it is used, problem areas that have been noticed or reported, and the expected traffic growth that may put pressure on the existing facility. They may be told that the study will look at reconfiguring existing terminal space as well as adding additional space. They should also be informed about the expected scope of the study, e.g., whether it will concentrate on the airside components such as gates and holdrooms, or whether it will be focused on the landside and curbfront components. In all probability the study will address both components and everything in between; if so, let the terminal users know that.

After these groups have been told what is being done and why, they should be questioned about any problems they are experiencing, what they would like to see addressed as part of the terminal planning study, and what they would like to see in terms of reconfigured or expanded facilities. In effect this is asking for their assistance in preparing the plan; this is the first step in making it "our plan" rather than "my plan" or "his plan" or even "their plan." This kind of communication at the outset gives everyone some ownership in the plan, and lets all terminal users know that they are part of the process. It will not only make it easier to obtain concurrence and support for the plan, but also help to develop a good plan that addresses all the concerns and meets all the needs of the terminal users.

The same kind of thinking and the same kinds of coordination should take place whether it is a terminal development plan, an airside capacity plan, or a comprehensive airport master plan. A master plan will involve a lot more people and many more organizations, including external groups such as elected officials, planning agencies, and community associations, but the essential process is the same: communicate and listen to what others have to say. And remember: if the key stakeholders and airport users have been included in the strategic planning process they will already understand why the planning is being done. All that remains is to educate them on the details.

For plans involving new runways, new flight patterns, new roadways, and other factors which could have a significant community impact, it is often effective to include the general public as a stakeholder. Normally this is done by working with representatives of community associations or special interest groups within the community. Community involvement in the development and evaluation of alternatives can help to ensure that the plan will be responsive to community concerns, and thus reduce potential community opposition to the proposed development.

Knowing Where the Land Mines Are

Early coordination and effective communication will help uncover the areas of concern—areas that may eventually be the basis for opposition to a project. If these "hot buttons" are known in advance, planners can be better prepared to address them, preferably as part of the planning study.

For example, if a community is sensitive to wetland issues, planners will know up front that special attention will have to be given to the potential for wetland impacts, particularly if any wetland areas will be taken for construction. In conjunction with an airport access roadway relocation project, for example, early coordination may let planners know that the community will oppose any incursion upon a particular sensitive wetland area. If that is known up front, additional work must be accomplished to see if the runway can be extended without adversely affecting the wetland. If avoidance is not possible, planners will know from the start that a given number of acres of wetland will have to be mitigated, probably by creating a new wetland area, preferably located in the same watershed. This also lets planners know that they will have to work closely with other governmental agencies having jurisdiction over wetlands in the airport area. Not having this kind of information up front can lead to extra work and project delays while such issues are being addressed.

The sooner that planners talk with the community, the sooner they will find out about hot button issues, and the sooner and more completely they can address them. If an issue such as wetlands can be addressed as part of the planning process, it reduces the likelihood of the unpleasant surprises that often interrupt the environmental approvals process and result in delays in getting final project approvals and an eventual AIP grant. Proactive planning also helps build a level of trust between the airport and the community.

If coordination and communication are launched early in the process, other state and local government agencies can sometimes assist in resolving airport issues. For example, local transportation planners can help to come up with some improvements to local roadways, or local traffic routings, to avoid putting more airport-related vehicles on local streets. If these issues and others like them are a possible result of the project, and a possible concern to local communities, they will have to be addressed at some point in the planning process. The sooner that these kinds of issues are identified, the sooner they can be addressed. Avoiding or resolving a local traffic issue early on in the study reduces the likelihood of its becoming a major issue in the environmental process or at a public hearing. That is not a good time to have to go back and address the issue; it will only take more time and more money. If the study has to be delayed to address local traffic issues, or other community concerns, it will delay the entire planning and approval process. If these issues are serious enough, it will take so long to address them that the original forecast may become out-of-date, and a good portion of the entire planning process may have to be repeated, beginning with the forecasts. This makes everybody look bad and it certainly does not help get the facility built when it is needed.

Coordinating Discretely
Be aware that discretion may be called for in coordination and communication. For example, one of the reasons a terminal development plan is being prepared may be that a new airline is coming to town, or that an existing carrier is planning a major service expansion. Because the airline business is so highly competitive, the carrier in question will probably not want to

have its expansion plans made public, so it will be necessary to be less than forthcoming with the current tenants. However, up-front coordination can still take place and much useful information can be obtained. In this case it would be stated that the airport is doing a terminal plan update because the terminal is getting a little crowded during peak periods (this is almost universally true of airport terminals, so this is pretty safe ground), and that it is necessary to take a long-term, big-picture look "just in case…." If anybody asks if there is a particular carrier in mind, the appropriate answer is that the airport is always working with airlines to obtain additional routes and flight frequencies. This may have a side benefit of stimulating some of the other carriers to revisit their current service patterns at the airport to see if there may be some expansion opportunities.

Public Involvement

The Master Plan AC notes that public involvement is the first task in a master plan study, after the consultant has been selected.

> Public involvement has its greatest impact during the early stages of the planning process, before irreversible decisions have been made and while many alternatives can be considered. When the stakeholders become involved before major decisions or commitments are made, the planners can better deal with issues of community concern and improve the chances of reaching a consensus on controversial matters.[2]

Building Trust

Airports are part of a larger community and planners must recognize that community and respond to its needs and concerns to produce an effective plan. Reaching out to the public at the outset of a planning study lets people know that the airport cares about what they think. If public involvement doesn't begin until alternatives have been developed, it tends to create an atmosphere of distrust. People get the feeling that key decisions have already been made and that they are only being informed because the law requires it. In this regard it is important to let the public know that they will have a role to play in the study and to let them know what that role is and how their views will be incorporated into the planning process. It is also very important to let people know why the study is being done and what significant issues and problems are being addressed. Sometimes people have the idea that the airport is expanding simply because it can, and a few may even express the view that the airport is being expanded as a form of job security (or higher salaries) for airport staff. A forthright statement of airport issues and planning objectives at the outset will help dispel these ideas, or most of them at any rate.

Consider the Many Publics

As noted in Chapter 5: Master Planning, the extent of the public involvement program will vary with the complexity of the study and especially with the extent of the environmental impacts. More specifically, the degree of public involvement will vary with the degree to which the facility improvements resulting from the plan will affect the community. Although the Master Plan AC provides some guidance on public involvement, much more detailed and more useful guidance is contained in the FAA's *Community Involvement Manual*.[3] This manual provides all kinds of information on everything from general principles of public involvement to program design and specific public involvement techniques, including the advantages and disadvantages of each.[4] It offers some very useful information (although some naivety or lack of first-hand experience shows in places) and should be consulted at the beginning of a planning study before any decisions are made as to how and when to involve the public. The manual notes that there are different "publics" and includes some guidance on how to identify and involve each of them. The publics listed in the manual are the

- staff of other federal, state, and local governmental agencies;
- elected officials at various levels of government;
- highly-visible leaders of organized groups or identifiable interests (e.g., air transport associations, airline pilots' associations, neighborhood groups, etc.);
- members of technical and professional groups;
- members of organized groups or identifiable interests (e.g., residents in proximity to the airport, airport users, etc.); and
- the general public not otherwise identified with any organized groups.[5]

The Master Plan AC includes tenants as part of the "public," although the *Community Involvement Manual* does not. The definition in the manual seems to be more accurate and useful because airport tenants are really stakeholders (rather than members of the public at large) and should be coordinated with on a more technical level, especially about the issues that concern them directly. In some cases a few airport tenants have attended public meetings and public hearings and spoken in opposition to a proposed plan or development program. This is not a good thing; it gives other opponents a more solid base for opposing airport improvements, especially if those directly involved in the operation of the airport raise safety as an issue. And this I have seen. Sometimes "internal" issues spill over into the public arena, but every attempt should be made to resolve these kinds of issues before plans are presented to the various publics noted above. It is not good practice to operate in a secretive manner, but on the other hand there is no point to a public exposure of dirty linen. It is usually not possible to please everybody so in these cases planners just have to make the best of it and address tenants' concerns as accurately and honestly as they can.

When is it Mandatory?

The manual lists cases in which community involvement is specifically required:

- Actions or projects involving the preparation of an environmental impact statement (EIS) or an environmental assessment (EA).
- Noise compatibility studies conducted under FAR Part 150.
- Planning studies including airport system plans and airport master plans.
- Facilities establishment, particularly if proposed navigational aids or other improvements could be interpreted as permitting or encouraging increased traffic or operations by larger or more noisy airplanes.[6]

Public Involvement versus Public Hearings

Note that public involvement is not the same as *public hearings*. Public involvement means, in a broad sense, telling people what is going on and giving them an opportunity to provide comments and other input to the planning process. This usually includes giving people the opportunity to review and comment on planning and environmental documents. Public hearings, on the other hand, are formal and according to the FAA manual,

> …consist of three major parts: a presentation summary of the main parts of the project or problem, an outline of the range of solutions including the recommended solution (provided there is one), and the public's reactions to the proposed course of actions.[7]

Note that the terms "public hearing" and "public meeting" are often used interchangeably—this is not correct. Any meeting with the public can be thought of as a public meeting, but a public hearing is a more formal event that conforms with the FAA requirements noted above, and for which a formal transcript is normally prepared. Sometimes whenever airport operators hear or see the term "public involvement" they immediately think that a public hearing is required and turn pale and begin to shake. Although public involvement is required under the conditions noted above, public hearings are only required specifically if an airport sponsor is submitting an application for AIP funding to build

- a new airport,
- a new runway, or
- a major runway extension.[8]

It should be noted that *public information meetings* are often held in conjunction with large or complex projects. These are not the same as public hearings in that they do not result in a written transcript and are not a specific requirement of any public involvement process. Rather, they provide an opportunity for citizens to discuss specific issues with knowledgeable airport representatives in an informal, typically one-on-one context.

Encouraging Productive Discussion

As noted above, the manual lists a number of techniques for getting the public involved, most of which I have personally either used or seen used, and they are all effective when used as noted in the manual. A couple of specific points should be emphasized to help amplify the manual's guidance. First, large meetings tend to attract individuals who like to get up in front of an audience and yell and scream and call people bad names. At times this can't be avoided and just has to be endured. Unfortunately these meetings are not usually very productive since people who have legitimate questions and concerns have a hard time making themselves heard, and also have a hard time getting their questions answered.

When a large public gathering is expected, at a formal public hearing, or less-formal public meeting for example, it is often more productive to have a separate area where the technical details of a plan or project can be discussed at individual work stations. If a hearing is being held in a large auditorium, the work stations could include various project displays such as graphs, charts, drawings, and aerial photographs that can be set up in a lobby area just outside the auditorium. These displays should illustrate various pertinent aspects of the plan, such as the forecasts, project layouts or renderings, noise exposure contours, wetlands, forest stands, and other environmental features. They should be manned by specialists or experts in each of the relevant fields, and may include both airport staff and consultants. This way people can look at all the aspects of the plan and see how it affects them and their community, and they can also discuss their concerns with knowledgeable staff. The exhibit area can be opened about an hour or so before a formal hearing or meeting is to take place so that the public will have adequate time to become educated on the plan details and potential impacts. Then they can go into the auditorium when the hearing starts to make their formal comments or ask questions "for the record," so to speak. The work stations or exhibit areas provide an opportunity for people to speak and/or ask questions who are not comfortable speaking in front of a large audience. For those who wish to address the larger audience, it is a good idea to have a sign-up list in the exhibit area so people who wish to speak can get on the agenda. When the hearing starts a moderator can deliver a formal statement of the plan, including what is being done and why it is being done, and announce the format for the hearing. It is usually a good idea to limit each speaker to about five minutes, and to let them know that if they have more to say they can have a formal letter entered into the minutes of the hearing, and that all questions and comments will be addressed in the final record.

In some cases a panel of experts sits on stage to answer questions from the general audience, but this is usually not a very good idea. First of all it can drag things out if the question or issue being addressed is complicated or highly technical. Second, it is sometimes hard to think quickly in front of a restive crowd of a few hundred people; the experts may say things that can be taken out of context and they can also make mistakes. When this (mis)information gets entered into the public record it can be difficult to straighten out some of the incorrect information. Remember: everything that is said in a public hearing will become part of the transcript or hearing minutes. So choose your words very carefully.

Speak Their Language

Another point to be emphasized with regard to public involvement is that, no matter what the format or who the audience, make sure all of the relevant information is presented to that audience honestly, accurately, and in a language they will understand. These considerations should be addressed up front as part of identifying which of the various publics will be addressed, what they are to be told, and more specifically, what they should know about the project. For example, don't use a lot of technical jargon when talking to the general public. In presentations of forecast information to a nontechnical citizens group, the language should be kept simple. Airport projects are technical endeavors, but their purpose and need, costs and benefits (pros and cons), and general highlights can be presented in common sense terms that are easily understandable by most people.

Honesty and accuracy mean not only telling the truth about the plan, but also fully describing its implications. For example, if a new runway is going to mean a change in flight paths, the public should be so informed. Also, if adopting a plan for a new runway is going to commit the airport to other improvements, such as an expanded terminal or reconfigured roadway system, this information should be made known. The latter is especially important for those who control the airport's finances, as well as for environmental resource agencies and local transportation and land use planners. The subject of actually preparing and presenting information is discussed further below, in the Presentation section of this chapter.

How Much Information?

There seem to be two somewhat different schools of thought about public involvement. One school says that the public should only be informed about things going on at the airport that will affect them directly, and in accordance with federal and state requirements for public involvement. This school feels that the public will not understand most of what is happening and that providing them with information that may be misunderstood or taken out of context will be self-defeating. This school has noted that in many instances airport opponents are more educated and more vocal—and are getting more legal support. Thus, in effect, the airport will be giving people the ammunition they need to successfully oppose airport development. The other school says that the community should be kept informed, even about things that don't affect them, so that they won't be confused or suspicious when they see that something new or different is going on or is planned. This school feels that keeping the public informed helps build a level of trust between the airport and the community it serves. In this latter sense it is helpful to think of public involvement as a component of the broader idea of public outreach.

In summary, there are many approaches to achieving public involvement and each method has its merits. Each approach must be carefully thought through based on the audience you are trying to reach and the nature of the information being presented.

Public Outreach

As noted in Chapter 5: Master Planning, the Pennsylvania Department of Transportation has published an excellent manual entitled *Partnering for Better Communities* that provides guidance for airport public outreach[9] programs. The basic premise for the manual is that, "Being a good neighbor is more than meeting regulatory requirements."[10] The manual includes guidance on various means of disseminating information to the public, such as Web sites, brochures and flyers, press releases, focus groups, advisory committees, and speaking engagements by airport staff. It also presents techniques for building bridges between the airport and the community by hosting events and programs that demonstrate that the airport is "…a good neighbor with ties to the community."[11] These include hosting career fairs and community appreciation days, as well as sponsoring education and training programs and awards programs. The manual includes references and testimonials from airports in Pennsylvania that have successfully implemented community outreach programs.

During my tenure at BWI Airport we adopted a number of these techniques and approaches and they seemed to be very successful in reducing community opposition to the airport's development, as well as its day-to-day operation. Before we began our community outreach efforts the airport did very little to communicate with the surrounding communities. When public meetings and public hearings were held, the audiences numbered in the hundreds and they were decidedly hostile. About five years after we began public outreach efforts, audiences numbered two or three dozen, and in some cases the audience was outnumbered by the airport's public hearing staff. This is not to suggest that our aim was to lower the number of public participants, but in this case attracting fewer people who were fired up to oppose our efforts demonstrated broader support for the airport in general and a greater acceptance of airport projects. Most airport operators who have adopted this approach feel that an ongoing, informative, and honest community outreach program pays off in the long run. Also, many planners have noted that working closely with special interest groups is more effective in communicating ideas and reaching agreements than trying to build consensus at a public meeting with 200 to 300 people.

To be successful a community outreach program should be continuous, not just undertaken when an expansion project is planned. Also, the community outreach program should involve everyone directly associated with the airport, including airlines and other tenants, fixed base operators, flying schools, and pilot groups, as well as the airport staff. If at all possible local planning and economic development agencies should also be invited to support airport outreach programs because airports are places of employment and generators of economic growth. Experience has shown that when the opposing views (for example the general public versus the pilots) are shared in this forum they begin to understand and appreciate opposing needs and it is easier to achieve compromise.

Dealing with Plan Opposition

In spite of everything airport operators and airport planners do to coordinate and communicate, almost any airport expansion project is likely to be opposed by members of at least one or two groups, and sometimes even more. These groups can include airlines currently serving the airport, other airport tenants, environmental resource agencies, local land use or community planners, real estate developers, elected officials, and the citizens living around the airport. Each of these groups has an agenda or a reason for opposing a particular project. Usually objections coincide, but at other times they may in fact work in opposite directions. The nature of some of these objections and ideas for dealing with them are discussed below.

Resistance to Change

Frequently a common theme pervades community opposition to airport improvements, and that is a resistance to, or even fear of, change. I once attended a short course in how to deal with an angry customer. One of the main points brought out by the course was that the thing people complain about is not the thing that is really bothering them. However, this doesn't always seem to be true. For example if someone is complaining about increased aircraft noise, it is a good bet that they are bothered by aircraft noise and don't want it to increase. But part of this opposition, whether from politicians on financial grounds, or from citizens on the basis of noise or traffic congestion, is partly grounded in their uncertainty about the future. They made it through today; therefore, today was a safe day. If tomorrow brings something different it may not be safe; it is unknown, and even if one survives, things will still not be the same. Resistance to change cannot be overstated, and should be kept in mind as you read the following sections.

Resistance to Competition

Occasionally an airline or group of airlines may oppose a project—for example, a dominant hub carrier may be opposed to a major terminal expansion project because the carrier does not want the increased competition. For example, an airline currently serving an airport may oppose the construction of a new international terminal because they plan to concentrate their domestic service at another relatively nearby airport, and use that domestic traffic to feed their transatlantic service from that other airport. Also, airlines are frequently opposed to any airport improvement that will be funded through the rates and charges established in the Basic Use and Lease Agreement (BULA), because they see it as an increase in their local operating cost to benefit another, potentially competing, airline. Airline opposition is usually not the kiss of death for an airport expansion project, provided that the local political leaders support the project. Airline opposition can make the airport's work harder, but it can be overcome.

Political Opposition

Obtaining the concurrence and support of local political representatives is often a different story. Consultation with local elected officials can be done at any point in the planning process, but it is much more effective to start discussions as early as possible. Obtaining the necessary approvals and concurrences is a lot easier if the elected officials feel that they have some influence in the planning process and the eventual outcome as well. Involving these officials early on allows you to identify their respective issues and concerns, and to address them in the planning process. This lets the officials know that their issues have been recognized and are being addressed, and it also shows them how they are being addressed. It requires a good-faith effort on the part of the airport planners and the airport operator to address these issues. Political concerns typically involve two major areas: community reaction and financial implications. The concern for community reaction is obvious; if an elected official supports a project that is opposed by a community, the citizens may not be likely to vote for that individual again in the next election. The financial implications are a bit more subtle, but just as serious. If a project is going to involve a large expenditure of public funds, it may cause taxes to increase to pay for it, or it may involve postponing some other project that is important to the elected official's constituency. It is important to note that community opposition may not kill a project if the elected officials know that there is a larger benefit to going ahead with the proposed development.

With regard to the financial aspect of development opposition, it is only fair to acknowledge that political opposition to a project may have a valid basis, particularly if their local jurisdiction is going to have to provide some of the funding for the project. Airport planners and operators must recognize that the airport may be one of many entities competing for the same limited pot of money. At a small airport that primarily serves general aviation activity, the local legislator may have to balance funding improvements at the airport against the need to fund improved police or fire protection services. At this point the legislator must make a decision on how many people, or more specifically, how many voters in his or her district, will benefit from each of these improvements. In other words, what is the value or return on each dollar spent?

Emphasize the Benefits

There are many reasons groups oppose airport improvement projects, and many of them are valid. However, the reason those airport projects are being pursued is because they will offer many benefits. It is up to the airport operator—specifically the planners leading the plan—to articulate those benefits so that the public and other stakeholders can appropriately weigh the pros and cons of a plan.

New jobs and tax revenue are one benefit that most people can relate to. Just as airports have to prepare an environmental document showing the potential impacts an airport improvement may have on the environment, so should they prepare an economic impact assessment showing the potential positive impacts the project may have on the economy. The key measures to be examined are: jobs created, revenues generated, and taxes paid. It is much easier to secure funding for a project if it can be stated that the airport should make the investment to build four new aircraft boarding gates because it will result in 25 to 30 additional flights per day in five new or underserved markets, resulting in 150 new jobs, $10 million in annual revenues, and $1.5 million in state and local taxes.

It should also be pointed out that these new jobs, revenues, and taxes are spread through the local economy. Some of the new jobs will be located directly at the airport, either by the airline, the airport, or other tenants, and others may result from an increase in taxi operators, hotel and restaurant staff, real estate sales or rental staff, and others whose businesses are either directly or indirectly related to airport activity. Taxes and revenues would be similarly distributed throughout the local area. In order to get an accurate estimate of potential economic benefits, the airport should do periodic airport economic impact studies showing the current contributions the airport makes to the local economy. An annual economic assessment would be ideal; a biennial assessment would also work in most cases. If they are done less often than that, the information tends to become dated and its usefulness may be limited.

To be fair, many economic impact reports produce numbers that are unbelievably large and people joke that the study showed that everyone in the county must work at the airport. Some people (including airport directors) express confusion about the use of such terms as "direct," "indirect," and "induced" economic benefits. Also, although all airports undoubtedly provide some degree of economic benefit, smaller airports often do not generate the revenues, taxes, or jobs generated by a shopping mall, especially one anchored by a "big box" store. Thus care should be taken when bandying economic impact numbers about.

That said, such studies can be quite useful. As a personal example, in my capacity as Planning Director for the Maryland Aviation Administration I began a program to measure the economic impact of each of the 35 or so airports in the Maryland aviation system. Initially, due to limited funding, the studies were conducted only every five years. The frequency was subsequently increased to every two years based on the response of many of the airport managers. They found the economic information generated by the studies very useful in demonstrating the community and regional benefits generated by the airports. For maximum effectiveness, economic impact study results should be expressed clearly and concisely, using language that the audience for such studies will understand. The American Association of Airport Executives (AAAE) has an airport economic impact analysis package for general aviation airports available on its Web site. According to AAAE, "The total economic benefits of airports (dollars and jobs) are measured in terms of the amount of money spent because of the airports, the amount of earnings for local residents, and the number of full-time equivalent jobs generated due to the airport."[12]

Present the benefits that are most relevant to your specific audience. Airlines often oppose projects that they feel will not benefit them directly, or will benefit their competitors even more. Other airport tenants may oppose improvements that may cause their lease rates to increase. People living near the airport often oppose any development they think will bring more air traffic, and thus more aircraft overflights or more highway congestion to their communities. In these cases it is critical to find out what their interests and concerns are so you can describe the issues and present the alternative concepts and plans in terms that will show them a benefit, or at least a significant mitigation of adverse impacts.

For example, airlines may be opposed to a taxiway improvement that will improve taxiway circulation in the area of the terminal that is used primarily by one of their competitors. In order to build the support of all airlines, planners must demonstrate how the project will benefit each of the carriers, perhaps by improving aircraft ground movements and airside traffic circulation overall. Improving taxiway efficiency in one area may also reduce taxi delays in other areas of the airport. If this is the case the supporting analysis should provide enough information to make this point. In other words, if the concurrence of an airline or other airport tenant is being sought for an improvement plan, they must be shown what is in it for them. It is often hard to sell people on something that is being done for "the common good" when money may be at stake.

Work With Elected Officials

In a democracy, elected officials answer to their constituents, at least in theory. Quite often it may be difficult to identify just whom that constituency consists of, but there is a constituency nonetheless. In many cases the local senator, representative, assemblyman, or councilman may support the proposed improvement, particularly if a good case can be made in showing the potential benefits, and especially if a significant portion of that benefit will accrue to his or her district. However, the people who live around the airport may not see it that way. Even if they are in a district that will benefit from the improvement, their portion of the district may have to bear the burden of increased aircraft noise and local traffic congestion, while another part of the district may reap the benefit. In some cases the additional jobs created as a result of an airport improvement project may not be important to the current local residents. At a public hearing for an improvement at BWI Airport, I once heard a man complain that all we (the State of Maryland, who owns and operates BWI) cared about was "…jobs and the economy"! The man was retired and getting a pension from a large corporation, as well as a Social Security check each month. Of course he was not interested in the creation of new jobs. That simply had no obvious relevance to his day-to-day existence;

Chapter 9 – Coordination and Communication

the only results he could see were increased noise over his house, and more cars on his local streets.

Thus it may be difficult for a local elected official to support an airport improvement project, especially if it will result in an increase in air traffic. In cases like this the politician may need some "cover" and the airport operator may be called upon to help. There are usually two things that can happen at this point. The local elected official may decide that he or she cannot publicly support the project, but also decide that they can get by relatively unscathed if their criticism is not too strident, i.e., not enough to kill the project. The local representative will know that other elected officials may support the project, and that his or her opposition will not be enough to stop development if the majority of others support it. In this case the airport operator must make a good enough case to obtain the necessary majority support. Alternatively the local elected officials may tell their constituents that they see some benefit to the project, but that they will ensure that certain steps are taken to mitigate any adverse impacts that may result from the project. For example, an official may state that he or she "…will see to it that a thorough environmental study is prepared and that it will examine closely any potential impact to the local community surrounding the airport!" What most constituents do not and will not realize is that, by federal law an airport improvement project cannot be approved by the FAA unless this kind of thorough environmental study is done. As discussed more completely in Chapter 3: Airport Management, Operations, and Finance and Chapter 5: Master Planning, any significant airport improvement must be shown on an Airport Layout Plan in order to obtain an FAA airport improvement grant, and FAA approval of that ALP constitutes a federal action; therefore, the conditions of the National Environmental Policy Act apply, and a thorough environmental document must be prepared.

In some instances a local elected official may write a letter to an airport operator stating his concern over the potential impacts to the community or area he represents, "strongly urging that a comprehensive environmental study be undertaken before any airport improvements are made." Such a letter may go on to state that mitigating measures should be undertaken by the airport as a condition to proceeding with the project. These measures could include such things as buying homes in high-noise areas at fair market value and establishing a soundproofing program if the homeowner chooses not to sell. This allows the official to go on record as expressing some concern for his constituents without actually coming out in opposition to the project.

In other cases a local official may be unalterably opposed to a project and will not only withhold support, but also vigorously oppose any proposed improvements, in spite of all the work that has been done and in spite of all the potential benefits that may result. In this case the planners and the airport operator will just have to live with it, and try to ensure that enough other political support is available to carry through. It is also a good idea to prepare a good fall-back plan or alternative in case political support cannot be obtained. Planners and airport operators should also beware that if too much attention is given to political considerations the plan may wind up (as one of the people I interviewed for this book put it) "as nothing more than a set of minor improvements to the status quo."

Work With the Public

Community opposition can often be difficult for planners because it is typically more visible—and more audible—than political opposition. For some perverse reason some people have a desire to berate their fellow citizens in a public forum—a place where they no doubt feel safe. Also, local newspaper, television, and radio people love to cover controversial topics, and they have even been known to stimulate controversies or confrontations where none exist. I distinctly recall addressing a local community planning group on the subject of impending airport expansion, having a very worthwhile and rational discussion of the issues, and being thanked profusely by a number of the local participants, only to read in the local paper a few days later that it was some sort of bloodbath where the local citizens vented their wrath on the airport officials. Nothing could have been further from the truth—in fact it took me a few minutes to realize that the article was actually referring to the meeting I had attended! That happens—planners and airport operators have to live with it and do the best they can.

Community opposition is also difficult to deal with because in a good many cases the local citizens' concerns are valid. A major airport improvement is often likely to result in more flights making more noise and putting more traffic on local roadways. Other impacts such as filling wetlands and cutting down trees may not be as obvious, but can be equally important. In order to move ahead with a project a plan will have to be developed to mitigate these adverse impacts to the extent possible. For example, the airport may have to limit the use of a new runway to certain hours of operation. It is not usually a good idea to propose this as a mitigation strategy up front; after all, it will likely reduce the benefit of building the runway in the first place, but the planners and the airport operator should be prepared to address this issue if it does arise as a result of the public participation process.

Just don't lie or try to deceive people—a lie may be exposed at some point in the process, and if it is, all credibility will be lost. It is important to establish a level of trust when dealing with anybody and everybody, especially local citizens, with respect to a potentially controversial project. Once that trust is violated, even accidentally, the path from there on out will be difficult. This is obviously important to a planning consultant who wants to maintain a reputation for honesty and credibility, and it is even more important for a planner who is an airport employee. He will have to live with these people for a long time and people have long memories. They may forgive, but they don't often forget. And bear in mind that the local media types seem to get their jollies by catching someone in a lie, especially a public official or employee. Maybe the media are so sensitive to deception because they do so much of it themselves.

Give a Little

An argument heard quite often from the local communities is that, "All the airport does is take, take, take and it never gives anything in return." Well, aside from jobs, that may be true. Oh—and don't forget—providing access to any point on the globe in a matter of hours. And fresh seafood and flowers too, come to think of it. But local residents do not often see these benefits, or they are not really benefits that affect their daily lives. And aside from things like safe and efficient air transportation, jobs, and income, there is not a whole lot an airport can do for the local citizens who are adversely affected by airport activities. There are some efforts, however, and although they are small things, they can help establish the airport as a member of the community. And even if they cannot muster community support for a particular airport improvement, they can at least blunt the opposition a little.

For example, the Maryland Department of Transportation, including the State Highway Administration and Aviation Administration, cooperated with Anne Arundel County to build a hiking/bicycling trail around BWI Airport. At one point on the trail the airport established a recreation area, complete with a paved parking area and a playground for children. The trail and observation area were an instant success and were both heavily used and highly praised by the local residents. At Raleigh-Durham International, the airport authorities built an aircraft observation area, complete with a radio tuned to the local tower frequency so people could both see and hear the local flight activity. These kinds of things are often a pain in the neck to the people who have to patrol and maintain them, especially when operating the airport itself is a major undertaking. However, they do help to engender community good will at a relatively low cost, and this can pay off when it comes to public reaction to a controversial project.

Don't Give Up

It is very important to maintain a dialogue with elected officials and the community, and especially with opposition groups. Establish a level of trust, respond to their questions, follow up on their complaints, and try to find some common ground. Let them know that you are a real person and not just a cog in a bureaucratic machine. As a planner you should convince people that you are interested in what they have to say. Sometimes the most important step in resolving a complaint is listening to it in the first place, before immediately responding with a defensive rebuttal. And remember also that public opposition to a plan does not mean that the planners (or the airport operators) should give up and set aside any ideas of airport expansion. If a project is needed and is worth doing, every effort should be made to see it through to a successful conclusion, even if it takes a long time and a lot of hard work.

Presentation

Airport planning involves presenting information to a variety of interested groups, such as airport executive management, the airport board or commission, chambers of commerce, economic development authorities, environmental agencies, airport planning peers (at a conference, for example), and the general public. But before coordinating and presenting begins, some thinking must take place regarding what to present and how to present it. When it is time to start the process, a decision must be made as to what kinds of information will be presented and how it will be presented. Much of this depends on the intended audience. Who they are, what their interests are, and particularly, what their hot buttons are, are all important. It should also be clear what they should get from the presentation, i.e., what should they remember once they've gone home? The purpose of the presentation should also be clear. Is it primarily a presentation to inform people about a certain subject—a terminal expansion plan for example—or is their feedback being solicited, or both?

Presentation Format

Before a presentation is put together it needs to be decided how the information should be presented, e.g., as an oral presentation, written report, brochure, pamphlet, or information sheet, etc. To a great extent this depends on the kinds of information being presented and to whom. If progress on a study is being shared with other airport offices or divisions and their feedback is being solicited on key study issues, something fairly informal may be appropriate. An example would be an oral presentation accompanied by handouts and/or mounted exhibits such as charts, drawings, or photographs, along with sufficient time for discussion about the various aspects of the plan or project. This type of presentation is actually a working session in many respects, with lots of give-and-take discussion. Thus it is usually most effective to use mounted presentation boards showing graphs and drawings; PowerPoint or similar projections can also suffice. The visual aids are usually replicated as smaller handouts that people can look at, write on, and take home with them for further examination. For some reason people seem to be a little more satisfied if they can walk away from a meeting or a presentation with something in hand. On the other hand, if interim findings are being presented to an airport board or local planning agency it might be best not to give them anything they can carry away—not unless you want to see it in the newspapers the next day.

Tailor Your Message to Your Audience

In order to communicate effectively it is necessary to speak the language of your audience—this applies to both oral and written presentations. When planning an oral presentation, remember your audience; speak to them and use terms on the graphics in a language and context they will understand. If you are presenting some forecast information to a nontechnical citizens group, keep the language simple and don't get caught up in jargon or you might just as well be speaking Esperanto. The same applies to written presentations. A report directed to the FAA, other airport divisions, other planners, etc., may contain a lot of technical terms. But if the report is directed to a legislative body, the general public, or even to the members of an airport commission, the technical terms should be translated or explained in a way they can be understood.

In all cases the aspects of the plan that will be of particular importance to the audience should be emphasized and shown or explained clearly in terms they can relate to and understand. For example, when discussing runway and taxiway improvement plans, airport operations and air traffic personnel will be interested in safety and workload, in addition to capacity improvements. When presenting options for new runways or new taxiway connections, be sure to include some discussion of how traffic will use these facilities, and how they will add to, or relieve, controller workload. If you are presenting a plan to smooth out a particularly complicated taxiway intersection, make sure you emphasize the changes in traffic flow between the existing and proposed facilities or facility improvement alternatives. In a sense this is a reality check because operations and air traffic personnel can let you know if it will really work.

Quite often it is most effective to prepare several forms of the same presentation. One form might be given to operations, maintenance, and air traffic personnel; a different one might be given to engineering and construction; and still a third one might be created for the commercial management, capital programming, and finance staff. The subject of all these presentations would be the same, whether they involve a new runway or taxiway, or a major terminal expansion, or whatever; the only thing that changes is the emphasis placed on the project details that are of interest to each group. Above all, make sure that the basic information is consistent and accurate in each of the presentations.

Written Presentations

Written materials are the usual means of presenting planning and analytical information. Written materials include the ubiquitous planning reports, as well as executive summaries, pamphlets, brochures, information sheets, and the occasional "white paper," which is usually prepared to announce policy changes or other world-shaking events. Written reports are the most common means of documenting the processes, methodologies, and results of planning studies; pamphlets and other condensed documents are used primarily to announce major findings to a broad audience. Planning reports are usually directed toward people who understand airports and airport issues; thus, they contain a lot of technical language and references. These reports, especially the reports that present the final results of a planning study such as a master plan, should thoroughly document all issues, methodologies, assumptions, alternatives, etc., that went into the planning process. It should be a complete reference for anyone who wants to get some information about any particular aspect of the plan or the process. For example, the final master plan should contain a description of how the forecasts were developed, not just the final forecasts themselves. Similarly, the final report should clearly document the purpose and need for the project (or projects) being recommended, as well as a thorough discussion of the alternatives considered and how they were evaluated. This information is particularly important if an EA or EIS will be prepared. The people preparing the environmental document should not have to go through a number of different reports or other study materials to get the information they need for the environmental document, as emphasized in Chapter 5: Master Planning.

For a major planning study the final report can be quite lengthy. Unfortunately that often means that not many people will read it. If the report is too long it is advisable to separate it into volumes. One volume could discuss issues, current conditions, inventory items, etc.; another could be devoted to the forecasts; another to the alternatives development and evaluation, etc. In this case a summary or overview report is usually prepared, which provides a general description of what was done, why it was done, how it was done, and what is being recommended. An alternative is to prepare a comprehensive report but put the technical details into separate appendices, which can then be printed as separate volumes.

Essential information related to the planning study is often produced in a condensed or abbreviated form for dissemination to wider audiences. These materials usually include a brief description of current conditions, a list of issues addressed, a summary of alternatives, and final recommendations. Executive summaries are usually prepared for upper management, airport commission members, and sometimes for other governmental agencies, planning groups, and elected officials. They contain a little more information than a brochure intended for the general public, but they do not include all the technical details, nor should they include too many technical terms or other airport esoterica. Highly-abbreviated brochures, pamphlets, flyers, etc., are used to disseminate information to a much wider and primarily nontechnical audience. These materials briefly summarize the kinds of information contained in the executive summary, and often rely more on visuals than words to convey information. For example, historical and forecast aviation demand would be shown on a graph, rather than in tabular or narrative form. Written materials for public circulation should be reproduced using quality services and paper. Remember, the quality of the materials is a reflection of the planning study and of the airport itself.

In all cases written materials should include graphs, charts, drawings, photographs, renderings, or whatever else is needed to convey the major points and findings described in the text. The guidance for visuals discussed below should be followed; the visuals should be clear and easy to understand, and should be used to emphasize major points, identify relationships, and help emphasize trends and issues. If the visuals are shown in color it is especially important to make sure that quality paper and reproduction services are used. Poor quality paper and printing tend to blur and fade color images, thus limiting the effectiveness of graphs, charts, photographs, and drawings.

Oral Presentations

The most important part of a successful oral presentation is knowing your subject. If you know what you are talking about, i.e., if you really *understand* your subject, you will be able to speak in a relaxed and casual manner, and not sound like you are simply repeating a memorized script, or are completely terrified that someone will ask a question that you don't know how to answer. Somehow audiences can tell if a speaker knows his subject and that can make a big difference in how they will react and respond. So make sure you know your subject and *do not* read your presentation from a script.

Above all, *do not read the slides* as you are showing them; your audience can read the information for themselves; your part is to add to and embellish the slide information. Remember that you are (or should be) simply *talking to people*. In fact it might be better off to think of it as talking *with* people. The audience is often more receptive if they feel they are being *included*, rather than *dictated to*. Presentations are most effective if the speakers look at people when they talk. A speaker should make eye contact with various individuals throughout the presentation, particularly when emphasizing key points or key components of the plan. This eye contact does two things: it lets people know the speaker is talking to them, not just as a group but as individuals, and it also lets the speaker know how people are reacting to what he is saying. Looking at people while giving a presentation also lets the speaker know whether or not the audience really understands what he is talking about. While speaking to an audience it is readily apparent whether they are really listening and understanding what is being presented, or whether they are looking out the windows, sleeping, or completely confused. If people hear, understand, and agree with what is being said, this intensity or interest will be very apparent to the speaker if he has established eye contact and sees heads nod in agreement (or shake in disagreement, as the case may be). This real-time feedback should be used throughout the presentation to help guide the speaker, letting him know when to add or omit information as appropriate.

As a brief example, if you are talking to an environmental or community group about a new runway and you see eyes glaze over (and that is not hard to see, believe me) when you talk about the aircraft delay costs to be saved, it might be a good idea to save that detail for another group that includes more financial types or airline representatives. Instead, shift your comments to those items of interest to that particular audience.

Listen!

While you are briefing the affected and interested parties, you should also be *listening*. This is the other half of coordination. Listen to the questions they ask and the general comments they provide. Find out what areas are of concern to them. This is not only a matter of being respectful (and meeting federal requirements), it can also generate constructive ideas that improve the overall project. There may be a way that the project can be done better, for example, by minimizing the environmental impacts, or by making other improvements so that when the project is completed some (or even all) of the environmental components of the airport can be made better than they are today. Listening to the operations and maintenance people can give you ideas on how to improve the plan so that the resulting facilities will operate more efficiently and be easier and less expensive to maintain.

Short and to the Point

Oral presentations can lose their effectiveness if they are too long, and this often happens when too many slides are used. Someone is invited to do a presentation and given a half-hour time slot to do it in, but the presentation winds up taking longer. As a result the presentation cuts into the following speaker's time and at conferences, for example, may cut into the lunch break or cocktail hour! This sometimes happens when a speaker has put too much information into a presentation—more than can fit into the allotted time. If you find that a presentation you put together is going to take too long, review it carefully and eliminate a few slides. The primary reason presentations take longer than expected is that each slide takes longer to cover during an actual presentation than it does during a practice run-through. When rehearsing or doing a dry run like this we all have a tendency to speak rather quickly, and usually stick to the information shown on the slide. In practice however we tend to speak a little more slowly and perhaps digress a little or repeat things in response to the audience reaction. For example if you have just made a point that registered well with your audience you will be able to see this in their facial expressions and body language. You will feel that you are on a roll and you will want to amplify or add something to what you have just said. There is nothing wrong with this, in fact, if you are on a roll and really cooking with your audience, it is a good thing. You just have to make sure you allow for it by giving some slack elsewhere in the presentation, perhaps by cutting something else out later.

Be Prepared

As noted above, oral presentations usually involve a couple of practice runs to make sure of the timing, sequence, etc. It is a good idea to do the practice run in a room that is the size of the room in which the actual presentation will take place. Practicing by looking at a personal computer (PC) screen will not give you a very good idea of how the slides will look when shown on a wall screen. Similarly, practicing in a small room, where the practice audience is sitting 10 or 20 feet away, may not give you an accurate idea of how the slides will look in a larger room or in an auditorium. Before giving the presentation you should check out the room. Are there windows? Do they have blinds that can be closed, and if so, do they work? Does the lighting give the place a sterile institutional glare like a Walmart, or are there dimmer controls so that people have enough light to take notes, without fading the colors or reducing the clarity of the presentation slides? Find out where the electrical outlets are located. This will determine how much extension cord will be needed, as well as indicate how the seating should be arranged and where the speaker will stand. Find out if there is a remote public announcement system or piped-in muzak; if so, remember to have it turned off during the presentation. The speaker should also decide where they will stand, whether a podium will be available, and whether a microphone and speakers will be provided. Many people don't particularly like to stand behind a podium while they are talking to a group; they prefer to move around, wave their arms, and point to slides, drawings, photographs, and other visuals. This helps keep the audience's attention and also helps keep them awake. It also makes you harder to hit with rotten tomatoes if the presentation is not going well. It is also a good idea to make sure that someone will be around who will know how to quickly fix all these mechanical and electrical things if they break down. And if you are using a slide projector, make sure you have a spare bulb along.

It is a good idea to have copies of the visuals available for the audience. As noted above, it seems to make people happy if they can take something away with them, and it at least gives them something to doodle on while you are talking. This is especially true for conference presentations. Those that show two or three of the slides on the left-hand side of the page, with lines for notes (or doodles) on the right seem to be particularly useful. A caution here: presumably the slides will be in color; if the handouts are done in black and white, make sure the color slides show up well in black and white. Often some of the detail is lost because the colors reproduce as shades of gray.

If your presentation is fairly detailed and being made to airport staff, it is particularly important to distribute materials such as draft reports or briefing papers prior to any meetings or presentations so that the audience has a chance to read and digest the information. Nothing is worse than asking a group for comments or suggestions without providing some relevant information beforehand for them to review. Meetings and discussions are much more effective if all participants are up to speed and all on the same page, so to speak.

Visual Aids

As the old saying goes, "A picture is worth a thousand words." Or as the Greek philosopher Heraclitus is quoted as saying several thousand years ago, "The eyes are more exact witnesses than the ears."[13] That seems to put it into the category of an eternal truth. What it means is that people remember more of what they see than what they hear, and they remember it longer and more accurately. Therefore slides, charts, graphs, drawings, photographs, and other visual aids should not be viewed as mere window dressing, i.e., some pretty pictures for people to look at during a presentation or while they are reading a report. If they are used properly, in oral presentations and in written reports, flyers, leaflets, or other handouts, visuals can highlight the most important points, identify relationships, and help emphasize the trends and analyses contained in both reports and presentations. Before putting any visual materials into the presentation, report, flyer, etc., make sure it is there to convey a message. Better yet, make sure it is conveying a message more effectively than could be done in words, or make sure it is enhancing (or explaining) something you have said or written. Don't put things in just to make it pretty or to show that you have good graphics skills. For example, in recent years consultants have had a tendency to fill their proposals with photographs, to help make their written presentations "more interesting," apparently assuming that people like to look at pretty pictures. This is all well and good if the photos add something to the proposal—if the proposal is in response to a request for some architectural work as part of a planning study it is certainly appropriate to add a photo or two showing the consultant's architectural skills. Or if the proposal is responding to a request to plan some general aviation facilities, such as a terminal, hangars, etc., it would be appropriate to illustrate a similar project that the consultant has done at another airport. But photographs of airplanes or earthmoving equipment? C'mon.

Designing the Graphics

Visual aids such as charts and graphs can be used effectively in presentations because they can strip a subject down to its essential points. They can focus attention to the essential information you want to emphasize and want the audience to remember. They can also present trends more cleanly and clearly than the same information presented in a table or extended narrative. To be effective the visuals should be simple, easy to understand, and illustrate important points, without unneeded detail and extraneous information. They should be accurate and should present information honestly. It is easy to distort the scale of a chart to create a false impression, but this does not show much in the way of the chart maker's integrity.

All charts in a presentation should use the same background color for each slide and the same color and font formats for titles, legends, and other written information—there should be a unified look to the presentation, even if it is not especially flashy. Sometimes it is effective to use one font or color for slide titles, another for key points, and yet another for additional detail or explanatory information. This usually works well as long as the same overall rules apply from slide to slide. This is especially important for slides in an oral presentation but it also applies to the visuals in a written report. Background and print colors should be chosen carefully, and remember that what stands out clearly on a PC screen may not show up when projected onto a wall screen. Before giving a presentation, test the slides on a projector to make sure that they are all legible. A medium blue color seems to work best for the slide background, and yellow, gold, and maroon or burgundy lettering generally shows up well. A black background, especially when used with bright red lettering, tends to look a little garish and seems to detract from the presentation. Make sure the background color is not so dark or so light that the print is not readable. Once the visuals have been completed it is a good idea to have someone else look at them—a disinterested third party—and see what impression they get from each of the graphics. Do they see what they are supposed to see? Do they understand it? If not you will have to make some corrections based on the reviewer's impressions. And one final word about color: it seems to be an unwritten rule that controversial items (alternative locations for a new runway for example) should not be shown in red. Apparently red has a tendency to inflame people's emotions and may incite them to violence.

Simplest is Best

The use of written information on any visuals should be kept to a minimum; the charts and graphs should be clear enough not to need much of an explanatory narrative. You can provide any needed explanation in your oral presentation or in the text if the visuals are being used in a report or brochure. An exception of course is what are called "word slides," i.e., slides used in an oral presentation to list major points or topic headings that highlight what the speaker is talking about. A very common mistake is to put too many words on one slide. Remember, what looks good on the PC screen may not show up as clearly when projected onto a wall screen. Words should be kept to a minimum, showing only what is essential. If the slide gets too busy but all the information (i.e., every word) is necessary, split it out into two or three slides.

Similar problems can be encountered when using numbers. Avoid putting tables as one of the slides in an oral presentation if at all possible. For example, if you are presenting forecast information with 20 years of historical data and a 20-year forecast, you will have 40 rows of numbers, plus a column for each item forecast, plus column headings. It will make for a very busy, complicated, and probably unreadable slide. Instead you might try showing four historical years and four forecast years, covering each period in five-year increments. If it is necessary for your audience to have the data for each year, give them a complete table as a handout. Similarly, it might add to the clarity if only total passengers and total aircraft operations are shown, and a handout is used to show the details for air carriers, commuters, general aviation, etc.

Graphs, Charts, and Drawings

As previously stated, graphs, charts, and drawings can be very effective in conveying information, especially information that may be difficult to put into words. Charts and graphs should be used to give quick impressions, not to make detailed calculations. Thus it is self-defeating to try to show too much information or too much detail on one graph, chart, or drawing. Visual aids have to be properly prepared and clear in their intent. For example, each visual should have a title that states clearly what it is, as well as concise captions and labels as appropriate for the information being shown. Sometimes the labels can be shown directly on a graph or chart but they should not add clutter which makes it difficult to get a good visual image of what is being presented. For example, if labeling each line on a graph adds too much clutter it may be appropriate to use a legend placed off to one side.

People seem to have a hard time with graphs, both in interpreting them as well as in preparing them. Quite often this is because the preparer tries to include too much information on one graph, but it also happens when graph segments, bars, lines, or surfaces are not clearly labeled. The scales on graphs should be captioned to show the subject and units used. The scales on graphs should be designed to aid in accuracy and clarity. In this regard it is usually better to start with a zero base point, especially for the "Y" (vertical) axis. It is also not a good idea to have a break in the scale for either the "X" or "Y" axes because breaks are often misunderstood. Use familiar intervals such as 5, 10, 15, 100, 200, 300, etc., instead of 3, 6, 9, or something similarly odd. I used to prepare graphs by hand on graph paper using a scale like 1 square = 3,333 passengers. It made pretty graphs and gave me some chuckles, but it drove most people nuts. The source of all data on a graph should be shown, usually at the bottom. Three-dimensional effects are frequently used for graphing data but they seldom seem to be used effectively. It appears they are used to make the graph more interesting visually, but it also seems they detract from the accuracy or ease of interpretation. Grid lines are helpful but they should not be overused because they can add to the clutter and cause confusion.

If many data points are involved, such as when presenting historical and projected enplaned passenger data covering a total period of 40 years, a line chart is easier to understand and interpret than a bar chart. Lines can be solid, dashed, dotted, colored, or any combination thereof. Too many lines on a graph can be distracting and confusing—three to five lines on a graph is generally considered an acceptable range. A bar chart can also be used to show a historical series if each time period is considered to be a separate entity. For example, a bar chart could be used to compare the volume of air carrier, commuter, general aviation, and military aircraft operations for a few representative historical years and several forecast years. If it is necessary to show a continuous progression of data however, such as aircraft operations by demand component for each of the historical and forecast years, a line chart should be used.

Pie charts are another simple, nontechnical, and attractive way to show component parts of a total, such as the aircraft operations demand components noted above. A pie chart should not have too many components—five seems to be the generally accepted limit. More can be used if the "slices" of the pie aren't too small—otherwise the chart will be difficult to read and interpret. When using a pie chart the actual value or percentage should be shown in each slice. A single pie chart should represent the grand total volume, or 100 percent, if percentages are being shown. Groups of pie charts should not be used to show a combined total or the percentage breakdowns for a series of items.

Drawings seem to be the most abused of all the visual aids, and this is usually because they contain too much information. An ALP, strictly speaking, contains so much information that when all of it is put onto one sheet it becomes virtually indecipherable, especially for a large airport. For a drawing to be effective it should show only those items relevant to the discussion. For example, if a drawing is being used to show alternative runway locations, it is not necessary to show a lot of detail about the terminal or about the airport's roadway system. If the drawing is intended to show conceptual runway or taxiway locations it may not be necessary to show all of the airport's safety areas, object free areas, and other zones.

Drawings should be shown to scale. Drawings that are going to be used later, to plot changes to configurations or to determine exact dimensions, should be shown at one of the common engineering scales such as 1:50, 1:250, 1:500, etc. If they are only going to be used as visual images, odd scales such as 1:30, 1:600, or those strange scales that architects use are normally fine. The important point is that *relative* sizes and shapes should be accurate.

In summary, it is a general requirement that planners coordinate but it is a *sine qua non* that planners actually *communicate* as part of the coordination process. A number of techniques can be used to present information; the particular technique used depends on the type of information being presented as well as to whom it is being presented. Planners have to let the various airport publics know what they are doing and why they are doing it. They also have to listen to what others have to say. The coordination/communication process can often gain support for future airport development, and in the very worst case it lets planners know what the sources of objection to a plan might be. And forewarned is forearmed.

Endnotes

1   *Airport Master Plans*, AC 150/5070-6B. Washington, D.C.: Federal Aviation Administration, 2005, p. 12.

2   *Ibid.*, p. 17.

3   *Community Involvement Manual*, FAA-EE-90-03. Washington, D.C.: Federal Aviation Administration, Office of Environment and Energy, August 1990.

4   *Ibid.*, Chapter 6.

5   *Ibid.*, p. 11,12.

6   *Ibid.*, p. 4.

7   *Ibid.*, p. 19.

8   *National Environmental Policy Act (NEPA) Implementing Instructions for Airport Actions*, FAA Order 5050.4B. Washington, D.C.: Federal Aviation Administration, April 2006. Accessed July 2008, from http://www.faa.gov/airports_airtraffic/airports/resources/publications/orders/environmental_5050_4/media/chapter4.pdf

9   *Partnering for Better Communities*, Pub. 427 (01-02). CH Planning for the Pennsylvania Department of Transportation, Bureau of Aviation. n.d., p. 1.

10 *Ibid.*, p. 1.

11 *Ibid.*, p. 17.

12 *GA Economic Impact Statements.* American Association of Airport Executives. Accessed January 2008, from http://www.aaae.org/products/900_GA_Economic_Impact_Statements/

13 Heraclitus, as quoted in Auden, W. H. (ed.), *The Portable Greek Reader.* New York: The Penguin Group, 1948, p. 70.

CHAPTER 10

MENTORING, MANAGING, AND TEAM BUILDING

One of the major concerns in the airport planning community is how to find, educate, and train young professionals in the field of airport planning. This chapter discusses how managers and experienced planners can identify promising candidates and how to train or mentor them so they can become leading professionals in the field by combining personal attention, progressive responsibility, and empowerment. This information also lets young planners know whether they are being mentored and trained properly. It also shows how a good mentoring program can incorporate training in management techniques for both staff and projects, and provides guidance on a number of effective management strategies. The chapter concludes with a discussion of how a comprehensive mentoring program combines with effective management to build a knowledgeable, dedicated, and efficient planning team.

Mentoring

One of greatest challenges to the future of airport planning that was frequently raised among the people I interviewed for this book was, "Where are the next airport planners coming from?" Frankly, I'm not sure where the current airport planners came from. Airport planners seemed to have just "happened." I started off to become a teacher and then realized that I didn't like kids. I didn't want to be like most of the teachers I had when I was in school, so I decided to try something else. I majored in Earth Science, and then got a graduate degree in Geography, because both fields seemed to offer the opportunity for variety, and I am easily bored doing the same thing all the time. At that time few schools offered planning degrees, thus most planners were geography majors. For example, I wound up almost accidentally as an airport planner because I always had an interest in aviation and I liked airplanes. As my career developed I guided myself; a career development path to airport planning did not, and still does not, exist.

Most airport planners seem to have a similar story; they really had very little in the way of formal guidance, mentoring, or career planning. The same can also be said for airport engineers and airport architects, and indeed they often wind up as airport planners also. These people started out to be something and wound up doing something else, specifically airport planning. They were lucky enough (or some may consider themselves unlucky enough) to be in a place at a time when a planner was needed, and *voila!*

Unfortunately, nothing seems to have changed much over the last 35 years. Although many universities offer planning degrees, none that I know of offer degrees in airport planning, although the International Air Transport Association does offer an online diploma in Airport Planning.[1] I don't know of any schools that even offer a degree in airport engineering, although many offer a few courses specifically devoted to airports. Some schools offer a degree in airport management, or something similar, and some even offer a course or two in airport planning. A number of schools offer degrees in transportation engineering or transportation management, and sometimes these programs include a course or two in airports and, more rarely, a course in airport planning.

It does not appear as though that will be changing much in the future, because the demand for airport planners is not that great; probably not large enough for airport planning to become a major at any large university and probably not even at a small college or aviation school. Just about the only "organized" aid to helping planners learn and develop is airport workshops and seminars. Conferences sponsored by such agencies as the Airport Consultants Council, Airports Council International – North America, Transportation Research Board, and American Association of Airport Executives usually include a number of discussion panels focused on airport planning issues. FAA regional offices also sponsor conferences that include airport planning issues—an example is the annual airports conference cosponsored by Penn State University and the FAA Eastern Region Airports Division.

Because there is no formal training for airport planners, it is very important for those who are planners now to learn how to mentor and teach new airport planners coming into the field. We have to let them learn from our mistakes and show new planners the fine points and "tricks of the trade" that we have picked up, either through our own experiences or the experiences that others have shared with us. If you are now a person who has a planning staff, even if it consists of only one person besides yourself, you may find the following discussion helpful. If you are now a beginning planner, and if you are any good at it, you may be supervising some planners yourself someday and may also get some benefit from this discussion. It may also give you some idea of what kind of boss you have.

Finding the Ideal Apprentice

The first step in mentoring a new planner is to find one, and that is not as easy as it may sound. To me, the most important qualities a new planner must have are imagination and interest. That does not mean having either one or the other—a good airport planner must have both. Those of us who are fortunate enough to be airport planners know that airport planning is rather unique and exciting, and most of us love airports. Airports are busy places, with people coming and going and everybody in a hurry. After all, aviation is all about speed and saving time. This frantic pace is reflected in airport planning because we don't have long lead times—airport customers want things *now!* The airlines are a particularly useful illustration: they don't do a lot of advance planning and they want to take advantage of a favorable circumstance as soon as they can. Thus, when they tell an airport manager or operations director that they need four new gates, they mean they want four new gates *now!* A potential candidate for an airport planning position has to share this feeling of urgency and thrive on the excitement it generates.

The other essential quality for an airport planner is imagination; planners have to see the airport, not as it is today, but what it will be tomorrow and for many tomorrows to come. An important part of this imagination is the ability to see the big picture—to see what the airport is all about, what it does, and who it serves. We always need to keep in mind why people use airports and what they expect from their airport in terms of facilities and services. We need to keep in mind why we do the things we do and why we recommend the plans we develop and recommend. I always used to tell my on-call planning consultants: When I give you a task, the first thing I want to hear you say is, "Why? Why do you want to build this? Why do you want to build it there? Who will use it? What will they use it for?"

Another important part of imagination is flexibility. An airport planner should be someone who says, "Just because we did this at another airport last year, it doesn't necessarily mean that we will do the same thing at this airport now." The world is not the same as it was a decade ago. Heightened security measures are one obvious difference; planning for a smooth flow of passengers through the terminal now involves providing for new passenger and baggage processing procedures and equipment. Yesterday's concepts and calculations for terminal space requirements are no longer valid and new ones must be developed. Security requirements are still evolving, thus terminal planning must evolve accordingly. The trick here is that the planner has to think ahead; if plans for tomorrow's airport terminal are based on the way terminals operate today, tomorrow's terminal is not likely to operate very efficiently.

Planners must always be thinking, "What's next? What kinds of things will be happening at airports and to air passengers (and their baggage) a decade from now and what can we do about it?" This doesn't mean only what can we do in terms of airport facilities, it means how do we change our thinking or our approach to solving tomorrow's airport problems today? How do planners solve problems that might not even exist today? This is where the planner has to be flexible and creative.

The combination of interest and imaginative thinking is what generates the enthusiasm to make a first-class airport planner. So when you are interviewing potential airport planners, try to find out if they have this kind of imaginative thinking. Ask thought-provoking questions and don't look so much for specific answers as good discussions. Find out what their interests are—the things that turn them on and get them fired up. It never mattered very much to me where airport planners went to school or what they majored in, as long as they loved airports, had active imaginations, and showed enthusiasm for the work they were being hired to do.

Sometimes the love of airports may be hard to judge since many people may not have had sufficient exposure, but most airport people I have known have had a passion for aviation since childhood. And yes, you need to find out if the person can communicate, both orally and in writing, but these kinds of skills can be developed through a formal education process. If you want somebody to do some aviation demand forecasting as part of their planning work, make sure they know some basics about statistical analysis, or at least can count to 20 without taking off their shoes. But as long as they have the basic skills, I never cared whether they majored in planning, engineering, architecture, political science, or art history. Just so they loved airport planning as much as I do. Again, the love of airport planning as a discipline may be hard to identify, since most young people, and probably most young planners, are not aware that airport planning exists, and that it may be a rewarding career field, but a fascination with aviation should be evident.

The Time Commitment
Supervisors and managers should keep in mind that the mentoring process involves a substantial time commitment—especially at the very beginning—but that it will pay off in the long run. Quite often a person's overall impression of an organization is based on their initial experience on the job. If the first days and weeks are interesting for the new employee, that positive impression will last a good while, and will shape the person's impression of the entire organization and of you as his or her supervisor. Because this initial experience is going to take a serious time commitment, you should plan ahead, before the new person arrives. Decide what you are going to do, when you are going to do it, and arrange your calendar accordingly. If you are not willing or able to make this commitment, you might want to think twice about how important this new person is really going to be, both to you and to your organization. Note that the amount of time that has to be spent with an apprentice will decrease as he or she gains experience.

The First Steps

When you select an apprentice and bring them into the organization, do all you can to make them feel welcome. Make sure that all "housekeeping" items are taken care of, including a computer and telephone that work. Having an office or desk all set up and functional may not make a person say, "Wow they are really glad I'm here," but *not* having a fully functional set-up will certainly give the opposite impression. Trust me, I have been there and my initial impression was correct.

Sit down with the new planner and review the kinds of things your organization does, its responsibilities, and how it functions. Once they understand the big picture, you can begin assigning them some work to do. Now I have been told by a number of people (and my own experience bears this out) that it takes about six months before new people fresh out of school can start performing useful functions. It takes about a year before they can really do things on their own, and two years before you can call them fully functional and useful employees. Sometimes you will be surprised and find someone who catches on very quickly and becomes a significant contributor much more quickly, and sometimes it may take a little longer than expected. And unfortunately in a few cases it may never happen; then you need to sit down with the person and help them decide what they really want to do.

One of the first things I like to do with a new planner is to take them on a tour of a few airports, both large and small, and point out the kinds of things that take place there. An orientation beginning with an ALP and/or an air photo is a good place to start, followed by site visits. Walk the person through a busy airport terminal and show them all the activities that take place there, how passengers move through the building, the kinds of things they do, and the kinds of things that are done to them. You should also point out the different uses of space in the terminal building and how space is an important factor in terminal planning—both in terms of providing enough space and in terms of how different spaces and different uses interact and complement each other.

This is an especially good way to start out because it helps people understand why we are in business in the first place. Our job as airport planners is to make sure that people can make that air/ground connection safely and conveniently. Watching an airport work and having someone point out significant facilities, uses, and other factors is a very good way to get a feel for what airports and airport planning are all about. Visiting different kinds or sizes of airports is also very useful because this provides an opportunity to point out the likenesses and differences between and among airports. Remember, "If you've seen one airport, you've seen one airport." I have always found it interesting to take new people to a couple of busier airports that comply with most FAA airport design standards, and then take them to a couple of privately-owned airports and show them how most of the aviation world really lives. Narrow runways and taxiways, dips, bumps, and some fairly interesting grades between the airfield and aircraft parking areas are always an eye opener.

The Real World of Airports

Another aspect of training that applies to many of us with experience, as well as to the new planners we are mentoring, is the process of learning how airports actually work and how decisions are made. Airport planners don't seem to have much experience in airport operations, i.e., the actual process of operating an airport day in and day out, month after month and year after year. In a sense, airports are not mechanical things; they are more like living organisms. They are a lot of different things to a lot of different people, ranging from airline operators, station managers, and other airport tenants, to general aviation aircraft owners and pilots and the passengers who are the ultimate users of aviation services. I don't think planners can do a good job of planning airport improvements unless they have a very good understanding of how an airport operates. Airport planners, and engineers, and architects as well, tend to see an airport as "our" facility—the one we are planning, or designing. This is especially true of those who are employed by the airport; after all, that is where we live for 8 or 10 or more hours a day.

However, it is very important to remember that our part in any facility is really only a very brief event in what we hope will be its long and happy life. We think that airport improvements get planned, designed, and constructed, and we often forget (or don't even consider) that the facility's life only really begins when our job is done. That is the point where the facility starts to be operated, maintained, and *used*. The understanding of day-to-day airport operations must include recognition for and accommodation of the facts that 1) these operations are continually evolving, and 2) proposed improvements must be constructed and phased-in with a minimum amount of disruption to ongoing operations. A comfortable and efficient level of service for both passengers and tenants should be maintained even during a major construction undertaking. Airport consultants seem to be particularly lacking in this regard, since they have a tendency to move from one project to the next without really getting involved in any particular airport and seeing how the kinds of facilities they are planning and designing are actually being used. They don't get to talk with the maintenance and operations people who make it work, nor do they very often talk with airport users and tenants. This is not intended as a criticism of consultants; typically they don't have time for this kind of close involvement with their client airports. Consultants working on projects in the design phase are a little better off because they do get chances to interact with operators and users at various points in the design process.

Planners who actually work at airports are generally better off in this regard since they have more opportunities to talk with these other kinds of airport people about their needs and wants. This is important in selling the plan, as discussed in Chapter 9: Coordination and Communication, but it is also important in preparing a good plan, i.e., preparing a plan that can be sold and is actually worthy of being sold. As discussed in Chapter 4: Strategic Planning, Chapter 5: Master Planning, and Chapter 6: System Planning, there is more to airport planning than the inventory/forecast/alternatives/plan process set out in the advisory circulars. A good plan is based on a solid understanding of what the customers, i.e., the providers and users of airport services, want and need in terms of facility improvements. There is also the idea of making the most of what you have through so-called "best management practices" before you invest in new or expanded facilities. Knowing how the airport works and identifying the problems encountered in the day-to-day operation of the airport will help the planner focus on the causes of some of the problems and will help in the development of effective solutions.

Effective Hands-On Learning
When it is time to stop touring airports and get down to business, I have found it works well to have the new person work with me on a task or two. You can assign a piece of something for the person to do, show them how to do it, and review it with them when it is done. Always be clear and consistent in what you tell them to do. If the job is done correctly, make sure you say so, and if it is done especially well, make sure you say that too. Usually there will be some mistakes the first time or two, and it may take longer for a new person to do something than it would for an experienced person to do it. Don't make a big deal out of the mistakes, especially during the early days of the mentoring process. Your apprentice will probably be nervous, self-conscious, and unsure of himself, and thus will be sensitive to criticism. Make sure your apprentice doesn't get into a situation where they think everything they do is wrong; provide positive feedback when and where you can. If, on the other hand, almost everything they do *is* wrong, you may want to point out nicely that they should think of another career. Overall, the mentoring experience should be positive and productive, so try to put a positive spin on things when you have the opportunity. Mistakes are to be expected; don't get into the habit of thinking—or ever saying—that you could have done it quicker yourself, so there was no point in having the new person do it. Remember, this is a learning experience, and if you can get some productive work early in the process, that's a bonus. And also keep in mind that you are trying to build self-confidence as well as technical skill, so give positive reinforcement when and where you can.

For example, you can have your apprentice dig up some socioeconomic data that will be used in the preparation of some aviation demand forecasts. To give them a break from data collection, if you are a consultant, you could also have them help put together a proposal and you could have them start by proofreading a draft that is being prepared by other staff members. This is a good way for an apprentice to get some experience in putting proposals together, and it is also a good way to get some good proofreading done. Remember, an experienced person is likely to see what he expects to see, rather than what is actually written on the page. If you are working for an airport, your apprentice could help review proposals as a way to become familiar with the sorts of things consultants present and how they present them. The apprentice could also review technical reports on a specific study that is underway—a report on terminal expansion for example. In this way the apprentice will see what kinds of data go into making up a forecast as well as see how forecasts are actually put to use in one component of airport planning.

Shaping Organizational and Interpersonal Skills

Another important part of the mentoring process involves engendering a feeling of respect for co-workers, both professionally and personally. We are all different; we all have our little quirks and foibles, but we are also human beings and we expect to be treated as such. Personal friendships are fine and personal antagonisms are unfortunate, but they should not affect how people work together to do their jobs. Mentoring in this regard does not mean teaching people to like each other; rather, it means demonstrating to people the importance of working together in spite of individual differences.

When I first started to work as an airport planner, I thanked a secretary for typing a letter for me. My boss called me aside and said, "You don't have to say thank you." I wasn't sure I heard him correctly so I said, "What?" And he said, "If someone is doing something for you that is part of their job, you don't have to thank them." I have never forgotten how especially rude and extremely ill-considered I thought that was. On the contrary, it is always a good idea to thank someone when they do something for you, whether it is part of their job requirement or not. It is especially important when working with new people who are just learning the ropes; it makes them feel appreciated at a time when they may be feeling particularly inept and perhaps fairly useless to the organization.

The mentoring process also includes making young planners aware of the "politics" involved in the planning, development, and operation of airports. This does not mean politics as in Democrat or Republican, rather it means the organizational (and sometimes personal) aspects of making decisions and getting things done. Organizations are like people in that there is a sense of pride in what they do, how they do it, and how they work with others. As discussed elsewhere in this book, many different organizations and entities are involved in airport planning and development. This includes agencies at the federal, state, and local levels, as well as the various groups within the airport itself, such as maintenance, marketing, operations, etc. Each agency has its own responsibilities and its own priorities; thus, each has its own way of getting things done.

Quite often planners are faced with turf battles in which two or more agencies squabble over whose ideas and requirements take precedence. For example, the airport operator may have some ideas of how the airport should be developed, but the FAA may favor a different approach. Or the FAA and the airport may be in agreement, but the community and its elected officials may have their own ideas. Within the FAA there are sometimes disagreements between the offices of Airports, Airway Facilities, and Air Traffic. Within an individual airport, planning and engineering may disagree on facility development issues, and both points of view may also be different from that of the marketing department. Mentors should make sure their apprentices are aware of these kinds of conflicts and the potential they have to delay airport development. In these situations the mentor should make sure his apprentice understands the role of each of the participating agencies as well as some of the background or history upon which the conflicts might be based.

Sometimes everybody comes out a winner, but more often than not a good deal of compromise is necessary to achieve a viable solution. Conflict resolution is an art unto itself and requires much more discussion than is warranted here, but many times conflicts can be resolved if all agencies agree on some common underlying goals. As noted in Chapter 4, preparing a strategic plan or at least developing some strategic goals at the outset of the planning process, and getting the key airport stakeholders to buy into them, will help give a common ground to reach mutually-agreeable solutions. Nonetheless, while compromise is often necessary, planners (and airport operators) should not compromise to the point where the effectiveness of the plans and follow-on development are seriously handicapped.

A Mentoring Plan
After your new apprentice has gotten his or her bearings and has a taste of how airports work, the next step in a mentoring process is to set out a program of what you want to do, how you intend to do it, what you expect the planner to do, and how you want them to do it. The mentoring and learning process for a young planner should follow three stages of classical learning: grammar, logic, and rhetoric, as described by Susan Wise Bauer in her book, *The Well-Educated Mind*.[2] This is really not as intimidating as it sounds; rather than being a formal program it provides a base or context for instruction. The *grammar* stage is where we learn basic facts. In the case of airport planning, for example, we learn about the FAA's advisory circulars and what they contain. We learn about airports—how they are owned, operated, financed, and managed. In short we pick up various pieces of what airports and airport planning are all about. In the *logic* stage we learn how to analyze the facts we have learned and how to discriminate and decide which information is appropriate for various uses. For example, we learn various forecasting techniques in the grammar stage and we learn which technique is appropriate for use in a specific situation in the logic stage. The *rhetoric* stage is where it all comes together. In the rhetoric stage we review the information we have learned in the grammar stage and combine it with the analytical skills we picked up in the logic stage to form our own opinions and resolve problems in our own way. This is the way we learn most things, and its effectiveness is demonstrated when people give opinions on things they know nothing about.

A mentoring program should follow a schedule, although it is hard to set up a firm schedule or program because everyone learns and progresses at different rates. For example, one person may catch on to all the airport imaginary surfaces in no time at all, while others (like me) never seem to quite get them down pat. But the person who is slow to pick up on that particular bit of esoterica may have no problem at all with performing demand/capacity studies or preparing demand forecasts. It is also difficult to set a firm schedule, especially if you are a planner working for a consulting firm, because many deadlines and unexpected duties tend to disrupt neatly-planned schedules. Nonetheless, a mentoring program should be established over the long term, and it can be effective if certain targets or goals are set up on a monthly, quarterly, or annual basis.

Mentoring by Objectives

When I was an undergraduate I was working on a degree in Earth Science Education. A couple of my courses dealt with how to go about teaching science in secondary schools. One of the main objectives of these courses was to teach us how to do lesson plans, i.e., a plan for each lesson, for each class, each day. We were also taught how to do unit plans, which were essentially plans for what we were going to teach in each unit. In Earth Science the units consisted of astronomy, meteorology, geology, etc. Unfortunately I didn't pay a whole lot of attention to what the professors were talking about, but I do remember a big emphasis being given to something called "behavioral objectives." For each lesson (and for each unit and for the entire course), we were to list the objectives for what we were teaching, i.e., what we wanted the students to learn from each lesson, from each unit, and from the course. Summed up, our class and unit objectives comprised what we wanted each student to learn during the entire year.

This got a little tricky because we had to write the objectives in such a way that we could observe and measure the results. Thus we couldn't just say that we wanted the students to understand how stars create energy. Instead we would say that we wanted the students to be able to describe the chemical process that goes on and to write the chemical equation that describes the stellar energy process. In other words we had to write the lesson objectives in a way that we could observe and measure changes in student behavior or actions that would let us know that they really understood how stars generate energy. An important part of this was for the teacher to let the students know what they were going to be taught in each lesson, what they were expected to learn from it, and what they would be able to do at the end of the lesson that they couldn't do at the beginning. It is also a good idea to let the student know why they should learn what you are trying to teach them, but I don't remember very much emphasis being put on this aspect of teaching.

Learning by Doing

This is not to say that you should adopt a formal classroom teaching approach since teaching airport planning to a young professional is by necessity a matter of on-the-job training. However, the ideas noted in the preceding paragraph provide a good way to approach mentoring because what you are really doing is teaching a person to become an airport planner, and you want to let them know what you are going to teach them, why they should know it, how they will do it, and what they will be able to do when you are done that they can't do now. For example, you may be teaching your apprentice how to determine some of what I have referred to as the airport's erogenous zones—examples are runway safety areas (RSAs) and object free areas (OFAs) as set forth in FAA AC 150/5300-13, *Airport Design*. The first step in the process is to let the person know what these areas do, i.e., why they were established in the first place. Then you show them how the RSA, for example, is dependent upon the type of aircraft (specifically the wingspan and approach speed) and the landing minima or type of approach (visual, instrument with visibility not lower than ¾-mile, or instrument with visibility lower than ¾-mile). Discuss why the width of the RSA increases as the aircraft approach speed and/or wingspan increases, and why the RSA increases as the visibility decreases. Somebody didn't just make these design standards up; there is a reason for them and they are important to the safety of aircraft operations. Once you have shown your apprentice where this information is located in the AC, let them walk through the process with you as you lay out an RSA for a particular runway. Then let them lay out the RSA for another runway while you look over their shoulder.

Next you can move to taxiway safety areas, runway protection zones, and the various other zones and surfaces around an airport, following the same process of showing the person where the information is located in the AC, and having them watch as you apply the criteria and lay out each of the appropriate zones or surfaces. This is an example of applying behavioral objectives to mentoring an airport planner. This approach should be applied to each and every thing you are trying to teach your apprentice. You show them what you want them to do, why they are doing it, how they should do it, and what it should look like when they are done. You can tell if your teaching has been effective by the outcome—if your apprentice lays out the appropriate zones and surfaces correctly, you have successfully taught them how to do it.

Thinking and Imagining

Mentoring becomes a little more complicated when it comes to the thinking part of airport planning. As noted throughout this book, planning is thinking, especially long-term thinking. How can you teach somebody to think and how can you tell if they are thinking—and thinking correctly? I don't have a definitive answer, and I don't know that anybody really does. In my opinion, the thinking part is based on asking questions—and literally questioning nearly everything. True, this is very subjective, but, if you have a lot of experience your thoughts, ideas, and feelings about something are valuable tools, as also discussed in Chapter 1: Overview of Airport Planning. It seems to me that you can train a beginning planner to think by encouraging them to ask questions. In airport planning they are the usual and obvious ones: Why are we doing this plan? Why are we doing it this way? What kind of facility should result? Who will use it? Why will they use it? How will they use it? These initial questions are followed by some more practical factors such as how much it will cost, who will pay for it, what environmental impacts are associated, and how efficient it will be. And perhaps the most important question of all, "What if...?" This is so important because planners deal with an unknown future. These kinds of questions are the result of macro or big-picture thinking. Macro thinking helps ensure that the planning process will encompass all necessary facets of the task at hand. In the macro context thought should also be given to the effect that a proposed improvement will have on adjacent facilities and seemingly unrelated operations, both currently and over the long run.

As you take your apprentice under your wing you should always be asking these questions, and answering them, or trying to answer them, as best you can. As an apprentice gains knowledge and experience they will start asking these kinds of questions too, and perhaps even providing some answers. This is often how you can tell if a person is "getting it" when it comes to airport planning. Does he or she ask questions? Are they good questions? Are they relevant?

Avoiding Boredom

One thing you should not do with a beginning employee is give them a pile of things to read and then leave them on their own. I have seen people receive a stack of advisory circulars to go through as a way to learn about airport planning and design. Or the company's human resources manual, which could even be worse than an AC. What an awful way to start a new job! A better approach is to show your new planner what the ACs and other resources are and what kinds of information are contained in them. They shouldn't have to memorize the information contained in the guidance materials, but they should at least know where to look for the relevant information. So don't say, "Look through this and then come see me." Instead, let them review the AC (one at a time, please) at their own pace, and give them other things to do in the meantime. For example, you could have them go through the AC on Airport Master Plans and walk through it with them briefly, pointing out the kinds of information it contains. Give them a couple of hours to read through it and then give them something else to do. Even if it isn't something all that important, it will give them a break—a chance to recharge their batteries after going through that dreary stuff. The airport tours noted above are a very good way to break the monotony.

Another way to break the monotony and provide a learning experience is to take beginning staff to meetings with you. They don't have to say anything, but you can introduce them and have them help you take notes of important points raised or discussed during the meeting. For this to be most effective, you should sit down with the person beforehand and tell them what the meeting is going to be about, note the important points you expect to be discussed, and tell them who else will be attending the meeting and what their interests or concerns might be. Then, after the meeting, review what happened, who said what, which decisions were made (and which ones were deferred), and try to sum it all up with a conclusion. Something to keep in mind: if you can't do this and present a coherent picture, maybe the meeting was a waste of time. In my opinion this is pretty likely, since I think most meetings are a waste of time anyway. (That is just my own personal opinion; I have always believed that a letter longer than a page and a meeting longer than an hour are a waste of time.) Taking somebody to a meeting with you can help give them an idea of what your organization or division is doing and how it relates to other things that other organizations or divisions might be doing. Hopefully it will also give them some idea of how to dress and comport themselves properly and professionally.

It is also a good idea to take (or send) your new planner to a couple of airport conferences each year. You need to screen the agendas first to make sure that there will be some substance to the conference topics, and some application to the kinds of work you and your apprentice are doing. Attending conferences is a good way to see what the rest of the airport and airport planning communities are doing, what their issues are, and what they are talking about in terms of solutions to current problems. It is also a good way for planners to interact socially, and this is especially important since airport planners constitute such a small community.

Empowerment

As your new planner gains experience in doing various tasks, and in learning how you and your group function and get things done, you can give them more responsibilities, and begin to broaden their professional experience and professional skills with other tasks. After a period of tutoring you will find that the new person can do some things on their own. When you sense that point, go ahead and "empower" them. Make sure you review their work and go over it with them if you find areas for improvement. You may also find that the new person has a new approach or new method of performing a task. Sometimes this makes managers and supervisors nervous, but keep in mind that you should be looking at the end result. If the new approach pays off and gives you an accurate and acceptable product, you may have just learned something yourself. Even after the new person starts functioning on their own, make sure they know that you are there to lean on or to support them if something unexpected arises. After all, you don't want the person to feel as though they are out on a limb with no support.

I have found that it also pays to have new people start doing presentations sooner rather than later in the mentoring process. A good way to do this is, once a task is complete and it is time to present the results to your boss, or the rest of your organization, or to a client, have the new person do part of the presentation with you. You can do the hard parts; what you are trying to do here is give the person some confidence in speaking in public and confidence in the work they have done. A self-confident employee will be much more productive and prove to be of much more benefit to the organization than one who is gun-shy. And the way you help build this confidence is to let them walk on their own, one step at a time, and always be there if it looks like they might fall. A next step that seems to work is for you to do the introduction and overview at a presentation and have your apprentice describe the technical work, with you again doing the summary and conclusions and taking questions. As the new planner gets more experience, they can do more of the presentation until they can do them on their own. The first few times they do presentations on their own you should also sit in to provide a comfort factor and to be there in case anything goes wrong.

This step-by-step approach also applies to the preparation of any graphics, drawings, or handouts that might be involved. Review with your apprentice the various ways of providing information visually, and help them learn which type of visual aid works best for different types of information. Having your apprentice help put a presentation together is a good way to help them focus on identifying and presenting the most important points. As you go through this "seasoning" process, you should always take the time to debrief afterwards and discuss how things went, in terms of the presentation itself as well as the information presented and the audience reaction. You should review the methods of presenting various types of information, discuss the reaction of the audience to the various points made, and review/summarize any ensuing discussions regarding the subject matter.

The Apprentice's Responsibilities

Young planners or apprentices also have some responsibilities as part of the mentoring process. As a young planner you should always pay attention to what your mentor is telling you or showing you. If there are parts you don't understand, it is your responsibility to ask questions and request additional information. The longer you work without really understanding just what it is you are supposed to be doing and why you are doing it, the longer it will take to reach a desired level of professional efficiency and personal satisfaction. You should also pay attention to how other staff members work and how they approach and accomplish their project assignments. No one does everything perfectly all the time, so you should observe others' mistakes and how they correct them. Observe other staff members' work habits to get some insight into how other people work. Try to identify good habits so you can copy them and bad habits so you can avoid them.

It is also very important to maintain a two-way flow of information between the mentor and the apprentice. If you don't understand the directions your mentor is giving you, make sure you let the mentor know which areas are causing you problems. If you don't feel that you are getting a good background or don't see how your assignment fits into the big picture, let the mentor know. Also let the mentor know if you are not being challenged by your assignments. Much of what airport planners do is sometimes considered mere grunt work and may not always be intellectually or professionally challenging; nonetheless, it has to be done. However, you should also find some things that challenge your thinking skills and if you are not getting them make sure you let your mentor know.

Managing

After your new planner or planners have started the mentoring program, you are faced with the challenges of management. Management has two components: managing staff and managing projects. They are related in that managing a planning staff effectively and efficiently will help ensure that projects proceed on schedule and within budget. They both require concentrated effort and close attention to detail on the part of the manager. In a broad sense the airport planner will be managing a staff with varying levels of experience and who are at varying points in the mentoring process. If you are working for an airport and have a planning staff, even if the staff consists of only two or three people, you have to manage their time and effort as well as their projects to ensure that everything is done on time and that the end product is a properly-prepared and effective plan. If you are working for an airport you will probably also be managing consultants on either on-call or project-specific consultant contracts. If you are a planner working for an airport consulting firm you will also have a planning staff with people and projects to manage to the satisfaction of the client. In any case, there are some things that I have found to be particularly important to make sure that your organization functions effectively and efficiently.

Managing People

An obvious key component of managing staff is to make sure that staff people with the proper skills are assigned to tasks for which they are qualified. Unqualified people usually produce unsatisfactory work and the consistent use of people outside their area(s) of expertise can lead to a breakdown of morale because the individuals involved are not likely to maintain an adequate level of job satisfaction (and could eventually decide to look elsewhere for more satisfactory opportunities). And as noted above, when staff people are assigned to a project they should be given clear guidance on what is required as an end product and how their piece fits into the whole.

Managers should also make sure each staff member is using his or her time effectively. Quite often we see people playing computer games, reading the paper, designing their next home improvement project, or something equally unrelated to their jobs. Now we can't expect everybody to work constantly throughout the day; some relaxation—some time spent clearing the mind, so to speak—is necessary, especially in a field such as planning which primarily involves thinking. However, short breaks in the daily routine should not be confused with perpetual goofing off. If you have people who make a habit of spending hours on end doing things that are not job-related, you should take them aside and find out what is going on and why they are not focusing on their job responsibilities. It could be that they are not challenged by the work they are given, or it could be that the work is beyond their capabilities. And frankly it could also be that they are just in the wrong field. In any case the manager should take the necessary action to correct the situation, either by finding work more appropriate to the individual's skills and/or interests, or by suggesting other places where they may find more satisfactory employment.

Much information, guidance, and how-to examples are available on the subject of time management, most of which involve keeping a chart showing how you have spent your time during a given week. Most that I have seen involve breaking each hour into fifteen-minute increments (or something very like) and reviewing the resulting information with a supervisor or manager. A big problem with this however is that such a detailed chart or time compilation takes a lot of time, and most people don't have that much time to spare. I have found it better to sit down twice a day—say at noon and the end of the day—and make a few notes about what you have done and accomplished during the preceding few hours. If you do this a couple of times each week, by the end of a month you will have a pretty good idea of how you are spending your time and whether you are using it wisely.

It is a good idea to meet with your staff individually to discuss broader issues such as job satisfaction, work environment, and career objectives. Human resources staff can give you guidelines to follow with regard to the types of questions to ask and what kinds of responses to expect, as well as how to respond to them; however, I have found that it is usually more productive to meet on an informal basis, such as over lunch or a drink after work. In a more relaxed atmosphere people tend to be more forthcoming and candid in a discussion of what they like and don't like, and how they feel they are performing. However you handle it, you should make sure your staff knows that your door is always open and that you are always ready to talk—and listen.

The most important thing in managing any task or project successfully is to be sure you and your staff share the same understanding of what is required as an end product. At the most basic level you will be doing whatever your employer or your supervisor tells you to do, i.e., you will be producing whatever is required to meet their needs. At the ultimate level, as an airport planner, you will be preparing a plan or an associated planning document that meets the needs of the airport sponsor and, in most cases, the requirements of the FAA. Thus it is critical that all parties concerned understand and agree on exactly what is required as an end product of your planning task or exercise.

Managing Projects
The initial thinking about the end product takes place in the Pre-Planning and Initial Needs Determination phases in the typical Master Plan process as discussed in detail in Chapter 5: Master Planning. By the time you get to the Study Design phase, when the consultant work begins in earnest, study participants develop a specific list of activities that must take place along with the products that are required as deliverables. It is fairly easy to set forth the end product or products for a large study such as an airport master plan or airport system plan. But sometimes we slip up on identifying the deliverables, and the exact form of the deliverables, when we are working on smaller or less complicated tasks. That is why it is a good idea to get all affected parties on board early in the process in order to 1) gain program support, 2) elicit valuable input, and 3) evoke a sense of team involvement. This helps

make the planning process run more smoothly and helps ensure a product that meets the airport's needs.

Prepare a work scope for each task, even for individual tasks that are being performed as part of a larger airport master plan study. Just as a consultant prepares a scope of services for a master plan study, they should also have a detailed scope for each of the tasks that must be performed as part of that study. The scope should contain a detailed list of exactly what will be done as part of the task, who will be doing the work, and exactly what the end product will look like or consist of. This information is needed to determine how much the task will cost and how long it will take to do the work. It is also the key to successful project management.

Schedule Challenges

Unfortunately, even though this seems like a simple, straightforward, common sense exercise, many studies (in fact I would venture to say *most* planning studies) seem to get off track somewhere along the line.

One of the most significant management challenges is to ensure that the project is accomplished on time. Although a schedule is almost always established and agreed to at the outset of a study, many studies (again, I could safely say *most* planning studies) wind up taking longer than expected. I did not pay as much attention to the study schedule as I perhaps should have; I tried not to be a stickler for on-time performance as much as for quality of the product. My rationale has usually been that planning is not typically done in emergency situations; I have always thought that the most important factor was the quality of the product, rather than the adherence to a time schedule. I believe that if you do a good job in planning you are plowing new ground. The example I liked to use was that planning is like turning over rocks, and every once in a while you turn over a rock and lo and behold you find a Gila monster under one of them. That little surprise could cause a change in plans, or at least a reevaluation of your position and intentions, which all ultimately impact the schedule.

To use a planning example, you may be working on a plan to develop an area for future hangar construction and, as part of the environmental investigation, you find that your favored site happens to contain some pre-Columbian artifacts. Additional work will have to be done to document the extent and importance of this archaeological find, thus blowing the planning schedule.

Again, when working with your planning staff it is imperative to develop a workable knowledge of task scheduling to ensure that they can produce what is required according to the established schedule. This will enhance the productive skills and capabilities of your staff tremendously. I have not heard of a sure-fire method to teach task scheduling, although I am sure there are some. However, it seems to me that the key is to have a complete understanding of exactly what the task requires in terms of both output, e.g., the final report or other deliverable, and input, e.g., the basic materials and information you have to work with. Inputs are the items collected during the inventory phase of a project. For example, for the forecasting task, the inputs include such items as current and historical data on passenger and aircraft operational activity. A workable schedule can be developed most effectively by having the sponsor sit down with the consultant (or the task manager sit down with his or her staff) and walk through the task step by step. Make sure all participants know what product is required, and then discuss how that product will be developed. This includes identifying any input materials required, as well as the sources of the input materials. Sponsors and consultants may not want to take the time to do this, but it will usually pay off in the long run. Quite often a study or a task is delayed because the needed data either were not available, or not available in a readily usable form. If a further search for the right data or further processing of existing data is required, it can add significantly to the time required to accomplish the task. If each task participant knows exactly what is required, what is available to work with, and how the work will be accomplished, it is easier to prepare a realistic schedule and to deliver a quality product.

Managing Reviews

I don't remember how many times my associates and I have gone through work scopes with consultants, come to an agreement on exactly what was to be done, how long it would take, and what the deliverables or final report would look like, and wound up with a product that was not what we expected. So many times study reports are delivered to the airport sponsor, the sponsor reviews the report and returns comments to the consultant, the consultant revises the report and returns it to the sponsor, the sponsor reviews the report again and makes more comments, the consultant revises again, and so on and so on *ad infinitum*. Finally the sponsor gives up and rewrites the report himself, as I have done many times. I have discussed this with planners at other airports and with consultants on many occasions, and the story is often the same. In fact most of the people who see this as a problem agree that it seems to be getting worse. I must also add that I think it is unfair for someone to review a report, provide comments to a consultant, then review the next draft and make new comments on old material, unless the previous comments were not addressed adequately. Except in extreme circumstances, a reviewer should only comment on a particular item once, assuming it has been corrected the first time. Consultants commit staff resources to a project and once something has been completed the staff members move on to the next phase of the project or to other projects. Having to spend more time on an item that has already been reviewed and approved causes schedule delays and potential cost overruns.

Speaking of reviews, projects are often delayed because the reviewers take more time than expected to review and respond to consultant reports, i.e., they do not meet the review deadlines established in the project schedule. People take vacations, get sick, and other problems arise, so sometimes delays are unavoidable. But remember that consultants also take vacations, get sick, or run into unexpected issues, so some degree of consideration and compromise is clearly called for. But tolerance should not be abused by either party, and project delays should be made up as soon as possible, and without sacrificing quality.

In many cases a review can be delayed by external factors; an external reviewing agency such as a local planning or environmental agency or the FAA does not review the report or other study product in the time allocated. Usually these agencies, particularly the FAA, will let you know up front how long to allow for their project reviews, e.g., 30 days, 60 days, etc. To avoid these kinds of delays, review times should be discussed with external agencies before the final project schedule is established.

Avoiding Delay Pitfalls

There are a few things that airport sponsors, consultants, and project managers can do to reduce and hopefully eliminate these little (and sometimes not-so-little) "glitches" that seem to occur so many times in so many studies. As discussed in Chapter 5: Master Planning, very close attention must be given to the detailed development of the Study Design in the Pre-Planning phase. This will help focus on exactly what is to be done. A similar focus should also be given to the list of deliverables developed as part of the Study Design. It is essential that sufficient time and effort be given to these items if misunderstandings and glitches are to be avoided.

One of my staff developed an interesting technique to help clarify study requirements: she would provide a table of contents for each report that a consultant was to prepare. She developed the table of contents within a few days of meeting with the consultants to discuss the study design, and forwarded it to the consultants for their concurrence. The consultants loved it, by all accounts. It helped both parties by giving an extra element of detail with regard to the contents and organization of the final product. It also gave the consultant a chance to look over her specifications and expectations, and ask questions and suggest modifications to ensure that both parties had a clearer understanding of what was required. Although I have used the airport sponsor/consultant relationship as an example, the same reasoning can be applied to the manager/staff relationship. If you are a manager, sit down with your staff and go through the steps required to accomplish the task at hand. Particularly if you have a relatively inexperienced staff member whom you are mentoring, make sure they have a thorough understanding of what they are supposed to accomplish and what you expect to see as a final product.

Budget Challenges

Another management challenge is to ensure that the work is completed within budget. Again, because planning deals with new ideas and explores the unknown in many cases, you can expect some surprises, which, to be addressed properly, may in turn result in a cost increase. The same process that is used to help ensure that each task or study is completed on schedule can be used to ensure that the task or study can be completed within the allocated budget. To repeat: each participant must know exactly what end product is required from the task, what inputs are needed, and how the task will be accomplished. The budget problem is especially critical if you are a consultant—if you overrun the budget on too many tasks you will lose money on the project, and if you overrun on too many projects you will be out of business. It is therefore particularly important to show beginning planners how to manage their own time and resources effectively. It is always a good idea, both for consultants and sponsors, to increase the initial budget estimate by a small amount to cover unexpected occurrences or unforeseen expenses. As already noted, planning often deals with unknowns that can cause delays and increase costs. Having a little reserve cash built into the project budget can reduce the impact of some of the minor glitches that can, when added up through the project, result in cost overruns. And if everything goes according to plan and no extra work is needed and the project comes in under budget, somebody is going to be a hero!

Project Reporting

A good way to help cost overruns—and to help keep the project on schedule—is to require periodic progress reports. The usual period for reporting progress is a month, but during a critical phase of a project biweekly or even weekly reporting may be appropriate. At times however, quarterly reporting may be sufficient—for example, on tasks that are nearly completed, or waiting for review or some other external factor. Simply preparing a progress report is not necessarily sufficient to ensure that tasks or projects are completed properly, on time, and within budget. The contents and quality of the progress report are extremely important to eventual success. A good progress report should contain several basic items: the work accomplished during the reporting period, products delivered, problems encountered, percent of work completed, and work expected to be accomplished during the next reporting period. As an airport sponsor you should ask these questions, and as a consultant you should be prepared to answer them. Again, this applies to sponsor/consultant relationships as well as to manager/staff relationships.

It may be adequate for some people to receive written progress reports, but it seems to me that in-person monthly project reviews are more effective. I have always had a hard time with these monthly progress or status meetings, and that could be one of the reasons why I didn't always get my projects done as well as I wanted, and on time, although most of my projects were completed within budget. More or less. The reasons why I didn't adhere to a firm project review schedule were two: I was too busy to spend time each month reviewing projects with four or five different consulting firms, and I have always hated meetings. Nevertheless, I suggest that you do as I say, not as I have been doing, and make your project reviews rigorous and regularly scheduled. This way you can make sure that the work stays on track. A slight slip can snowball through the course of a study and leave you with a serious problem at the time you should be looking at a successful conclusion, so it is imperative that potential problems be identified and addressed promptly.

How these project reviews are conducted is also important. The sponsor should be quick to spot any errors, delays, cost discrepancies, or other aspects of the project that "just don't look right." The consultant should be forthright in addressing any issues raised by the sponsor. Project reviews should not be conducted in a confrontational atmosphere; instead, they should be focused on the task at hand with a view to developing a clear picture of the project status and critical issues. If any issues are discovered, whether with the schedule, the cost, or the quality of the product, they should be resolved to everyone's satisfaction. Or at least as close to unanimous satisfaction as you can get. The main point here is to identify any issues and determine how they should be resolved before they become problems.

On a day-to-day basis project management can be helped by preparing minutes for every meeting held. The minutes should include the date, the attendees, the subjects discussed, and the conclusions reached. Where appropriate they should also include a summary of action items, due dates, and responsibilities. Typically, in meetings involving consultants, the consultant is designated as the party responsible for preparing the minutes. In fact most consultants include in their proposals the fact that they will prepare the minutes for all project meetings and distribute them for review to all attendees. Generally minutes are produced within a week of the meeting date. Also, the minutes should end with a note to the effect that unless somebody raises a question or contradicts what is presented as a conclusion within seven days of the date of the minutes, the minutes will stand as written. Bear in mind that this management aid will not be effective if the meeting attendees do not read the minutes in a timely manner.

Another tip on managing, whether you are managing your own staff or managing a consulting firm working on a project for you, is to avoid constantly looking over their shoulder or riding them closely as the work is being accomplished. And above all, don't be a micro-manager. Give your staff, or your consultant, clear direction on what they are to do and when it is to be done, and then let them go do it.

To summarize, whether managing a project or a task you should begin by identifying the product that is desired or expected as the outcome. In an airport/consultant situation the airport's representative sits down with the consultant who will be in charge of the project and identifies and specifies exactly what he expects as a product. The discussion should also cover what is to be done, why it is to be done (the purpose of the project), how it will be done, who will do it, and how long it will take. The consultant takes this information back to his staff and assigns each element of the project or task to an appropriate staff member, discussing again what is to be done, why it is to be done, how it will be done, how long it will take, and what is expected as a final product. One of the main reasons projects get off track or delayed is because these questions were either not asked at the outset, or they were not answered properly or correctly. And this leads directly into the next section of this chapter, Team Building.

Team Building

Team building involves showing each member of the team how they fit into the whole, and how their work fits in with other people's work to produce the desired outcome. I'm sure management experts can turn the subject of team building into a book and develop presentations with lots of touchy-feely exercises, but to me it is as simple as that. Yes, we all have to be aware of other people's sensitivities and quirks; after all we are all human and we usually act like it. But team building or teamwork doesn't necessarily involve everyone sitting down and working together on a common problem or issue. It involves understanding what is being done, why it is being done, and who is doing the various components. As noted in Chapter 4: Strategic Planning, people in bureaucratic organizations such as large airports and large consulting firms tend to become focused on their specific tasks and organizational rules and procedures, thereby losing their sense of purpose and mission; they lose sight of how their function fits into the whole.

Teamwork versus Personal Friendships

Many people I know seem to think that working as a team, or being a *team player* means that all staff members get along well with each other, sometimes even to the point of socializing over lunches and happy hour festivities. They also seem to think that team players should always agree with each other on various aspects of a current project. If somebody disagrees with a planned approach to a project, or with some particular aspect, they are accused of not being a team player. It is true that people who get along well together help create a more pleasant working environment, but I think that some dissension is necessary to making a project work. Remember, this is *planning*. All participants in a planning project—sponsors, consultants, and individual staff members—should challenge each other throughout the process. They should ask questions such as, "Why are you doing that? Is that the best way to do it? What if...?" This is an effective way to help build a team, and it also helps to ensure a better product by stimulating thinking about alternatives. Planning is a world of ideas and the more ideas people have, the better the chance of coming up with an effective and implementable plan that meets the airport sponsor's goals. In an orchestra, for example, many of the musicians may get along well and some may socialize together. Others can't stand each other and only speak when necessary. Still, the sounds they produce can be magnificent. It is the job of the conductor—or the airport planning manager—to make sure each person plays his part in the manner expected.

Understanding the Bigger Picture

Each person on the team should understand exactly what they are doing and how their piece fits into the final product, or into the complete puzzle, if you prefer. The manager should try to communicate that big picture among his staff to help generate an air of importance and excitement to the work being done. Specialized staff members, such as forecasters and airspace analysts, often do not get to see the whole picture, they just see their part of the project. Understanding how their particular piece fits into the entire package often helps them do a better job, and also lets them know why schedules and due dates are important. Good managers should also let their staff members know how important their work is to the successful completion of a project. Anybody who has worked on an airport expansion project, a terminal addition for example, knows how proud they feel when years later they walk through that terminal and see all the activity taking place in a smooth and efficient manner, and know that they had a part in it.

Just as you mentor each apprentice airport planner by going step by step through the process, the manager should also take the team members through the process that will be followed to complete a project. In this way each person can see not only how their piece fits into the whole, but also how important it is for them to have their work done on time. They can also see who is working on other elements of the project that may affect what they do or how they complete their task, and see how their work fits into elements that other staff members are working on. Working together in this way can be considered "coordinating" and coordination is an essential component of team building as well as successful project completion.

The Benefits of Diverse Skills

Another key component of team building is realizing how you aren't supposed to know everything and it is not a bad thing to admit that there are some areas of airport planning in which you are not an expert. We all have our strengths and weaknesses; sharing them with others is usually a good thing. That is why complex projects require a number of people who are specialists in the various subject areas included in the study. A good airport planning manager should be able to carry on an intelligent conversation about any aspect of airport planning, or at least be able to ask intelligent questions, but he does not have to be an expert in all areas. He only has to know how all the pieces fit together to produce the desired outcome or product. Similarly, the airport director does not have to know all the intimate details of runway or fuel farm design, capital programming, security, etc., but he should understand how all those things fit together to make the airport work.

When you or any of your staff sit down together and somebody says that they really don't understand how forecasts are developed, that makes the person who does understand forecasting feel important—that they are an important part of the team and have a significant role to play. The same thing is true for other elements of airport planning, from airside capacity studies and other analyses to terminal planning and highway/curbside traffic studies. Having these kinds of individuals with diverse specialties available, and having them play an active role, helps to ensure a quality product. In a sense, an airport planning team can be thought of as being similar to a symphony orchestra. The music director or conductor is in charge of the orchestra. He knows (or thinks he knows) what the composer intended when a particular piece of music was written. Each of the orchestra sections has a part to play—the first violins, second violins, cellos, horns, etc. Each has a necessary contribution to make. Each orchestra member knows what his part is and how it fits in with what the other people in his section are playing, and how each section's part fits into the whole concerto or symphony. The members of each section rehearse together to ensure that they are all playing from the same sheet of music—literally. During rehearsals individual orchestra members can voice their ideas on how a particular piece should be played, and often these ideas are discussed among the other section members and with the conductor. Some conductors are receptive to suggestions and some are not.

Leading through Inspiration

However, the conductor is ultimately in charge—he is the boss and his word is final. His job is to ensure that each section and each musician produces exactly the sound that he wants at the tempo he thinks is appropriate. As part of his job he makes his ideas known to the orchestra members and tells them what he expects in terms of their performance. Some conductors simply tell the musicians, "Play it this way because I want it this way." They get what they want through intimidation. However, the better conductors explain why they want the piece played in a particular way; what they feel the composer intended; and what kinds of tones, textures, and colors they are looking for. They lead through *inspiration*. Each of the section leaders, or principals, works with the individual members of their section to ensure that they perform as expected. Thus each musician gets a clear idea of what he has to play, how he has to play it, and how his playing will fit in with the orchestra as a whole. Thus the orchestra functions as a team to produce a musically-gratifying result.

Team building then is the result of mentoring—ensuring that each staff member becomes efficient and effective in their particular specialty—and also managing—ensuring that staff resources are used efficiently and effectively to produce the desired result. Team building shows individuals how to work with each other and respect each other personally and professionally. Building an efficient and effective team takes time, patience, clear communication, and the ability to inspire staff members to work toward a final vision. It is up to the manager to ensure that staff members work together to complete projects that meet all technical requirements, on time and within budget.

Endnotes

1. Airport Master Planning Training Program, International Air Transport Association. Accessed January 2008, from http://www.iata.org/training/courses/tapp08

2. Bauer, Susan Wise, *The Well-Educated Mind*. New York: The W. W. Norton Company, 2003, p. 8.

CHAPTER 11

CONCLUSION

Think!
In this book I have aimed to shed some light on what I believe are the critical aspects or significant points to be considered in airport planning. The most important is that planning requires thinking. Airport planning is not just a matter of following the FAA advisory circular guidance as though it were a cookbook. While it is necessary to follow the FAA guidance, planners must think while they are doing it. As the planning process progresses, the planner should always consider, "Why am I doing this?" "Who will use it?" "Why is it needed?" "How will it be used?" The ACs can provide guidance on how to answer these kinds of questions, but they will not do your thinking for you.

Flexibility
The second point to keep in mind is that the future never happens exactly the way we expect it to, and sometimes it doesn't even come close. Plans should be developed with future uncertainties in mind and some flexibility should be retained with respect to timing, phasing, facility size and/or location, funding sources, and other factors. Alternatives should always be considered as part of the planning process and evaluated as part of a "what if" scenario analysis.

Overlapping Phases
The third point is that planning is not necessarily a linear process, where first we do A, then we do B, etc. As discussed in Chapter 5, a number of planning program elements, such as the inventory, the public involvement process, environmental considerations, and forecasting can begin as soon as the scope of work is approved by the FAA and the grant has been awarded. Perhaps the most critical of these is the environmental aspect. As discussed at various places in the book, and especially in Chapters 5 and 8, environmental factors should be considered throughout the planning study. This will make the resulting plan more likely to be implemented in a timely manner, and, more importantly, it will help ensure that critical environmental factors are addressed and that subsequent facility development and operation will not result in serious environmental degradation.

Completeness

Speaking of the environment brings me to the fourth major point; planners should make sure that the planning is completed in a competent and thorough manner before proceeding to the formal environmental documentation process. Poor or incomplete planning is almost guaranteed to result in excessive delays and cost expenditures. It is especially important for the plan to identify and clearly document the purpose and need for the project, as well as the alternatives considered. Also, keeping environmental considerations in mind throughout the planning exercise will help ensure that the planning documents are complete and will withstand scrutiny by reviewers and the general public. This approach also supports subsequent environmental documentation.

Judgment

The final point brings me back to thinking. Planners today have all kinds of analytical tools. Personal computers and simulation models are readily available to help them analyze data, prepare forecasts, and develop and evaluate alternatives. We can generate hundreds of tables, dozens of reports, and mounds of awesome graphics. But at some point we have to be able to answer the question, "What does all this mean?" Don't forget that we learn things and develop ideas through our experiences and the experiences of co-workers, airport staff members, consultants, the FAA, airline representatives, and even friends and neighbors who fly frequently. Airport planning requires judgment; not every good decision can be fully quantified or "proven." Use the full range of tools available, but recognize the value of human judgment.

Your Most Important Tools

We are all human and we all make mistakes. And no one can foresee the future, convenient though that would be in the airport planning business. Just do your best and have confidence in yourself and your ideas. Always remember that the most valuable tools you have are your brain and your imagination. Use them well.

BIBLIOGRAPHY

Aeronautical Information Manual. Washington, D.C.: Federal Aviation Administration. Accessed May 2008, from http://www.faa.gov/airports_airtraffic/air_traffic/publications/atpubs/aim/Chap1/aim0101.html

Aeronautical Information Publication: Official Guide to Basic Flight Information and ATC Procedures. Washington, D.C.: Federal Aviation Administration, March 15, 2007.

Airline On-Time Statistics. Washington, D.C.: Bureau of Transportation Statistics (USDOT). Accessed May 2008, from http://www.bts.gov/programs/airline_information/airline_ontime_statistics/

Airport Aviation Activity Forecasting. Washington, D.C.: Airport Cooperative Research Program, Transportation Research Board, 2007. Accessed June 2008, from http://onlinepubs.trb.org/onlinepubs/acrp/acrp_syn_002.pdf

Airport Design, AC 150/5300-13. Washington, D.C.: Federal Aviation Administration, 1989. Accessed April 2008, from http://www.faa.gov/airports_airtraffic/airports/resources/advisory_circulars/media/150-5300-13/150_5300_13.PDF

Airport Improvement Program (AIP), Funding for Airport Planning and Development, Overview. Washington, D.C.: Federal Aviation Administration. Accessed June 2008, from http://www.faa.gov/airports_airtraffic/airports/aip/overview/

Airport Improvement Program (AIP) Handbook, FAA Order 5100.38C. Washington, D.C.: Federal Aviation Administration, June 2005. Accessed June 2008, from http://www.faa.gov/airports_airtraffic/airports/aip/aip_handbook/

Airport Master Planning Training Program, International Air Transport Association. Accessed January 2008, from http://www.iata.org/training/courses/tapp08

Airport Master Plans, AC 150/5070-6B. Washington, D.C.: Federal Aviation Administration, 2005. Accessed April 2008, from http://www.faa.gov/airports_airtraffic/airports/resources/advisory_circulars/

Airport Recycling Specialists, home page. Accessed August 2008, from http://www.airportrecycling.com/

Airport Rescue and Firefighting Station Building Design, AC 150/5210-15. Washington, D.C.: Federal Aviation Administration, July 30, 1987.

Airports Benefit-Cost Analysis Guidance. Washington, D.C.: Federal Aviation Administration, Office of Policy and Plans, 1999. Accessed December 2007, from http://www.faa.gov/airports_airtraffic/airports/aip/bc_analysis/media/faabca.pdf

APO Terminal Area Forecast 2007. Washington, D.C.: Federal Aviation Administration. Accessed July 2008, from http://tafpub.itworks-software.com/taf2007/default.asp

Architectural, Engineering, and Planning Consultant Services for Airport Grant Projects, AC 150/5100-14. Washington, D.C.: Federal Aviation Administration, September 2005. Accessed April 2008, from http://rgl.faa.gov/Regulatory_and_Guidance_Library/rgAdvisoryCircular.nsf/0/87be820a72d12407862570a6006b4f29/$FILE/150-5100-14d.pdf

Assurances, Airport Sponsors. Washington, D.C.: Federal Aviation Administration, March 2005. Accessed May 2008, from http://www.faa.gov/airports_airtraffic/airports/aip/grant_assurances/media/airport_sponsor_assurances.pdf

Assurances, Non-Airport Sponsors Undertaking Noise Compatibility Program Projects. Washington, D.C.: Federal Aviation Administration. Accessed May 2008, from http://www.faa.gov/airports_airtraffic/airports/aip/grant_assurances/media/nonairport_sponsor_assurances.pdf

Atkin, Peter, *Trash Landings – How Airlines and Airports Can Clean Up Their Recycling Programs*. National Resources Defense Council, December 2006. Accessed September 2008, from http://www.nrdc.org/cities/recycling/airline/airline.pdf

Aviation & Emissions – A Primer. Washington, D.C.: Federal Aviation Administration, Office of Environment and Energy, January 2005. Accessed July 2008, from http://www.faa.gov/regulations_policies/policy_guidance/envir_policy/media/aeprimer.pdf

Aviation Investment and Reform Act for the 21st Century (AIR 21), (HR 1000). Washington, D.C.: U.S. House of Representatives. Accessed May 2008, from http://thomas.loc.gov/cgi-bin/bdquery/z?d106:h.r.01000:

Aviation Safety and Capacity Expansion Act of 1990, CIS-NO: 90-H643-3. Washington, D.C.: U.S. House of Representatives, Committee on Public Works and Transportation. Accessed April 2008, from http://thomas.loc.gov/cgi-bin/bdquery/z?d101:HR05170:@@@D&summ2=m&

Barry, Brian W., *Strategic Planning Workbook for Nonprofit Organizations*. St. Paul, MN: Amherst H. Wilder Foundation, 1997.

Bauer, Susan Wise, *The Well-Educated Mind*. New York: The W.W. Norton Company, 2003.

Bradford, Robert W., J. Peter Duncan, and Brian Tarcy, *Simplified Strategic Planning*. Worcester, MA: Chandler House Press, 2000.

Bryson, John M., *Strategic Planning for Public and Nonprofit Organizations*, 3rd Edition. San Francisco: Jossey-Bass, an imprint of John Wiley & Sons, 2004.

Collis, Roger. International Herald Tribune, July 26, 2007. Accessed January 2009, from http://www.iht.com/articles/2007/07/26/arts/trfreq27.php

Community Involvement Manual, FAA-EE-90-03. Washington, D.C.: Federal Aviation Administration, Office of Environment and Energy, August 1990.

Consideration Of Cumulative Impacts In EPA Review of NEPA Documents. U.S. Environmental Protection Agency, May 1999. Accessed August 2008, from http://www.epa.gov/compliance/resources/policies/nepa/cumulative.pdf

Current Aviation Excise Tax Structure, Taxpayer Relief Act of 1997, Public Law 105-35. Accessed August 2007, from http://www.faa.gov/about/office_org/headquarters_offices/aep/aatf/media/Simplified_Tax_Table.xls

de Neufville, Richard, and Amedeo Odoni, *Airport Systems Planning, Design, and Management*. New York: McGraw-Hill, 2003.

Definition of Navigable Waters of the U.S. (33 CFR Part 329). http://www.usace.army.mil/cw/cecwo/reg/33cfr329.htm#329.4

Delegations of Authority, FAA Order 1100.154A. Washington, D.C.: Federal Aviation Administration, June 12, 1990. Accessed July 2008, from http://rgl.faa.gov/Regulatory_and_Guidance_Library/rgOrders.nsf/0/5b3290986c1763598625717f0051c024/$FILE/1100.154a.pdf

Elgun, Serdar Z., M. Issapour, Y. Dathatri, and A. Filios, *Retrofitting Airports by Harnessing the Sun's Energy*, (n.d.) presentation at Farmingdale State College, State University of New York, Solar Energy Center. Accessed September 2008, from http://www.faa.gov/airports_airtraffic/airports/regional_guidance/eastern/airports_news_events/hershey/media_08/airportdesign.ppt#256,1,Slide 1

Engineering Brief No. 75: Incorporation of Runway Incursion Prevention into Taxiway and Apron Design, memorandum. Washington, D.C.: Federal Aviation Administration, November 2008. Accessed June 2008, from http://www.faa.gov/airports_airtraffic/airports/construction/engineering_briefs/media/EB_75.pdf

Environmental Desk Reference For Airport Actions. Washington, D.C.: Federal Aviation Administration, Office of Airports, October 2007. http://www.faa.gov/airports_airtraffic/airports/environmental/environmental_desk_ref/

Environmental Stewardship and Transportation Infrastructure Project Reviews, Executive Order 13274. Executive Order Implementation. Washington, D.C.: U.S. Department of Transportation, September 18, 2002. Accessed July 2008, from http://www.dot.gov/execorder/13274/eo13274/index.htm

Federal Aviation Administration. Accessed July 2008, from http://www.awp.faa.gov/ops/awp600/runway/definitions.pdf

Federal Aviation Authorization Act of 1996, House Report 104-714 – Part 1. Accessed April 2008, from http://thomas.loc.gov/cgi-bin/cpquery/?&sid=cp104v6n3H&refer=&r_n=hr714p1.104&db_id=104&item=&sel=TOC_134897&

Federal Aviation Regulations (FAR), Part 1, Definitions and Abbreviations. Washington, D.C.: Federal Aviation Administration. Accessed February 2008, from http://www.airweb.faa.gov/Regulatory_and_Guidance_Library/rgFAR.nsf/0/7B29C0FFCE0C430A86256EDF00478339?OpenDocument

Federal Aviation Regulations, Part 77, Objects Affecting Navigable Airspace. Washington, D.C.: Federal Aviation Administration. Accessed April 2008, from http://www.airweb.faa.gov/Regulatory_and_Guidance_Library/rgFAR.nsf/MainFrame?OpenFrameSet

Federal Aviation Regulations, Part 91, Sec. 91.155. Washington, D.C.: Federal Aviation Administration. Accessed May 2008, from http://rgl.faa.gov/REGULATORY_AND_GUIDANCE_LIBRARY/RGFAR.NSF/0/074608A2FA18B48A86256EEB006704EF?OpenDocument

Federal Aviation Regulations, Part 91, Sec. 91.319. Washington, D.C.: Federal Aviation Administration. Accessed May 2008, from http://www.faa.gov/airports_airtraffic/airports/airport_safety/part139_cert/media/part139_wcorrections.pdf

Federal Aviation Regulations, Part 150, Airport Noise Compatibility Planning. Washington, D.C.: Federal Aviation Administration. Accessed May 2008, from http://rgl.faa.gov/Regulatory_and_Guidance_Library/rgFAR.nsf/ MainFrame?OpenFrameSet

Field Formulation of the National Plan of Integrated Airport Systems (NPIAS), FAA Order 5090.3C. Washington, D.C.: Federal Aviation Administration, December 4, 2000. Accessed June 2008, from http://www.faa.gov/airports_airtraffic/airports/ resources/publications/orders/media/planning_5090_3C.pdf

Forecasting Aviation Activity by Airport. Jenkintown, PA: GRA, 2001, incorporated for Federal Aviation Administration, Office of Aviation Policy and Plans, 2001. Accessed June 2008, from http://www.faa.gov/data_statistics/aviation_data_statistics/ forecasting/media/af1.doc

GA Economic Impact Statements. American Association of Airport Executives. Accessed January 2008, from http://www.aaae.org/ products/900_GA_Economic_Impact_Statements/

Galbraith, John Kenneth, as quoted in *The New York Times*, March 15, 2009.

Heraclitus, as quoted in Auden, W.H. (ed.), *The Portable Greek Reader*. New York: The Penguin Group, 1948.

Higher Visions For Airports. American Planning Association, Transportation Planning Division. Accessed May 2008, from http://www.apa-tpd.org/airports.html

Horonjeff, Robert, and Francis X. McKelvey, *Planning & Design of Airports*, 4th Edition. New York: McGraw-Hill, 1994, 1983, 1975, 1962.

http://forms.faa.gov/forms/faa1800-31.pdf

http://web.mit.edu/aeroastro/www/labs/AATT/reviews.html

http://www.airweb.faa.gov/Regulatory_and_Guidance_Library/rgFAR.nsf/ MainFrame?OpenFrameSet

http://www.apa-tpd.org/airports.html

http://www.bts.gov/programs/airline_information/airline_ontime_statistics/

http://www.faa.gov/airports_airtraffic/airports/resources/forms/index. cfm?sect=airportmaster

Instrument Procedures Handbook. Washington, D.C.: Federal Aviation Administration. Accessed May 2008, from http://www.faa.gov/library/manuals/ aviation/instrument_procedures_handbook/

Intermodal Surface Transportation Efficiency Act of 1991 – Summary. Accessed September 2008, from http://ntl.bts.gov/DOCS/ste.html

Intermodal Transportation – DOT Could Take Further Actions to Address Intermodal Barriers, GAO 07-718. Washington, D.C.: U.S. Government Accountability Office, July 2007. Accessed September 2008, from http://www.gao.gov/new.items/d07718.pdf

Intermodal Transportation – Potential Strategies Would Redefine Federal Role in Developing Airport Intermodal Capabilities. Washington, D.C.: U.S. Government Accountability Office, July 2005.

Introduction to the Clean Water Act. Washington, D.C.: U.S. Environmental Protection Agency. Accessed August 2008, from http://www.epa.gov/watertrain/cwa/

Bibliography

J.D. Power and Associates, *2008 North America Airport Satisfaction Study*^{SM}, press release, May 2008. Westlake Village, CA. Accessed June 2008, from http://www.jdpower.com/corporate/news/releases/pressrelease.aspx?ID=2008050

Lurie, Carol, and Sarah Townsend, "How Do Airports Stack Up?," *Airport Consulting*, Winter 2007/2008, Airport Consultants Council, Alexandria, VA.

Massport, Logan Airport. Airport Programs, Environmental. Accessed August 2008, from http://www.massport.com/LOGAN/airpo_envir_data.html

Mintzberg, Henry, *The Rise and Fall of Strategic Planning*. New York: The Free Press, 1994.

Model Reviews, MIT Modeling Research Under NASA/AATT. Massachusetts Institute of Technology. Accessed June 2008, from http://web.mit.edu/aeroastro/www/labs/AATT/reviews.html

Napier, Rod, Clint Sidle, and Patrick Sanaghan, *High Impact Tools and Activities for Strategic Planning*. New York: McGraw-Hill, 1998.

National Environmental Policy Act (NEPA) Implementing Instructions for Airport Actions, FAA Order 5050.4B. Washington, D.C.: Federal Aviation Administration, April 28, 2006. Accessed July 2008, from http://www.faa.gov/airports_airtraffic/airports/resources/publications/orders/environmental_5050_4/media/chapter1.pdf

National Plan of Integrated Airport Systems, 2009-2013, Report to Congress. Washington, D.C.: Federal Aviation Administration. Accessed January 2009, from http://www.faa.gov/airports_airtraffic/airports/planning_capacity/npias/reports/media/2009/npias_2009_narrative.pdf

New England Regional Airport System Plan, n.d. New England Airport Coalition. Accessed March 2008, from http://www.faa.gov/airports_airtraffic/airports/regional_guidance/new_england/planning_capacity/airport_system_plan/

Partnering for Better Communities, Pub. 427 (01-02). CH Planning for the Pennsylvania Department of Transportation, Bureau of Aviation. n.d.

Passenger Facility Charge, FAA Order 5500.1. Washington, D.C.: Federal Aviation Administration. Accessed August 2007, from http://www.faa.gov/airports_airtraffic/airports/resources/publications/orders/media/PFC_55001.pdf

Pehrson, John R., "Air Quality Regulations Compliance: Act Now," *Airport Magazine*, September/October 2005, AAAE Service Corporation, Inc., Alexandria, VA.

Planning and Design Guidelines for Airport Terminal Facilities, AC 150/5360-13. Washington, D.C.: Federal Aviation Administration, 1994.

Poh, Eileen, *Airport Planning and Terminal Design*, presentation for the Strategic Airport Management Programme, April 9-13, 2007. Accessed May 2008, from http://clacsec.lima.icao.int/Reuniones/2007/Seminario-Chile/Presentations/PR07.pdf

Policies and Procedures for Considering Environmental Impacts, FAA Order 1050.1E, CHG 1. Washington, D.C.: Federal Aviation Administration, March 20, 2006. Accessed July 2008, from http://rgl.faa.gov/regulatory_and_guidance_library/rgorders.nsf/0/2bb5c3876ba31261862571810047a403!OpenDocument&Click=

Polluted Runoff (Nonpoint Source Pollution). Washington, D.C.: U.S. Environmental Protection Agency. Accessed August 2008, from http://www.epa.gov/owow/NPS/MMGI/Chapter1/ch1-1.html

Procedures for Abatement of Highway Traffic Noise and Construction Noise (23 CFR Part 772). Washington, D.C.: Federal Highway Administration. Accessed July 2008, from http://www.fhwa.dot.gov/hep/23cfr772.htm

Program Guidance Letter 07-03 Revised and Updated Requirements for Letter of Intent (LOI) Requests, November 20, 2006. Washington, D.C.: Federal Aviation Administration. Accessed May 2008, from http://www.faa.gov/airports_airtraffic/airports/aip/guidance_letters/media/pgl_07_03.pdf

Revision to Guidance on Review and Approval of Aviation Forecasts, memorandum. Washington, D.C.: Federal Aviation Administration, 2004. Accessed June 2008, from http://www.faa.gov/airports_airtraffic/airports/planning_capacity/media/approval_aviation_forecasts_2004.pdf

Root Causes of Amtrak Train Delays, Report Number CR-2008-076. Washington, D.C.: Federal Railroad Administration, September 8, 2008. Accessed January 2009, from http://www.oig.dot.gov/StreamFile?file=/data/pdfdocs/Amtrak_Root_Causes_Final_Report_9_8_08_with_508_charts.pdf

Runway Length Requirements for Airport Design, AC 150/5325-4B. Washington, D.C.: Federal Aviation Administration, July 1, 2005, p. 2. Accessed April 2008, from http://rgl.faa.gov/Regulatory_and_Guidance_Library/rgAdvisoryCircular.nsf/0/b5f123f1451fe9468625724100785f60/$FILE/150_5325_4b.pdf

Spill Prevention, Control and Countermeasure Plans (SPCC). Washington, D.C.: U.S. Environmental Protection Agency. Accessed August 2008, from http://www.epa.gov/region5/oil/plan/spcc.html

Stormwater Program National Pollutant Discharge Elimination System (NPDES). Washington, D.C.: U.S. Environmental Protection Agency. Accessed August 2008, from http://cfpub.epa.gov/npdes/home.cfm?program_id=6

The Airline Handbook – Online Version. Washington, D.C.: Air Transport Association, 2001. Accessed February 2007, from http://members.airlines.org/about/d.aspx?nid=7951

The Airport System Planning Process, AC 150/5070-7. Washington, D.C.: Federal Aviation Administration, November 11, 2004. Accessed August 2007 and June 2008, from http://www.faa.gov/airports_airtraffic/airports/resources/advisory_circulars/

The National Environmental Policy Act of 1969, Pub. L. 91-190. Washington, D.C.: U.S. Congress. Accessed July 2008, from http://www.nepa.gov/nepa/regs/nepa/nepaeqia.htm

TransSolutions, Inc., *TransSolutions' Team Selected to Lead Research Project for Airport Planning and Design*, press release, April 28, 2008. Fort Worth, TX.

Travel Industry Association of America, *Multi-Billion-Dollar Economic Loss from Deteriorating Air Travel System Hits Small Businesses Hardest*, press release, June 26, 2008. Accessed August 2008, from http://tia.usdm.net/pressmedia/pressrec.asp?Item=905

U.S. Department of Agriculture, Business and Cooperative Programs. Accessed June 2008, from http://www.rurdev.usda.gov/rbs/busp/rbeg.htm

U.S. Department of Agriculture, Rural Development Housing & Community Facilities Programs. Accessed June 2008, from http://www.rurdev.usda.gov/rhs/cf/brief_cp_direct.htm

U.S. Department of Agriculture, Rural Development Housing & Community Facilities Programs. Accessed June 2008, from http://www.rurdev.usda.gov/rhs/cf/essent_facil.htm

U.S. Green Building Council. Accessed August 2008, from http://www.usgbc.org/

Vause, Jordan, *Wolf: U-Boat Commanders in World War II*. Annapolis, MD: Naval Institute Press, 1997.

Virginia Department of Aviation, State Funding Programs for Airports. Accessed June 2008, from http://www.doav.virginia.gov/Downloads/Airport_Grant_Program/Airport%20Program%20Manual/10%20Airports%20Revolving%20Fund.pdf

Virginia Resources Authority, Revolving Loan Funds. Accessed June 2008, from http://virginiaresources.org/revolvingloan.shtml

Vision 100 – Century of Aviation Reauthorization Act, (HR 2115), Public Law 108-176, Title III, Subchapter A, December 12, 2003. Washington, D.C.: U.S. House of Representatives. Accessed June 2008, from http://frwebgate.access.gpo.gov/cgi-bin/getdoc.cgi?dbname=108_cong_public_laws&docid=f:publ176.108.pdf

Voluntary Airport Low Emissions Program (VALE). Washington, D.C.: Federal Aviation Administration. Accessed July 2008, from http://www.faa.gov/airports_airtraffic/airports/environmental/vale/

Webster's II New Riverside University Dictionary. Boston: Houghton-Mifflin, 1998.

Wells, Alexander T., and Seth B. Young, *Airport Planning and Management*, 5th Edition. New York: McGraw-Hill, 2004, 2000, 1996, 1992, 1986.

Wendell Cox Consultancy, *The Public Purpose*. Belleville, IL. Accessed January 2009, from http://www.publicpurpose.com/ic-hsramtrak.htm

Wetlands Definitions. Washington, D.C.: U.S. Environmental Protection Agency. Accessed August 2008, from http://www.epa.gov/owow/wetlands/what/definitions.html

Yu, Roger, "Airports Go for Green with Eco-friendly Efforts," *USA Today*, September 18, 2008. Accessed September 2008, from http://www.usatoday.com/travel/flights/2008-09-16-green-airports_N.htm

Lynn S. Bezilla

Airport Planning draws from Lynn Bezilla's 37 years of airport planning experience, including 20 years as Director of Planning and Environmental Services at Baltimore/Washington International Airport (BWI). He was responsible for all facility planning, forecasting, environmental analysis, and capital project development at BWI, as well as at Martin State Airport, a reliever for BWI. Lynn was also responsible for preparing airport system plans for the State of Maryland.

Previously Lynn worked for several consulting firms and the Metropolitan Washington Council of Governments in Washington, D.C. He began his career as an airport system planner with the New York State Department of Transportation.

A native of Pennsylvania, Lynn holds a Bachelor of Science in Earth Science from the Indiana University of Pennsylvania and a Master of Science in Geography from Penn State University.

He resides in Columbia, Maryland, with his wife, Rena.

Made in United States
North Haven, CT
05 January 2023

30688664R00200